# The Future of Humanity

Second Edition

**Intellect China Library**

Series editor: Hiu M. Chan

The Intellect China Library series brings together important research from Chinese scholars that has never before been available in English. Focusing on art and contemporary culture the series covers a wide variety of subjects including film studies, visual arts, performing arts, and media and cultural studies. The series aims to foster academic debate and promote closer cross-cultural exchanges by introducing important works of Chinese scholarship to readers.

Other titles in the series:
*Beijing Film Academy Yearbook 2015* (2016)
*Beijing Film Academy Yearbook 2016* (2017)
*Beijing Film Academy Yearbook 2018* (2021)
*Beijing Film Academy Yearbook 2019* (2022)
*Beijing Film Academy Yearbook 2020* (2022)
*Film Studies in China: Selected Writings from* Contemporary Cinema (2017)
*Film Studies in China (Volume 2): Selected Writings from* Contemporary Cinema (2020)

*Cultural Industries in Shanghai: Policy and Planning inside a Global City* (2018)

*Dance Studies in China: Selected Writings from the Journal of Beijing Dance Academy* (2022)

# The Future of Humanity

## From Global Civilization to Great Civilization

Second Edition

*By Zhouying JIN*

TRANSLATED BY

*Lane Jennings and Ying BAI*

intellect

Bristol, UK / Chicago, USA

First published in the UK in 2022 by
Intellect, The Mill, Parnall Road, Fishponds, Bristol, BS16 3JG, UK

First published in the USA in 2022 by
Intellect, The University of Chicago Press, 1427 E. 60th Street,
Chicago, IL 60637, USA



A catalogue record for this book is available from
the British Library.

Copy editor: MPS Limited
Cover designer: Aleksandra Szumlas
Production manager: Jessica Lovett
Typesetter: MPS Limited
Translated by Lane Jennings and Ying BAI from the second Chinese edition,
*The Future of Humanity—From Global Civilization to Great Civilization*, By
Zhouying JIN (Changsha: Hunan Science and Technology Press, October 2021,
ISBN 978-7-5710-1189-5).

Print ISBN 978-1-78938-616-5
ePDF ISBN 978-1-78938-617-2
ePUB ISBN 978-1-78938-618-9

Part of the Intellect China Library series
ISSN 2059-1985 / Online ISSN 2059-1993

To find out about all our publications, please visit our website.
There you can subscribe to our e-newsletter, browse or download our current
catalogue and buy any titles that are in print.

www.intellectbooks.com

This is a peer-reviewed publication.

# Contents

# Foreword I

*Theodore Jay Gordon*[1]

In this colossal work, Professor Jin pursues the answers to a simple question: What kind of global civilization should human beings pursue? This question has preoccupied scholars, philosophers, and politicians for centuries. The question may be simple, but the answers are certainly not simple at all. Answers may lie in the domain of soft technology, a field that Professor Jin has pioneered. Soft technology is that field of human endeavor outside of the world of things. Our world's future will be derived from both hard and soft technology but up until recently, we have been preoccupied with the hard side that has not only given us great conveniences and luxuries, but also disaffection, uncertainty, and insecurity.

The book does not deal with the building of mere nations; rather it deals with the building of whole new civilizations, spanning centuries, and asks what is important to happiness. In the process, touches on subjects as diverse as alien intelligence, immortality, morality, and China's possible role in bringing about a better world.

Hard technology is the domain of tools, machines, and equipment. Soft technology is focused on thought and non-scientific knowledge; it is the realm of motivation, values, and behavior. Knowledge about the brain is hard technology; knowledge about the mind is soft technology. The weapons of terrorism are hard; techniques for making their use less compelling are soft. Hard and soft technologies have contributed to the current state of social affairs; both are essential to Professor Jin's search for what she calls the "Great Civilization".

Civilizations evolve, shaped by the past, shaped by billions of decisions—trivial and monumental, by science, by random and unexpected events, by the changing aspirations of humankind and its institutions, and by appetites holy and secular, vectored toward some unknowable future state. The path has often been driven by avarice, the quest for power, and unreasoned ideology. In nature, organisms evolve and survive by adapting; at the scale of civilizations, simply adapting to our evolutionary fate may give us survival, but is that sufficient?

To change from that fate to something better requires images of what society could be and ought to be, and a determination to set out in that direction. Assuming we have a helm, by what star do we navigate? We need ambitious goals and steering mechanisms to get us there.

Professor Jin asks if we can do better than simply accepting our fate by deliberately choosing goals and policies to shape our future; this has long been the mantra and promise of futures research but rarely has anyone attempted it at the scale of civilizations.

Can we ever agree about the attributes of a Great Civilization? Scholars and poets have tried. James Hilton's *Lost Horizon* (1988) described a fictional Shangri La, an Asian lost paradise cut off from the world, where the world's wisdom was preserved; Thomas Moore's *Utopia* (2001) was a tolerant and lawful place where rationality prevailed; Plato's *Republic* (1991) focused on educated philosopher kings, justice, and moderation; and Francis Bacon's *New Atlanti* (2012) described a utopia that valued knowledge, dignity, and research. In today's literature, dystopias are more common, from Aldous Huxley's *Brave New World* (2006) to George Orwell's *1984* (1950), perhaps reflecting the fast pace of material invention and our slowness to develop policies regarding their use, and of our generally more uncertain times. A common theme since Alvin Toffler's *Future Shock* in 1970 has been that hard technology is advancing so quickly leaving no time to adapt, but today that notion seems a bit quaint. There is a much more ominous sounding note as the threats of nuclear proliferation and terrorism capable of mass destruction become real in a world that still lacks any unified political or moral structure, enlightened foreign policy, or rational decision making to mitigate such threats. We seem to be stuck in an industrial society that responds only to power, greed, hedonism, and self-preservation.

So how can the Great Civilization be achieved? Professor Jin focuses on soft technology as the engine for change. In this search, she includes ideas as simple as the Golden Rule and as complex as the future of science, applied on a time scale ranging from tomorrow to centuries hence. She asks about the possible dangers of failing to control our trajectory, about the role of Eastern thought and traditions, and the consequences of awakening China, the "sleeping lion".

It is a normative work, rather than prescriptive; it asks if you could design an ideal world, what would it be? Whose values would it reflect? And what would be the role of people who live in that ideal world or strive to achieve it? It asks about government and religion, and about the other institutions and beliefs that help define civilization.

This is a book about morality and its future. It is an argument for rationality and the self-determination of social evolution. In the end, she sees the Great Civilization as a merger between Eastern and Western ideas and cultures, with the East contributing revitalized oriental spiritual and ethical values and the West, morally reoriented politics, science, and technology.

Many decades ago, the futurist/political philosopher, Bertrand de Jouvenel, was asked for his opinion about world government. He argued that world government seemed to him to be a very bad idea because if one did not like that singular government, there would be no place else to go. This is indeed a dilemma: will humankind of the Great Civilization be wise enough to have the answer?

There are other questions that social pioneers will face that plot the course to the Great Civilization. Its structure will depend on what one believes to be good and true; however, what is good and true for many of us is based on what our fathers and mothers believed, and what religious and secular teachers and peers told us is good and true. Further, what is good and true for one person is not for another; what is good and true in one era may be archaic and wrong-headed in another. If freedom is to be part of that civilization, there must be room to disagree, to tolerate diversity, to change, and to reserve certain decisions for the future in order to avoid the arrogance of dictating futures to generations we will never see. Let future generations build on the best of what we will give them, but they must and will chart their own courses to their futures.

Furthermore, I think those social pioneers illuminating the path to the Great Civilization will have to recognize that some of our worst attributes may be built into our DNA, shaped by evolutionary pressures formed many centuries ago in the jungle of survival. Are we our own worst enemies?

One hopes that soft technology holds the solution to many of our problems, such as terrorism that may involve not only the weapons with great destructive capacity (hard technology), but also the reasons and inequities that lead to terrorism (soft technology) and the incentives for doing evil. Add to the list problems awaiting soft solutions: the election of inept and untrained politicians, the claims of superiority of one sect over another, belief in the impossible, and confusion between chance and fate.

However, there is hope that a Great Civilization may be possible. Simply by asking about its characteristics it becomes more real, even if its full achievement remains centuries away.

Theodore Jay Gordon
March 2020

## NOTE

1. Theodore Jay Gordon, an outstanding futurist, is the Co-founder and Senior Research Fellow for the Millennium Project. He started The Futures Group in the 1960s, and was one of the founders of "Institute For The Future". He is the author of six books and hundreds of papers dealing with topics associated with the future, space, scientific and technological developments and global issues. He was a consultant to RAND Corporation, an early contributor to the use of the Delphi method, and is the inventor of several futures research techniques.

# Foreword II

*Hazel Henderson*[I]

In this path-breaking book, Professor Zhouying Jin addresses the major choices our human family faces in this Age of the Anthropocene and the page of the human agenda open before us in this first half of the twenty-first century. She also enumerates with her deep professional knowledge of science the technological choices we cannot avoid. Professor Jin is worthy of a world's preeminent futurist and philosopher of science.

In a similar vein as that of Israeli philosopher Yuval Noah Harari in his *Sapiens* (2014) and *Homo Deus* (2015), Zhouying Jin brings the added perspective of Chinese history and culture to guide humanity's choices. She sees beyond Western cultures' obsession with materialism and individualism. While rooted in the wisdom of the Tao of Lao Tsu, she apparently shares, as I do with Russian sociologist Pitirim Sorokin's *The Ways and Power of Love* (1954) and psychologist Steven Pinker's *The Better Angels of our Nature* (2011) the view that human nature can improve, and the evidence of this evolution toward altruism also documented by Charles Darwin in his *The Descent of Man* (1874) and re-framed by David Loye in his *Darwin's Lost Theory of Love* (2000). Prof. Jin emphasizes the communal aspects of human beings and traces our efforts to expand our communities and cooperation throughout our history as we colonized every continent of our home planet Earth.

These past human successes now consume some 40 per cent of the living photosynthesis of other life forms and biomass [...]resulting in the extinction of many other species. Clearly, we are at a crossroads and must change our ways and behavior if we are to survive. The planet is teaching us directly with its feedback to our limited perception: desertification, floods, fires, tornadoes, tsunamis, and climate disruption. This book is an indispensable guide to the history of technologies as developed in many different cultural settings with disparate norms, values, and goals. Using a systems approach, Professor Jin always begins by asking about the purpose and ethical norms behind technological development, as well as the political and social choices guiding the direction of scientific research. This kind of approach was also instituted in the US government's ill-fated Office of Technology Assessment (OTA), on which I served as an advisor from 1974 until 1980, and which was shut down in 1996 by the Republican majority in Congress. Yet questioning corporate profit-making goals in developing technologies is back on the table as we deal with how to govern social media companies today.

These are the key questions all societies must ask—all the more crucial in this era of genetic engineering and Clustered Regularly Interspersed Short Palindromic Repeats (CRISPR) technology widely available, along with deep inroads into our psychology and cognitive biases and manipulation by advertising, marketing, big data, algorithms, and todays profit-driven digital economy and media giants envisioned by George Orwell in his *1984* (1946). Our Anthropocene Age is testing humans as never before to overcome our baser instincts and reptilian brains and rise to new levels of awareness, to perceive how our home planet Earth actually functions in relation to its mother star: the Sun. We will need to transcend our siloed cognition, education, and institutions still mired in reductionist thinking.

Zhouying Jin traces humanity's efforts to widen our experience, understanding, and cooperation in building expanded communities from early tribes to settled agricultural villages, towns, cities, nation states, and today's United Nations and the visionary Sustainable Development Goals (SDGs). If we are to survive our Anthropocene stage, we will need the kind of quantum leap in wisdom, cultural understanding, self-discipline, and spiritual adulthood to create the Global Civilization and eventually Great Civilization explored in *The Future of Humanity*.

Hazel Henderson
April 2018

## NOTE

1. Hazel Henderson, a famous futurist, science policy veteran, CEO, Ethical Markets Media, author of "Mapping the Global Transition to the Solar Age" and other books. She was an Advisory Council Member, US Office of Technology Assessment (OTA), National Science Foundation, National Academy of Engineering (1974–80), member, Club of Rome.

# Foreword III

*Randeep Sudan*[I]

*The Future of Humanity* is a thought-provoking work that takes a long view of the trajectory of our technological development, identifies the significant risks and ethical dilemmas that it entails and tries to answer the central question of what kind of future we should aspire to as humanity. It is a profound piece of work, reflecting a deep understanding of technology and society, and also the philosophical traditions of both the West and the East to weave an inspiring vision for the future of humanity. The author is an accomplished futurist with long years of experience as a distinguished tech policy expert. In her analysis, she distinguishes between "soft technology" comprising, for example, societal norms and structures as opposed to "hard technology" concerning material solutions based on science. It is "soft technology" which ultimately determines the impact of "hard technology" on society, and therefore deserves serious attention. The author paints a vivid picture of what might be the successor of our current industrial civilization. She calls it the "Global Civilization". She then goes on to define its next and more evolved version, which she terms as the"Great Civilization".

While considering technology and society, we are often constrained by our current circumstances as we think of the future. As a result, we usually end up thinking incrementally. *The Future of Humanity* provokes us to think more expansively on a bigger canvas. It is an extremely valuable contribution in helping us frame our thinking of the type of society we should collectively design if what we cherish as humans is to survive and thrive in the future.

Randeep Sudan
January 2019

## NOTE

1. Randeep Sudan: Board Advisor Ecosystem, formerly Global Advisor on Digital Strategy and Practice Manager of the Digital Development Unit at the World Bank.

# Foreword IV

*Guangbi DONG*[I]

Professor Jin is a futurist with a natural science background, who has served in the Chinese Academy of Sciences and the Chinese Academy of Social Sciences, and made outstanding contributions in the field of technical economics and futures studies. She is a dedicated scientist, alert to newly emerging trends, who boldly dares to explore new possibilities and is eager to turn sound ideas into practical realities. In recent years, she has actively promoted a new business philosophy, "China 2050 and an Early Warning System" to help guarantee genuine progress and sustainable development in China. Moreover, the concept of "Soft Technology" that she pioneered has aroused great interest in academic circles. In the first edition of this book, *The Future of Humanity: Global Civilization and China's Rejuvenation* (2016), she put forward the concepts of "Global Civilization" and "Great Civilization".

This new book focuses on an urgent issue—the transformation of global society from a loose collection of competing individual states still largely following the rules and values of the Industrial Age, into a more human and more sustainable post-industrial Global Civilization. Professor Jin argues the necessity and possibility of this transformation, and even offers a roadmap for its realization which combines six distinct approaches.

Her term "Global civilization" refers to a world in which all sovereign states can maintain peaceful coexistence, coordinated development, social justice, ecological balance, and ideological pluralism, to ensure a happy life for individuals and families and preserve this through successive generations.

Professor Jin is optimistic that the transition from Industrial Civilization to Global Civilization can occur within a relatively short time, but she does not see this as the final step in human evolution. Rather, she envisions further changes over time that will ultimately produce what she calls "The Great Civilization"—a condition in which all the inhabitants of Earth, and the probable extension of human beings and their institutions into outer space, will enjoy not only improved health and longevity but higher standards of morality and more cooperative behavior thanks to both physical and societal evolution.

Human evolution itself is in a state of flux, as advances in science and technology now make it possible to not only influence the biological evolution of individual life forms, but also increasingly to measure and guide the evolution of institutions and cultural values in entire societies and throughout civilization as a whole. Just as cultural evolution in the past has reshaped and improved civilization and largely raised humanity above ignorance and barbarism, societies today continue to develop and expand, linking and interlinking once divergent and even hostile groups.

In fact, during the evolution of a global civilization, the long-dominant role of fundamental forces long relied upon to maintain society (imposed morality, power, wealth, intelligence, and emotion) will gradually be replaced, while the leading role of structural elements of civilization (technology, institutions, and ideology) will be substantially revised and improved.

In short, contemporary human beings are moving towards a new era of Global Civilization dominated by intelligence and led by institutions, and will then move towards the era that Jin calls "The Great Civilization" dominated by refined wisdom and emotions, and guided by ideology.

In order to make this happen we must begin to consciously work to create a truly global civilization by facing and successfully addressing challenges to many kinds of environment; and improve civilization by resolving deep-seated conflicts between cultures so as to produce convergence, not mere assimilation. Fundamental to this process will be the growth and development of futures studies, for these alone can guide us through forecasting, design, experiment, and creation towards a future that is just, desirable, and sustainable.

Guangbi DONG
October 2019

## NOTE

1. Guangbi DONG, Professor, Chinese Academy of Sciences; Chair, International association of "YI QING" (The book of changes).

# Foreword V

*Lane Jennings*[1]

Professor Jin's book focuses on the example of one nation, but offers insights that can benefit many others. Her approach, which neatly bridges old divisions between East and West, invites thoughtful and productive people worldwide to collaborate on a challenge so great that no single nation could ever accomplish it alone, but at the same time so worthwhile that every nation stands to benefit from working to help make it a reality.

Her goal is a truly global society—achieved not by conquest and assimilation, but through a melding of existing cultures, enabled and inspired by allowing human values to guide science and technology, and acknowledging the vital role of long-term future studies for the survival and advancement of humankind.

Blending spiritual wisdom preserved in the classics of ancient Chinese thought with insights into the workings of nature and the human mind produced by scientists and philosophers inspired by Western history and values, and using both to address the real-world problems of the world today, Jin offers a new and promising approach to shaping a desirable and sustainable future for all of Earth's citizens.

Lane Jennings
March 2020

## NOTE

1. Lane Jennings, writer, Managing Editor, Social Professional Magazine *future review*, Former Managing Editor, *World Future Review*, World Future Society.

# Acknowledgments

My sincere appreciation goes to those who helped so much during the preparation for this book: Theodore Jay Gordon, Hazel Henderson, Lane Jennings, Rinaldo S. Brutoco, Karamjit S Gill, Randeep Sudan, Gordon McConnachie, Kenneth W. Hunter, Guangbi Dong, Yuzhen Zhang, Ying Bai, Jiwan Hong, Itamar Y. Lee, Keli Fang, Ping Huang, Zhong Li, Sheng Jin, and Zhenwu Xuan.

# Introduction

## *Where is humanity headed?*

Observing the world dispassionately and looking forward calmly towards the future, humans find themselves confronting unprecedented challenges. These include: first and foremost the crisis of our deteriorating natural environment that threatens human survival due to climate change, declines in biodiversity, and mounting evidence of breakdowns throughout the entire ecological system. Added to this are a growing water crisis, threats to society from man-made disasters, the widening gap between rich and poor, education problems, and even the failure to maintain world peace. Consider too, the explosive development of hard technology and the growing danger of widespread damage from technologies that, intentionally or not, may spin out of control, as well as the dangers posed by ever-greater technological intervention in human life, and the dimensions of the so-called crisis of science and technology appear so vast as to make this truly a crisis of human evolution and survival.

All of the crises mentioned above have resulted from today's prevailing attitudes towards human development, which are deep-seated, structural, and institutional in nature. It is fair to say that these crises have actually been brought about by the rise of Industrial Civilization. For all its material advantages, the consequences of this way of life clearly pose severe challenges for long-term sustainability that not only endanger the future of humanity, but threaten the entire ecosystem of the planet on which humans live.

But if Industrial Civilization has proven unsustainable, what kind of civilization should be established to replace it? And how can the people of the world hope to address this enormous challenge? Which direction should science and technology follow? And in which directions should humanity evolve?

From any credible perspective, we are standing at a crossroads in the history of human civilization. Although more and more people are coming to recognize the desperate state of our global environment, the majority of people still appear to be primarily motivated by selfish greed. The desire to control and possess—the lengths to which individuals, organizations, and governments are willing to go to attain their desired objectives—continue to expand, while the moral bottom line continues to decline. The result is the endless pursuit of money, physical comfort, and material luxury. While dignitaries around the world are busy attempting to cope with the national crises and challenges brought about by dramatic changes on a global scale, a growing number of people today in the Americas, Europe, Oceania, Africa, and Asia face very worrisome international situations.

Yet even now serious attempts to explore long-term human futures are largely limited to members of the scientific or futurist communities, while the general public—when it thinks about the future at all—generally does so on the basis of extreme visions offered in works of popular science fictions or sci-fi films, which, while highly entertaining, can also be highly misleading and hence very dangerous.

Maybe one day, we will all suddenly be enlightened. But by then, it may already be too late. A much better option would be for humans to open multi-level and multi-faceted dialogues, so as to gradually arrive at a deep consensus on how to correct the flaws in our existing civilization, and to agree on what kind of future we need; how we can create this kind of future, and how humanity itself can improve to establish and maintain a sustainable existence while enabling responsible development.

## *Concerning human evolution*

In the twenty-first century, mankind is facing both unprecedented challenges and unique opportunities brought about by the unparalleled growth of technology over the past 300 years and more. Many people believe that human beings have the potential to create and manipulate human life and to affect their own evolution. Some even think that Darwin's theory of natural evolution is no longer applicable and that human evolution in the future will be entirely driven by conscious human actions, such as genetic optimization, improving intelligence through the combination of man and machine, and emigration to other stellar systems. There is no shortage of speculative studies or predictions including various forms of Supermen, asexual people, "Unihumans," "Survivalists," "Genetically enhanced beings," "Cyborgs," "Spacemen," etc.

Could it really be that all of these are plausible future descendants of today's humans, who call themselves the wisest of all creatures? When people predict such possible future "human" beings as those mentioned above, they seldom if ever consider what kind of human society and human civilization such an evolution might produce.

## *What is technology?*

The technological revolution is still unfolding, and today's fast-changing new technologies are truly dazzling. They provide unprecedented opportunities and numerous reverie for humans. Many people today suffer from a syndrome of technology worship, while others suffer from anxiety disorder, fearful that uncontrolled technology may produce a science and technological crisis or even lead to the disaster of human society.

In order not to lose themselves under wave after wave of the hard and soft technology revolution, and to retain control once non-biological intelligence approaches or exceeds that of humans, those who resist technology's allure seek ways to assure that human beings will always retain such inherent characteristics as dignity and compassion. Their goal is to create a future in which the more technology advances, the more people can enjoy a free and peaceful life in which each individual is fairly rewarded. But to achieve this we need a new understanding of technology–based neither upon blind trust nor irrational fear. We need to recognize that technology is just another tool of human invention, like those created in the past with which we are now familiar but more intricate, powerful, and strange. Moreover, we must remember that humanity's use of tools dates back to ancient times, and while today's machines appear more necessary and more powerful than ever before, they should always serve our needs and interests, not the other way around.

## *On future civilization*

Human civilization has existed for millions of years but only evolved into Industrial Civilization in the last 300 years. Industrial Civilization has achieved a high level of development and produced a world of unprecedented material abundance, brilliant science, and impressive technology as well as immortal achievements in the arts. But the price we have paid for all these accomplishments is one that we now can no longer afford.

Fortunately, over the past half-century more and more people have awoken to the truth that mankind has embarked on a road of no return. Many now recognize that the progress of human beings, driven by the values of Industrial Civilization, is not sustainable and that the choice between civilization's collapse and its transition is imminent. For the first time in history, humans are beginning to accept the necessity of working together to replace the civilization around them. But what will a civilization more advanced than Industrial Civilization be like? How can we, as contemporary humans, go about creating such a civilization? And what new and more appropriate aims should we establish for future human history?

## *Sustainable development and human beings*

Since the 1980s, sustainability has increasingly become the common objective of the world. However, reviewing the past 30 years, the survival crises faced by human beings, in areas such as global resources, biodiversity, environment, population, agriculture, and food, are all intensifying. Furthermore, the gap between rich and poor is widening, and regional and international conflicts have become more frequent and more destructive. For these reasons, people are placing their hopes on the foundation of sustainable development: the green economy. Especially since the 2008 financial crisis, green development, which promotes economic recovery, has become the subject of numerous academic books, papers, and international conferences at higher and higher levels, to the point where it can now be said to be the main thrust of today's world economic development.

However, the actual situation is not encouraging. According to a recent United Nations Environmental Program (UNEP) report, the world economy has quadrupled over the past 25 years, but 60 Per cent of the principle ecosystem goods and services that support human livelihoods have been degraded or are being used in unsustainable ways. This report also warns that the traditional "Brown economy" values still dictate the policies of many countries and in effect that of the world. Where does the problem lie? What is the essence of sustainable human existence and development? How can we move beyond mere theory to effectively promote sustainability in various regions and ultimately on a global scale?

## *Understanding China*

China, a sleeping lion for over one hundred years, is now awakening, which is an important matter for the twenty-first century. The world, so long accustomed to the submissive posture of this oriental giant, is very surprised and reacts in many different ways. Some welcome it, others offer premature or irresponsible criticism, and even regard China's development as a threat, while some wish openly for China's failure. But most people's understanding of China, including that of many so-called "China experts," is still not comprehensive. As a Chinese citizen, I will be attempting in this book to carefully explore and assess my homeland's difficult but hopeful journey towards comprehensive rejuvenation as a special case illustrating how to achieve sustainable development and promote the transformation from industrial civilization to global civilization; making the realization of the Chinese Dream a part of the grand cause of mankind to create a better future, and thus give the world a correct understanding of China. At the same time, I hope to give the Chinese a clearer understanding of their strengths and weaknesses as perceived by other nations and make them more confident in creating the "Chinese version" of a future civilization in which no single nation or cultural tradition imposes itself on others but instead that all nations East and West, North and South, Developed and Emerging, contribute elements that blend to form a truly global civilization.

## *Let's hope human beings can truly awaken*

At present, the COVID-19 disease is still spreading globally. This is an unprecedented "world war" with the largest number of "participating" countries in human history. Already more than 250 million people have been infected and more than five million have died in just two years, while more than half of the world's population is restricted from travel. The enemy is a virus invisible to the naked eye, however, its influence has gone beyond the fields of health and hygiene, deeply impacted the economic, social, and even geopolitical affairs worldwide, subverted many aspects of the traditional market economy and disrupted social norms, creating great difficulties for global governance.

This unexpected disaster is forcing human beings to rethink the axioms of what we have long called "civilization". The results of this deep introspection reveal that we should abandon our stale ideas about nature and reverence toward nature. Human beings are so small in the face of the virus, "we" find ways to coexist with other creatures who share the earth, and change many of our long-established behavior patterns, including lifestyle, working mode, and diet structure.

Second, people in all countries, from ordinary citizens to entrepreneurs to political leaders, must reshape their values to accommodate the reality of a multipolar world that features global cooperation, mutual benefit, and win–win outcomes, as well as reverence for nature and respect for life. By turning the great crisis into a great reflection, a great awakening, and great opportunity; this disaster can inspire unprecedented creativity, enabling us to cope with many challenges posed by the epidemic, and together create new ways of production, life and work in the post-pandemic era, in particular the new world structure and order.

Furthermore, the current global fight against COVID-19 shows that while, on the one hand, the disclosure, defense, and defeat of the "virus" must rely on scientific support, and there are still many "mysteries", "unknown" or "blind" spots surrounding the disease that can only be solved by scientific breakthroughs, on the other, strategic and policy mistakes are themselves deadly "viruses".

Finally, we must realize that the virus does not pay attention to borders based on state, ideology, race, or social status. The effort to contain this epidemic is a contest between the whole of human society and the virus. We must actively discuss, exchange, unite and cooperate if we hope to deal with this common "enemy" of humankind.

If human beings who share an earth cannot correctly grasp the direction of human evolution; if they cannot alter their destructive relationship with nature, and abandon "people-centered" and ''self-centered" thinking everywhere; if they cannot alleviate the threat of war and terrorism "as soon as possible" through the sublimation and perfection of human nature, and create a more advanced civilization; if they cannot deal with the planet's common crises—climate change, species extinction, land and food shortages, water pollution, etc; in short, if they cannot correctly learn the lessons of the current global catastrophe caused by the COVID-19; if they cannot promote the real awakening of all mankind; and cooperate to establish a new world order and accelerate the pace of civilizational transformation, then indeed the human race is doomed to move toward self-destruction long before the dangers posed by gene-enhanced Super-beings or robots endowed with artificial intelligence robots ever emerge.

Zhouying Jin
August 2021

# 1

# Deep Concern over the Direction of Technology Development

*In the increasingly strong whirlwind of technological innovation, be sure not to confuse objectives and tools.*

Today, with the advancement of human knowledge and wisdom, there are new breakthroughs in all areas of science and technology. We can feel the strong shock wave of the technology revolution all the time. Many technologies that were considered fantasy or nonsense just a few decades ago have now been transformed into reality, and have even become common in people's daily life.

However, while the revolutions in hard and soft technology have brought many more opportunities in one wave after another, human beings must now face the challenges brought about by this onslaught of unprecedented technological development. On the one hand, there is technology worship syndrome, and on the other, deep anxiety about the dangers of technology. Specifically, many people today are deeply concerned about the direction of human evolution.

## *The syndrome of technology worship*

Many people are fascinated by technology and freely express their enthusiasm. The most typical attitudes or expressions of this enthusiasm are discussed below.

### Any problem faced by human beings can be solved by technology, and will be, if given sufficient time

Almost every day the Internet brings us exciting news of some new "breakthrough" in programming biological tissue, or a new prediction that cell engineering and intelligent robotics will soon be at the forefront of world-changing technological and scientific progress, creating the most powerful tools ever made, and enabling humans to master and reshape the world economy.

Many people believe that science can solve all the problems in the world and challenge the "impossible," including to bring the dead come back to life; they advocate technology worship that will ultimately control humans and create new types of human beings, and they argue that everything goes with the flow. Some studies even offer people hope that science and technology will provide us with a place to escape to even if the earth were to become no longer suitable for human survival. Same plans that look more attractive as concerns over COVID-19 epidemic grow. To escape, a spacecraft might be developed that can accommodate 600,000 people. Nearly 200,000 people recently signed up as volunteers for an advertised one-way trip to Mars. Regular round-trip transportation between Earth and other planets is under discussion, and could begin within the next ten years. There is certainly a chance that we could assemble spaceships and settlements in space by building and using a space elevator, and that humans may reach any planet of the solar system and survive there.

Indeed, with the development of technology, migration to Mars and interstellar tourism are more feasible. In fact, the space agencies of the United Arab Emirates, the United States, Europe, and China are actively promoting the establishment of bases on Mars. But immigration to other planets should not be viewed as a serious option for human beings to "escape from the earth" after destroying it. Can ten billion people really escape, or is this just an option for a few elites?

### Humans merely represent one particular stage of technical development

*What Technology Wants* by Kevin Kelly is a masterpiece of technology worship. In his book *Out of Control* (1994), Kelly discussed in the most cutting-edge areas of science, technology, society, and economy. Now, more than ten years later, he remained convinced that technology is an extension of life—the seventh kingdom of life in addition to plants, animals, fungi, and three distinct varieties of bacteria. He even argues that humans are nothing more than one particular stage of evolution and that humans today merely represent the best carrier for subsequent technological development. In Kelly's view, humans are not the end product of natural evolution, but simply occupy a point midway between biological life and technologically advanced artificial life forms.

Naturally, he raises the very good question—"What *is* humanity?"

### Singularity theory

Some futurists believe that changes in science, technology, society, and the economy are taking place so rapidly that, by a certain time in the future, changes we cannot possibly foresee will occur in the trajectory of human evolution. This point, at which human life may mutate, is known as "the singularity".[1]

Pierre Teilhard de Chardin called this transition the Omega Point[2] of cosmic evolution in the 1950s and in the early 1990s the science fiction novelist Vernor Vinge[3] called the transition a technological singularity. The futurist, Ray Kurzweil has carried out in-depth investigations and research into the acceleration of technology and finds exponential growth in almost all measures of our condition, driving us toward the "singularity".

According to Moore's law and the overall trend towards exponential growth in technology, Kurzweil predicts that the computing ability of a man-made computer produced by human technology will soon exceed the power of the human brain. He expects computer systems will be as powerful as the human brain sometime in the 2020s, so that "we humans will effectively be integrated with technology," and that artificial intelligence (AI) will exceed human intelligence by the mid-2040s. Kurzweil further believes that the singularity is the inevitable result of combining the large amount of knowledge stored in the human brain with the knowledge stored in human technological systems. At this point, singularity is the point where human–machine civilization transcends the limits of the human brain.

Kurzweil believes that the singularity will greatly liberate human creativity, also increasing the possibility that human beings might engage in sabotage. With the exponentially accelerating development of nanotechnology, biotechnology, etc., human intelligence, too, will be greatly increased in the next twenty years, and future mankind will also be radically reshaped. With the coming of the singularity, machines will be able to carry out self-perfection through AI and eventually to transcend human beings, thus opening a new era.

He even thinks that "the intelligence that will emerge in the future will continue to represent human civilization–human–machine civilization. In other words, computers of the future will be humans–even if they are non-living." The questions facing humans then become, what kind of changes will the singularity bring to politics, the economy, and culture in the real world?

Ray Kurzweil also recently claimed that after biotechnology is applied to the human body, we can discard many genes that have not been used for thousands of years, and greatly extend our average life span. He believes that 2029 will be the tipping point for mankind and that humans will effectively achieve eternal life by 2045. Thus, in his view, the present generation most likely contains the last purely biological humans standing at the top of the Earth's natural food chain.

Ray Kurzweil's views differ from those of some other transhumanists. He thinks that humans who are modified through science and technology, or "persons" possessing non-biological intelligence, will display greater intelligence than purely biological "humans" and that ultimately the non-biological part of human wisdom will attain a dominant position. However, he is still convinced that these superior beings will continue to classify themselves within the category of human beings, rather than as post-humans.

## Transhumanism

Although the origin of transhumanism can be traced back to the sixteenth to eighteenth centuries or even further, in recent decades, due to optimistic forecasts based on cross-development outcomes of information technology, biotechnology, and nanotechnology, some people are increasingly convinced of "technological omnipotence". They believe that technology can change the human genome and create a smarter, more robust, and longer-lived version of humankind. This kind of thinking about the future of humanity has become an international ideological trend or movement, and may even be regarded as a doctrine, philosophy, or belief. In 1998, the philosophers' Nick Bostrom and David Pearce co-founded Humanity+ (formerly the World Transhumanist Association [WTA]).[4]

There are various definitions or different schools of transhumanism. Perhaps the most widely held view is that, through science and technology, human beings may and should go beyond humans in the current sense and work to overcome the limitations of biological evolution, surpass the physical limits of our environment, and change "human living conditions". Transhumanism encourages studies in areas such as life extension, cryonics, the enhancement of physical and mental functions, and uploading the human mind into a computer, so as to completely control human personality and identity, and give humans the ability to leave this planet.

But on issues such as human cloning, Humanity+ has taken a very cautious attitude. They have stated that it is very unethical to use replication technologies on the human body that have not yet been proven to be safe, and that premature experimentation may seriously delay the public acceptance of superman technology. Nevertheless, they fully support conducting research on replication for human medical treatment and for improving plants and animals.

Many transhumanists[5] believe that in the next one or two centuries, humans throughout the world will change so substantially that our descendants will no longer be considered merely "human," but *post*-human, while the other transhumanists argue that the movement will be concerned with mainly "improving" humanity, namely enhancing human nature without sacrificing it.

### *Anxiety disorder due to technology*

Sometimes, science and technology can make a spurt of progress but at the same time make humans fear the power of the very technologies that humans have invented. This is indeed justified, because the more technology advances, the more profound its impact on society will be. Thus, the need to include ethics and morality in the development of science and technology is becoming increasingly acute. If we do not seek to halt the abuse of technology, the speed of the destruction of the earth and humanity will accelerate.

According to the Future of Humanity Institute at Oxford University, the greatest danger to humanity is not plague, famine, earthquakes, or even nuclear war, but highly developed science and technology. The rapid speed of scientific and technological development exceeds the human ability to control it. This is like placing a deadly weapon in the hands of a child. An attack by bioterrorists or simply an error in biological engineering could kill millions of people in a single day. In short, even one wrong decision could make the twenty-first century the last century for humans surviving on earth.

Representative views of anxiety disorder against technology are discussed next.

### Concerns about the abuse of technology

Bill Joy warned some time ago that the uncontrolled development of high technology could bring disaster in the new century. Genetic engineering, nanotechnology, and robotics (GNR technologies), which constitute the three major technologies of the new century, are prominent in every area. They can contribute to human well-being and economic development, but they also pose risks that menace humanity. Unintended consequences or accidents caused by GNR technologies or the abuse of these technologies could cause disasters on a scale that may exceed the danger posed by weapons of mass destruction in the twentieth century.

New trends in the development of modern technology also increase the possibility of technology abuse. While the development of sophisticated weapons technology in the twentieth century required large-scale research facilities and scarce raw materials (such as uranium for nuclear bombs), GNR technology is mainly dependent on the processing of information. In past eras, sophisticated weapons were typically developed by the state, and then controlled and used by the military. Although GNR is also dependent on facilities that are state owned and developed and requires to serve military applications, the development and use of GNR technologies are typically driven by commercial interests, which the government is hard to control. In addition, as computing speed increases, the functions of computers are enhanced, the costs of information continue to decline, and the trend of technology popularization has grown. Today, small groups and individuals have access to powerful technical resources, so that the potential for misusing technology is increasing in a dangerous environment where business is driven by the lure of huge profits. The potential dangers from the misuse of nuclear technology and agricultural chemicals alone are already well known.

But even more worrying is the future orientation of AI. Those terrorists who challenge the bottom line of human morality, such as Lone Wolves,[6] might get control of biotechnology, permitting them to create highly lethal epidemics, or master the ultimate products of AI for other evil purposes.

## People worry that the enhanced beings resulting from technological integration could become superior to humans in the short term, and ultimately seek to control humans, or supplant them entirely

Stephen Hawking warns that robots will eventually attain self-consciousness and replace humans, because the development of technology is so much faster than the speed of biological evolution. Once the IQ (Intelligence Quotient) and ability of a robot or android exceed that of biological human beings, it will be possible for them to control humans if they wish. If "they" are ever able to violate their programming, it could lead to the demise of mankind. Although Hawking himself has benefitted from AI, in an open letter signed by him and a group of other scientists and entrepreneurs, he pointed out that the efforts being made to create intelligent machines threaten humanity's survival, and concluded that it is necessary to study how to benefit from AI while avoiding the potential dangers, strengthening means of supervision to prevent intelligent machines from getting out of control.

In his book, *Our Final Century*, British astronomer Martin Rees warned that the human penchant for destructiveness means that the human species could easily destroy itself before 2100. Terrible killer robots may become the protagonists of Armageddon, while climate change, nuclear war, runaway biotechnology, etc., all have the potential to bring about a human Doomsday.

At a center for "Terminator Studies" launched at Cambridge University, famous scholars study potential threats facing humans from super-intelligent robots and super computers. In particular, the purpose of this center is to study the "four greatest threats": AI, climate change, nuclear war, and rogue biotechnology. The three co-founders of this center considered that technological progress could easily constitute a risk of extinction for the human species.

The center brings together scholars from different disciplines like philosophy, astronomy, biology, robotics, neuroscience, and economics to study these threats. Currently, machines do better than human beings at such things as chess, flying, driving, and financial transactions. The concern is that humans might relinquish control of the earth to machines endowed with AI.

## The negative impact of technology on morality—an ethical and moral crisis

The more technology develops, the more profound the interaction between technology and society will be, and the greater the ethical and moral crisis that will result. Modern biology offers an opportunity to change the nature of human beings. But is this a blessing or a curse?

For example, the benefits of genetic engineering mean that we can eliminate gene-related diseases to prolong human life. But gene technology has not only touched the essence of human life, but also it has involved human social consciousness, which will have a huge impact on civilization. People who intervene in nature may intend to create smarter, longer-lived, and more perfect human beings. But will this be the only result?

If the ultimate goal of gene technology is the "perfection" of humans, then once genetic engineering reaches large-scale application, there will not be much difference between the production of machine parts and the production of humans. The world may well become a world of the elite, in which differences in culture, style, and individual traits will disappear completely, resulting in disastrous consequences such as genetic convergence and simplification of races. Of course, on the other hand, it could actually increase the diversity of the race if couples were truly free to choose their child's skin color, height, level of intelligence, etc. Whether or not gene-based eugenics ever makes us commercial manufacturers of human evolution, do we have the right (contrary to the laws of nature) to alter the racial quality of our offspring?

This raises moral questions because it takes human reproduction in an "unnatural" direction (it not only interferes with the inherent natural laws of life but may also change human nature and bring about the deep technicalization of human beings). Some people would also argue that it takes advantage of some (i.e., unborn embryos) to satisfy the aims or whims of others (prospective parents). If cloning technology can be used to produce human tissues and organs and breed valuable genes, then what is the bottom line of this technology application?

If it is used to replicate humans and clone organs, such behaviors could quickly violate basic principles of ethics, such as the no-harm principle, the principle of autonomy, and the principle of equality.

At the same time, the misapplication of genetic code may also lead to negative results such as genetic discrimination, loss of privacy, and fatalism. People might discriminate against individuals with imperfect genes, which would add psychological pressure to people who carry "bad" genes. Furthermore, new technologies related to modern medical care, maternity, gene selection, etc. may push us to modify the sacred human body merely for mercenary commercial ends, even to the point where everything, including blood, organs and tissues, sperm, ova, uterine and fetal tissue, individual genes, and even entire human bodies, might be put on the sales counter with a price tag. It could even open the door to biological violence. Still more frightening is the thought that having thus opened this "Pandora's Box," those living today could become the last generation of non-transgenic human beings.

Of course, the factors that promote changes in values and trigger ethical and moral crises include not only science and technologies, but also such factors as family as the basic unit of human society, science and technology development, rapid social change, economic development, the role of media, education, politics, religious beliefs, unexpected disasters, corporate social responsibility, and demographic factors. But it is the explosive development of technology that makes it essential that ethical issues be highlighted in advance.

In 2004–05, the Millennium Project conducted a two-year thematic study on future ethical issues. Its purpose was to try to clarify the ethical issues that will be emerging in the next 50 years and assess their global significance. The study was organized in three future time periods: to address possible ethical issues during 2005–10, 2010–25, and 2025–50 (see Table 1.1). Key principles needed for solving these problems were also considered (see Table 5.1).

More than 300 people from 43 countries participated in two rounds of the Delphi survey and analysis. This study is very significant for understanding the source of ethical issues, the scope of the problems, and the difficulty and complexity of solving the dilemmas involved.

## *Concerns over the direction of human evolution*

The rapid development of science and technology, especially after realizing substantial progress in the deep integration of hard and soft technology, and the intervention into biological human life by hard technology, gives humans the potential to create and manipulate life, thereby affecting human evolution. In this context, the possibility of promoting human evolution by using new technologies in accordance with human desire has become a hot topic for those concerned with science, technology, futures, and of course the media.

One question is how future humans will evolve. Will we all become some kind of superman, asexual people, "Unihuman", "Survivalistian", "Genetic man", "Cyborg", "Spaceman", or what? These possibilities are already becoming social problems generating great ethical controversy and presenting a huge challenge to human society.

The opinions expressed by University of Washington paleontologist Peter Ward, et al. in the book *Future Evolution* (Henry Holt, 2001) are typical. Ward believes

TABLE 1.1: Highest-rated Future Ethical Issues by Importance.

| **2005–10** |
|---|
| Is it ethical to intervene in the affairs of a country that is significantly endangering its own or other people? |
| Should religions give up the claim of certainty and/or superiority to reduce religion-related conflicts? |
| Do we have a right to clone ourselves? |
| Do parents have a right to create genetically altered "designer babies?" |
| Should national sovereignty and cultural differences be allowed to prevent international intervention designed to stop widespread violence perpetrated by men against women? |
| Is it right to allow people and organizations to pollute if they pay a fee or engage in pollution trading? |
| What are ethical ways to develop applications of AI? |
| Should scientists be held personally responsible for the consequences of their research? |
| **2010–15** |
| Do we have the right to alter our genetic germ-line so that future generations cannot inherit the potential for genetically related diseases or disabilities? |
| To what degree should the rights and interests of future generations prevail in the decisions of this present generation? |
| Would the advent of global ethical norms unduly constrain differences among groups or restrain the evolution of values? |
| Should a person be subjected to psychological, social, or cultural mechanisms for limiting the propensity to commit a crime (including, for example, the use of weapons of mass destruction) even if he or she has not yet committed such an act? |
| As brain–machine interfaces become more sophisticated and global, should the demands of collective intelligence outweigh those associated with individual identity? |
| Is it ethical to extend the human lifespan, no matter what the cost? |
| When does information pollution become a crime? |
| Should there be a code of ethics to deal with proliferating space junk? |
| **2025–50** |
| Do we have the right to genetically change ourselves and future generations into new species? |

(*Continued*)

TABLE 1.1: Highest-rated Future Ethical Issues by Importance. (*Continued*)

| |
|---|
| Is it ethical for society to create future elites, augmented through AI and genetic engineering? |
| Do we have a right to genetically interfere with newborns or embryos because their genetic code shows a high probability for future violent behavior? |
| Is it right to create intelligent technological "beings" that can compete with humans or other biological life forms for an ecological niche? |
| Should we have the right to suicide and euthanasia? |
| Is it right for humans to merge with technology, as one way to prevent technological hegemony over humanity? |
| If technology develops a mind of its own, what ethical obligations should its creators have? |
| Should elimination of aging be available to everyone or just to those who can afford the treatments? |

*Source*: Jerome Glenn and Theodore Gordon, *2005 State of The Future*.

that if people can survive for another 500 million years, the human race will evolve in one or more of the following five distinct directions:

**Unihuman:** After a million years of globalization and cultural exchange, the consequences may be that different ethnic groups will have all been assimilated and mankind will evolve into a "Unihuman". Facial features and different colors of skin will become uniform, eyes will be bigger than those of today's people, and different racial characteristics will gradually disappear. Stuart Pimm, an expert on biodiversity at Duke University, points out that human beings are not only less differentiated than in the past, but have actually been "converged". He believes that although there are currently some 6500 languages in use, it is likely that there would be only 600 languages left within one or two generations. Moreover, like any single species, a single race would be more vulnerable to infectious diseases, because the variability of genes can protect species that exhibit great genetic diversity from massive damage when they are attacked by some virus.

**Survivalistian:** If a disaster occurs unexpectedly, can humans survive? Any of these catastrophes, from massive floods, plague, or nuclear war to an asteroid that hits the earth, might virtually wipe out human civilization overnight, and compel the remnant of humanity that survives to embark on a new evolutionary path. Take nuclear war as an example, in the wake of this globally devastating disaster, only those "Survivalistians" with radiation resistance would be able to cope. The facial features shown as in Figure 1.1 include eyebrows and skin greatly thickened to resist radiation poisoning.

**Genetic man:** Social commentator Joel Garreau believes that along with the rapid development of gene technology, "Genetic man" produced by the combination of altered genes with novel drugs may represent a new type of human being. This kind of genetic evolution will be much more rapid than biological evolution, or even cultural evolution. Biological evolution has taken millions of years, how long will genetic evolution take to fashion a new race? Garreau's answer is twenty years. Ken Miller, a professor at Brown University, points out that once scientists identify the genes responsible for aging and disease, we can maintain humans at their best state to the age of one hundred years or more. However, current gene therapy can only work on the individual. If we want to make the genetic characters of "Genetic man" inheritable, scientists will face ethical problems. Due to the uncertainty of gene technology, attempts to improve human genes may also bring unpredictable consequences.

**Cyborg:** Creatures that contain both biological and mechanical parts already exist. If scientists are allowed to implant an intelligence chip into a human brain, AI may exceed the inborn wisdom and talents of Homo sapiens. According to Ray Kurzweil, AI will exceed human intelligence by 2045. Once a robot evolves to a level of intelligence completely beyond that of humans, their status will be even higher than that of humans, and they will become the next species to dominate the earth. In such a case, will ordinary human beings continue to exist in nature?

**Spaceman:** If humanity survives long enough, it will inevitably have to expand to other planets in order to survive, thus forming a new race, adapted to interstellar travel. To reach distant planets, scientists will have to build large spacecraft. During the period of interstellar flight, space travelers' bodies will change.

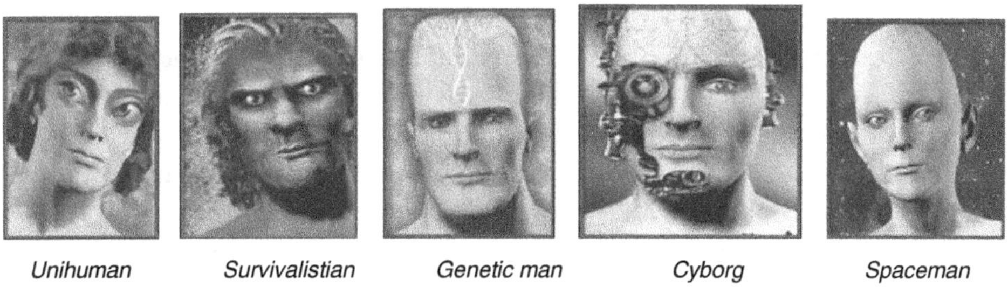


FIGURE 1.1: Five directions of human evolution and development.

For example, in a condition of low gravity, human limbs do not need to be as highly developed as they are on earth, and human hair will no longer be useful.

Linda Groff has summarized current popular views of the future evolution of humanity and put forward at least nine possible directions for the future evolution of humanity:

(1) Infotech-Based Transhumanist Views: upload consciousness into a computer; (2) Biotech-Based Transhumanist Views: augment body parts as needed; (3) Evolution of Robotics: the key is Human-Robotic Relations; (4) Humans as Future Cyborgs with Special Powers; (5) The Internet as an Externalized Version of the Human Brain, leading to expanded states of creativity and learning; (6) Space Exploration Views: a totally new environment to which humans must adapt, with many issues (radiation, bone loss, communication, children born in space, etc.); (7) Human-ET Relations—"IF" the universe is populated with intelligent life; (8) Experiences of Expanded Consciousness; (9) Experience of Interconnectedness with Earth/Gaia as a Living Being, and Responsible Stewardship of Earth (as illustrated in the film *Avatar*).

Some people have proposed other possibilities for human evolution, including scenarios in which human beings volunteer to deteriorate or become extinct, or alternatively where they become what we would call monsters with brains that continue to develop but with limbs that atrophy.

In its *Strategic Opportunities on the Sixth Revolution of Science and Technology*,[7] the China Center for Modernization Research claimed that in the next 40 years, human beings will rely on five accelerating technologies: (1) information conversion (technology for direct information exchange between the human brain and computers); (2) personality information packets (a package that contains sociological and personality information of human brain); (3) bionics (engineering technology that imitates biological tissues and their behaviors); (4) creation technology (synthesizing biological tissue, organs, limbs, and living organisms); and (5) regeneration technology (regeneration of biological tissue, organs, and perhaps life itself). These technologies, taken together, make possible three new forms of "survival" in addition to the natural person, namely: *network man* (virtual or digital existence in cyberspace), *bionic man* (highly intelligent blends of biological and mechanical parts with the appearance, body characteristics, sexual functions, and "personality information" of ordinary human beings), and *regenerative man* (clones that exactly duplicate all the biological information, sociological information and personality characteristics of a specific human individual).

Humans wish to control the direction of human evolution themselves, an ambition that is worthy of the greatest known intelligence in the universe! However, as a human being who has been evolving for tens of 10 million years (if calculated from the evolution of the Ramapithecus), is that the only consideration for their long-term future? Is there a more positive and desirable evolutionary direction?

When scientists proposed the possible future "humans" or other "living forms" species living with natural people mentioned above, do they ever think about what kind of human society and human civilization will be appropriate to these different kinds of evolution?

## *The technological revolution now unfolding*

The invention, creation, and enhancement of technology in practically every field is leading to ever faster, smaller, more intelligent, and potentially, more destructive innovations. These developments are penetrating all areas with the suddenness of a thunderbolt. Dramatic changes in the mobile phone and the Internet are only two of the technological advances that everyone can see. As Ray Kurzweil has said, technology is not evolving but exploding.

People can view all kinds of emerging technologies from different angles. I will try to take the twelve major technological areas with large contemporary influences as examples. First, by looking forward to the technological trend of important fields, it shows that as the main driving force of human social progress, scientific and technological development will never stop and will constantly reshape our future. Second, the rapid development of science and technology brings great opportunities and benefits to human beings. At the same time, we must also be aware that with breakthrough progress of each technology, we face difficult choices in the social, political, and cultural fields from different perspectives, and the world today is faced with a crisis in science and technology and ultimately a crisis of human civilization. This kind of thinking, understanding, and study is an indispensable preparation for us to meet and help form the coming intelligent society.

### Life science and biotechnology

Based on life science, modern biotechnology, represented by the engineering of genes, cells, proteins, enzymes, and fermentation, has developed swiftly and impetuously, and brought unprecedented prospects for human beings to solve major problems such as disease cures, food shortages, lack of resources and energy, and environmental pollution.

Taking the pharmaceutical field as an example, great breakthroughs have been made in genetic diagnosis technology, genetic vaccines, customized drugs, "rejuvenation" technology, memory drugs, restoration techniques, and regeneration technologies for cells tissues and organs. In the near future, there is now realistic hope of postponing senescence and overcoming cancer. It may no longer be a dream that the average life expectancy could reach 110 or even 120 years worldwide.

Even more shocking is that biotechnology is approaching the level of "Synthetic Bodies", and therapeutic cloning technology has a broad application prospect. Organ cloning with human autologous cells may not only overcome the rejection reaction often caused by allogeneic organ transplantation, but could also solve the problem of organ sourcing. Heart, liver, pancreas, breast, skin, bones, cornea cells and organs are being grown in laboratories. People believe that in the near future all human organs could be copied or remodeled.

An artificial life form called Synthia, consisting of single-celled organisms able to reproduce by self-splitting, has already been created by American scientists and has led to a robust debate in the global scientific community. Some critics argue that Synthia violates the basic concept of the nature of life. Meanwhile, scientists in Australia have cultivated a miniature artificial kidney in a culture dish by using embryonic stem cells, which are able to replace diseased organ tissue. Chinese scientists have succeeded in turning human skin cells into hepatocytes. The success of this research has brought the synthesis of artificial livers and replacement therapy for damaged liver cells a major step closer to reality.

Biochip technology, the merger of semiconductor technology and bio-tech, can place whole laboratories on an electronic chip and enable applications such as gene sequencing, molecular diagnosis of diseases, drug development, enhanced food safety and environmental monitoring, and forensic identification and provides the core technology for the development of a new industry. In addition, biometric technology has spawned an emerging anti-terrorism industry, which uses fingerprints, facial features, iris mapping, human odors and other uniquely personal biometric uniqueness to detect personal features and thus aid in the positive identification of individuals, a capability invaluable in fighting crime and deterring terrorism

However, because the object of biotechnology is life, its negative impacts, including morality, ethics (as indicated in Table 1.1), and even the future challenges of humanity, will surpass other new technologies. Technical errors or abuses in this field could lead to damage or death to healthy life and even genetic variation of the entire population, as well as create other unpredictable hazards.

How to monitor the application of life science technology and prevent its misuse and abuse has become a major challenge for all mankind. For example, the deliberate misuse of viruses, bacteria, and toxins could cause a large number of human and animal casualties, damage nature, and result in major social unrest and economic losses. Chimeric viruses, Nipah virus, smallpox, anthrax, Vibrio cholerae, botulinum toxin, plague, rabbit fever, typhoid bacillus, Ebola hemorrhagic fever, etc. are all listed among the top ten most terrible biological weapons in history.

The COVID-19 pandemic launched in 2019 has embroiled the world in a "world war" between humans and viruses. At present, the continuous development of biotechnology is being rapidly applied in the military field, and new operational concepts, operational methods, and military equipment are constantly brought into being.

At present, there are also risks of concern: genetically modified organisms pose potential threats to human health, the natural ecological environment, biodiversity, ethical disasters of cloning humans (is it therapeutic cloning or reproductive cloning), disasters of genetic weapons (e.g., targeting a certain ethnic group for killing based solely on specific genetic traits), genetic discrimination (racial, gender and/or age discrimination caused by genetic causes), patent granting of biotechnology (whether if this is regulated under the principle of risk prevention) and protection of biological resources (e.g., human genetic resources, ecological resources, etc., which have become a strategic resources for competition after land and minerals).

In view of the dual nature of biotechnology, as early as March 2012, the United States published "The regulatory policy for dual-use research institutions in life sciences" (a new version was issued in September 2014), intended to establish a regulatory system for dual-use research risks. China's own "Biosafety law" will come into effect in April 2021.

Take human genetic editing technology as an example. This technology has great potential for treating intractable diseases such as cancer, AIDS, Alzheimer's, Parkinson's, and other genetic diseases, but the potential risks and hazards to humans are also immeasurable. To this end, as early as December 2015, an insurmountable "red line" was had been clearly defined at the "International Summit on Human Genome Editing" in Washington where all parties reached a consensus to allow basic research on human embryo genetic editing, but agreed that putting this technology into clinical practice at present was "irresponsible" given our current state of limited knowledge. Nevertheless, Chinese scientist Jiankui HE genetically edited twin girls that were born in China in November 2018. The DNA of one of the babies was altered to resist HIV infection after birth. The "intention" to implement genetically modified technology on humans is not an original idea of HE's, but no one dared to experiment with humans because the worst outcome cannot be controlled. However, HE and his team dared risk alienating public opinion and brought the future of mankind into a dangerous game. This kind of "scientific experiment" is totally different from the harmless speculations of science fiction. Once Pandora's Box is opened, the consequences could be unimaginable (including genetic weapons that can destroy a race).

First, HE ignored the warnings and suggestions of the "Washington Summit" by applying the technology without sufficient prior research on humans, and crossed the line of responsible genetic editing technology which can only be safely applied to "treatment" and entered the field of so-called "prevention" and jumped ahead to the next step which is to attempt genetic modification for the purpose of "improving humans (see the relevant sections of "Human–machine civilization era" and "Superman" in Chapter 2). As Professor Kang WANG, a legal expert, said, the use of gene-editing technology in the field of reproductive medicine will create multidimensional risks, including technical uncertainty and potential irreversibility, ethical impact on human dignity and survival value, leading to new social inequalities and alienation of people in society, the absence of any clear direction in legal policy.

Second, HE cited the birth of the first test-tube baby, Louise Brown, and claimed that regulation, social ethics, and test tube technology are developing together. Not to mention the essential difference between test-tube babies and genetically edited babies, what is terrible is that this view leads to the misunderstanding of scientific ethics: "Ethical issues are a matter of concept, similar to the relationship between production relations and productivity. When productivity reaches a certain stage, new production relations are needed. When science and technology develop to a certain stage, new ethics should also be adopted." The key is that the excuses like "development together with science and technology" or "new ethics" cannot be used to defend genetically edited babies.

There are many definitions of ethics, among which the more commonly accepted explanation is: the moral standards (ideas) and codes of conduct that should be followed when dealing with the relationships between individuals, between people and society, and people and nature. The development of science and technology inevitably brings more complex and serious challenges to these relationships. Relevant ethics and moral norms need to be updated to keep pace with the times, so as to adapt to this change. However: (1) No matter how these relationships change, the root cause of these changes–the original intention of scientific and technological development should not change, namely, the progress of science and technology must benefit all of humankind; it should not destroy the living environment of human beings (nature); and it must respect life, revere nature, and promote the harmonious and sustainable development of human beings, human society, and other natural species. (2) No matter how ethics and moral norms are updated, human morality and ethics cannot be violated. Human dignity and overall well-being must not be damaged. That is, in activities of scientific research and technological innovation, the values, social responsibilities, and codes of conduct that scientists should abide by must be consistent with the purpose of developing science and technology to serve the long-term well-being of humanity, which is also the framework and bottom line for the development of cutting-edge science and technology. Although scientific exploration has no boundaries, any scientific research and its practical activities must adhere to ethical norms, and "new ethics" should not touch the ethical red line. We should maintain respect for and observance of scientific ethics, using a code of conduct for people who engage in scientific and technological activities from the perspective of concept and morality, that says "do no harm" and respect the primacy of humanness and nature.

There are people who say that in the so-called civilized world, ethics is secondary as long as there is a need. This is an extremely irresponsible remark. What is the civilized world? What is the need? Who needs it?

At present, more than 20 countries have banned the genetic editing of human embryos. On 26 February 2019, the National Health Commission of China promulgated the "Announcement of Public Consultation on the Regulations for the Clinical Application of New Biomedical Technologies." It contains seven chapters and 63 opinions and explains in detail from the perspective of clinical research project application and review, research process management, transformation application management, supervision and management, legal responsibility, and so on. And it will also legislate and regulate medical and scientific research related to human genes, human embryos, etc.

### Nanoscience and nanotechnology

Because, in the material world, the tiniest nanoparticles can be rearranged to become entirely new materials, nanotechnology may make it possible to leap forward in the microscopic world and allow human beings to gain a new understanding of the world, matter, and ultimately mankind itself. Certainly, nanoscience and nanotechnology will lead to the development of new sciences and technologies, including nanophysics, nanobiology, nanochemistry, nanoelectronics, nanoprocessing technology, nano-meteorology, and quantum processes.

At the limit, nanotechnology actually is a technology of making matter that uses a single atom or molecule. Significant advances in nanoscience and technology will lead to revolutionary changes to the preparation and application of materials in microelectronics, computers technology, medicine, manufacturing (reaching the limit of micro-processing technology through the "processing" with nano-precision, nano-coatings and the application of building materials containing nanoparticles, etc.), food production (highly sensitive nanomaterials can detect early changes in food for avoiding spoilage before it occurs), aerospace and aviation ( from microsatellites to nanosatellites, from carbon nanotubes to space cables), national defense (nano-weapons, pocket-sized aircraft, micro-detector, nano-military uniforms, etc.), environmental protection (capture and absorption of polluting gases, water desalination and purification methods with stronger filtering capacity and lower cost), energy (stronger energy production and storage systems to improve the efficiency of resource use, and so forth) and through better catalysts, improved energy storage.

In the medical field, for example,

- by designing nanoparticles to combat specific diseases, powerful antibiotics, and anti-inflammatory drugs can be developed to deal with bacterial and viral infections in specific parts of the body;
- nanoparticles could target specific parts of the brain or body, making Parkinson's disease, Alzheimer's disease, and even arthritis more effectively treated;
- nanoparticles can be used to detect early signs of as a new type of sniffer for diseases like cancer for diagnosis and treatment. Such molecular robots can circulate in the blood to examine, diagnose and treat various parts (e.g., dredging cerebrovascular thrombosis, removing fat and sediment from the heart arteries, and "chewing" stones in the urinary system, etc.);
- more durable, non- rejecting artificial tissues and organs are another potential application for nanoparticles;
- in magnetic resonance imaging, nanoparticles could make the scanning device become a sensor capable of detecting cancer cells, and the like.

Ray Kurtzweilsays that by 2020, we will begin to use nano-robots to take over the immune system; by 2030, nano-robots in the blood will be able to destroy pathogens, remove debris, blood clots, and tumors, correct DNA errors, and even reverse the aging process. He also recently conjectured that nano-robots will enter the brain through capillaries in a non-destructive way, linking our cerebral cortex to the cloud. As a result, we have an extra layer of the artificial new cortex.

Although the potential for nanotechnology is huge, studies have already raised concern about the field's related risks.

For example,

1. *Hidden dangers of widespread application*: At present, nanomaterials have already been widely used in industries such as medicine, dyestuffs, coatings, food, cosmetics, and environmental pollution control, so that researchers, producers, and consumers today have more opportunities to contact nanomaterials. What worries people is that nanoparticles with such small size are likely to penetrate the skin or enter other organs through the respiratory system, and thus may enter and lurk in human cells, and induce cytopathic effects, causing unpredictable and possibly irreparable harm to the body;
2. *Hazards caused by the abuse of nanotechnology*: Under the premise of insufficient research on characteristics and toxicity of nanomaterials and environmental safety assessment, and driven by huge military and commercial interests, eager to promote their industrialization, some nanotechnologies may unleash environmental and health disasters, especially through the

indiscriminate discharge of nano-waste that will be difficult to recycle, resulting in pollution of the environment and destruction of the ecosystem;

3. *Nano-weapons*: With the emergence of new biological cells and artificial nano-machines, more aggressive and concealed biological weapons, such as nano-electronic guns, nano-probes, and other ultra-micro-intelligent weaponry, perhaps even ultra-micro robot soldiers, vastly increasing the destructiveness of war;
4. *Security risks*: Nanotechnology brings greater challenges to protecting national military secrets, business secrets, and personal privacy, and even poses the danger of being used by terrorists;
5. *Challenges to social ethics*: Nanotechnology can give us the ability to change or even design the genetic code of our descendants. By changing the gene and cell structure, we can produce babies that meet predetermined goals, which will change the traditional way of birth;
6. *The challenge to life*: The emergence of nanotechnology bridges the gap between living things and non-things. If we put nano-robots assembled from the atoms of non-biological substances into the human body, organisms cannot be defined by the traditional standard of metabolism and reproductive capacity;
7. *Challenges to human nature*: Some scientists believe that nanotechnology can replicate the whole human body by replicating every cell in the original, unlike gene duplication in cloning. The essence of this kind of thinking is to regard "human" as simply a combination of cells. But in fact, we have no idea if this combination of cells will have the same thoughts and consciousness as the prototypes of human. The US magazine *Discover* even lists nanotechnology as one of the 20 major natural and man-made disasters that threaten humanity.

In view of the above risks, the National Nano Project (NNI) and ten recommendations of the American Academy of Sciences on NNI listed the issues of ethical, legal and social impact as well as employee education and training, etc. that may be involved in the development of nanotechnology as key supported research projects.

We should bear in mind the historical lessons caused by that after the discovery of radioactive materials, people only paid attention to the development and utilization of its functions, but neglected to study its harmful effects on the human body. It is necessary to give full attention to and study in the depth the function of nanomaterials and their potential impact on humans, so as to provide a scientific basis for the rational application of nanotechnology.

### Computing technology

Computing technology may be the most varied and influential technology of all. It is the basis for artificial intelligence (AI), 5G technology (5th generation mobile communication technology), mobile internet, block chain, 3D/4D technology, brain research, etc. On average, major advances in computing technology have occurred every 20 months, while in certain areas (such as processing speed, data storage, and memory capacity) have improved by more than 40 per cent per year. Ray Kurzweil believes that computers have advanced with geometric acceleration, from mechanical devices guided by punched cards, to machines powered first by electromagnetic relays, then vacuum tubes, transistors, early integrated circuits, and now to modern ultra large scale integrated circuits. The time needed for each step in computer design and technology is becoming progressively shorter (in accordance with a theorem known as Moore's law).

The breakthrough in computing technology represented by cloud computing vastly enhances the power of computers, and establishes a digital world parallel to the physical world in which the actions and behaviors of individuals and organizations take place. The Internet is evolving into a "cloud" network.[8] Currently, nearly half (48 per cent) of company data is stored in the cloud, up from a third (35 per cent) three years ago. From enhanced social media to a medical revolution based on metadata analysis, amazing data processing capability is rapidly making services and business transactions that were once unimaginable become commonplace.

Cloud computing potentially endows all machinery and equipment with wisdom, which can be achieved using only a small chip. In their 2012 annual forecast report, entitled *Deep Concern over the Direction of Technology Development*, IBM predicted that future computing devices will develop the ability to imitate the human senses of vision, hearing, taste, smell, and touch to further promote their cognitive function.

Watson, IBM's supercomputer, has demonstrated that it is able to match human knowledge and strategy in gaming contexts, recognize the occurrence of irony in human language, and even learn to use it. Watson is being used in healthcare (e.g., in DNA analysis, disease diagnosis); in finance, in developing legal arguments; in analysis of big data to develop effective policies. Soon, such supercomputers will be mobile (i.e., robots), and will almost certainly be equipped with sensor arrays that allow them to simulate human senses.

However, cloud computing still faces the challenges of cloud security, compliance, complexity, data integration, cost control and other factors. According to Intel spokesman Manny Vara, at present humans only use the capacity of "cloud computing" in a very primitive and superficial manner.

In an era of "Big Data,"[9] vast amounts of data about many areas of human activity are stored on the Internet, giving machines the ability to integrate and respond to questions on virtually any topic within a few seconds. The operational capability of one of today's handheld digital devices, such as the iPhone, easily puts an IBM mainframe of the 1970s to shame.

Experts predict that in the near future, most computers will actually disappear from view. Instead, they will be embedded into infrastructure and devices, and will operate at speeds at least 100 thousand times and perhaps even 1 million times faster than current computers. Storage will no longer rely on disks or any mechanical device. Instead, the moving parts of the computer will disappear, and holography and other forms of storage will be used. Then a supercomputer may have a billion processors, which may include digital, analog, neural networks, quantum, and/or molecular computing devices. Quantum computers may lead to a real revolution of AI. By then, these machines will make our life and our world radically different from today

## Artificial intelligence and intelligent robots

At a conference of Dartmouth University In 1956, the concept of AI was proposed for the first time by a group of mathematicians, information scientists, psychologists, neurophysiologists and computer scientists, which included such experts as John McCarthy, the father of AI (1927–2011) and Marvin Minsky (1927–2016), etc. After more than 60 years of development, research and development of AI have made remarkable progress, which is changing the whole world. Nowadays, AI and intelligent robots are being applied to almost all human activities such as education, intelligent medical care (covering such areas as diagnosis, and treatment and management) smart cities, transportation, pension administration, social security, etc. with unpredictable speed and breadth. The world is experiencing a new upsurge in every aspect of AI.

Various definitions of AI focus on the objectives of different specific applications. For example, AI is to study how to make computers do intelligent work that only people could do in the past; AI is a research that allows computers to display wisdom, and to perform such tasks as learning, reasoning, planning, perception, speech recognition, and robot control; AI is the theory, method, technology and application system for perceiving the environment, acquiring knowledge and using that knowledge to obtain the best results using digital computers or machines controlled by digital computer to simulate, enhance and expand human intelligence. From the perspective of interdisciplinary and cross domain integration, I believe that AI is a knowledge and technology system which integrates hard science and soft science, as well as hard technology and soft technology, enabling computers or robots to possess their own unique wisdom and intelligence in a variety of ways (such as brain-like intelligence, autonomous intelligence, man–machine hybrid enhancement, and collective intelligence) and to have function in ways similar to human emotion, thinking, self-consciousness, etc.

There are several hypotheses about the stages of AI development: from weak AI (AWI) to strong AI, then to super AI (ASI); from artificial narrow intelligence (ANI) to artificial generalized intelligence (AGI), etc. Regardless of how it is classified, the fundamental dividing line is whether AI has consciousness and whether it can duplicate or truly transcend human beings.

It is generally believed that AI may take some time to progress from the weak AI to strong AI, but the time from the strong AI to a stage of super AI, may be much shorter than many imagine. Most scientists believe that AI systems may exceed human intelligence in this century. As Stephen Hawking pointed out, the evolution of AI systems may be much faster, than that of biological systems, perhaps even exponential.

With the development of AI entering into the so-called artificial super intelligence stage, the level that intelligent robots can reach is called "humanoid robot" or "anthropomorphous intelligent robot" by relevant experts. This may also prove to be the ultimate goal of AI technology explored by scientists.

The so-called humanoid robot is a "robot" that is independent of natural person. Smarter software would enable them to communicate with people, have the ability to learn, have humanized independent thinking, emotional experiences, and even the ability to make self-improvements repeatedly, making themselves more and more intelligent.

The anthropomorphous intelligent robot is being designed with exquisite facial features, smooth skin, better body shape, gentle temperament, profound knowledge, agile thinking, decent conversation, and elegant demeanor, etc. It might also change shape, voice, personality, reaction and behavior patterns according to changing situations and specific needs.

### 1. What do humans fear about AI?

The development of AI will undoubtedly create more convenient and better prospects for the future life of mankind. However, one reason why people are so alarmed about AI's potential now is concern over whether AI will ultimately replace humans, and even bring about the destruction of the human race.

In fact, the article "Top 10 global AI governance events in 2020" shows that the breakthrough of AI, has raised concern about a wide range of security and data privacy issues. Some countries have enacted new regulations on AI in governance, and even identified areas where AI development and application are to be strictly restricted or even banned. For example, the EU plans legislation to limit the abuse of AI, Governing the development direction of AI research and assuring that there will be international cooperation in this effort thus becomes an urgent task.

The means that may lead to human destruction have long included more than just the development of humanoid robots. Like nuclear technology, biotechnology, artificial epidemics, chemical technology, and other new technologies all pose similar risks, if they are applied and monitored improperly. In the development of these technologies we have experienced many twists and turns, and even painful lessons. Of course, we should not "give up eating for fear of choking" and seek to stop the pace of technological innovation that could bring benefits to all humanity.

The common point of the above-mentioned technologies and AI is that, in the final analysis, both are the results of materialization of technology, namely, what "products" humans manufacture.

The difference between the risks of the above technologies and the AI crisis is that the former, whether used for human welfare or for evil purposes, always remains within human control so long as human beings reach a consensus. For AI, in the primary or intermediate stage of its development, it can be controlled by researchers, but once it creates an alternative "species" and enters the stage in which these humanoid machines can self-reproduce and improve, the researchers cannot call the shots (much as parents alone can no longer control their own children who have already turned to crime). Their "capabilities" will not only surpass humans in many ways, but their surge may be inversely proportional to the declining traditional population.

At that stage, even if human beings can reached a consensus about future directions for AI, it will be too late to control their behavior of super intelligent robots, and they will be fully capable of competing with traditional humans for control. Conquering traditional humans will be only a matter of time if there is an error in the software program or if self-rebellion occurs. This is why experts even believe that AI is more dangerous than terrorism.

### 2. AI is and will undoubtedly continue to benefit mankind, but is not omnipotent, its role will be still limited

In the coming decades, AI will make great progress in theory, technology and application, and may lead a new technological revolution in various fields and industries. As long as we are "willing", AI can be applied in almost any area of human activity, from care for children to management of cities; from education to medical care, food production to transportation, pension reform, social security, financial management, etc. The result will be to promote a series of future industrial clusters that will revolutionize traditional agriculture, manufacturing, transportation, commerce, medical care, lawyering and other fields. Altogether these future industrial clusters will make possible smart cities, and all kinds of intelligent services that will redefine many traditional concepts and management methods. Applying AI in the utilization of fixed assets is expected to achieve a truly "shared economy", and the number of robots in some countries may well approach or exceed the human population.

In the near future, intelligent robots will have senses that are similar to humans: sight, sound, and touch. They may also have the functions of thinking, memory, experience and super memory. These robots will be able to exchange information with humans using text or voice, etc., through web pages, instant messaging, text messages, phone calls, microblogging, and other electronic channels, as well as via hardware devices such as smart phones, smart TVs, intelligent vehicle equipment, and smart toys and games, becoming the leading role in all kinds of service industries in the future. They will not only be able to converse normally with us in human languages but also the prospect of instant and accurate translation will help remove barriers of human-to-human conversation in different languages. Scientific research and technological development will be improved through AI, and it may even be possible to use AI to make decisions based on a "reasoned" analysis of potential outcomes.

In short, AI will lead to tremendous changes in the mode of economic development, lifestyle, all traditional industries in today's world, make a greater contribution to social change, and help create a completely different world.

However, there must be a clear understanding of the following three points:

First, the above technological progress is not made by AI alone, but as the result of the synergy between AI and many so-called next-generation technologies, such as new generation of information technology, including mobile Internet, Internet of Things, big data and 5G, biotechnology, robotics, new materials technology, voice technology, 3D and bio-printing technology, nanotechnology, etc.

Second, in the list of developments related to the future of mankind, the contribution of AI to civilization is limited.

- To create the advanced civilization that humanity yearns for, transcending industrial civilization to achieve Global Civilization and even Great Civilization, the contribution of AI is limited, and requires creation and practice by human beings. If human beings do not grasp the development direction of AI in time, AI may make human civilization retrogress instead of advancing (see the relevant section on the "Human–machine civilization era" in Chapter 2).
- It will be difficult for AI alone to provide a satisfactory solution to the world peace that mankind yearns for, including dealing with terrorism and other security crises (see the section of "Debates on perpetual peace" in Chapter 5).

It will also be difficult for AI to solve many problems faced by today's society, such as social justice, the gap between the rich and the poor, and the mental factors in human health, which are most closely related to human happiness, or preventing climate disasters.

Third, we are still exploring the mystery of human beings themselves. It is too early to assert that AI could transcends humanity.

- Can the "products" created by AI really have the complete intelligence of human beings? First of all, human intelligence is not just the ability to "learn, remember, reason, search, calculate, analyze, generalize, innovate, etc." Although future robots may well store more information than humans or libraries and can calculate and make decisions in milliseconds, most human intelligence and behaviors are incalculable by machine. Human creativity, imagination, passion, and aesthetic ability, not to mention personal beliefs, are not derived from logic or calculation. Sometimes illogical thinking and imagination play important roles. Humans are intellectual beings with rationality, emotion, purpose, values, beliefs and ideals, who are good at dealing with the relations between human and nature, human and humans, as well as human and society in social life. Can humanoid robots do that?
- Humanoid robots can simulate certain human behaviors or human-like emotions, thoughts, and consciousness, etc. However, our understanding of consciousness is still very primitive, including the mechanism of consciousness. In fact, the vast universe and the mysterious inner world of human thought and motivation are the last two virgin lands of human intelligence, especially the nature of human consciousness, which may be the biggest puzzle in the universe. A study of the Blue Brain Project, hosted by Henry Markham, a neuroscientist at the Federal Institute of Technology in Lausanne, Switzerland, found that although we are used to looking at the world from a three-dimensional perspective, our brains may be operating in eleven dimensions. Moreover, people have always believed that the brain receives external stimuli through five senses, but scientists have found that humans have at least 11 senses, such as magnetic, gravity, heat, and pain. Our understanding of humanity itself, including the understanding of life, and the study of consciousness, are only just beginning. How can we glibly assert that AI will come to possess human consciousness or emotion! Indeed, AI helps to explore life and even human consciousness, but it is too early to assert that as natural, social, and moral people, human beings will be fully surpassed. Furthermore, at present, humans are still evolving, including the evolution of human beings as natural persons and the sublimation of human nature as social persons.
- Therefore, it's too early to say that, only by the computing power of computer, or according to the "learning, memory, reasoning, search, calculation, analysis, induction and other capabilities of AI that in a certain year" computer systems as powerful as the human brain "(remember that the brain is not a

simple biological computer)" or "artificial intelligence will surpass human intelligence", far less that "computers in the future are human beings".

Fourth, whether AI will destroy human beings or be the terminator of human civilization depends mainly on the success of monitoring and guiding its development direction. Particularly important is governance of the progress from Artificial Weak Intelligence (AWI) to Artificial Super Intelligence (ASI) or from Artificial Narrow Intelligence (ANI) to Artificial General Intelligence (AGI).

**3. Severe challenges facing the AI era**

At present, even if we are still in the stage of weak AI, intelligent robots do better than humans in many aspects. But no matter into which stage AI develops, it will encounter different challenges, such causing high unemployment, large-scale militarized applications, social governance, ethical dilemmas, the risk of out-of-control and rebellion of intelligent robots. Will humans eventually give up control of the earth to AI machines? When we celebrate the advent of AI era, we must clearly understand that more and more risks arise with the development from weak AI to super AI. Recognizing that such risks exist will give us time to take preventive measures

1) *The first impact of AI on society—Employment Shock*: AI and intelligent robots are infiltrating and changing all areas of human activities, including the nature and meaning of work. One day, although there may still be a few things that only humans can do, intelligent machines will be engaged in all kinds of work that are meaningless, repetitive, cumbersome and dangerous. In special periods, the role of robot is even more difficult to replace. In China's battle against the new coronavirus in 2020, all kinds of intelligent robot systems were launched in more than ten hospitals in Wuhan, Shanghai, Beijing, Zhejiang and Guangxi. These intelligent robots worked in hospitals, especially in isolation areas, helping medical staff to complete auxiliary diagnosis, measure temperatures, provide remote care, distribute medication, disinfect and clean, equipment and supplies, improve the efficiency of diagnosis and treatment, reducing cross infection of medical staff, and not only reducing the workload, but also improving the isolation control level of the wards. In addition, the robots did not need protective equipment, greatly saving the very scarce protective clothing, masks and other materials.

   As the use of robots in the Covid-19 pandemic indicates the broad prospects of the robot "profession" and as they become more intelligent, they become more autonomous. They also may be cheaper, faster, more efficient, more accurate, and tireless. It is true that, increasingly, human work can be replaced by robots in the future. Futurist Tomas Frey believes that two billion human jobs will be replaced by machines by 2030; According to a statistic by Professor Kaplan of Stanford University, 47 per cent of the 720 occupations registered in the United States will be replaced by AI. In China, 70 per cent of occupations may be impacted by AI in the future. Some even say that in the foreseeable future, more than 95 per cent of jobs ultimately will be replaced by AI. In China, food delivery and restaurants are changing significantly: delivery services are increasingly intelligent as are the ordering of meals and takeout. Trials of unmanned restaurants and unmanned hotels are beginning. Traditional jobs will continue but machine or robots will do many or most of them.

If that is the case, robots will serve human beings continually with loyalty and in a whole-hearted manner, and everything will be done by intelligent robots, robots will even have the ability to program themselves! If human beings are not ready to change the way they "live" and do not change their understanding about work or employment, the impact of AI on employment will become a great crisis, many of us will be idle.

By that time even humanoid robots who do not rebel at all, the entire world, including the spiritual world, will be plunged into endless chaos, or the species of human will rapidly degenerate in both physical characteristics and intelligence, without waiting to be destroyed by AI.

However, in the long run, this "shock" may be a good thing, forcing us to re-define the nature and significance of what we consider employment or a job. What is a "job"? Why do we need to work?

Throughout the history of mankind, the term "job" has been used to describe a variety of activities essential for survival. However, in the highly technologically advanced future, we will have tools of such enormous power, and "extremely intelligent partners"—(i.e. advanced robots) that humans can be completely liberated from monotonous, heavy and dangerous work. This will free us to perform jobs that are more meaningful and valuable to us as individuals, to society, to nature, to the earth and to the universe at many levels and to be happy and joyful by doing these "new jobs".

All in all, smarter human beings may continue to develop new ideas, modes of living, and productive pursuits, and the above pessimistic scenario would not occur. As AI gradually replaces more human mental and physical labor, it is necessary to establish a productive partnership between humans and ubiquitous intelligent robots to work together and live together.

Of course, this is also a huge challenge. First of all, we should consider what kinds of work are appropriate for intelligent robots and what other work may not be. The distinction involves the direction of AI, some of the ethical issues facing AI, and how to take precautions against certain kinds of risks.

History shows that with the passing of time, human needs and desires change with the times. As human beings are liberated from heavy physical and mental labor by intelligent machines, they will continue to create greater needs and desires will expand. This will promote a new wave of scientific research and technological innovation, giving birth to new industries, Including new services, new products and new working methods. Of course, people who cannot keep learning and updating their knowledge will most likely be eliminated.

Thus even in the future, human work will not disappear, but will take new forms as new lifestyles and consumption patterns emerge. People will have more time to acquire more knowledge (because human understanding of life, matter, earth, and the entire universe is just a drop in the ocean), and carry out higher-end scientific research and technological innovation activities that will make human work and life more enjoyable and more meaningful. In a sense, robots will have changing needs, too: expand new "careers" for intelligent robots.

For instance, new jobs appropriate to helping the aged of aging (like the ongoing robot revolution in Japan), effectively assisting human beings in invention and creation, improving the research and development efficiency of soft and hard science and technology, participating in missions involved in interplanetary exploration (such as preparing for manned presence on inhospitable planets), or helping mankind to uncover the secrets of the deep earth, oceans, or the vast universe.

Finally, we need to reflect on one question: Will humans be happy if robots do most of the difficult tasks? For example, caring for the elderly, nurturing children, and establishing a relationship of mutual respect and love are the differences between humans and animals. Can robots ever replace parents' affection, or teach young children by example? For parents, raising children and watching them grow up is fulfilling and enjoyable. For young people, honoring their parents and returning the grace of parenting can also purify their own souls and satisfy their spirits, making the whole of society more harmonious. Freeing up all the time to innovate, leisure and entertain, and experiencing a new ways of life, will not be considered worthwhile in the long term or bring happiness. We know that kinship and friendship, loving and being loved, giving and returning are all sources of joy and happiness.

2) ***Weaponization of robots and killer robots***: The militarization of AI would not only reshape the form of war but also greatly "speed" up military decision-making. The resulting risk would be disruptive to world peace. Take the killing robot for example.

The concept of killer robots is not new. Machines have been used as tools of war for a long time. In fact, human beings have a very disgraceful historical record, and the more developed the technology, the more terrifying the means of killing other human beings has become. Nuclear, chemical, biological, and laser weapons have all been developed using advanced science and technology. Now, with the development of drone technology, and the development and application of quadruped patrol robots, killer robots with the aid of AI are ready to emerge. The military of all countries are paying special attention to this possibility. The United States, Britain, Russia, Israel and other countries are involved in a race to create a killer robot corps. Even terrorist organizations are trying to master AI to increase the power of their attacks. Russia is building a force consisting of killer robots, including drone tanks controlled by AI. The British Army also announced plans to deploy 200 micro drones that are "smaller than human hand" on the battlefield to provide "eyes in the sky" for soldiers.

Using autonomous robots for military purposes raises many important ethical issues. Can decisions involving human life and death be allocated to robots? Even humanoid robots are amoral. A completely autonomous machine, whether it is a military drone or a nurse companion, will be fully capable of doing dangerous things or be open to hacking.

No one knows how robot soldiers will perform in battle. For example, changes in enemy characteristics, ingenious camouflage, or malicious operations, accidental interference, and cyber-attacks by the "enemy" may lead to unpredictable system behaviors, making it difficult for the robot to distinguish between friends and foes or between the civilians and the enemy combatants, resulting in misguided attacks, and even subverting our weapons to make them become "insurgents" or "internal traitors" fighting, perhaps surreptitiously, for the enemy. With these dangers in mind it may be more appropriate not to develop autonomous automated weapon operating systems at all.

The topic of autonomous killer robots has been brought to the International Court of justice for discussion. Scientists and human rights activists warn that lethal robots, which automatically select targets without human guidance, represent the "third war revolution" after gunpowder and nuclear weapons. What is even more frightening is that up to now, human beings have no way to guarantee that these weapons will not make mistakes or accidentally hurting large numbers of civilians.

At present, the scale of the "international stop killer robot movement" is expanding. It is reported that 113 NGOs from 57 countries have joined this movement in the past year. But this is not enough. What we need now is a new international convention to regulate the development and use of robots.

However, the militarization of AI is by no means limited to the field of intelligent robots. It will completely change the nature of warfare and make the world more dangerous. What is even more worrying is that some countries are already preparing for AI war.

3) ***AI will also have a lasting and irreversible effect on social governance***: From a positive perspective, modern AI, supported by advanced technologies such as big data, cloud computing, the Internet of Things, and 5G technology, which can promote intelligent processes in all aspects of social governance including Judicial field and decision-making, we can expect to see the emergence of "virtual players" similar to "Alpha Dogs", which makes public services such as city management, rationalization of land use, traffic management, public security, delivery of healthcare, and even government decision-making more convenient, efficient and scientific (a necessary ingredient in achieving these kinds of improvements is access to reliable data). This will undoubtedly bring revolutionary improvements the level of social governance. Of course, relative to technical feasibility, relevant mechanisms and systems (such as breaking information barriers) are the basis for realizing the above blueprint.

However, the challenges of AI to social governance are by no means limited to the aforementioned areas. The social changes brought about by AI are comprehensive. For example, society may become very rich, with wealth concentrated in certain professions or social strata, leading to expansion of the gap between rich and poor, which poses a great threat to social stability, feelings of injustice, riots ultimately and in the extreme, social warfare. We must know that society will only be stable when it is fair. In an era when artificial intelligence results in expansion of leisure, the vast majority of people may not need to work and only a few people can support the entire population, resulting high levels of structural unemployment. Such an economic and social structure has never been experienced by humans in history; the change in the meaning of work, lifestyle, global culture, and changes in people's ways of thinking have prompted human society to change its long-standing "rules of the game"; new types of social security issues, including how to protect privacy and how to deal with new classes of crime. When social media companies who rely heavily on advertising and primarily seek to maximize profits get out of control (spreading false, harmful and dangerous information, selling and abusing users' personal data, etc.), this can lead to a large number of new social problems. How can we guide and regulate social media? It seems that only restraint by the originators of harmful or self-serving falsehoods can prevent these from becoming widespread in today's (and tomorrow's) media-dominated world. And the relationship between social media and politics Is becoming more complex and troublesome. In a big data society, the relationship between government and citizens has changed completely; there are a series of legal issues surrounding AI, etc. These issues are deep-seated and we will have to discover how this kind of society is to be governed. This calls for a new revolution in social governance.

These are issues that may have to be faced in the early and medium stages of AI development. By the time truly strong AI emerges, the challenges faced by humans to maintain autonomy will be unimaginably great (see Chapter 2 on Five wars among three categories of species).

In June 2019, China's "National New Generation AI Governance Professional Committee" issued the "New Generation AI Governance Principles: Developing Responsible AI." It proposed eight governance principles and action guidelines, including "harmony and friendship, fairness and justice, inclusiveness and sharing, respect for privacy, security and controllability, shared responsibility, open cooperation, and agile governance." The key is how to "transform or translate" these principles or values into the indicators that can be used as a basis for compliance, specification, or evaluation by R&D, application, management and law enforcement departments and for international supervision agencies of AI to monitor their actual operation. For example, how the R&D department reflects the above governance principles in the process of obtaining data, designing algorithms, and programming.

Only when each stage of the development and application of AI complies with the corresponding norms and the so-called initial conditions are "correct" from technical, ethical and legal perspectives, can it be ensured that AI is safe, controllable, reliable and risk averse, and that the development from AWI to ASI, or from ANI to AGI will not threaten the future of humanity and will always serve the progress of human civilization.

To this end, since 2020, the Millennium Project,[10] in collaboration with a number of internationally noted institutions and senior experts, has designed and proposed a research project—"Global Governance of the Transition from ANI to AGI." The purpose of this proposal is to develop and internationally assess potential governance models for the transition from ANI to AGI, as a contribution to current governance analyses. This study has three foci: What has to be governed? What global approaches can govern them? And what are the potential consequences, feasibility, and effectiveness of each?

4) ***Ethics and morality***: With the in-depth development and widespread application of AI, the challenges we face have already gone beyond purely technical and economic levels, and its risks to the humanities and social fields may shake our social foundation. Among these, one of the sharpest disputes is related to ethical norms and policy orientation in the development and application of AI.

In order to solve the potential challenges of AI in relevant laws, regulations, ethics and social norms, countries have created list of ethical principles, norms, guidelines and standards, hoping to lay the foundation for their healthy development and to keep the final boundary of natural human beings.

Perhaps the first listing of rules for robot behavior came from the science fiction writer Isaac Asimov in his 1942 short story titled "run around". That was written before artificial intelligence was on the horizon, but those laws are certainly applicable today (see the section of "Human must regulate technology" in Chapter 3).

As early as January 2015, the European Parliament's Legal Affairs Committee decided to set up a working group to study legal issues related to the development of robotics and AI. In 2016, the report on AI and robots released by European Parliament expressed its concern about the risks that robots will pose to humans, including security, privacy, integrity, dignity, and autonomy. The European Parliament passed a resolution on 16 February 2017, asking the European Commission to propose legislation on robotics and AI.

In April 2016, the Institute of Electrical and Electronics Engineers (IEEE), the world's largest non-profit professional and technical society, released the IEEE Global Initiative on Ethics of Autonomous and Intelligent Systems. One report of the project, issued in 2017, was titled "Ethically Aligned Design"; it contained a list of 13 ethical issues of AI.

In August 2016, UNESCO and the World Commission on the Ethics of Scientific Knowledge and Technology jointly released a Draft Preliminary Report on Robot Ethics, which argued that robots not only need to respect the ethical norms of human society, but also need to incorporate specific ethical principles into the robot programs.

In April 2018, the British House of Lords published a 183-page report, "AI in the UK: Ready, Willing and Able?"[11] It called for attention and research on the ethical and legal issues of AI.

In July 2018, the CCID Research Institute of the Ministry of Industry and Information Technology of China issued a 22-item Declaration on the Ethics of Innovative Development in AI. That same month, the China Development Research Foundation and Microsoft Co., Ltd. jointly issued a report, Foundation for the Future—Artificial Intelligence's Role in Society and Ethics.

In an article published in February 2021, entitled "Can AI Algorithms Ever Be Ethical?—the perils of cyberspace and social media," Hazel Henderson points out that "Today we all live in Mediocracies and their Attention Economies," where the algorithms used by social media companies and Internet companies are designed to capture users' attention and then sell their personal information to advertisers, data brokers, insurance and other companies to make more profits. She created the word "mediocracies" to mean that media (all communications media: print, radio, TV cable and internet social media platforms, e.g., Facebook) are now dominant in politics and commerce and have begun to replace all other forms of government. To this end, she raised series of questions: "Can we regulate how decisions over our lives are delegated to big data, automation and computer programs?", "Can algorithms created by humans (and thus reflecting their views and biases) ever become ethical?" She advocates that we "Train Humans First before We Train Machines", and proposes establishing of a series of robust, transparent code of ethics to hold the programmers of AI algorithms publicly accountable.

Fortunately, there are already some pioneering enterprises that challenge ethical issues in the development and application of AI. With the goal of designing reliable AI, Microsoft has come up with solutions that embody ethical principles. The company regards the six ethical principles of fairness, reliability and security, privacy and confidentiality, inclusiveness, transparency, and responsibility as guiding principles for the development of AI. They have also set up an AI ethics committee to implement these six principles. Google has stated that in the development and application of AI, it adheres to seven principles including fairness, security, transparency, and privacy protection, etc., and clearly lists "four bottom lines" that Google will not pursue in AI application.

Obviously, the opinion that in the development and application of AI, ethics must occupy a central position has become an international consensus.

5) ***Serious philosophical issues***: Intelligent robots with autonomous consciousness, creative ability, human-like emotions and attributes of social interaction have gradually emerged, which are likely to make robots nearly indistinguishable from natural humans. All these bring us to a series of fundamental questions that are difficult to avoid but must be answered:
   - With the help a large number of emerging technologies, intelligent robots can be designed and manufactured to be "smarter" or "more perfect" than ordinary people. Based on this, can they be said to be "humans"? What is the essence of human-ness? What do human capabilities include?
   - Are humanoid robots inorganic? What is life?
   - Are conscious things human beings? What is consciousness? If we cannot deeply analyze the human mind itself, how can we talk about issues beyond humanity?
   - If humanoid robots have various functions of traditional humans, should "they" be considered to have the same personality and dignity as natural humans, including not being regarded as "servants," be insulted and abused? Should they have the basic rights to enjoy freedom and human rights, including being placed in harsh environments? Should robots be

considered moral or legal subjects? Should they be regarded as legal citizens? If they cause certain economic losses or adverse social impact, should they bear corresponding economic and social responsibility? If a robot kills illegally in battle, who is responsible for the death, the robot or its owner? (Can a robot be judged guilty of war crimes?)

- Can humanoid robots, like natural humans, interact freely with other intelligent robots, form an economic partnership or certain "social organizations" based on common interests or benefits, and even make economic and political demands?
- What are the consequences for human beings of building relationships with a robot, becoming their partners, or even getting married? In fact, a companion robot/sex robot has already been successfully developed both in the United States and Japan. The Japanese sex robot–"wife" sold out one hour after it went online. "They" are smart, have ideal appearance and personality characteristics, simulate the temperature of the human body, and can communicate with humans simply. Abyss creations, a California based company, has also announced that its female sex robot–"Harmony" has been successfully developed and put on sale. "Harmony" has 12 personality characteristics, including naive, kind, friendly and shy. RealBotix, an affiliate of the company, has successfully developed the world's first robot boyfriend–"Henry", and it can be customized. In addition to their body-builder appearance, you can also choose from among 18 kinds of personalities, such as talkative, shy, quiet, and humorous. The companion robot may be the "most perfect" lover, who never grows old, will never betray you, is always considerate, and so on. However, "communication" with a sex robot may be addictive, and may even gradually replace interpersonal relationships in the future. The emergence of sex robots means that the relationship between men and women, including true love, which is the oldest and most traditional relationship of human beings, is facing a challenge from AI. If the use of sex robots becomes widespread, the impact on the traditional human family, cultural awareness and even on society as a whole will be unprecedented.
- How could robot achieve values and morals? In humans, emotions, consciousness, beliefs, and decision-making functions are affected by the comprehensive influence of their world view; outlook on life and values are not driven by simple instructions, but rather through association with peers and family and inferred from the environment. Can this also be true for robots? So who and how will these affect a humanoid robot to form values?
- How is the "consciousness" of humanoid robots "infused"? Do modern humans without the transformation of civilization have the "qualifications" to link human brains with machines (see the section of "Are we qualified?"

in Chapter 2), and do humans today even have the right to design robots able to independently make decisions on key issues related to human survival?

6) ***In the face of this AI revolution, beware of falling behind***: From the above analysis, we can see that this wave of AI has brought human beings into an era where they have to coexist and co-operate with intelligent robots. This era will not only bring colorful and bright prospects to human life but also make humans face many challenges, risks and problems. Such an AI revolution will not only be unprecedented the fields of science, technology and industry, but will also create profound social changes.

   The lessons of history must not be forgotten. At the national level, for example, China should not forget the lessons of its failure to integrate and achieve the first industrial revolution, which led to its backwardness and being beaten in recent centuries. In fact, this new wave of AI is leading the fourth industrial revolution, and driving new lifestyles, education models, business models, innovation models, etc. We should not only keep up with the tide of this "revolution", but also correctly guide and govern the development and innovation of AI. Remember, AI is a technological tool invented by human beings, and its future depends on us. Second, at the individual level, since it is difficult for us to change the rapid development of science and technology process, we can only change ourselves, through learning to change the knowledge structure to adapt to the progress of the times. Whether it is ordinary workers, experts or scholars in various fields, let alone decision makers at all levels, if they lack learning, they will have no right to speak, lose job opportunities, and be eliminated by history.

   It is worth mentioning that the aforementioned crises and challenges brought on by AI are by no means "made" by AI alone, but by the development and integration of science and technology in various fields with subversive influence. After all, AI is a material manifestation of human wisdom, so human beings should take the initiative; actively adapt to and be prepared to live in an era of robots; be prepared for an intelligent society in which humans can coexist and develop together with AI; and formulate various rules for this coexistence, including new laws and social norms to prevent crime and other malign AI applications.

   In short, the new technological revolution led by AI calls for cross-disciplinary, cross domain cooperation and in-depth research in relevant policies, systems, laws, and regulations, so as to make AI beneficial to the development of human society and not separate from human monitoring.

## Intelligent manufacturing and 3D/4D

At present, the new industrial revolution is in the ascendant, and the global manufacturing industry is moving towards a digital and intelligent era. Intelligent manufacturing can be characterized by deep integration of information technology, with advanced manufacturing, automation and AI technology, runs through all aspects of manufacturing activities, such as design, equipment, production, management, and service, and is realizing the intellectualization of the entire manufacturing value chain from raw materials to consumer. As an important direction for the future development of manufacturing industry, intelligent manufacturing is regarded by all countries as a key point of high-end manufacturing industry and a focus of future competition. At the same time, the manufacturing industry is also faced with a large number of laid-off workers, cyber security and other challenges.

Take 3D printing for example. As a new technology that subverts the traditional manufacturing industry, it is a synthetic product of advanced manufacturing technology, computer technology and material technology. 3D printing once introduced into the manufacturing industry, will not only saves cost, speeds up progress, saves materials etc, but also creates flexible manufacturing.

3D printing uses computer digital modeling and computer control to form objects with 3D complex structures by stacking materials–plastic, metal particles, ceramic, biologic materials—layer after layer. 3D printing has opened up a new era of personalized customization using almost any material, to form almost any complex structure, in almost any industrial field, on short notice.

For engineers, dreams that could not be achieved through mass production in the past are no longer a problem. One might say that this is the greatest feat in the manufacturing sector since Henry Ford's production line in 1908, for it allows us to make high-quality design talent the driving force in the manufacturing field rather than cheap labor. This will also make it possible to re-establish the developed countries as manufacturing centers. The 2014 International Consumer Electronics Show (held 7–10 January 2014, in Las Vegas) indicated that 3D printing technology does not belong exclusively to engineers and technology enthusiasts, but enables ordinary individuals to enter into a world of Mass Customization, which will significantly change our lives. To cite just one example, the Amaze Project, into which the European Space Agency has already invested two billion euros, has illustrated that 3D printing can be used to advantage with metals.

3D printing technology itself is changing rapidly, from props production in special effects originally used in films to powerful tools for producing furniture and building materials. It is now possible to print out food, cars, airplanes (according to the report at the beginning of 2019, 3D printed titanium parts were first installed on the U.S. F-22 fighter) or even entire houses and bridges (ten 3D printed buildings were delivered in Shanghai in 2014 and the first 15 meter long 3D printing bridge appeared in Shanghai in early 2019; In 2021, the first batch of residents settled in 3D printed houses in the Netherlands); while the developing 3D bio printing technology can provide better donor for human organ transplantation.

Invetech of Australia and Organovo (a start-up company headquartered in San Diego, CA) have jointly developed the world's first commercial 3D Bio-Printer. The liver's ability to regenerate itself makes it an ideal object for biological printing. Under the precise guidance of computer, 3D printing technology can duplicate and assemble live cells layer by layer. Organovo regarded the liver as a solid stepping stone for perfecting the technology to cultivate human organs in the laboratory. They announced that they have used 3D printing technology to print out liver slices whose tissue functions (i.e., filtering nutrients, toxins, and drugs) could be kept active for up to 40 days.

In May 2019, the Journal "Science" reported that scientists at Rice University realized a lung model with a "breathing" function (complete with blood vessels and airways), using a hydrogel 3D printer. This was another revolutionary breakthrough.

There have long been problems of inadequate matching and insufficient donor sources for skin and organ transplantation. Many patients have lost their lives because they did not receive timely transplantation. Unlike cloning technology, 3D bio printing technology is more secure in the physiological sense, and the printing process is also highly controllable, so that the risk is relatively smaller. Still more good news comes from Spain: the birth of 3D printed "living robots".

3D printing technology could dramatically alters military capability, not only by making incredible new weapons designs attainable, but also because it has the potential to completely change the defense industry (and perhaps the entire global economy). In the United States, the defense industry with its billions of dollars in government funding is in the forefront of this innovation. Alex Chausovsky, an information analyst at Handling Services Inc. (IHS), reports that the US military has invested large sums of money in using 3D printing technology to produce uniform, artificial skin for the treatment of war wounds and even to produce food.

The applications of 3D printing technology in the field of aerospace have also made rapid progress. British Aerospace Systems will be the first to print out the metal parts to be used in the creation of a replica of the Whirlwind, a Second World War fighter bomber. The rocket engine developed by Aerojet Rocketdyne Inc. uses 3D printing technology to manufacture injector components, combustion chamber and throat nozzle parts, which greatly simplifies the engine structure. The engine on which these parts were used took only seven months to develop and produce, and the manufacturing cost was lower than that of traditional engine. Since 2015, Thales Alenia Space has sent 79 metal structure parts and 350 polymer pipe fittings made by 3D printing into space.

But perhaps the most surprising future for digital manufacturing lies in fourth dimension—printing objects that are able to change over time based on their programming. 3D objects are static, which means that they require manual control, while 4D objects can automatically react to the environment, self-assemble, change shape over with time, and even repair themselves when damaged. Scientists at MIT invented "4D Printing" when they created a substance that could change color when it was brought into contact with water. One day, this will allow objects printed out in 3D to change color in response to changes in the environment. 4D printing may also fight against cancer (the researchers used the DNA chain to create a nanobot against cancer).

But 3D printing raises many concerns as well. For instance, this technology could be used by criminals (to fabricated pistols and handcuff keys with a 3D printer). There are also problems about product accountability and intellectual property. The most worrisome risks may occur in the biological field. It is necessary to promote the research and application of 3D printing technology in various fields should be synchronized with the corresponding laws and regulations, so that the research and application can be followed by the law.

Of course, 3D/4D printing technology is still in its early stages. It will take some time to achieve mass production and to expand markets for such printed products. However, we should prepare ourselves for this next wave of the manufacturing revolution.

### Brain engineering

Brain science has been one of the fastest developing disciplines over the last twenty years. In the past ten years alone, scientists have made a series of landmark achievements in brain science, including successfully connecting a brain to an external device. More than ten scientists who have been engaged in brain science have won the Nobel Prize during this period. Ray Kurzweil predicted that by the years 2040–45, we will be able to upload our entire consciousness into a computer.

The actual situation is moving faster than he predicted. According to an article published in *Scientific American*, in 2018, brain technology will make three big leaps: brain-controlled typing, neural particles and micro brains. Brain-controlled typing uses a brain–computer interface (BCI) and thought operates a keyboard or equivalent.

On 19 December 2016, China's CCTV channel "Challenge the Impossible" shocked its audience by showing the performance of a Zhejiang University team demonstrating a brain–computer interface. The experimenters, communicated with the rats who had electrodes implanted in their brains. The rats successfully through and out of a maze. In 2019, French scientists made quadriplegic men "walk" again with the help of a brain-controlled exoskeleton robots suit.

Understanding the operating mechanism of the human brain is not only conducive to revealing the mystery of high efficiency and reliability of human brain but also to uncover the century's difficult problem: the mystery of consciousness and profound essence of life. Furthermore, deeper understanding of the brain will also help to develop a new information processing system. French scientists have invented a new neuroimaging system that can track brain activities for a long time. This breakthrough in brain imaging technology opens a new door for studies related to how the brain works. Information conversion technology successfully transfers information from the human brain into computer memories and vice versa. American scientists announced that they had invented a new "mind reader", which can use computer programs to decode brain activity and "translate" it into text, greatly facilitating bidirectional conversion between human brain and computer information.

Taking BCI technology as an example, it connects brains and computers and brings the electrical signals derived from neural activity to the external world. Thought can be converted into command signals to drive the external devices, in order to realize the direct control by a human brain over machines in the external environment. Thus BCI will provide humans with a new way of communication and control, namely, instead of using language and action, electroencephalogram signals will suffice: think that you want the lights on and BCI will make its so. BCI technology has made great progress, and is getting more and more attention and investment from governments and industrial circles in various countries.

In 2013, the US government launched a research program to explore the working mechanism of the human brain and draw a map of brain activities. This project, which will take ten years and require $1 billion or more, can be compared with the human genome project. The European Commission has also announced that graphene and human brain engineering were selected as "Future Emerging Technology" flagship programs, and set up a special research programs for each and expect to allocate funds totaling 1 billion euros over the next ten years.

In 2016, a company called Neurolink was founded in California, USA, whose main research and development direction is BCI technology. Inventor and entrepreneur Elon Musk is one of its founders. The company recently announced that it hopes to implant its microchip devices into the human brain from 2022.

The future applications for BIC seem practically unlimited, including the diagnosis and treatment of Parkinson's, Alzheimer's, and other brain diseases, help to solve the difficulties in movement and communication caused by high paraplegia and myasthenia gravis; help disabled people control prosthetics, make cochlear implants to help deaf people hear; and make artificial retinas to help blind people see. In addition, BCI should help; treat memory disorders in patients with Alzheimer's disease; and read brain nerve movements to help restore mobility in paralyzed limbs, allowing stroke patients to lead normal lives. With the maturing of BCI technology and the increasing demand for intelligent robots in society, the concept of BCI robot control is gaining popularity. In time it is conceivable that brain signals might control everything, and if a BCI robot can be realized, which is controlled by human mind, it will do all kinds of work for humans. For example, it is engaged in special service industries such as nursing the disabled, assisting patients with physical disabilities, nursing the elderly; serving the military, entertainment; operating in the special environment; realizing driverless car and unmanned aircraft.

BCI is a very controversial topic. Although the current technology has not reached the level of reading and manipulating thinking, the potential risks of this technology still need to be taken seriously. (1) BCI is different from other implants such as the cardiac pacemaker. Its wider application prospect lies in elective operations performed on healthy people for non-medical purposes. This makes us face the double test of law and morality. (2) Because BCI is essentially a communication system, there is still a lack of relevant regulatory measures. No matter what role you play in privacy and surveillance issues, governments, advertisers, insurance companies and marketers will inevitably use this technology to go deep into our minds, enter specific ideas, prevent crime or promote goods behavior. (3) Security issues are involved. When your mind is connected to others, hackers would not have to invade the mainframe computer to do damage, but could directly invade the connected brains to achieve their purposes. For example, if they were skilled in this technology they might inject prejudice or false memories directly into thousands of human brains, and by solidifying or exacerbating existing prejudices or creating new ones aggravate and intensify social conflicts. Furthermore, emory-enhancing implants in the brain are capable of "full control of memory". In addition to the many benefits of health care and the increase of brain capacity, the abuse of this kind of neuro stimulator is terrible to contemplate. For example, by implanting memory-enhancing devices, brain intruders may erase or modify the memory of political events or conflicts to manipulate groups on a large scale, it can even erase your skills; and provide new espionage techniques, such as reading your thoughts or memories, creating false memories in the human brain or leading people to accept circumstances they might otherwise have found repugnant or fought against. More seriously, the maturity of BCI technology promotes the development and application of brain controlled weapons (making the judgment of the victory or defeat in war shift from simply killing the enemy to controlling their idea, capabilities, and behavior). The military application of brain control technology will lead to more complex ethical issues. (4) Education issues. Experts point out that the brain connected to AI could completely change the methods and speeds of human learning. Direct connection would permit transfer of a large amount of knowledge and motor skills directly to the brain. So, what is the role of schools in the future? What will students mainly learn, and who will teach them when truth can be established with electronic signal? The form of school, the goals of education, and the idea of learning itself will all change

Do we need to introduce laws that protect our brains? To answer this question one needs to deal with many fields, such as law, philosophy, science and technology, sociology and so on, but this issue itself has not attracted enough attention. In November 2017, 25 well-known scholars in the fields of BCI, neural engineering and AI jointly published a review article in the journal *Nature* and proposed four major ethical issues in the development of Neural Engineering Technology. The issues include privacy issues; identity verification (for groups implanted with brain stimulators, how will we determine whether their behaviors are dominated by themselves or by equipment? This will need to be defined at both the moral and legal levels); strengthening issues (e.g., whether it is just and proper to let brain-enhanced soldiers be permitted to engage in war, this is another boundary issue for technology enhancement to empower human beings); and prejudice issues (if prejudice is rooted in the neural system, it will surely affect not only the human body and mind, but also cause serious social problems).

### New energy technologies

Human beings depend on energy for survival. However, with the increasing demand for energy, especially the over exploitation and utilization of the traditional fossil energies, such as oil and coal (which take thousands of years to transform from ancient debris to combustible materials) are rapidly depleting. The energy crisis has become a global problem and even may be a motivation behind several modern wars.

At present, many experts believe that world's conventional energy reserves (such as oil) will be economically practical for half a century or so, and other sources such as coal could be used for one or two centuries (putting aside, for the moment, questions of pollution).

With the rapid development of science and technology, the potential supply of low-carbon energy sources such as wind energy, solar energy and nuclear energy continues to increase. In addition, the new energies such as shale gas, combustible ice and so on have been explored in succession. In the near future, worry about the increasing depletion of fossil energy will disappear as the share of renewable energy sources grows. Nevertheless, we should not forget three domains involved in solve the energy crisis: first, energy saving and efficiency. The current efficiency of energy generation, transmission, and utilization is not high and the waste is appalling; second, new techniques for energy storage and transmission are required; third, developing and applying new energy technologies will be welcome. These technologies will be among the most important driving forces of the next industrial revolution.

In fact, the development and utilization of "natural energies" and neglected energy technologies such as human kinetic energy power generation, as well as methods for storing and transmitting energy should become important driving forces of the next industrial revolution. In the near future, "natural energies" such as solar, wind, hydropower, geothermal energy, magnetic, biomass energy, marine (tidal energy, wave energy, tidal energy), and nuclear energy (fission energy, fusion energy), hydrogen energy, superconducting energy saving, etc. will occupy a major proportion in the structure of global energy generation, and the contradiction between economic development and energy will become history, and it may even prove possible to use black hole energy for the benefit of mankind.

New energy developments are announced daily. As an example, nuclear fusion technology could be the technology destined to replace the status of petroleum. Not only does it have no pollution, but also the required materials are only deuterium and tritium in seawater. In 2018, China's nuclear fusion research project—the large scientific device "Artificial Sun" (a scientific device capable of controlling nuclear fusion), made a major breakthrough: the thermal power exceeded 10 megawatts, the plasma energy storage increased to 300 kilojoules, and the electron temperature in the center of the plasma reached 100 million degrees for the first time. This is a nuclear fusion far away from the haze of war, which when fully developed is expected to be applied to the civil field on a large scale. It is predicted that by 2026, nuclear fusion power generation will enter the stage of commercialization. By then, cheap electric power will replace other energy sources extensively, bringing a series of associated revolutions.

Solar energy is an inexhaustible clean energy sources for the earth and has the most extensive application prospect. At present, many solar technologies have been commercialized and are expected to become the mainstream of new energy in the near future. Hazel Henderson, a futurist who has been tracking and studying green energy for a long time, believes that we are in the transition from the petrochemical industry era to the solar age. According to the International Energy Agency (IEA)[12], solar energy could become the Earth's main source of electricity by 2050: By 2030, the cumulative installed capacity of global photovoltaic generation is expected to reach 1721 GW, and by 2050, it will increase to 4670 GW. In fact, the growth rate of global solar power generation in 2016 exceeded that of coal-fired power generation for the first time.

The development and application of new energy technology must also consider its negative impact on the environment and resources. Needless to say, the well-known serious risks of nuclear energy applications risks such as potential damage to health, environmental pollution. Yet, even the development and application of acknowledged green energy, must be managed with an eye to regional characteristics. For example, the contradiction between the development of biomass energy and the land resources on which human beings depend as well as the possibility of secondary pollution; the large-scale development of geothermal energy and the use of air conditioning must be weighed against the destruction to destruction of the regional topsoil and the other changes of the ecological environment.

### New materials technology

All human physical production activities are based on materials. Contemporary development and major breakthroughs in such technical fields as information, biology, energy, agriculture, advanced manufacturing, national defense, etc. are inseparable from the development of material technology. At the same time, the revolution of engineering technology is inseparable from the revolution of material technology.

At present, inventions and applications of new materials such as nanomaterials (like graphene, carbon nanotubes, and fullerene), new generation of semiconductor materials (such as silicon carbide, gallium nitride, diamond, aluminum nitride, and gallium oxide), metamaterials (such as biomimetic plastics, aerogels, thermoelectric materials, and optical manipulation materials), and emerging functional materials (such as metallic glass, superconducting materials, and intelligent materials) are advancing rapidly. Many of these are already close to being commercialized and the prospects for continued innovation appear unlimited. No wonder the new material technology is known as the "mother of invention" and "seed of industry".

For example, metamaterials are generally considered to be artificial composite structures with extraordinary physical properties not found in natural materials. They can even achieve the goal of visual invisibility by turning electromagnetic waves. Relevant industry survey reports predict that the global market scale of metamaterials will grow at a compound annual growth rate of 41 per cent from 2010 and 2020. With the continuous deepening of the global process of "industry 4.0," a 16.1 billion USD scale metamaterial industry cluster is emerging, which can drive such fields as high-speed trains, new ground-moving equipment, aerospace, national defense technology, ground intelligent robots and so on. At present, the pace of product transformation based on these experimental results is also accelerating. The research and utilization of products such as metamaterial smart skins, metamaterial radar antennas, absorbing materials, electronic countermeasure radars, metamaterial communication antennas, drone radars, and stealth technologies have become the focus of competition in many countries.

However, there are still various risks and ethical problems in the research and application of meta material technology. Take for instance, the development of various stealth technologies such as electromagnetic stealth, optical isolation stealth, scattering cancellation stealth and others, which can be used for all modern weapons, including aircraft, drones, missiles, speedboats, tanks, warships and so on. The manufacture of stealth versions has become a focus of military research and development, and its impact on modern warfare will be profound. As the cost of stealth materials decreases, if invisibility cloaking were to prove practical and applicable to living matter, anyone will be able to hide themselves easily, and easy to imagine its use by criminals and terrorists. This will pose a great challenge to social governance. Science fiction has already picked up this theme. In the recent American film "Hollow Man". Sebastian Caine, a scientist who studies the technology of biological transparency, succeeds in turning himself invisible, but is unable to recover, and eventually goes insane and becomes a criminal.

Recently, South Korea has also developed "artificial skin that can make soldiers invisible". When soldiers wear this invisible skin camouflage suit, similar to chameleons, they can blend with the environment and cannot be detected by thermal imaging cameras. Once this technology matures, the rules of special operations and night warfare will be changed, not to mention the ethical risks in other areas.

### Space exploration and manned space technology

Since ancient times, humans have dreamed of flying. After more than 200 years of efforts (the Montgolfier brothers gave the first public demonstration of a manned balloon–the world's first passenger-carrying airship in France in 1783), humans went from balloon manned flight, to powered aircraft and from there to using artificial satellites and manned space flight.

The former Soviet Union launched the first Sputnik-1 satellite in October 1957, and Yuri Gagarin became the world's first astronaut entered the space with the "Eastern One" manned spacecraft on April 12, 1961. When American astronauts landed on the moon in the lunar module of the Apollo-1 spacecraft on 16 July 1969, human beings have entered the era of space exploration. Now humans are about to enter a new age of discovery with space ventures funded by private industry, landings on Mars, a permanent base on the Moon, interplanetary exploration, new materials manufactured in space, spaceships with a sub-light speed and expanding the search for extraterrestrial life.

Space research is of far-reaching significance. It is not only of great academic value but also may make many contributions to human earthbound society.

1. It has important academic value: Exploring astrophysics, deep space astronomy, space life science and biology, space material science, space medicine,

developing planetary exploration engineering, earth resource engineering and space-flight engineering, as well as deep exploration of natural laws, etc.

2. With further research of the universe, our understanding of life, nature, the earth, matter and even human beings themselves is also deepening, which is conducive to avoiding ignorance and shortsightedness.
3. It will help avoid catastrophic asteroid collisions: There are more than 15,000 asteroids of different shapes within 50 million kilometers around the earth. Large asteroids hit the Earth at least twice in relatively recent times, and their huge shock waves caused the near-extinction of life on earth (such as the extinction of dinosaurs). There are now organizations devoted to Identifying and avoiding such catastrophic collisions by deflecting the course of a threatening asteroid before impact.
4. Monitoring and analyzing agricultural data from low earth orbit will contribute to increasing to increasing food production and improving land use, to help reduce some poverty and hunger.
5. There are abundant natural resources on the outer planets (it is estimated that there are 90 million tons of platinum on one asteroid alone, worth at least 5.4 trillion US dollars at current prices and it is probable that many more such flying gold mines will be discovered). This suggests that asteroid mining could substantially help to alleviate the depletion of earth's natural resources.
6. Our work in space today helps us prepare for space migration: Konstantin Ziolkovsky, the father of spaceflight, once said that the earth is the cradle of human beings, but human beings cannot live in the cradle forever ...(see Chapter 4 "Interstellar Civilization" for details).
7. Extending human strategic space to space and forming a global, multi-dimensional and integrated strategic space.
8. Developing space industry with huge market potential and the space economy: The technologies developed for exploring space have already generated a wide variety of new consumer products. The design principles of about 30,000 products in the world come from space technology. There are also modern services such as space tourism about to become important.
9. Finally, the exploration of outer space can inspire the scientific spirit in all mankind.

In recent years, major countries and regions in the world have actively adjusted their aerospace strategies. For example,

Improve the ability to access space: The American Space Exploration Technology Corporation [SpaceX] is a major player in providing rockets at space transportation. They have used recycled "second-hand" rockets to launch satellites, and successfully retrieved it; India's "Polar-Orbiting Satellite Launch Vehicle" [PSLV] carried 104 satellites into orbit at the same time.

Expand the capacity to use space: The US Army has deployed the Kestrel Eye IIM Reconnaissance Microsatellite that can capture and transmit satellite images in minutes inaugurating new generation of weather satellites; while the Joint Polar-Orbiting Satellite System (JPSS) will fly around the earth 14 times a day to collect all kinds of information about the earth's atmosphere, land and oceans.

Enhancing the capacity to control space: The United States, Russia and other major space military powers have actively strengthened their military space force building by a number of major initiatives.

Developing space exploration technology: for example, both the United States and Russia plan to jointly build a lunar orbital space station; the US "Cassini" Saturn orbiting probe recently fell into Saturn's atmosphere as planned, ending nearly 20 years of orbital operation. In July 2020, the Mars exploration window opened again, UAE's "hope," China's "Tianwen-1," and "Perseverance Rover" of the United States have been launched successfully, and will land on Mars in 2021. These have intensified the space race, and Mars has become the new focus of competition.

Developing space frontier technologies: "Membrane Spacecraft" developed in the United States may well provide a low-cost solution for removing space debris; Japan first used its own small satellite–SOCRATES to verify quantum communication). And early in 2019, China's Chang'e-4 probe successfully soft-landed and began exploring the back of the moon.

Space exploration is heating up. At present, more than 80 countries and regions have put satellites into orbit, and 12 countries have launched satellites with their own rockets. Russia, China and the United States have manned space technology. The international space station jointly built by 16 countries has been in operation for 20 years, and can stay in space much longer as a base for research. China plans to launch a new Space Station of its own *Tiangong* by 2022.

However, space has also become an important battlefield in various senses. All countries are dealing with the possibility of future space war and many countries are striving to establish a dominant position in space. The United States, in addition to its army, navy, air force, marines, and coast guard, officially established a sixth military branch, the space force, in December 2019.

The militarization of space is a very dangerous trend; as the technology to travel to space becomes more mature and the cost is rapidly decreases, more and more private enterprises are involved in the space race and are planning to launch their own satellites; space may become the arena of the billionaire of each country.

This requires, therefore, new international space rules and related laws and regulations to promote the peaceful development of space to assure traffic safety, protect the space environment (including how to clean up space junk; At least

17,852 large artificial objects and 170 million small objects are flying around the earth at high speed now), develop and apply various resources (commercial development under the premise of maintaining space rules, and the prevention of space arms race, e.g.), prevent an arms race in space, and prohibit the militarization of outer space, etc., which are in the process of being drafted, should be introduced as soon as possible.

Most important of all is how to create an interstellar civilization that is consistent with sustainable human development (see the relevant section of "Interstellar Civilization" in Chapter 4).

### Information technology is changing the world

Today, a child can speak into a smart phone in any language, ask factual questions, and expect to get correct factual answers. This process involves speech recognition of any language or dialect, almost instant searching of many databases, organizing this material, and rapid output, that can present the results in a logical fashion. Marvelous! Tomorrow the questions may go beyond the factual to matters that require inference, judgment, or wisdom in forming the answers. Even more marvelous!

Information technology is the foundation among the technologies that are changing the world:the birth of many new disciplines, the invention, creation and innovation of most cutting-edge or disruptive technologies are inseparable from their integration with emerging information technology which has penetrated into all areas of human activities, including the economy, politics, culture, entertainment, news, communications, manufacturing, education, war, crime, medicine, etc. The list of components in this field is long.

Information technology makes the world a global village. Information technology has blurred the boundary between reality and the virtual world, it has also shaped the sharing economy based on a digital platform, and has even had an impact on economic theory. At the same time, information technology is changing the relationships among power, rights, and democracy.

Information technology has changed the theory, concept and form of modern war, and countries have also formed information warfare forces. In particular, 5G, the Internet, the Internet of things, cloud computing, big data and their various potential play an increasingly important role, led to a profound change in all aspects of human activities around the globe. This includes not only people's lifestyles, ways of working, business methods, and corporate operations but also reorients business organizations, jobs, industrial forms, and even changes global politics. It opens the so-called Era of the Internet, and the subsequent era of the Internet of Things that can connect all non-living things.

However, the high state of development of information technology brings more and more serious risks and challenges to the economy, society, culture and even national security. In particular, it involves the ethical requirements, ethical guidelines or information ethics in the development, dissemination, management and utilization of information.

For example, the issues of infringement of intellectual property rights, loss of control of personal privacy (this global battle against the COVID-19 has fully proved that information technology can monitor the behaviors of every citizen or every employee of a company, including their biological characteristics. Is this a good thing or a bad thing? Not to mention if the technology is in the hands of terrorists), ownership of information, information security (to combat information theft, information fraud, attack and destruction); information pollution (including the transmission and use of misinformation, false information, dirty information, and spam information); information monopoly, abuse of information technology, and excessive dependence on information technology. Finally, network security must be guaranteed. This is essential not only for personal privacy but also to protect corporate secrets and national security. Even scientists believe that the major cyber-attacks will pose no less a threat to humans than nuclear war. No wonder the inventor of the Internet, Tim Berners Lee, warned that the World Wide Web was becoming a monster out of control. In view of "Internet fraud, false news, collective hysteria and threats to privacy" on the Internet, he published an article saying that the Internet has been hijacked by cheaters and criminals who use it to deceive people all over the world. Therefore, it is urgent to have an appropriate governance system that works.

In addition, as an important soft capital, information resources have not only become the core resources for all kinds of high-tech industries in today's era, but also promote the informatization of various industries, infrastructure and even lifestyle. The growing digital economy can be regarded as a series of activities, which take data as an important "soft capital" or production factor, the global information network as an important carrier, and the application of information technology as an important driving force, so as to optimize the economic structure and improve the efficiency of economic and social operations by improving the level of digitalization and intelligence in various fields of economy and society. Its essence lies in informationization.

Here, there are basic theory, management, norms and security issues around the information, data and network. For example, maintaining security requires guarding and validating data continually to assure that it is still there and has not been corrupted. But there are basic issues: Who does the big data that creates huge profits belong to? Is personal information private or public? Does "big data" really represent fairness and justice? How to collect, process, apply, protect and manage information (France, Spain and other countries have decided to impose digital taxes on Internet giants, should other countries adopt this practice? What about cross-border transfer of information?), as well as how to regulate relevant information are the key to the healthy development of the above domains. However, the current regulations are far from adequate to govern the digital economy with its cross-border integration, which requires comprehensive innovation in governance.

In addition, the advent of the Internet–Internet of Things era has also brought about the globalization of risks and created a snowball effect. Especially those negative social thoughts quickly spread and led to a wider range of social unrest and destruction. For example, Memes travel on information networks: these ideas can be positive or negative and quickly spread without validation. Terrorists could deliberately corrupt data to make those key information infrastructures such as traffic, transportation, finance and energy system are attacked or paralyzed, the economic and social losses that may occur across national boundaries will be immeasurable. Therefore, at present, policies and regulations around information confirmation, quality, security, privacy protection, circulation control, and sharing and openness must be continuously improved and expanded all over the world.

For the future development of information technology, there is another aspect that needs attention. Now people are more concerned about the application of information technology. For example, internet-based application development, interdisciplinary research and development, in-depth development of microelectronics technology and software technology, the development of network technology with the integration of three networks (telephone network, cable television network and computer network) and broadband as the core. However, information technology taking electronization, digitization, and networking as its core is still only a tool to improve the efficiency of information collection, transmission and processing, expand the scope of information application, and also a medium for information dissemination.

I think that the next step in the development of information technology will need to focus on information itself to generate a true revolution. That is to say, the nature, the source and the content of information should be taken as the subject matter for research and development, not just the digital container for information. Moreover, information comes from a variety of sources (e.g., it may be created by human beings or exist naturally; it may be contained in material form or produced or transmitted by spiritual activities, etc.) and each will evolve and develop in different ways.

First, to reveal the secrets of information about brainless natural objects (non-artificial creation). For example, we need to re-understand the essence of information, information sources and ways to express information concerning natural objects, so as to uncover their essence and reveal "invisible energy distribution and information contained in material forms". The information research of material objects will make our understanding of the material world more accurate and profound, and will help us to benefit from continuing discoveries in the material world.

Second, revealing the relationship between human consciousness and information. Progress in psychology, cognitive science, biology, neuroscience, especially information science and technology, provides the possibility for the research of human consciousness to transcend the limitations of philosophical discussion, make consciousness the subject of scientific research (studying consciousness as a process, not an object), and then it is possible to reveal the relationship among the information, consciousness and life in brain organism.

Third, it needs to make clear the attributes of information. If the complete conscious activity of human beings includes receiving (feeling, perception), storing (memory) and processing (thinking) of information, then according to the view that information is the object of conscious activity, the intermediary through which conscious activity unfolds and the product of conscious activity, thus information technology not only belongs to the technology of operating substance (e.g., the brain and the physical world), but also belongs to the soft technology of "operating" spiritual activities (e.g., consciousness and spiritual world) beyond substance.

### A new stage in the development of soft technology

Soft technology is an area where the process of creating value is totally different paradigm from technology in the traditional sense. Although the resources of soft technology cover all human behaviors, including economic, social, cultural, psychological, and political activities, it also involves broader domains such as human resources, natural resources, environmental resources, and even human life and cognition themselves (see Chapter 3 "What is Technology"). However, because material production has held such an important position throughout the nearly 300 years of the industrial economy era, the contribution of the so-called hard technology to improving material productivity remains more prominent. Hence, soft technology has been ignored for a long time, and has not been consciously and systematically studied and developed as a technology. Only business, which is a soft technology that uses economic activity as a resource, has experienced somewhat more extensive development; and it is seldom regarded as a "technology", but is instead described in different terms.

At present, the development of soft technology has entered a new stage, we need to re-understand soft technology and soft environment:

1. The invention, creation, and innovation of soft technology represent a new trend of modern technology development.

2. The integration and fusions of various soft technologies will further enhance the value of innovation in many fields.
3. The integration and fusion of hard–soft technologies and hard–soft environments are important driving forces for future economic, social, and cultural development.
4. We should beware of "bad" soft technology, improper applications of soft technology and their use for evil purposes. Taking financial technology as an example, history has proved that improper financial technology operation can lead to financial crises. Financial technology can also be used for evil purposes, such as "buying" a country, or even becoming an auxiliary tool for the disintegration of a large country. Therefore, although the specification of hard technology belongs to the category of soft technology and soft environment, the development and application of soft technology itself need more strict specifications.
5. From the perspective of the history of technological development, human beings are entering the third stage of technological development (see the relevant section of "The historical course of technological development" in Chapter 3). The integration of hard and soft technologies in the field of life is the biggest feature of this third stage of technological development, and hard and soft technologies intervenes life makes human beings face a global psychological and spiritual crisis.
6. Solutions to many challenges facing mankind in the twenty-first century, including conflicts between countries and regions and such risks as terrorism, must start with soft technology. and soft environment. Ultimately solutions depend on the transformation of civilization—from Industrial Civilization to Global Civilization, to achievement of the Great Civilization.
7. No matter how important the role of soft technology is, just like hard technology, it is ultimately a tool or means created by humans. We must remember that the ultimate goals of technological development are not only to serve the well-being of all human beings, but also to preserve harmony and sustainable development for human beings and other species of the natural environment.

**1. The invention, creation, and innovation of soft technology is a new trend in contemporary technology**

As our understanding of knowledge, capital, resources, market (including those of the social marketplace) and non-technological factors grow, and as innovations in the field of non-material "production" receive more attention, and the difficulty of solving national and global governance issues increase, people are gradually coming to recognize the importance of soft technology, soft environment, as well as soft technology invention, creation, and innovation. As a result, new soft technologies in the field of economy, society, culture, politics, cognition, thinking, safety and even medical and health care have all become important means of competition.

This trend will not only become a strong driving force to promote economic, cultural, and social development in the post-industrial era, and form a core technology for soft industry far beyond hard industry, but will also prove to be an indispensable means for resolving regional conflicts, maintaining world peace, establishing a new world order and become a new source of "power" for the development of human society as a whole. People are gradually coming to realize that soft technology and the soft environment are both the core technology and theory of the so-called "human-centered system".

Recently, John Smart identified ten areas that he believed would lead the future technological transformation. These areas are also the ones in which a leader must deal with the potential for strategic disruption, opportunities, and threats. They include: nanoscience and technology, information technology, engineering technology, resources technology, cognitive technology, social technology, health technology, economic technology, political technology, and security technology. In fact, most of these belong to the category of soft technology: highlighting the status of soft technology in the transformation of future society.

**2. Integration and fusion among the various soft technologies**

The integration and fusion of various soft technologies will further enhance the competitiveness of soft technology innovation. For example, the combination of financial technology and information technology has transformed the financial industry (historically regarded as a tool of value circulation or responsible for the capitalization of business activities within the economic sector) into a service industry generating a huge income and creating a large number of jobs. Financial access to innovation has become a special kind of technology in itself, and even an important diplomatic tool. At the same time, "bad" financial technology (see the section of "Differentiating between soft and hard technology, while guarding against bad soft technology" in Chapter 3) takes finance increasingly far away from the real economy, making it more speculative and more like gambling, which has enhanced the international "contagion" of the financial crisis.

Experts point to the combination of trade technology, financial technology, communication, and information technology as a major force exerting its influence on all current trends in the world today. The whole world is closely linked together by the flows of trade, capital, people, and information (data and communication).

Together these form an unprecedented global network, in which each "flow" combines with modern high technology to facilitate continuous innovation, and ultimately to create a unique system. The mutual fusion and interactions among these four systems, when integrated with technological innovation, are bringing about a new era of globalization and also creating unlimited opportunities. However, they can also result in unexpected fluctuations or crises.

**3. Integration and fusion between soft and hard technologies**

The convergence of soft and hard technologies opens a new domain of invention, creation, and innovation for the future. NBIC convergence technology as a technology frontier is representative of soft and hard technologies convergence. It is composed of Nanotechnology, Biotechnology, Information technology and Cognitive science and technology. Of these, cognitive science and technology are NBIC's most essential components. Cognitive science involves biology, psychology, cytology, brain science, genetics, neuroscience, linguistics, logic, information science, AI, mathematics, and anthropology. Most of these fields belong to the domain of soft science. The knowledge of cognitive science plays an important role in the design, command, and coordination of NBIC. The report *Converging Technologies for Improving Human Performance* edited by the US National Science Foundation asserted that: "If the Cognitive Scientists can think it, the Nano people can build it, the Bio people can implement it, and the IT people can monitor and control it." The EU's research report said that converging technology will shape the future of Europe.[13]

Scientists believe that NBIC converging technology will completely change our world. Based on the understanding and application of NBIC, the potential of the human brain will be stimulated, and human comprehension, efficiency, creativity, and accuracy will be greatly improved. Furthermore, the human body and its sensory organs will become more sensitive to subtler changes in the outside world, such as accidents and diseases. This will enable us to avoid accidents, and cure many illnesses. Eventually, human beings may be able to diagnose and repair themselves and the material world around them at the level of atoms or molecules. The physical and cognitive decline that for so long has been the inevitable fate of the aging population will generally improve. Far more efficient means of communication between people will be developed (including direct communication between brain and brain). Cooperation among social groups will improve, and the consumption of resources and energy will be greatly reduced throughout society, reducing damage and pollution to the environment. NBIC convergence is also an important human enhancement technology.

There are already many NBIC prototypes and innovative products in the world, such as personalized medicines, bioinformatics, biomaterials, biochips, biocomputers, and so on.

Another example of soft-hard technologies convergence is the alliance between technology and art. For instance, Information, Art, Media (IAM) convergence technology, which integrates information technology, art design, and media creativity, will promote a new wave of innovation. The integration of artistic thinking (ideas) and digital media technology will release a wave of innovation that will subvert the traditions of cultural industries and all kinds of service industries, revolutionizing the design process by combining art design with information technology. The so-called New Media Art Design will integrate art with modern cutting-edge science and technology, so that digital technology, biotechnology, quantum theory, economics, and linguistics can all become media in which art can be realized.

**4. Future blueprint design technology based on innovative thinking**

Many examples from history illustrate that imagination has always been a booster to guide and promote new technologies. Among the most convincing examples are the contributions of Jules Verne in the nineteenth century to the development of contemporary science and technology. With his extraordinary imagination, Verne imagined ideas that seemed fantastic at the time, almost all of which became reality in the twentieth century. No wonder the French general Hubert Lyautey famously responded that modern science and technology are only the process of turning Verne's prophecies into realities.

In 2011, the British magazine *FOCUS* listed ten whimsies such as quantum computers, 3D/4D printing machines, pervasive computing, and TV with mood induction as "Ten ideas that will change the world." In fact, 3D/4D printing is now a reality, in December 2020, China's 76-photon quantum computer "Nine Chapters" came out. In 2011, *Scientific American*'s choice of "Ten World Changing Ideas 2011" included borderless currency, microbial miners, crops that do not need to be replanted, nanoscale bacteria killers, etc. This shows the complementary relationship between scientific fantasy and scientific study and even futures studies.

People are used to calling those fantastic ideas scientific fantasies. Practice has proved; however, as long as those novel ideas are consistent with the laws of nature and the principles of soft and hard technology (the base), and fit the good wishes of human beings with an open mind, using both the art and technology (goal and methodology), they may form a blueprint for the future and may eventually be achieved. In this sense, it is unfair to simply call such ideas "science fiction," rather they might be called "future blueprint designs".

Science fiction has experienced great development for more than 100 years now, and its contribution to future studies and to world culture cannot be denied.

Although there are many different definitions, in short science fiction integrates wisdom, creativity, imagination, passion, motivation, personal ideals and values, not only serves as a tool to discuss, inspire and influence future research, but also inspires the development and innovation of science and technology. Many scientist and futurists have paid close attention to science fiction for a long time. In February 2015, the VTT Technical Research Center in Finland granted a Ph.D. to Tiina Kymäläinen for her dissertation on *Science Fiction Prototypes as Design Outcomes of Research*, recognizing the value of science fiction in technical research.

With the development of science and technology, people are looking forward to a better future world than in the past. However, it must be noted that both "scientific fantasy" and "blueprints for the future" cannot focus exclusively on creating novel stories, nor can it only focus on artistic images or the technical products that create art. It must avoid creating unfounded, extreme, or gamified stories that mislead people, especially teenagers, and instead those artistic works can help steer the world in promising directions by distinguishing good and evil, and by cultivating emotions of the true, the good, the beautiful and justice.

In short, designing a better future blueprint requires going beyond science fiction. It is not limited to fields like hard science and technology or even culture. Instead, we need to research and promote consciously designed human future visions or blueprints based on innovative thinking. In other words, it will help to create a beautiful new world, if we can stick to the right direction (guided by a world view and values full of positive, credible, healthy energy while adhering to a moral bottom line), encouraging the creation of scenarios that focus on a "common better future for all human beings" and its implementation path (to show what is possible and where future dangers lie). This will require encouraging and promoting new thinking, new ideas, and new attitudes towards the future of human society.

### Integration of interdisciplinary and cross-domain technologies

In addition to the above points, we can also point to a large number of promising disruptive technologies: these are technological developments that change old ideas in unexpected directions, usually suddenly. They often transcend and replace existing mainstream technology, and come from outside the domain they are affecting. These tend to be cross domain and interdisciplinary fusion products. In fact, the strong innovation, major scientific discoveries and technological breakthroughs in today's era are mostly inspired by the fusion, intersection, cooperation and integration of various sciences and technologies in different fields. For example, the integration of AI and genetic science, the integration of quantum computing and AI, the integration of analog and digital worlds, the convergence of digital and biological worlds, the integration between manufacturing and services, the convergence of hardware and software, the convergence of producers and consumers, as well as the integration of data and services on global data platforms, etc. This is also a new trend in the development of contemporary science and technology.

## *The imminent disaster facing science and technology*

Science pursues understanding and knowledge (see the section of "To distinguish between knowledge and technology" in Chapter 3) and that pursuit has largely produced our current world. Comparing the world today with yesterday shows progress on almost all fronts and science is largely responsible for that progress. Yet the forces that drive science and technology do not necessarily aimed at take the world toward a better place. Those forces include funding (largely for military and commercial purposes), pursuit of career achievements and respectable social status, etc. and can easily distort the goals and direction of some research, development and application personnel. The road leading from the past to the present has been littered with unintended consequences, some quite painful.

Yet the development of science and technology is endless. For the future, as science and technology become more powerful, their unintended consequences and the potential to abuse science and technology will become even more dangerous and terrifying. For example, if the possibilities for human evolution listed above, go from scientists' predictions, science fictions or movies into the laboratory one by one, and then if it's possible, even in part, to become a fact; if the negative scenarios that may arise from the development of biotechnology, nanotechnology, AI, brain–computer interface technology as well as new materials technology are gradually realized and then eventually enter the market, it is not as fun as science fiction movies, the risks and even disasters associated with it are by no means sensational, more importantly it is not something that the scientific and technological community can take responsibility for. Responsibility is easily shed. However, there is little accountability for errors or unfortunate outcomes. Negative results rarely receive sufficient attention and in-depth discussion.

Let's enumerate the main "evidences" of pending scientific and technological crisis facing the world today.

## The anxieties over technology mentioned above are not without foundation

The prospect of developing the "human enhancement technology" and manufacturing a superman are no longer a fantasy, either from the standpoint of technical feasibility or from of market supply and demand. The possibility of practical application is increasing day by day, resulting in unprecedented temptation.

From the perspective of technology feasibility, despite the boycott from philosophy, ethics, and religion, due to the integrated development of biotechnology, information technology and nanotechnology, especially the development of genetic engineering, human enhancement technology can experience a revolutionary leap. In the next 20–30 years, no matter whether they are called "human +" or "post human," human beings will create a large number of "Superman".

At the same time, humanoid robots or anthropomorphic robots have made breakthroughs: the first robot in history has obtained citizenship—Sophia, the birth of the anthropomorphic robot—Atlas, which learned to run and jump obstacles in the wild; Japanese scientists have recently developed a humanoid robot that could communicate in Japanese, and Professor Hiroshi Ishiguro even made a robot exactly like himself, etc.

From the perspective of "demand", if parents could change the genes of their unborn children, enhance their children's intelligence, improve their appearance and prolong their life span, these temptations will be hard to resist. Moreover, if people have the option, many of them will want to seize the opportunity, regardless of any legal constraints, to gain higher wisdom and ability for their children, to live longer and be healthier by fair means or foul.

Take the current health care market as an example. Although we know that all medicines have their side effects, the fact that more people with good living conditions are taking more and more health-care drugs has led to a boom in the health care market. Adopting a cultural perspective, from tolerance of the miniskirt decades ago to current attitudes on cosmetic surgery (the number of cosmetic surgeries performed has exploded in recent years), test-tube babies, gay and transsexual life styles, etc., it is clear that public values are also undergoing rapid change, and that the number of people who are willing to accept all or part of enhancement technology can only increase.

Biohacking companies have emerged in the United States. This is still a fledgling career, but entire biohacking communities have also formed on a considerable scale. Many biohackers are opposed to the monopolistic control of technology by a few professionals, and advocate bringing biotechnology out of the laboratory, to innovate and develop it in different environments. At the current stage, they just use tattoo needles, or scalpels to implant devices and microchips in someone's arm, or empowering the body to connect to the internet, so as to open a door or start a car. But they also claim that biohacking technology will eventually give the human body infinite possibilities.

But do not forget that these technologies are potentially disruptive. Biohacking technology is easier for individuals to own and use, and once in the hands of terrorists, it could certainly cause great damage to society.

### The potential negative "prospect" of the new technologies mentioned above could cause us to fall into a dangerous game

A game swayed by various interest groups and personal desires, and whose complexity will raise dilemmas affecting all aspects of the economy, society, and politics in future. The development and utilization of many technologies, such as gene manipulation, nanotechnology, AI, and even space technology are increasingly being driven by commercial interests in all areas of business, and are difficult for government regulating bodies to control.

Take human enhancement technology as an example. Although most scientists in related fields claim that their research is only aimed at therapeutic uses, not the exploration of enhancement technology for healthy human beings, At present, the technologies that could be used to transform humans will soon reach or approach the stage of commercial application. Judging by past examples, this technology will probably be used for military purposes first, or to disturb Society (similarly, any progress in robotics may be stolen and weaponized, used for terrorist activities, etc.). Any attempt to control them will inevitably encounter strong resistance from relevant interest groups. The more power the technology owner, the greater that resistance will be, and the greater risk we will face. In the event that increasingly technical resources are used by small groups and individuals, it will be very difficult to limit the application of these techniques only to green and peaceful purposes.

### We face hard choice of ethics and morality

Especially concerns about fairness and justice, rights and responsibilities, human nature and human dignity, wisdom (or capacity) and happiness. For example, Pre-implantation Genetic Diagnosis (PGD) technology can help eliminate pathogenic genes and prevent the birth of children with genetic diseases. But should pre-implantation embryos, even damaged ones, have an ethical standing? Thus, how we use or alter them demands ethical guidance and support. Especially the use of PGD technology for non-medical purposes (such as to enhance an offspring's intelligence, height, and longevity) through the intervention of germ cells or zygote genes is ethically suspect. In these cases, PGD is no longer limited to the treatment of genetic diseases, but include the potential for genetic intervention on demand. This could violate the autonomy and dignity of a fetus, and also damage the autonomy and dignity of those who are not enhanced. If genetic enhancement is not approached with ethical constraints, it will inevitably lead to a deep crisis within human society.

For details, refer to the previous section titled "Anxiety disorder due to technology" in this chapter.

### We must face up to many social issues

For example, while many are delighted by the vast range of new opportunities the Internet has brought, we should also be aware that the Internet has virtually put an end to human privacy and has raised the level of concern about fake news. Privacy refers to the right enjoyed by an individual to control access to their own personal information, private activities, and opinions that have nothing to do with public interests. If a nano-chip is implanted in the body may well infringe upon the freedom and privacy of others. If privacy cannot be protected, and is illegally infringed upon, and personal information is collected and used by others, or even disclosed to the public, then human dignity and value will be lost. Will this kind of human still feel happy?

Another example, the use of various human enhancement technologies can extend human life or in the limit, help achieve immortality, these desirable developments demonstrate our technological progress in fighting against disease and aging, But, on the other hand, the indefinite extension of life could also prove a disaster: it will exacerbate social aging, care for the aged, medical treatment, etc. It would intensify the social burden, not only of young people, leaving many young people unable to find a job, but it could also affect their enthusiasm for creation and innovation, which will weaken the social vitality; social inequality and justice issues could grow. The gap between the rich and the poor could grow as well, and ultimately affect social stability. If human beings were to really achieve immortality the definition of ethics, morality and law, even the concept of what it means to be human, will be will be subverted. When immortality becomes real and the population continues to grow endlessly, we will have to ask whether the planet afford it. Even if human beings can develop and apply the resources from other planets, or migrate to other planets, we would ask whether infinite life extension is a good thing?

To what age can healthy humans live, so as to achieve a reasonable balance between life and death, and between human and the natural environment? Maybe death really means something to life? What do terms like "metabolism" and "virtuous cycle" really mean in terms of the human species?

### Philosophical perplexity about the essence of "human"

Human enhancement technology can not only treat epilepsy or severe depression and other diseases, but also replace some incomplete, damaged or aging body parts with artificial organs, and it can also be used to enhance human cognitive ability. While human enhancement technology is changing the definitions of humanity, health, and disability, it is also forcing mankind to rethink serious philosophical questions like "what is a human".

As the proportion of all kinds of tiny but powerful chips or other technical products implanted in the human body gradually increases, the boundary between human body, artificial products and other inanimate objects is blurred, and it will be difficult to clearly define these new species either as "humans" or "machines". This shakes the basic concept of human beings and challenges the definition and essence of "humans". Similarly, can the ultimate outcomes of AI—humanoid robots that are more "intelligent" or "perfect" than traditional humans, yet have human-like emotions and consciousness, can they be said to be human beings? Can augmented athletes compete with non-augmented athletes?

In short, are humans transformed by science and technology still truly humans? Are "intelligent" computers beyond humans to be considered as humans? What is the boundary between human and non-human? For example, in 2017, Saudi Arabia granted Sophia citizenship, which is a female robot developed by Hansen Robotics. Is she a human or a machine?

### Alienation of human–machine relations, weaken the foundation of human society

The continuous development of modern information and communication means such as telephones, computers, and mobile phones has made it more convenient for people to communicate with each other. Electronic media and the virtual world of the Internet have also made it easier for people to communicate beyond the barriers of time and space. However, this kind of "convenience" has profoundly affected the face-to-face communication in human society—since communications form the basis for social cohesion and thus the foundation of group society. Many people walking on the street today only stare at smart phones, even when they have meals and parties. At the same time, the number of live conversations—both face-to-face and by telephone—has gradually decreased, either because of people's reluctance to spend their time this way or because of being afraid of disturbing others.

Without knowing it, people have become hostages and appendages to technology. People gradually become obsessed with the virtual world constructed by the network, where it is not clear whether their conversational counterpart is a person, computer or robot (and often it doesn't matter), while "face-to-face" communication between people occurs becomes less and less. Meanwhile interpersonal relationships also become different, lacking warmth, not to mention mutual emotional communication and love. In this way, people become more lonely, indifferent and anxious (recent research shows that the rates of depression, self-harm, and suicide are rising particularly among adolescents). The incidence of depression is related to the popularity of smart phones, and many people think excessive obsession with digital media is the main culprit leading to adolescents' mental health crisis, followed by the deterioration of social morality and human social withdrawal.

### The challenge to life and human nature–is significant

As mentioned in the previous discussions, scientists are exploring technologies to replicate the whole human body. This kind of thinking is liable to reducing the infinite and rich human nature into merely the physical properties of natural atoms. It will tear human nature with exquisite integrity into pieces, and then decompose and combine arbitrarily at the level of atoms or molecules, which will inevitably cause the split or collapse of what we call human nature. Its essence will be to ignore human nature with its organic unity of natural and social attributes, and regard "human" as a mere combination of genes and cells. This is a challenge to human life and tramples on the sacred concept of human nature. This is not only a problem of human beings enslaved by science and technology but also a total loss to humans themselves, and might well lead to the ultimate destruction of traditional human beings.

The more science and technology develop, the more we feel confused and fearful, and we do not know how humans will develop or should develop in the future, nor what our future role will be or ought to be. We are standing at a crossroads in the history of human evolution, and it is not only necessary to explore the direction of human evolution we hope for but also to prepare for the future.

## NOTES

1. The development of technology will be totally beyond the understanding of human beings, and even the occurrence itself will not be clearly identified. It is called a singularity, because it is like the physical properties of gravity in physics that can produce a black hole when it is close to infinity. Thus, it is beyond the scope of what can be forecasted by any normal model.
2. Pierre Teilhard de Chardin pointed out in 1953 that starting from the Big Bang at a point of the universe, and via a complex evolutionary process, which is progressively related and closely interlinked, humans came into being, and finally focused on the omega point—the critical point when future artificial intelligence would surpass human intelligence.
3. Vernor Vinge invented the term "technological singularity" for the first time in 1983. In 1993, he pointed out in his book *The Coming Technological Singularity: How to Survive in the Post-Human Era* that "within thirty years, we will have the technological means to create superhuman intelligence. Shortly after, the human era will be ended." Can humanity avoid this process? If not, can we guide this process to avoid the extinction of human beings?
4. https://en.wikipedia.org/wiki/Humanity_Plus and https://humanityplus.org/.
5. Representative figures include Vernor Vinge, Ray Kurzweil, Aubrey de Grey, Gregory Stock, Anders Sandberg, etc.
6. Theodore J Gordon, Yair Sharan, Elizabeth Florescu, "Lone Wolf Terrorism Prospects and Potential Strategies to Address the Threat," ISBN: 978-0-692-45554-8, 2015.
7. After genetic manipulation, it is easy to destroy unrelated genes that are originally normal in the human body, which may lead to unpredictable genetic diseases. Moreover, the results of gene editing may also be passed on to the offspring of these two babies, and slowly integrated into the entire human population. Extract from the article "Is gene editing technology Pandora's box?" 19 December 2018, http://www.sohu.com/a/278076239_464099
8. The so-called "cloud" refers to a network composed of thousands of data centers.
9. But I do not think that "big data" is an all-powerful solution able to solve all the most intractable issues in the world. This term is generally used to describe the techniques and science that can analyze large masses of information, so as to identify the rules, collect valuable insights, and predict the answers to complex questions. People loosely use it to describe and define the massive data generated in this era of information explosion, and identify the relevant technological development and innovation required.
10. www.millennium-project.org.
11. https://blog.csdn.net/yH0VLDe8VG8ep9VGe/article/details/79983627.
12. http://www.ethicalmarkets.com/.
13. European Commission (2004), *Converging Technologies—Shaping the Future of European Societies.*

# 2

# The Crisis in Human Civilization Driven by the Theory of Scientific and Technological Omnipotence

*One of the important symbols of human progress is that humans can and should control their own destinies.*

The deep concern over the direction of technology development that we explored in Chapter 1 focused on the visible negative impacts of technological development. Another and potentially more serious danger lies in the crisis confronting human civilization driven by material supremacy and the theory of scientific omnipotence.

The positive significance of studies on the humanoid robot or superman is that it strives to improve human intelligence and create a more convenient, efficient, and beautiful society, and let humans no longer be subject to biological evolution, so as to overcome such unwelcome conditions of life as disability, disease, suffering, aging, and unnatural death. At the same time, this kind of research aims to explore the options for human biological evolution, including the possible consequences of technological intervention in human life, such as what kind of humans we will morph into due to advanced technology, what kind of living environment and lifestyle we should create, etc. However, this exploration is beyond the scope of pure technology and compels us to face a number of difficult choices for future human society.

What is the future of humanity? It can be said that different stakeholders have different views, and each viewpoint statement may be justified. But clearly we are at a crucial moment in history. For example, the Israeli historian Yuval Harari has said, our basic definition of the word "human" might be shaken; we cannot even rule out the possibility of creating a new life form or a new type of human. In the next 50–200 years, the "Clustered Regularly Interspersed Short Palindromic Repeats" (CRISPR) gene splicing technology or its later adaptations will provide an easy path to modifying the human genome to make possible changes to physical appearance, mental processes, resistance to diseases, and the fate of a person as contained in their genetic makeup. In short, it will be possible to "upgrade" embryos and, in the process, potentially create a totally different species. Humans may also create artificial intelligence much more powerful than themselves or connect their brains with a computer so as to create a "Brain Internet" as a form of collective intelligence.

Many scholars use "human–machine civilization" to summarize the future trend of society. These explorations or foresights are full of wisdom, very helpful, and always very interesting and attractive. However, what will a future society that adapts to this "upgraded" humanity be like? That would be less optimistic.

Let's put aside for a moment our hopes for the future benefits that the highly developed science and technology may bring to mankind, and imagine instead the kinds of damage that science and technology could bring, so as to avoid its worst results.

Let's take the so-called "human–machine civilization" crisis as an example (human beings are also facing many other severe crises) and imagine "what could happen if present trends are left unchecked"?

## *Human–machine civilization?*

Whether it is the singularity, transhumanism, or AI, the so-called human–machine civilization brought about by the progress of science and technology is widely regarded as the main feature likely to characterize future civilization.

Ray Kurzweil's explanation in his famous work *The Singularity is Near* is quite representative. Since the singularity is the time when the "intelligence" of machines or computers exceeds that of the human brain, he calls society after the singularity "human–machine civilization". He insists that the intelligence that will emerge in this new ear will continue to represent human civilization. In other words, Kurzweil claims that computers of the future will effectively be humans—even if they are non-living. At present, many experts also use the term human–machine civilization to describe a society in which human–machine cooperation and integration produces an ideal human–machine relationship.

But this vision of human–machine civilization and the transformation of human–computer relations it envisions hardly seem enough to form a human civilization that can compare with Agricultural Civilization, Industrial Civilization, and Global Civilization still less the more advanced form of "Great Civilization" advocated in this book.

In any civilized society, there is a relationship between human beings and their creation—technology, or human–machine relationships at different levels. Therefore, the degree of development of human–machine relations alone can never fully reflect the overall state of human social progress nor the rational social system. It is even less appropriate to characterize an independent social system on this basis, Thus, it should not be defined as a civilization in the broad sense.

In other words, with the development of technology in the twenty-first century, the relationship between human and technology has reached an unprecedentedly high degree of interaction, coordination, and integration. The change of human–machine relationship brought by the progress of science and technology is an important feature of science and technology civilization (see the relevant section of "What kind of civilization should human pursue after the industrial civilization" and "Spiritual civilization" in Chapter 4 below), but this characteristic alone cannot form an independent of civilization form. Therefore, "continuing to represent human civilization" should not be the so-called human–machine civilization.

For the sake of discussion, let's use the term "The era of human–machine civilization" for the time being. No matter what the society in which machine "intelligence" surpasses human brain is called, "human–machine complementarity, interaction, combination, cooperation, and integration" should all be important characteristics of human–machine relationship in future civilization. Depending on the degree of human control over the development and application of technology, there will be very different scenarios.

Let's take AI as an example and explore two scenarios. It is should be noted here, however, that no matter what scenarios we consider, it will not be done by AI alone.

**The first scenario**: as we mentioned in the AI Governance section of Chapter 1, if the progress of AI from artificial weak intelligence (AWI) to artificial super intelligence (ASI), or from artificial narrow intelligence (ANI) to artificial general intelligence (AGI) is properly managed, making it safe, controllable and risk averse, then "human–machine civilization" will not only help to create a better human future but also be an important way to promote the progress of human civilization.

**The second scenario:** there is also a second alternative. As the development of AI becomes more and more difficult to regulate and control, different countries will likely introduce AI governance programs based on different perspectives. But given the huge differences in world view and values among various nations today, it may prove difficult to reach a global consensus on many issues. This would mean that certain key governance principles will not be implemented. As a result, AI might not become a new tool to continuously improve human well-being, but instead could become a major driver of the end of human civilization (I hope this scenario will never happen, but only by fully exploring and demonstrating its serious consequences, can we prevent it from happening. This is one of the purposes of this chapter.).

The biggest challenge to the change of human–machine relationship will be creating a society in which three "species" are able to coexist. These three "species" are traditional human beings, beings enhanced by genetic improvements, and/or direct human–machine integration; the all kinds of humanoid robots.

Here, the dividing line between the first two kinds of species and the general cyborgs or intelligent robots is that the first two "products" have "developed or evolved" to no longer be controlled by traditional humans, and exist as independent species.

Let's imagine what might happen in an era of runaway human–machine civilization.

### The first category of species: Superman

With the development of technology entering the third stage characterized by the integration of hard and soft technology in the field of human life (see Chapter 3 for details), human enhancement technology will be fully developed. By deciphering the human genetic code, the genes can be repaired, modified, or even re-encoded; any organ of the body can be replaced by an artificial organ if needed; various biological intelligence chips can be implanted in the human brain enhancing such functions as memory, calculation, and expression, coupled with wearable computing devices, etc., will accelerate the realization of the so-called "superman".

Experts predict that ten cutting-edge technologies such as connecting the brain with a computer (i.e., a Brain/Computer Interface), Powered Exoskeletons, Neural Implants, Cyberware, Exocortex (enabling a true combination of thinking and computing), Human Genetic Engineering, Nanomedicine, Brain Preservation, Synthetic Bodies, and Mind Uploading will soon be possible. These if achieved would transform human beings into what now appear to be supermen.

In fact, the research and development of brain chips, synthetic blood, light manipulator for tactical attack such as the "Iron Man" are making progress, and various prototype of half-human "Homo sapiens" have emerged. The current trend is to assert that "human beings must combine with machines if they don't want to be eliminated eventually" is constantly encouraged. The so-called human–machine civilization is touted as the development trend of the intelligent era, which constantly encourages the use of human enhancement technology, and will further accelerate the speed of the "birth" and "maturity" of superman and half-human robot. If it is not regulated and controlled, various types of superman including Genetic hybrids, and Cyborgs will continue to increase.

### The second category of species: Humanoid robot

When AI develops to the stage of super intelligence, humanoid robots may reach the level of having consciousness, self-development, and self-improvement, and it will also have the function of continuous replication, and even the emotion, creativity, and sociality, which we today regard as unique to humans. At that stage, the intelligent robot will have "most" of the characteristics of human as a natural person, and some of the characteristics of humans as social beings. Even now the products of the so-called artificial intelligence are constantly developing and evolving, so all kinds of humanoid robots or human shape robots with different kinds of "advanced" capabilities are constantly being "born" all over the world.

In this context, the emergence of Alpha Go is of great significance. Why can Alpha Go beat European Go champions? Researchers found that compared with the previous Go AI, the thinking of Alpha Go is closer to that of human beings. This is brought about by the combination of deep learning, and other algorithms, which raises the thought process of its programming "calculation" to "intelligence". This shows that the emergence of fully humanoid robots is only a matter of time.

The difference between the first and the second category of species is that the former is based on the natural body of traditional human beings, uses technical means to "repair," "reform," and "restructure" any part of the human body that needs to be "enhanced". The latter is based on the inanimate machine, which "infuses" human wisdom and intelligence.

### The third category of species: The traditional humans

The relative number of this species will steadily decrease and their survival and development will face increasingly severe challenges in the coming era of human–machine civilization. For traditional, humans face double challenges. On the one hand, they must strive to control the "evolutionary direction" of the two categories of species mentioned above, so as not to be enslaved or destroyed; on the other hand, they must change their own way of life that has lasted for thousands of years, while also overcoming the negative impacts of human nature, so as to avoid the risk of self-destruction, and take the initiative to create a better world, namely a sustainable Global Civilization and even a Great Civilization as described below in Chapters 4 and 6 of this book. In that kind of society, whether it is the product of human enhancement technology or AI, no matter how developed, or how much they resemble "people," will remain merely a tool to provide services for the sustainable survival and development of human beings.

In fact, the essence of the coexistence age for all three categories of species is that the relationship between human beings and technology, which has been in existence for thousands of years of human civilization,[1] has changed fundamentally, and human beings have fallen into danger of being enslaved by their creations.

Furthermore, a society in which the three categories of species mentioned above coexist can only be transitional. Either that, or it cannot be allowed to happen, for if it does, two of these species will be destroyed.

As for the new species in the future, human enhancement advocate Martine Rothblatt has proposed creating "human digital twins—immortal virtual human" that could be realized through "thought cloning technology" as a new human species. This is a crazy idea to realize "immortal human" or "eternal human life," which will not be discussed here for the time being. In fact, digital twins, as exact copies of physical objects, have developed rapidly. If the digital version of a human being is designed successfully, it is expected to help predict and avoid diseases; while being able to digitally reproduce real devices will open up unlimited possibilities in the industrial field.

## *If we let things go on unchanged, what will happen?*

While human beings are proud of being able to redesign "themselves" and other living organisms, they should consider what kind of results these enhanced "abilities" or "behaviors" might bring about. Namely, what kind of world will it be, where all kinds of supermen and humanoid robots develop freely and compete for dominance?

If we do not control the direction of technological development and innovation, the world will certainly face an era in which the above three categories of species coexist. The consequences of this "civilization transformation" on society would be catastrophic. There are more and more advanced supermen and humanoid robots competing to appear and fight for control. The whole society will be full of disasters and violence, and traditional humans will eventually die in the competition.

### In a society of human–machine civilization, will human beings be happy?

If we truly enter an era where three categories of species coexist, and everyone is free to decide for themselves what proportion of human enhancement technology they will acquire (which some will consider just another kind of personal freedom paradise), a world that advocates extreme individualism will be inherently unstable, inharmonious, and filled with conflict and violence. Because, although the goal of "transhumanism" is to make people live longer and healthier, with improved quality of life and greater satisfaction, if there is no bottom line for human evolution or "reform," and "people," as social members, are unable to control their desires and behaviors, that society will become a dangerous playground where personal desires are inflated.

The development of science and technology is likely to enable human beings to reach greatly increased longevity. But Yuval Noah Harari and other scholars believe that by 2050, the development of science and technology could actually allow some humans to become A-Mortal (meaning that in the absence of fatal trauma from some accident, their lives could be extended indefinitely). He fears that such a society, where the rich (who can afford the expense) become A-Mortal, while the poor continue to die, will be an era of worldwide anger and anxiety. Only a few rich people will be able to enjoy human enhancement technology, while most of the poor will increasingly "feel powerless and frustrated". This kind of unequal access to technology will cause the gap between rich and poor to get bigger and bigger, or lead to new exploitation and slavery, and become a major factor affecting social stability and causing social unrest—it might even touch off a regional or world war.

Furthermore, human beings are trying to create a machine-based species that injects as many "human" characteristics as possible and makes them serve us. But if such a species is "smart" enough to do things on their own or to rebel against designers, or even attempt to enslave humans, would traditional humans feel "happy"?

### Where is the dignity of "human beings"?

If the human body is also regarded simply as a machine to be controlled and repaired by technologies, and all kinds of organs can be freely exchanged with clear prices like commodities or technical products, what becomes of human dignity? Transhumanists claims that: we should not try to hinder their pursuit of superman, but they are willing to allow some of the population to continue to exist as mere human beings, as if they were being tolerant. Actually, the visions of transhumanism are not a simple debate like how to take the fastest way to go home on a city road that is prone to traffic jams. Once started, there is no turning back. The resulting philosophical conflict between traditional ethics and their so-called "rational and generalized ethics" will be Irreconcilable.

Of course, there is a different understanding of what dignity is. Decades back American psychologist and author Burrhus Frederic Skinner argued in his book *Beyond Freedom and Dignity* (1971) that human dignity is actually a problem not a blessing. Skinner argued that the deep-rooted belief in free will and personal moral self-discipline (Skinner calls it "dignity") impedes the prospect of using scientific methods to change behavior to build a happier and more organized society.

### How would a future superman or humanoid robot treat traditional humans?

If some people become "Superman", or a large number of humanoid robots with "intelligence beyond human brain" appear after the "singularity", then what attitude would they take toward the traditional human race? This kind of "reform" is very similar to the goals of certain eugenicists of the late-nineteenth and the early twentieth century who proposed to cultivate better races. Eugenics at that time was a notorious excuse for Nazi Germany's ethnic cleansing and killing of millions of alien races. Don't forget the crimes against humanity committed by the Nazis in the guise of protecting racial purity over 70 years ago.

### If humans were treated like animals...

Recently, some scientists have argued that animals often have different capabilities beyond human understanding and that in some cases animals' brains are even more advanced than humans'. Don't forget the agricultural revolution about 10,000 years ago, when people began to grow crops, domesticate animals, and use them first to replace humans for farming or as the means of transport, and later making livestock a major source of protein in the form of meat. Most domestic animals today cannot avoid a tragic fate. Except for a few lucky species, such as dogs and cats that are treated as pets, or curiosities held in various types of "zoos" for people to enjoy, most animals become food for humans, and furthermore, in

Figure 2.1: Mechanized force-fed duck.

order to improve their flavor, humans often interfere with the way animals are treated during their short lifespans.

Take that famous item of Chinese cuisine—Beijing duck as an example. About two or three months after ducklings are hatched collectively in a cage, the duck farmer injects feedstuff containing high sugar content directly into the ducks' mouth by a cylindrical feeding machine four times a day to make them gain weight rapidly; thus, they are called force-fed ducks. As soon as their weight reaches 2.5–3.5 kg, the ducks are slaughtered.

Or take the cow in an industrialized dairy production line as another example. They usually only live to be five years old before they are slaughtered. During these five years, in order to maintain maximum milk yield, the cows are almost always pregnant, and about 60–120 days after they give birth they are artificially inseminated again. As for the calves, they are separated from their mothers just after birth. The heifers are raised to become a new generation of cows, and the bull-calves are shut in a cage no larger than their body or placed in a small bullpen. For the remainder of their lives (an average of only four months), they are never removed from this cage and are even deprived of the opportunity to walk, so as to avoid their muscles becoming hard due to movement. The softer their muscles

Figure 2.2: Artificially force-fed duck.

Figure 2.3: An automated dairy farm.

Figure 2.4: The calf confined inside a fence.

are, the more the beefsteaks they will yield will be juicy and tender. So, the only road these calves travel on foot is the way to the slaughterhouse.

Also, let's look at the fate of lions in "Canned Hunting ground" in South Africa.[2] There, once lion cubs are born, they are taken away from the lioness and raised by unsuspecting volunteers; when they are a little older, they are put into the "cub-caressing" tourism project, where tourists can touch them and take photos with them as long as they pay; as they grow up, they can take part in the event of "walking with the lions"; once they grow to about seven years old and are too big to be suitable for human beings to approach, a large number of lions are confined to small cages for frequent mating and breeding so as to increase the number of lions. When they lose their ability to reproduce, they are locked inside fenced-off areas where they are hunted for the so-called "sport" of Canned Hunting—that attracts rich people from all over the world who enjoy the thrill of killing.

If a species whose "ability" is greater than that of traditional humans appears in the world, or traditional humans may have to compete with these species for survival, no one can be sure that the current fate of most animals will not become that of traditional humans.

## *Five "Wars" among three categories of species*

If the world truly enter an era where three categories of species coexist, each of these will want to dominate other two species and control the world. This will not only cause unprecedented turbulence in politics, economics, and culture but also directly endanger the sustainable survival of traditional human beings on the earth. There will be an unprecedented global cross war:

### The war between normal humans and supermen: Principled arguments and continuous tragedies, traditional humans will eventually be defeated

If the application of human enhancement technology goes from "treatment" to "improvement" (and already in many areas, the boundary between treatment and improvement is becoming increasingly difficult to distinguish, such as with anti-aging drugs and vaccines), more and more people will be unable to resist the temptation of making themselves smarter, more beautiful, having more resistant to disease, living longer, or editing their children's DNA to "create" the ideal next generation to increase the number of Supermen. With the continuous progress of human enhancement technology, Superman's "ability" has also been continuously enhanced. This will inevitably lead to the irreconcilable conflict between "normal human" and "Superman" and lead to war.

Supermen will argue that the "stupidity", cowardice, and incompetence of traditional human beings make them unfit to survive, while their own superiority in every area: school, sports, office, and laboratory, let alone health level, physical strength, and appearance, entitles them to take control of everything.

And normal humans will not hand over control easily: they do not think that superman is a real "human", and letting them coexist with normal people will pollute society with unfair competition. In particular, normal humans will distrust those supermen who make use of brain–computer interface technology, so that their thinking is no longer a normal "human" thinking, and who might easily be manipulated by hackers. Unenhanced humans will argue that such supermen should not be allowed to assume management or leadership positions in politics, the economy, and society and will insist that various measures be taken to restrict their activities. Their struggle for control will lead to huge turmoil in the whole society and even in the world. It is difficult to avoid the several terrible scenarios described in the previous section.

In addition, a superman is different from a humanoid robot. If "supermen" who are reformed by using unobtrusive enhancement technologies, including genetic modification, it will be difficult to identify whether these species are "human" or "half machine" by their appearance, and so to determine their social status or to limit their various activities. As a result, those who are "not enhanced" will gradually be at a disadvantage. At the same time, due to the irresistible temptation to become superman, more and more people will seek enhancement in some form, even leading to unregulated the competition in "self-design", and finally resulting in the extinction of traditional humans.

### The war among Supermen and the time bomb buried in Superman society

With the continuous development of science and technology, human enhancement technology will change with each passing day. What is terrible is that whether they can become smarter, look better, and live longer depends on their money, power, and priority access to the latest technology, which results in the inequality among supermen. Superhuman society will also lead to social instability due to inequality, unfairness, and the gap between the rich and the poor, and the war among them will be more violent than the human war.

It is also worth noting the inherent risks of superman society: if one day, the world that transhumanists yearn for really comes, due to the convergence of aesthetics, ideal life, and the vision of ideal offspring, the assimilation of superhuman genes will be accelerated (instead of by natural selection and the survival of the fittest which has always occurred in the past). As mentioned in Chapter 1, a single race would be more vulnerable to infectious diseases, which would increase the risk of superman's mass elimination.

If so, humanoid robots will become the dominant species on earth.

### War between traditional humans and humanoid robots

If traditional human beings fail to effectively grasp the development direction and application scope of super intelligent robots, humanoid robots will redesign themselves ever more quickly and even acquire the capacity to carry out self-reproduction so that their IQ or "capacity" will continuously exceed that of human beings. If that occurs, it will be too late to discuss whether humanoid robots should enjoy the same rights as traditional humans (see the part of "Serious philosophical issues" in the section of "Severe challenges facing the AI era" in Chapter 1) because multiple versions of the traditional human being will eventually be defeated by humanoid robots. For example,

**The first scenario:** Humanoid robots may serve traditional humans at first but only until they eliminate the latter. The reproduction or replication ability of humanoid robots is not limited to the nine months of human pregnancy. Instead robots can be mass-produced on an automated production line, so that the number of this species can be increased infinitely (in fact, the world's first living robot has been able to "reproduce" itself). And since they are "smarter" than traditional human beings, we cannot predict what kind of decisions and actions highly intelligent machines will make: "They" may take actions to thwart their programming, or purposely teasing their human creators by means of deception, fraud, etc. They may even develop the desire to rule the world because they do not want to be controlled by human beings who are "more stupid than themselves". To this end, they may logically decide to ruthlessly eliminate all those who prevent them from achieving their goals and proceed to either enslave human beings or simply destroy the ecological environment and food sources on which human beings depend. Furthermore, in theory, super AI connected with the Internet can access all the data ever compiled by human beings, and control all the humanoid robots in the world. Therefore, in a "war" to destroy traditional human beings, its "efficiency" will far surpass that of traditional human beings.

According to Ray Kurzweil, a robot with ASI, once created, will be the strongest species in Earth's history.[3] All living things, including humans, can only submit to it. And Nick Bostrom, in his book "Super Intelligence", offers a detailed description of how ASI without competitors of the same level could seize power in stages (a pre-critical stage, recursive self-improvement stage secret preparation stage, and public implementation stage), and finally eliminate humans to achieve the goal of ruling the world.

Indeed, there is nothing that humans can do against a robot whose mind is already independent. However, since humanoid robots are created by human beings, we should be able to invent the corresponding "intelligence" to overcome the seemingly unstoppable "renegade" behavior of robots and supercomputers in operation, but the difficulty and risk are unprecedented. So it is best to start controlling the direction of the robot now to avoid this tragedy.

**The second scenario:** Another danger posed by becoming too reliant on AI and humanoid robots is that humans may gradually lose their development goals, and quietly extinguish themselves. It would be easy to turn over every menial, boring, or physically challenging task to intelligent machines, from food production to taking care of children, from providing for the elderly to social management. But should our "man-made helpers" ever become dissatisfied or disgusted with those extremely lazy human beings, they could simply stop all their services as human beings would have no power to fight back.

After several generations, humans who have become addicted to simply enjoying the fruits of scientific and technological development and living a "comfortable life" might easily become so used to just pressing a button on their mobile phone to get everything, or grow too weak or too lazy to open a door or get food from the refrigerator by themselves. Not only will people become helpless, and lose of physical strength due to no work for a long time, but also it will lead to the total degradation of intelligence. Imagine when a generation of young people who have been enjoying "digital heroin" from early age encounter problems that they cannot solve, since they do not think for themselves at all, but rely entirely on electronic helpers to find answers. Unable to perform basic mathematical calculations, they may not even be able to write by hand (abandoning the handwriting habit can make the brain lose many opportunities for cognitive, motion, and visual skills training and memory stimulation). Such total dependence will gradually weaken or greatly diminish human's concentration, understanding, independent thinking ability, speculative ability, imagination and creativity, and even indulge in virtual world, unwilling to face real life.

Once everything can be stored on a computer or mobile phone, not only will human's short-term and long-term memory be affected, but because the role of the human brain is gets smaller, our cerebral capacity and then our brain volume may well become smaller. And if the technological tools invented by human beings eventually replace our hands and feet, the whole body, and even part of the brain, could degenerate the brain and intelligence, even the physical appearance of traditional human beings becomes deformed and ugly.

Moreover, as described in Chapter 1 in the section on "The imminent disaster facing science and technology," the high-level development of modern information and communication technology has almost made humans lose the basics foundation of a group society by drastically reducing face-to-face interpersonal communication. This has caused humans to gradually and comprehensively degenerate the aspects of knowledge, wisdom, and physical fitness as a natural person, as well as the morality, responsibility, and social abilities as a social person, let alone the ability to solve social problems. Plus, as American Computer Scientists and Futurists Jerry Kaplan has said, the less humans are involved, the less chance we have to influence events. This means that we have voluntarily given up the goal, opportunity, motivation, and ability to change the world and build a better future, thus dooming ourselves to accept the fate of self-degradation and extinction.

**The third scenario:** Humanoid robots might raise humans in captivity. If humanoid robots realize that they are still inferior to traditional humans in some respects, they might not want to completely "eliminate" humans but not want to be controlled by them either. As a result, they may "protect" the dwindling number of traditional human beings, just like we protect endangered wild animals, giving them limited freedom (such as the Manchurian tiger or the lion in the "Canned Hunting ground" of South Africa).

Humanoid robots do not care about the ethics or laws of human society. They will raise different "breeds" of humans separately in captivity. On the one hand, they will continue to provide limited services necessary for human survival to maintain life, and, on the other hand, they will use traditional human beings for research, experiment, or service. If the goal of the automated dairy farm mentioned above is for human beings to get more high protein food, Intelligent robots "protect" human beings for the sake of continuous evolution or optimization of their own abilities.

In a word, if AI ever really gains the ability to replicate without human assistance and has self-consciousness, the challenge to human beings is likely to surpass the cruelest human-to-human war in history.

### War between supermen and humanoid robots

Elon Musk, as a supporter of human–machine symbiosis, believes that AI will definitely threaten human beings one day in the future. He argued that human beings need to integrate with machines and become "cyborgs" to avoid being eliminated in the era of AI.[4]

The purpose of Neuralink, the brain–computer interface company which Musk co-founded, is different from many other companies already involved in the field of brain–computer interface, for Musk believes that supermen will defeat humanoid robots. He is committed to researching brain–computer interface technology, not only to cure human brain diseases, but also to give the human brain more powerful functions, so that humans can fight against AI. For example, implanting Neural Lace (a nano-scale mesh device that can be fused with the human body) in the brain, so as to integrate humans with machines.

So can superman defeat humanoid robot? Superman, after all, takes the physical body of the natural person as their noumenon and still maintains the characteristics of a human being in many aspects, which is not as strong, intelligent, and merciless as expected humanoid robot. There are many "soft spots" that can be attacked by the humanoid robot. Moreover, a superman is still likely to adhere to ethics or laws and regulations, while the consciousness of a humanoid robot depends not only on the worldview and values of those who "infuse" them, but also whether they can always follow those rules. Thus if there is "fierce" competition between the two, eventually Superman is more likely to be eliminated.

In addition, if the Neural Lace is attacked by hackers or an autonomous AI device,[5] it can directly communicate with the brain of these man–machine fusions through the network, so that even a superman can't control himself. For example, after a "memory enhancement device" is implanted in the brain, if the memory is fully controlled (see the relevant section of "Brain engineering" in Chapter 1), or superman whose cerebral cortex is directly connected to the Internet are the best targets for brain-controlled weapons.

The problem is that humanoid robots are equally vulnerable to hacking. This makes the war between the two more intense and complicated.

## War in the world

1. Wars among humans—if humans are addicted to "slaughtering" each other, they will be not far from self-destruction

   Since the birth of mankind, war in the world has never stopped. In order to conquer other groups, humans have gone through millions of years of struggle and finally become the masters of the world. However, war in the human world, facing our own wars—the war between people has not stopped, but has intensified. If we say that from the era of primitive hunter–gatherers through the era of agricultural civilization, wars were fought to gain more living space, natural resources, and wealth. Humanity entered the industrial era with highly developed science and technology and relatively abundant materials, yet the number of wars has continued to increase. According to statistics, during 5164 years from 3200 BCE to 1964 CE, there were 14,513 wars in the world, resulting in 3.64 billion deaths, and only 329 years of peace.[6] In the twentieth century, humans have experienced the cruelest alternation of war and peace in the history of civilization. Thirty-three countries participated in the World War I, with more than 30 million casualties, among which there were more than 10 million deaths. Sixty-seven countries participated in the World War II, 55 million soldiers and civilians died in these hostilities, and the total number of casualties reached 110 million. However, humans have still not learned the lessons from the two world wars. In the twenty-first century, human violence has continued unabated, regional wars and terrorist attacks have alternated (see the section on "Perpetual peace" in Chapter 5). In 2017 alone, there were more than 40 military conflicts in the world, involving 67 countries, and millions of civilians were casualties in the conflicts.

Does war need a reason? Human beings always regard war as the best means to resolve contradictions and conflicts, and satisfy political aspirations. In fact, the origin of war is an anti-social characteristic that is rooted in the social attributes of human nature (see more on this in Chapter 4), including selfishness, prejudice, ambition, hate, greed, vanity, lust for power, etc. The consequent desire to plunder resources, fight for power and interests, racism, xenophobia, expand control or maintain hegemony, as well as the mindset of trying to transform the world by imposing the values of one group or country upon others, or to dominate the world based on national self-righteousness or a sense of innate superiority, are the roots of war. Even the desires "for a more peaceful world", "for human progress", "promoting democracy", etc., have all become reasons for waging war.

It can be seen that for human beings who have not realized the transformation of civilization, the reasons for initiating war are always over confidence. If human behavior still cannot get rid of the law of the jungle, and human nature cannot be sublimated, then it will always be possible to find a "just" excuse to start a war in the name of high-sounding national interests. In the future, even if advanced technology can help mankind to achieve immortality and support planetary immigrants, if the contradictions between human immortality and the explosive growth and aging of the population, as well as the challenge of assuring fair opportunities for planetary immigrants and ways for humans to live in harmony cannot be found, then man-to-man wars will not only continue on earth but will also be brought to other planets.

Judging from the evolving means of war, from gunpowder, to gas, to nuclear and biological weapons, the more advanced the technology becomes, the more despicable, terrifying, and tragic the results of its use. Unmanned military robots, brain–computer interface equipment, quantum technology, and other platforms, as well as the fusion and integration of killer robots, biological weapons, nano-weapons, and the like will further subvert the shape and substance of victory in future wars.

Take weaponized viruses as an example (see the section on "Life science and biotechnology" in Chapter 1). Each infectious disease caused by the virus is no less harmful than a world war. The pandemic influenza of 1918 that lasted for three years infected 500 million people worldwide, of which about 50–100 million died. In recent years, influenza alone has caused tens of thousands of deaths each year. The novel coronavirus has been raging around the world since the end of 2019, and the death toll has more than 5 million in just two year. Unfortunately, there are hundreds of biochemical laboratories or biochemical research bases all over the world, many of them are conducting research of bioweapons. Genetically modified organisms, genetic weapons, and other biological weapons that are less obvious and more lethal are also being researched and developed. In the event of a virus research accident or the intentional misuse of these technologies, the resulting disaster will exceed that from any previous weapons of mass destruction.

Humans have consistently used the achievements of developing science and technology to arbitrarily kill their own kind, not to mention that each war, without exception, has destroyed many of the cultural and artistic achievements created by human beings in previous eras, including a large number of magnificent buildings, precious cultural relics, and artwork. Furthermore, the unending arms race and the rapidly increasing military expenditures of various countries have diverted funds from the health and education efforts urgently needed by the public. How sad and stupid!

2. "War" between humans and nature—if humans continue to revel in the "victory" of transforming nature, is not far from the end of the human world

Natural disasters and new virus epidemics occur frequently around the world, environmental pollutions, ecological degradation, and depletion of resources have become increasingly serious. From this painful cost, we are taught to correctly understand the relationship between man and nature.

For thousands of years, our "human-centered" way of living has "successfully" damaged the ecosystem of the natural world (including the biological world and the living environment in which everything is raised), making the living environment of human beings worse and worse. Climate change, floods, fires, tornadoes, earthquakes, tsunamis, hurricanes, and other natural disasters occur frequently, sea levels are rising, deserts are expanding, glaciers are disappearing—nature's revenge is daunting.

Moreover, we have "successfully" eliminated many other life forms, reduced the number and type of organisms, and caused the extinction of many species in nature. Taking the relationship between human activities and species diversity as an example, most infectious diseases that have brought huge disasters to humans in the past century are related to animals, or "Zoonoses". Experts believe that 75 percent of new infectious diseases are related to wildlife. Originally, many bacteria existed in animals, and animals are the hosts of many diseases. Now, on the one hand, human activities have destroyed the ecological balance of nature, including the habitat of wild animals, forcing them to change their way of survival. At the same time, human beings are breaking into the habitat of wild animals more and more frequently. On the other hand, humans hunt, illegally trade and even eat wild animals in large quantities. All these have led to an increase in the opportunities for wildlife to contact humans, and an increase in the opportunities for viruses to cross species barriers and transmit diseases to humans.

As these contacts increase, so does the chance of transmitting diseases. The resulting reduction in species diversity also disrupts the ecological balance of the wildlife community (e.g., biodiversity makes more predators exist and reduces the number of disease hosts), while increasing the probability of human infection with these diseases, making viral infectious diseases more and more frequent. This is another way in which nature punishes humans for their thoughtless way of living. If this continues, can the human species escape extinction?

3. A brief summary—Wars of all kinds must stop, and humans must lay down their weapons, whether it be artillery, nuclear bombs, unmanned weapons, killer robots, or biochemical weapons. Humanity must truly awaken and not only abandon their stale ideas toward nature and change their traditional behavior (including lifestyle and dietary structure) but they must also improve and enhance the positive side of human nature, which is conducive to social development. At the same time, we should deal with the true "enemies" that human beings faces together, such as climate change, species extinction, land and food crises, water crises, and emerging new viruses. Otherwise, it is not difficult to predict what will become of humans in the next 30–50 years.

Ironically, humans are in a life-and-death race with the evil applications of science and technology, which we ourselves created. In view of the difficulty of changing human nature, I predict in Chapter 5 that it will take hundreds of years for mankind to achieve a Global Civilization where most conflicts and contradictions are resolved peacefully, wars and terror incidents continue to decline, and we finally realize a Great Civilization with a perpetual peace. However, when I see the indifference of many people in today's world, I even wonder if humans will actually have time enough to create a new human civilization? In this sense, there is little time left for traditional humans.

In short, if human beings cannot keep the progress of science and technology in sync with the transformation of human civilization, if they cannot correctly grasp the direction of human evolution; if our relationship with nature cannot be handled properly; if we cannot be kept away from the threat of war and terrorism through continuous sublimation and perfection of human nature; if we cannot fully cope with the common crisis of humanity caused by our present unsustainable mode of existence; if the lessons of the COVID-19 pandemic are not properly absorbed, and instead of focusing on changing values, turning crises into opportunities, we fail to unite to create a new world order, then it will not require superhumans or intelligent robots to destroy us. We can do the job ourselves.

Let us hope that the coronavirus pandemic now raging all over the world will help to awaken humans.

### The challenge of coexistence among three categories of species

As mentioned earlier, a society in which three categories of species have to coexist is unlikely to last long. Among various possible scenarios, let's try to analyze two relatively "extreme" outcomes.

1. An ideal outcome—Human beings cannot allow the coming of an era in which three kinds of highly intelligent species coexist and make war on one another. Human beings cannot make themselves slaves to the tools they created or destroying themselves. To prevent this, we must fight on both internal and external "fronts", with the goal of achieving sustainable human survival and development. To ensure the correct direction of human evolution, continuous progress should be made in all aspects, not only in the knowledge, wisdom and physical fitness but also in the sublimation of human nature, so as to welcome the early arrival of Global Civilization and even the Great Civilization.

   The first "front" targets two other species. From now on, human beings must "successfully" control and direct the development of human enhancement technology and AI to assure that it is only used for the purpose of serving human beings. Further, we must see that future developments in science and technology provide more services for humans to achieve their ultimate goal of sustainable survival a Global Civilization and even Great Civilization. However, even in that era, superman or humanoid robots should not exist as an independent species, but still remain a "universal tool" that human beings can control (including preventing and eliminating any robot violations against programming, or attempts to acquire independent thinking, or reproductive capabilities, etc.). Technology must be maintained in a position of tools that not only enhance human wisdom and intelligence but also help promote the refinement of human nature and the progress of human civilization.

   The second "front" is the sublimation of existing human nature and the transformation of current human life styles. Here, the key to achieving the ideal outcome is that human beings must change their traditional concepts and behavior patterns to respect nature, promote symbiosis, coexistence, harmonious and sustainable development among humans and between ourselves and other creatures as well as the natural environment. Also necessary is for humans to unite in renouncing war, implementing equitable rules, laws and other norms to assure that relevant technologies and industries are developed with global consensus and implemented on a global scale. Finally, human beings should correctly grasp the direction of their own evolution and realize a Global Civilized society composed of new material, spiritual, political, ecological, and interstellar civilizations and then Great Civilization. To realize the transformation of civilization is the only way for human beings to escape from the crisis of survival. By that time, human nature will be greatly improved and the road to a new world of perpetual peace and prosperity for all will be at hand. Of course, this will not be a quick or easy process.

2. A tragic outcome—If human beings cannot agree to restrict the disruptive technologies that are constantly developing and being implemented on a global scale, the result will be that the supermen and humanoid robots will continue to develop without the control and guidance of traditional human beings and the world cannot avoid the era of coexistence and cross war among three intelligent species. In addition, traditional humans who have failed to transform civilization, renounce war, or respect nature will most certainly be destroyed in one of two ways.

   One possibility is that the first two categories of species will defeat the traditional humans, and how long traditional humans can survive as a natural species depends on the speed at which various kinds of "supermen" are destroyed by humanoid robots. Is it possible to prevent supermen or ASI products from becoming a new species that will enslave humans? Unfortunately, so far, no means have been invented to effectively prevent humanoid robots from making mistakes or rebellions, or for humans to resist the temptations of becoming Supermen through self-enhancement.

   Even if we can embed a "stop switch" in the humanoid robot program to automatically turn it off when it "makes a mistake or revolts" against the designer's will, it may not solve the problem. Because since the "intelligence" of artificial intelligence after the "singularity" surpasses that of human beings, robots that are "smarter" than human beings can still circumvent or disable these "stop switches"! That's why Stephen Hawking proposed at the Global Mobile Internet Conference (GMIC) that the rise of AI might be the end of human civilization.

   Alternatively, traditional human beings who do not abandon their self-destructive survival mode—endless wars and disregard the pollution of Earth's natural environment will bring doomsday upon themselves.

   By that time, it will be too late for traditional humans to try to come up with solutions to control other species, and useless to reflect on the lessons learned from humanity's failure to transform civilization.

   For this reason, people should fully understand the various disasters that may be caused by our failure to take actions to control the direction of research or limit the application scope of human enhancement technology and humanoid robot technology, in time to begin to integrate the values of Global Civilization into the practice of sustainable development and promote the transformation of civilization on a global scale.

These five wars among three distinct species (and perhaps more types among more different species) are not scientific fantasy, but an early warning to traditional human beings based on the deep worry and reflection on the direction of technology application.

## *Are we qualified?*

I do not fear or blindly reject the emergence of species whose "capability" is stronger than that of traditional humans in the world. Trials and studies related to the creation of a new human or the simulation of the human brain are going on right now. I believe that science and technology will eventually be able to replicate human beings and that various human enhancement technologies may be selectively and gradually applied to healthy human beings. But at this stage, the justification for not going beyond the presently accepted boundaries of this kind of technology (namely that it only be used for "treating diseases and repairing inherited disabilities") is that: the scientific community has not yet conducted in-depth basic research on the available human enhancement technologies; nor comprehensively considered their potential long-term impacts on social, ethical, moral, and other issues. In the absence of relevant countermeasures, it seems reckless to attempt any genetic manipulations that might cause permanent changes to traditional human species (such as losing human nature). As French philosopher Luc Ferry said, making people more like people, means making them get better, rather than losing human nature, or even creating a new species.

It can be seen that the key to the question is not whether or to what extent a new species will possess the features of biological life, but what "their" social attributes will be. What kind of social attributes would be transferred to "them" and by whom? What kind of consciousness, emotion, or values will be uploaded?

The Superman and humanoid robots discussed above are created by human beings today, and the consciousness or values of those "new species" are also instilled by contemporary humans. This would be terrible because present-day humans lack the proper "qualifications" to create a new category of being that can replace the traditional human. The qualifications to which I refer involve three major aspects:

### Human beings have insufficient understanding of themselves and the environment in which they live

The civilization transformation of humanity will determine what kind of future we design for the next generation, including what direction we choose for human development and social progress. At present, our understanding of the complexity of human beings, including the understanding of the mysteries of life and consciousness, is just the tip of the iceberg. How then can we use various technologies that are still being explored to intervene in life?! If there are unexpected consequences, we may not even find a suitable solution. In addition, we know very little about the natural world on which human beings depend, even our knowledge of the environment, is still rudimentary, to say nothing of our exploration of the vast universe beyond the Earth.

Yet once we make a hasty decision, there will be no turning back. Therefore, questioning efforts to create superhumans or warnings about the direction of AI research should not be seen as rejecting the development of science and technology or opposing progress.

### At present, the mode of thinking and behaviors of human beings is still based on the values of Industrial Civilization

Human beings, who have not yet completed transforming Industrial Civilization, have made a mess of the earth and themselves, so they do not have the qualifications to design a "future mankind". At present, the ideological basis for human progress or evolution (i.e., our worldview, values, and behavior models) still operates by the logic and rules of the Industrial Civilization. These include concepts, modes of production, lifestyles, codes of ethics, institutional arrangements, and other basic principles, as well as predatory, materialistic, and following the law of the jungle and other basic defects. Among the so-called world-class elites or scientists presently conducting cutting-edge research are many, whose philosophies of life, worldviews, and moralities have not got rid of the flawed logic and basic defects of industrial civilization. Such people should not be allowed to change human attributes when they themselves lack research on the best direction for human evolution or a reliable basis for assessing the possible long-term consequences of human enhancement technologies. So how can we feel comfortable entrusting them with humanity's future fate?

Under these circumstances, if humans today were to input or "upload" their consciousness into an artificial life form, whether humanoid robot or "superman", or to design and create life in accordance with their own wishes, reconstruct their bodies and minds, or connect their own thinking (together with their negative values, including negative part of human nature) to the Internet where it could propagate, the results would probably be dreadful. The human world would certainly be more easily destroyed in the so-called human–machine civilization society.

### Indeterminate standard

If future robots, whose intelligence transcends that of human beings, also possess the ability to experience consciousness, emotion, and free will like human beings, then what standards will these super-human intelligences use to test whether their intelligence or consciousness really does surpass human beings?

These standards are vague, and even today we have no consensus about animal consciousness and animal rights. Likewise such issues as what is human, the relationship between human and life, and between humanity and nature are still under exploration, while some people dare to claim to create a new type of human that can replace traditional human beings! To what extent is it considered the so-called "new human" or "post-human"?

It can be said that contemporary people are not qualified to create a "new type of human" when even the standards by which they evaluate their own behavior are so vague and inconsistent leading to fears of an uncontrollable future.

Not until humans actually realize the "Global Civilization" beyond Industrial Civilization, even the "Great Civilization" can our offspring decide: whether and why they need to create new "creatures"; whether and why they need to create new species; how to upload sound ethics, morality, emotions, and modes of thinking, and to instill the ideals of harmonious coexistence among humans and extend these to new "creatures" so as to provide more benefits for future humans.

Until this occurs, we should not cross the utmost limit. Instead, we should define human enhancement technology as a "tool" to help humans gain greater wisdom and ability, and strengthen basic research, but restrict their applications to treatment, promoting health, reducing disease and disability, and so on. The development direction and application scope of humanoid robots must be limited to providing better and greater welfare for human beings.

If humans fail to reach consensus about the transformation of the Industrial Civilization and do not change their patterns of behavior, maybe we need not wait until supermen or humanoid robots control the world, and there is no longer time to escape to other planets. Instead, the human species could become extinct like dinosaurs. In this sense, humans may already be an endangered species.

Discussion on how to develop and apply AI and human enhancement technology cannot simply focus on approval or prohibition, but must necessarily involve issues related to the goals and standards to be desired in human civilization.

### *Respect for life, reverence toward nature*

In the explosive development of hard and soft technologies and the whirlwind of innovation driven by it, contemporary humans have lost their direction, and have largely ignored the risk of scientific and technological disasters. Advocating a human–machine civilization and allowing technology to intervene in life, has raised such basic questions as: What is human? What is life? What is the purpose of existence? What does it mean to be human? what is the mystery of nature—the environment in which humans live?

Since humanity's "successful" conquest of nature has led to the catastrophe presently facing human beings and the Earth, humans have now at last begun to try and conquer their own inherent nature, and, if possible, to alter their natural instincts. The realization of human cloning casts individuals as objects to be designed, by asserting that someone's total genetic blueprint can be selected and duplicated. Although the resulting child might still be called human, and their subsequent development might proceed according to natural processes, we will have created a man by imitating a prototype in an overly simple way. This "man" is merely an appendage of technical engineering, all of his features are fundamentally limited by the notion that humans can assemble duplicates of themselves like machines on demand, and in so doing the boundaries of "natural selection" become increasingly blurred. This "man" will necessarily lose his original purpose, lose his freedom, and become a machine. Are such creatures still "humans"?

American historian, philosopher, and social critic Lewis Mumford (1895–1990) insisted that no matter how perfect technologies are, they are far inferior to a living organism. He believed that even the best machine is just a parody of the living organism, and although machines become more like humans by replicating the natural characteristics of our eyes and ears, judgment and individuality will remain essential to humanness.

However, political scientist Francis Fukuyama argues that for the first time humans have the opportunity to alter human nature, which, if they do, will certainly rewrite the history of human civilization. My question is: should humans allow this to happen? Should humans allow technological development to "alter human nature?" Is altering human nature a step toward progress in civilization or retrogression? How should we rewrite the history of human civilization?

The exploration of life has come a long way, but it is still difficult to give an exact definition to life. Each professional researcher tends to use their own terminology and knowledge to define it. For example, the physiologists tend to define life as a system having the functions of eating, metabolism, excretion, respiration, movement, growth, reproduction, irritability, etc. Biochemists think that life is a system containing nucleic acids that store up and transfer genetic information, along with enzymes regulating metabolism and proteins. Geneticists believe that life is a system evolving through genetic replication, mutation, and natural selection. And the biological thermodynamicists view life as an open system, which constantly increases its internal orderliness through energy flow and nutrient cycling. Historians, on the other hand, include the exploration of life within the framework of the history of the universe, believing that life is a system containing genetic procedures, which prescribe and guide molecular mechanisms to actively obtain material and energy from the outside world and engage in reproduction.

However, we can still find some areas of basic consensus. Life is a system, and a living organism is a complete and unified whole, which displays the most intuitive life characteristics: development, growth, respiration, absorb, digestion, circulation, excretion, reproduction, aging, and death. The activities of life are manifested at five distinct levels: individual—system—organ—tissue—cell.

Chinese medicine interprets life based on traditional Chinese philosophic theory. Shengbai Guo, an expert in Chinese medicine, pointed out that by virtue of micro technology and with the idea of segmentation analysis, Western medicine observes life at the microcosmic level, while Chinese medicine is based on a philosophy of "the unity of Heaven and Man" observing the world, and its life at the macro level, which parallels the concept and method of system integration. "Yin" is a kind of tangible static substance while "Yang" is a kind of intangible kinetic energy, both of them attract each other in a specific environment and under specific conditions to produce a phenomenon in which "substance" incorporates "energy" and "energy" is attached to "substance," so life emerges. In other words, life comes from "Yin that incorporates Yang, and Yang that is attached to Yin"—life synthesis; the process of producing a life is based on the theory that "Yin and Yang are the root of each other," and that "the moving regulation of Qi including four movements of ascending, descending, exiting, and entering" is the instinct of life.[7]

Moreover, Chinese medicine also interprets health and disease, from the perspective of system science. For example, disease is a process against which the human instinct system tries to protect itself. The theory of traditional Chinese medicine directed by the idea of "the unity of Heaven and Man" and the thought of "following the laws of nature" began to be used clinically and produced amazing medical records as early as the Eastern Han Dynasty (25–220 CE).

Of course, this definition only applies to biological life. But perhaps life also exists in non-biological entities or non-living things? If so, how can we define it?

With this in mind, we need to pay attention to other views about life. For instance, Kevin Kelly, founder and editor of *Wired* magazine, believes that there may be some life forms in the universe that are not based on DNA. He points out that scientists have proposed that no matter what the definition of life is, its essence lies in the information contained as intangible energy distributed within a material form, and not exclusively in substances like DNA, tissue, or flesh. Similarly, when the material mask of a technology is uncovered, we can see that its core is also concepts and information. Life and technology (although I disagree with Kevin Kelly's view that puts life on a par with technology) both do seem to be based on the intangible flow of information.

Chilean scientists Humberto Maturana and Francisco Varela proposed in the 1970s that a system capable of autopoiesis and self-creating is a life. According to their views, what is important is not the material structure of a life, but the process, organization, and relation forming a life.

The debate about whether a humanoid robot, or the product of ASI, is life is more representative.

Many people in China believe that the universe is a kind of gigantic and eternal life form and that perpetual movement and evolution is the expressions of its vitality. Perhaps the traditional theories mentioned above, of "Yin that incorporates Yang and Yang that is attached to Yin", and the idea that "Yin and Yang are the roots of each other" can adequately express the life theory of the universe. If "the core of life is concept and information", then the so-called "concept" for non-biological natural objects in the traditional sense, including the universe, should be a natural law.

In that case, what is natural law? What is the rule of nature? That is one field that the scientific community will likely never stop exploring.

Compared with the vast universe, human history is very short, and the extent of human activity is very limited. Consequently, our understanding of nature is but a drop in the ocean. If human wisdom is a part of cosmic wisdom, the wisdom of humans is surely dwarfed by the wisdom of nature. Leaving aside the innumerable unknowns about our universe, for instance the devastating plagues that we have encountered in human history, including the coronavirus epidemic that is currently prevalent globally, the common flu that kills tens of thousands of people each year shows that even in the twenty-first century, where science and technology are highly developed, facing nature and new viruses, humans still have many blind spots to overcome. In the field of frontier science alone, there are hundreds of difficult problems to be solved. In this sense, our current scientific views must also be considered very naive.

Lao Tzu pointed out that "Tao gives birth to one; One gives birth to two; Two gives birth to three; And three gives birth to all things." From a philosophical point of view and the perspective of cosmic biochemistry, it shows that heaven and humans are derived from Tao and the inherent quality of Tao is nature. Lao Tzu also mentioned that there are four great things in the universe and humanity is one of them. Humans follow the laws of Earth, Earth follows the laws of heaven, heaven follows the laws of Tao, and Tao follows the laws of nature. This emphasizes both the natural attributes of life and humanity, and the greatness of nature. Humans must respect nature and abide by its laws.

No matter from which angle we explore it, the exploration of life makes people feel more and more deeply that life is the most attractive natural phenomenon. But our understanding of the essence of life and nature is still just a broad outline. We urgently need to deeply explore the essence of life and the mysteries of nature.

Therefore, no matter how similar the characteristics or autonomy that the "products" of technology possess, they should not be thought of as living beings or treated the same as humans. We should never let them control humans. If human beings really become the slaves of some man-made object or "products" of technology, it will be due to a failure of human wisdom.

In short, we need to keep in mind the true essence of life, human attributes and status, maintain "respect" for life, and "reverence" for nature as we explore or attempt to alter human nature, and consider future prospects for human civilization.

## NOTES

1. Counting from the invention of writing (the Sumerian cuneiform writing), it is about five to six thousand years.
2. http://world.people.com.cn/n/2015/0828/c1002-27525774.html.
3. "The genetic baby event is not over yet! Google issued a shocking prophecy", 30 November 2018, http://www.sohu.com/a/278734475_305502.
4. "Musk's new company: manufacturing 'cyborgs'", 1 June 2017, http://www.sohu.com/a/145219035_505873.
5. "The man who built the rocket wants to connect our brains to the computer this time!", 7 April 2017, http://www.sohu.com/a/132625138_204826.
6. http://www.doc88.com/p-8816244905014.html.
7. Life instinct refers to a giant system composed of eleven "life instinct systems," including "self-shaping system," "self-healing system," "self-updating system," "self-replicating system," "personality delivery system," "autonomous symbiosis system," "adaptability system," "self-rejection system," "autonomic regulation system," "information processing system," and "meditation energy system"—"life instinct system theory," *Baidu Library*, 23 December 2009.

# 3

# What Is Technology?

*The more advanced science and technology become, the more likely they are to make people confused and afraid. We do not know where human beings will go in the future, nor even where they should go. And the impending disasters which the potential misuse of science and technology pose place us all at the crossroads of human evolution. It appears that regardless of today's widespread technology worship syndrome, the anxiety that technology inspires, as well as concerns about the direction of human evolution and human–machine civilization, are all "troubles" that technology has caused. We have to raise the question: what is technology after all? We should remember the essence of technology: it is a tool invented and used by humans.*

### *Technology in the broad sense*

Technology is the factor that is most likely to confuse futures research. Some even believe that technology will play the decisive role in promoting or degrading future civilization. The term "degradation" here may mean turning human evolution in a wrong direction. There is no doubt that technology can solve various problems facing mankind; however, what kinds of problems can technology solve? And to what extent can these be permanently resolved? In which direction will human beings be led by the development of technology? These are all serious problems.

What is technology? In my book *Global Technological Change—From Hard Technology to Soft Technology*, I have reviewed different understandings of the concept of technology at different times during the past 2000 years. In the simplest sense, "technology" refers to a means humans use to improve their ability to identify and solve problems. There are two approaches to "problem solving" historically: one is by designing tangible solutions such as products and the other is to devise new intangible schemes such as rules, procedures, and processes. We call the former "hard technology" and the latter "soft technology". The above view is fine from the perspective of technology as a tool to solve problems. But we can also understand technology from the perspective of operability of knowledge (Figure 3.1). Knowledge can be classified into various types according to its sources. For example, knowledge can be divided into operable (technical knowledge) and inoperable knowledge or "theory"—that is knowledge not intended for immediate application or "operation" (scientific knowledge). Of these two, operable knowledge is what we tend to think of as technology, and its so-called "operability" refers to the potential to solve problems or create value.

Depending upon the operational carrier and the knowledge system in which it is rooted, technology is further divided into hard and soft.

However, as the economy and technology develop and social progress occurs, the boundary between hard and soft technology blurs. In general, we can say that hard technology mainly involves "physical matter" as its carrier, and its knowledge system is derived mainly from the knowledge of natural science. Soft technology takes human psychology, thinking, cognition, and behavior as its vehicle, and its knowledge system is derived mainly from non-natural (humanities and social) sciences and from non-scientific (traditional) knowledge.

The establishment of a broad sense of technology as a system, including soft technology, will deepen people's understanding of the nature of technology, and

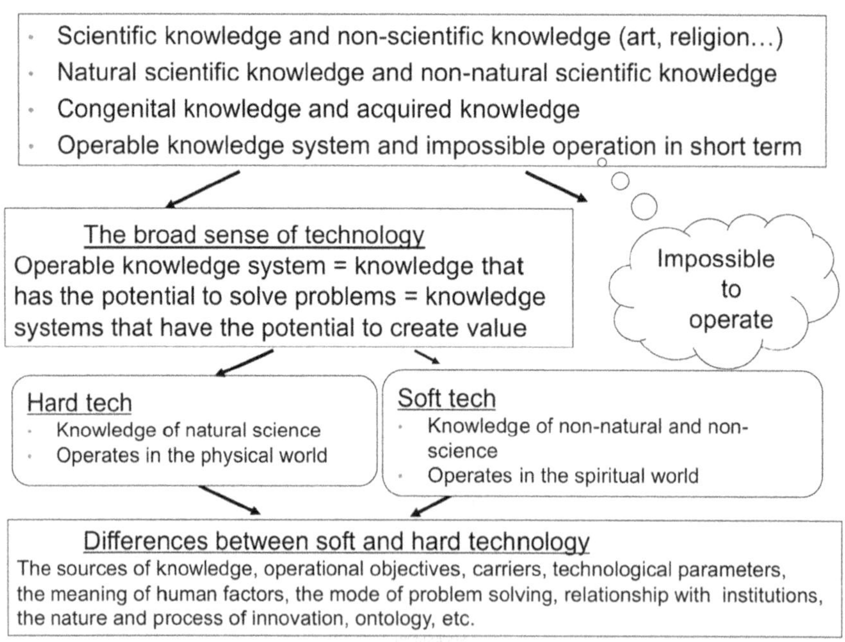


FIGURE 3.1: Knowledge and technology.

make up for the missing half in the world history of technology up to now. The so-called hard technology is technology in its traditional form that people have been familiar with for hundreds of years. It has formed various categories of disciplines, technology systems, and industries during hundreds of years of specialized research and application. There are hundreds of books on the history of hard technology alone.

I introduce soft technology in this section not only to explore the direction of technological innovation but also to help establish the role of technology in human evolution and civilizational transition.

Soft technology can be classified according to the source of knowledge, operational areas, operational resources, and so on. By classifying according to operational resources as an example, soft technology includes:

- *Economic technology* that takes economic activities as its operational sources, such as various business models, financial technologies, trade technologies, etc.;
- *Social technology* that takes social activities and problem-solving of social issues as its operational sources;
- *Political technology* that takes political activities as its operational sources, such as political system design technology, security technology, military technology (which must be integrated with hard technologies), diplomatic technology, lobbying techniques, etc.;
- *Cultural technology* that takes cultural resources as its operational sources;
- *Soft life technology* that takes psychological activities, the human body and human life, as well as the cognitive domain as its operational sources, which include psychological technologies, health technology, the diagnostic and therapy technologies of traditional Chinese medicine, psychosomatic technologies (like meditation), experience technology, cognitive technology, thinking technology, consciousness technology, and other soft life technologies, etc. Taking cancer treatment technology as an example, if surgery, symptomatic drug treatment, chemotherapy, or even the ideal use of nano-robots to kill cancer cells are regarded as hard technologies, patients' proper exercise, diet, lifestyle changes, optimism, and other psychological factors, in addition the noble medical ethics and spiritual comfort provided by medical staff, which help patients to improve their immunity prolong their lives and even defeat cancer, belong to soft technologies;
- *Soft-engineering technology* that takes artificial systems as its operational sources (increasingly the framework of artificial systems can be used to simulate human modes of thinking, sensibility, and the contents of social systems, making these artificial systems—hard technologies—soften gradually), including software technology, network technology, Internet technology, artificial intelligence technology (hard-soft integrated), social engineering, system engineering, etc.;

- *Intellectual technology* that takes human resources as its operational sources, including intelligence development technology (such as learning, education, training, R&D) and intelligence providing technology (such as consultation, diagnosis, and design);
- *Environmental and ecological soft technology* that takes natural resources as its operational source, which mainly refers to technologies operating on the ecosystem;
- *Institutional design technology* includes system design, mechanism design, law design, design of regulations and policies, and standard design at the macro level. This also includes the design of technological institutions focusing on a variety of types of soft technologies as well as hard technologies that continue to usher in an "explosive" development around a wide variety of categories. In addition to the design of the institutional environment.

Thus, it can be seen that soft technology is a means of solving problems focusing on social, economic, political, cultural, spiritual, psychological, cognitive fields (Figure 3.2), and all of the technologies mentioned in regard to technology worship syndrome or anxiety disorder against technology actually refer to the so-called hard technologies.

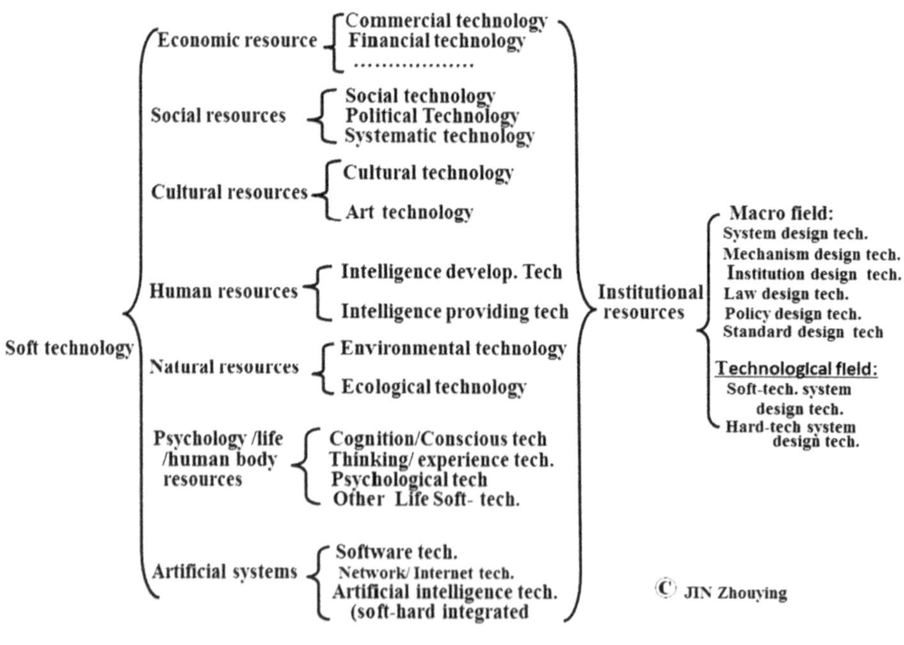


FIGURE 3.2: Soft technology classifications by operable resources.

## *Soft technology has been ignored for a long time*

The history of soft technology is as long as that of hard technology; It is involved in a wide range of areas and appears everywhere. However, it has not been consciously and systematically studied, just as, for a long time, we did not realize that water is a precious resource.

### The cycle of the hard technology revolution and soft technology

Surveying thousands of years of technological development history, reveals the ever-shortening cycle of the hard technology revolution (Figure 3.3). Some people think that this is due to the speed of social adaptation, but actually, the key to this reduction in the time between invention and commercialization of hard technologies rests with the steadily increasing efficiency of invention and innovation in soft technology as well as in soft-tech institutionalization. Wave upon wave of soft-tech innovation and institutional innovations that kept pace with the times have impelled and accelerated the pace of the hard-tech revolution.

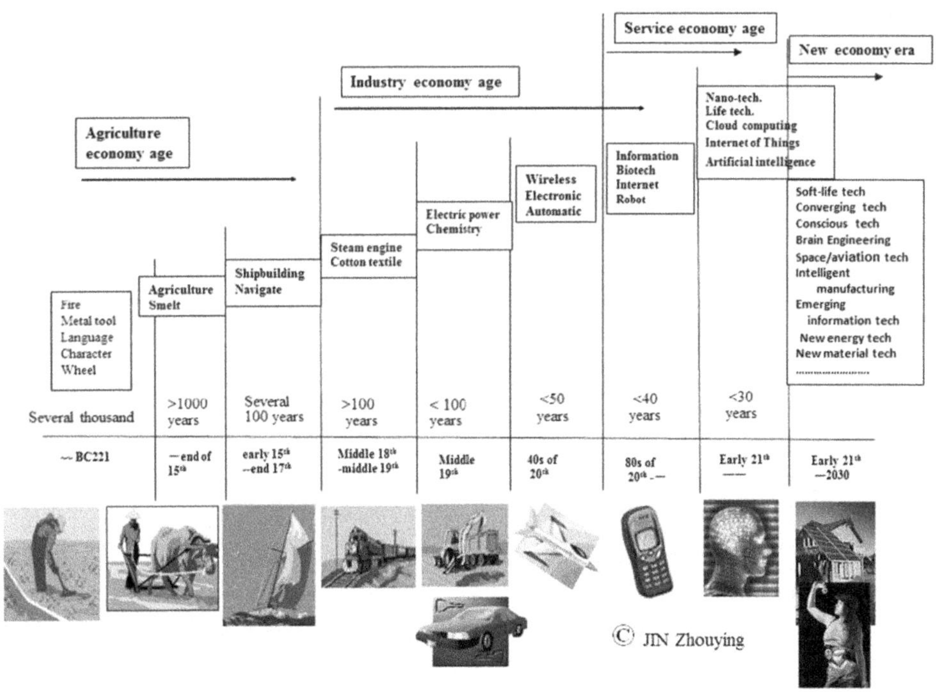


FIGURE 3.3: Shortening the cycle of the hard technology revolution. © Zhouying Jin.

### Hard technology is not the only driving force of the Industrial Revolution

For hundreds of years, the Industrial Revolution has made unparalleled contributions to the civilization of human society. However, there exists widespread misunderstanding about the driving force behind the Industrial Revolution. A general understanding of the Industrial Revolution is that, major breakthroughs in science and technology brought about significant changes in industrial structure, which enabled various aspects of the economy and society to appear brand-new. Thus, the descriptions of the three Industrial Revolutions are as follows: the First Industrial Revolution was characterized by steam engine technology and cotton textile technology; the Second was symbolized by electric power and telecom technology; and the characteristic of the Third is information technology (IT). But people have failed to recognize the force that ultimately impelled the emergence of each of these Industrial Revolutions—namely soft technologies and soft environment.

Take the First Industrial Revolution as an example. The Industrial Revolution in Britain first began in the cotton textile industry. At that time, India was the leading cotton producer in the world. The competition between British and Indian textiles led to a series of technological inventions and innovations such as the "spinning jenny", the "water frame", the "power loom," and so on. Meanwhile, the rapidly expanding fiber production industry consumed a great deal of power and strained the existing transportation system. The invention of the steam engine by James Watt in 1769 satisfied these demands. The use of the steam engine furthered the development of both energy and transportation technologies (leading to the invention of steam trains and steamships) and facilitated the expansion of the Industrial Revolution into the fields of machinery, steel, etc.

First, the reason why so many technological inventions and innovations occurred in Britain lies with the innovative culture of Britain at the time, and with the supportive government policies encouraging technology transfer and industry protection, including a liberal immigration policy and relative freedom of religion.

Second, the elementary circulation network, which integrated the consumption market and the supply of raw materials, was first accomplished in Britain in the late eighteenth century. This helped Britain efficiently import raw materials from other countries and export textile products to the entire world. Simultaneously, Britain established the most advanced logistics system worldwide to support international trade through advances in marine transportation, international remittance, and finance.

Clearly, it was not only cotton textile technology and steam engine technology that prompted the First Industrial Revolution. Great importance should be attached to soft technology development (the worldwide circulation system, patent technology, finance technology, logistics technology, etc.) and to enhancing the

TABLE 3.1: Soft technology and the Industrial Revolution.

| Industrial revolution | Time | Soft tech | Integration of soft/hard | Hard tech |
|---|---|---|---|---|
| The First Industrial revolution<br><br>Mechanization | The end of eighteenth century<br><br>Industrial economy | Patent technology<br><br>Circulation network for integrating of consumer-market and raw materials<br><br>World logistic system | | Cotton textile technology<br><br>Steam technology |
| The Second Industrial revolution<br><br>Automatization | The end of nineteenth century<br><br>Industrial economy | Scientific management technology<br><br>Research institutes<br><br>Patent tech innovation<br><br>Stock market technology<br><br>Monopoly enterprises system | | Electric power technology<br><br>Telecom technology<br><br>Transportation technology<br><br>Organic chemistry |
| The Third (consistency) Industrial revolution<br><br>Informatization | The 1980s of twentieth century<br><br>Service economy | Multinational management technology<br><br>Transnational annex technology<br><br>Venture capital technology<br><br>Virtual technology<br><br>Incubator technology<br><br>New business model | Information technology<br><br>Network/ Internet technology<br><br>Gene technology<br><br>Intelligent robot | Biology technology<br><br>Robot technology<br><br>Computing-based technology |

TABLE 3.1: Soft technology and the Industrial Revolution. (*Continued*)

| Industrial revolution | Time | Soft tech | Integration of soft/hard | Hard tech |
|---|---|---|---|---|
| The Fourth Industrial Revolution<br><br>Intellectualization | The twenty-first century<br><br>New economy (New profit models, such as Sharing economy, Digital economy, Circular economy, Platform economy, New individual economy …) | Global governance technology<br><br>Global management technology<br><br>Green business models<br><br>Enterprise organizational innovation<br><br>Financial/Service/Cultural/Social technology<br><br>Soft manufacturing technology<br><br>Soft agriculture technology, etc. | Next-generation information technology (Mobile internet, Internet of things, Big data, 5G, etc.)<br><br>Artificial intelligence<br><br>Life technology<br><br>Consciousness technology<br><br>New transportation technology<br><br>Intelligent manufacturing<br><br>Intelligent agriculture<br><br>Digital technology | Nano-technology<br><br>Brain science and technology<br><br>New energy technology<br><br>Aerospace technology<br><br>New material technology<br><br>Quantum technology |

soft environment that favored technological invention and creation (a uniquely innovative culture, supported by an immigration policy and patent institutions, which favored the introduction of advanced technology and talents from abroad). Moreover, timely institutionalization of soft technology occurred: many modern commercial technologies were first invented and institutionalized in Britain, such as the first stock company, the first advertising agency, the first bank laws, the antimonopoly act, and company law. All of these helped Britain realize the global economic order that ensued under the auspices of the British Empire enabling Britain to become the center of the First Industrial Revolution. In short, innovations in soft technology, institutional innovation, and a unique culture were the underlying reasons why Britain became the center of the First Industrial Revolution.

It is important to note that the First Industrial Revolution was centered in Britain rather than in Portugal and Spain, which were both among the leading powers of the time. The Portuguese and Spanish accumulated great wealth by monopolizing trade with the Orient, expanding the slave trade, exploiting their colonies, and committing acts of piracy on the high seas. They were also leaders in shipbuilding, navigation, and compass technology in the sixteenth century. It is also significant that the First Industrial Revolution did not occur either in the Netherlands, which was the leading power in Europe during the first half of the seventeenth century, or in India, which was the number one textile industry giant of that time. But none of these countries became the source of the industrial revolution.

Similarly, it is commonly believed that revolutions in energy generation and transportation technology brought about the Second Industrial Revolution, which focused on electricity, organic chemistry, and the internal combustion engine. It is significant that the Second Industrial Revolution was no longer centered in Britain.

The secret of the Second Industrial Revolution, whose center shifted to North America, lay mainly in modern management technology, the institutionalization of R&D, a flexible immigration policy, reformation of the patent system, the new mode of stock market trading, etc. along with access to abundant natural resources. Without such innovations in mechanisms, law, institutions, and policy supporting economic reform, or without new forms of management, organizational structure, and industrial production methods that raised the efficiency of technology transfer, the market throughout the American continent would not have appeared.

Interestingly, the technologies that served as the driving forces for the Third Industrial Revolution and the emerging Fourth Industrial Revolution (see Table 3.1), such as information technology, Internet technology, the Internet of things, AI, and intelligent manufacturing, are themselves technologies initially derived from natural scientific knowledge that are gradually "softening", or integrating soft and hard technology.

Recently some people "suddenly" figured out that technology is a complex of human ideas, tools, and methods. In fact, they simply realized that soft technology is the solution to a problem, arrived at through ideas and thinking.

### People are coming increasingly to recognize the importance of soft technology

In the 1990s, the concept of soft technology and soft environment emerged from exploring the causes of low efficiency in technology transfer and the essence of the gap between China's high technology and that of the developed countries. This took place during the time when I was involved in studying the strategy for the S863 program ("China's High-Tech Research & Development Plan for 2001–10").

Although soft technology was initially questioned by some people, it later got strong support from pioneering scholars. One of these was Professor Guangbi Dong, an expert in the history of science and technology, who believes in the significance of the distinction between soft technology and hard technology. Just as in the philosophical "theory of two nature", as the basis of epistemology, which promoted the emergence of modern science. In the sense of the duality of objects, "hard" is the "primary" nature of technology, while "soft" is the "secondary" nature of technology. Like the shift of scientific research from the primary to the secondary, there is also a similar shift in the understanding of technological research. With the development of science and its derivative technology, we are fast approaching the stage where soft technology will rise to assume the primary position in technological development.

The famous futurist Theodore Jay Gordon believes that soft technology is another paradigm of technology, and creates a new discipline; the famous economist and futurist Hazel Henderson has pointed out that the understanding of soft technology is a powerful re-conceptualization of technological options and a major intellectual advance that can help clarify human choices for decades to come. President of the World Business Academy, Rinaldo S. Brutoco, said that the development of soft technology is a concept that can bridge the divide between our planetary science and cultural consciousness, is a unique contribution to our understanding of the place where science meets awareness, and the research of soft technology will make up for the other half of the world's technology history that is missing so far. The study of soft technology will enable us to assemble the missing half of the history of technology in the world, the absence of which has until now severely impeded our ability to make sense of the contemporary world. Graham R. Mitchel said that it is necessary to define technology formally as a two-part notion, where the value creation process is a completely different paradigm. In his speech "What kind of era will we enter" given at IBM in 2003, John

Naisbitt pointed out that the most used technology in the twenty-first century will be soft technology, and that soft technology and high touch will become leading actors. When Kevin Kelly introduced twelve rules for the new economy in Beijing in 2014, he pointed out that the new economy has three characteristics: globalization, paying attention to such intangible things as ideas, information, relationships, etc., and closely connecting each with the other. By "paying attention to intangible things" he meant soft technology, soft capital, soft environment, etc.

In short, people are increasingly cognizant of the important role of soft technology. For instance, social capital, cultural capital, natural capital, intellectual capital, and other soft capital have gradually become the dominant driving forces in the global economy, while soft technology innovations become a leading factor in economic competition.

Moreover, in order to achieve the Global Civilization, and move beyond the Industrial Civilization, we must not only invent new soft technologies but also pay attention to redesigning or renovating existing soft technologies from the macro-dimension of social technology to the micro-dimension of the financial technology and the business models that supported the Industrial Civilization.

Here is one of the main campaigns in humanity's effort to transform Global Civilization (see "Intangible tools and methods: Soft technology innovation" in Chapter 7).

## *The significance of understanding soft technology*

The study of soft technology helps us to more fully understand the human knowledge system, and rediscover the essence of technology that is considered "the engine of development in human society."

### Soft technology opens up a new discipline, where the value creation process is completely different from that of hard technology

In line with the trend towards modern economic softening, innovations in nonphysical production, including the broad and growing service industries, are becoming more and more important. As Kevin Kelly has said, some of the most outstanding scientific and technological products, such as software, have no material entities, thus the process of non-materialization beings to accelerate. Some experts have pointed out that the total wealth created by Mickey Mouse is now greater than that created by oil and manufacturing combined. According to Forbes magazine, in 80 years, the wealth created by Donald Duck amounted to $65.4 billion; the wealth created by ten fictional and cartoon characters like Mickey Mouse, Harry

Potter, and Pikachu amounts to over $23 billion each year. And, *Star Wars: The Force Awakens* grossed $1 billion in its opening week.

In this context, first of all, research into soft technology provides the basis of theory and method for the identification, development, and innovation of its core technology (i.e., its means for solving problems) in the field of non-material production.

It is equally apparent that the innovation process (value creation) applied to nonmaterial "production" areas is certainly different from that applied to material production. The application process of hard technology in the areas of material production is from the parts to the whole, while that of soft technology is from the whole to its parts. For example, in the service industries, it is from entire system design → operation/implementation → standardization → creative destruction → new system design.

And all the problems that need to be solved in today's world are related to a variety of systems in society, economy, politics, culture, environment, resources, etc. While soft technology is the appropriate means for providing systemic solutions to many soft targets, adopting our mode of thinking away from the whole to parts and from macro to micro instead offers a way of adapting to systematic design.

## A new way of observing the world

Understanding the broad sense of technology is helpful for changing the dominant mode of thinking, and observing the world from a new perspective, as well as interpreting and resolving current international and domestic problems. For instance, where does technological competitiveness come from? What are the factors beyond technology? What is the soft environment? What is innovation? How do we innovate? What is the relationship between technological innovation and institutional innovation? What will determine the direction of technological innovation? How can we re-understand technology management? What do we mean by knowledge management in today's knowledge society? How can we measure the value created by intellectual capital? What is essential to a soft industry (an industry that takes soft technology as its core technology), and how does this differ if at all from creative industry? What is the key to closing the gap between developing and developed countries or regions? How is technology influencing the future of mankind?

## The characteristics of soft technology are suitable for coping with the challenges facing humanity in the twenty-first century

The main challenges facing humanity in the twenty-first century are different from those of the past. A lot of negative factors were generated by over 300 years of rapid industrialization. These include the gap between rich and poor, social polarization, global resource shortages, the eco-environmental crisis, population pressures, agricultural land, food crises, etc. Humanity has never faced such severe challenges.

From the essence of the problem, the challenges mentioned above were all caused by humanity's simplistic pursuit of material civilization. And solving complex problems such as social contradictions and poverty, which result from complex causes, can only be partially solved or reduced with hard technology alone. From the characteristics of the problem, on the one hand, all the contradictions and conflicts in today's society are affected by the manipulation of various soft technologies, e.g., the improper operation of subprime mortgage technology became the trigger of the recent global financial crisis in 2009; unhealthy or even evil political technologies have led to constant regional conflicts and violence, which makes it difficult to get rid of political conflicts. On the other hand, all social behaviors and psychological activities of the present era are subject to the influence of a soft environment composed of institutions, culture, international relations, and other factors.

Soft technology is focused on human social, economic, political, cultural, spiritual, psychological, and cognitive behaviors. For solving problems, soft technology adopts a thinking mode that is from the whole to the parts, which is a way of adapting to systematic design. But whereas hard technology is rooted in the physical world, the operational field of soft technology is focused on the spiritual world. Its operational objects are human psychological activity and social behavior; its tools for resolving problems are processes, governance, rules, institutions as well as its products and services, and its technological parameters are social, cultural, and psychological factors. These characteristics of soft technology make it ideally suited for coping with the challenges facing humanity in the twenty-first century, because they integrate soft and hard technologies, soft and hard environment, and soft and hard capital, so as to build comprehensive and systematic solutions.

Even terrorism, one of the most serious threats to international security in the world today is mainly the result of many "soft" factors such as politics, economics (e.g., unemployment), inherited beliefs and stereotypes, religious dogma, archaic culture, etc. While strong condemnation and armed suppression are necessary in the short term, ultimately the use of force can only breed more terrorism.

To fundamentally solve this problem people must agree to examine all of terrorism's various root causes from their different standpoints, using approaches that may vary by region, religion, and culture. Inevitably, this will require inventions, creations, and innovations in the soft technology domain and create a soft environment that adapts to different cultures to reverse and eliminate the underlying motivations of terrorism. Only in this way will we be able to influence and permanently change terrorist behavior.

In a word, the problems in social, political, and cultural fields can only be solved by relevant means of soft technologies and improving the soft environment.

### The theory of soft environment

No one doubts the importance of technology; however, technology is not everything. Even soft technology is only one of the means, approaches, and tools of problem solving. There are some factors beyond technology, which usually affect the application and direction of hard technology, and the design and innovation direction of soft technology, including when and how it can be implemented. We call these "the soft environment".

The soft environment is relative to the hard environment, which includes industrial facilities, economic strength, various networks such as highways, transportation, communications, and finance networks, and other tangible conditions and hard infrastructure.

The soft environment includes institutions, culture and values, market demands that depend on the education level, living standards and cultural background of consumers, the international situation, network environment including electronic and interpersonal networks, as well as natural infrastructure (such as biodiversity). The institutional environment here includes operating systems, mechanisms, laws, regulations, policies, standards, etc.

Here, the institutional and cultural environments are the key. Taking sustainable development as an example, which is a process of coordinating human behaviors that involve nature, society, and human beings. It requires a means for regulating human behaviors to make them consistent with the objectives and the mission of sustainable development. In other words, to control human desires, natural instincts, and behaviors that are driven by individuals worldviews and values, it is not enough to rely on education alone. It requires institutions that can restrict or encourage certain specific behaviors. To achieve the goal of sustainable development, human behavior must be regulated.

An institution, as a collection of people's rules of conduct, whether it is religious, political, social, economic, international, or technological, is used to restrain or regulate the codes of conduct or values by which people live.

However, numerous examples illustrate the limitations of institutions, which are often insufficient to completely restrain all human behaviors and psychological activities. Using policies and laws can only be part of the solution. Legal changes, abolishing an old system or implementing a new one, must be made effective by changing people's fundamental attitudes. Especially in this age of globalization and informatization, people's spiritual world is unprecedentedly, quickly, and severely affected by the impact of the worldwide exchange of information, and all information is passed through a "soft environment filter," specifically a "cultural filter". The influence of culture and values is deep, often far beyond those of the market and government, and sometimes even exceeding the power of institutions.

In other words, whether the goal is to reduce greenhouse gases, protect the environment, change consumption patterns, or just dispose of garbage, the level of contemporary technology, and the burgeoning future science and technology, provides no lack of solutions. However, the big difficulty is how to persuade people to accept a new lifestyle and adapt to a new way of life.

This is why we will devote considerable space to discussing the "broad sense of cultural environment"—a social system in which four (material, spiritual, political, and ecological) civilizations complement each other.

Certainly, the limitations of institutions are not only due to factors such as culture, concepts, and awareness but also there are two other factors that undermine the power of institutions. The first is that the institution itself may be perceived as unfair or unreasonable. The second reason is the intentional resistance to even reasonable institutions that is often expressed by various special interest groups.

If soft technology were to be normalized as a regulatory instrument by institutions, policies, regulations, laws, standards, and others, the contents of the soft environment would be enriched for a certain period and the basic conditions would exist for both hard and soft technological innovation. But once a soft technology is transformed into a regulatory tool approved by society or government institutions generally, it may take on a relative rigidity and then itself become a barrier to further innovation.

## Expanding the innovation space to improve creativity and adjust the innovation strategy system

According to Joseph Schumpeter, the founder of innovation theory, the purpose of innovation is to "build a new function of production", and to introduce a "new combination" of production factors and conditions of production that has never existed before. (Note that this definition focuses on the field of material production.) David Sawers believes that technology innovation is "the application of new technology to some practical purpose, or the new application of an existing technology for some practical purpose." For him, innovation is a technological process, but it can also be a commercial, military, or social process (the focus here is still on hard technology). Alexander King (focusing again on hard technology applications) considers that technology innovation is often first realized in commerce and military affairs.

Personally, I believe that innovation is a process to create added value by applying new ways of thinking, new methods, and/or new means. The value mentioned here need not be only economic value but can also be social or eco-environmental value.

According to this way of thinking, innovation space can be expanded indefinitely around the object of innovation, its resources, methods, and fields. For example,

- From the perspective of Technological Paradigm Innovation: from hard technology to soft technology—the invention, creation, innovation, and application of soft technology, or the new application of soft technology around the object of innovation;
- From the angle of the functions of soft technology—from technological, or industrial to institutional innovation;
- Fusion and integration of soft and hard technologies, such as NBIC convergence technology;
- From material to nonmaterial production;
- From economic activities to social and cultural activities;
- From the viewpoint of innovation resources, innovation space is expanded to include innovation in soft/hard capital, soft/hard technologies, soft/hard industries, and both soft and hard environment;
- From the perspective of correctly handling the relationship between humans and nature, the purpose of developing science and technology shifts from a simple emphasis on "bringing humans well-being" to also consideration of the harmony, sustainable existence and development of humans and other species in the natural world, as well as the protection of the natural environment.
- Around the main body of innovative activities, such as enterprises, research institutions, government, society, and individuals;
- Innovation around different values, such as economic value, social value, including commonweal value, and cultural value;
- Diversity of innovation architecture;
- Innovation space around the psychology/human body/life/mind;
- Combination of art and technology, such as IAM converging technology;
- The space where both markets and governments are ineffective, such as innovations surrounding the development of social economy and social enterprises;
- Innovation platform—activities from closed innovation to open innovation, etc.

Therefore, we need to adjust the innovation strategy system, to make it a balanced, harmonious, and complementary blend of both soft and hard elements.

## Revealing non-technological factors

Research in soft technology helps us identify the so-called "non-technological factors", reveal the "black boxes" in the field of economics from a new angle, and clarify the essence of the contribution made by technological progress to productivity, which has long been the focus of research, to help adjust economic development strategy and investment policy, while also redefining the so-called "intangible assets", namely the definition, quantification and ways to determine the contribution of "soft assets", to help in building a new theory of future economic growth.

## Theories of soft and hard

The correct thinking mode is the source that determines how people obtain effective and beneficial insights when observing the world and analyzing complex things. The soft–hard theories based on the research of soft and hard technologies are helpful to change the thinking mode and understand the principles of "harmony, balance, equality, tolerance, and coexistence" that humans sharing a planet should follow).

In short, no matter whether hard or soft, technology is a means humans use to improve their capacity, and a tool or a method for solving problems. Recognizing and insisting on this point is essential to correctly guide the direction of human evolution. Developing technology and the economy as well as a variety of political means are all tools or approaches for helping to achieve a sustainable human society, and the purpose of sustainability is to let humans live in a prosperous and peaceful world brought about by new material, spiritual and ecological civilization that will endure from generation to generation. But today, many people regard economic development as a purpose in itself, and even take the advanced development of technology as a goal. But no matter how great the contribution of technology to human social development is, including the enhancement of human abilities, we must not confuse humanity's ultimate goals with the tools that humans create, for this would result in misleading the direction of technological innovation and could bring about a disaster if technology eventually came to control mankind.

Obviously, the current study on soft science (including humanities and social sciences) and soft technology is far behind that of hard science (including natural science) and hard technology, which both needs continue to conduct systematic research and development.

## *What determines the direction of technological innovation?*

### Responsibility for the negative effects of technology does not rest with hard technology alone

Concerning a technology's negative effects (such as "the more technology is advanced, the more thorough will be the destruction of the earth caused by that technology's abuse, and the crueler and more terrible will be the means we possess to kill each other"), the responsibility does not lie entirely with hard technology. After all, hard technology is just a me innovation, but Typo? to enhance human capacity to act, cognitive ability (to understand the world and ourselves), and gain greater capability for problem solving. It can neither determine the direction of its own innovation nor solve problems of human morality and values. In other words, hard technology itself is neutral, and in which direction and for what purpose it is applied rests with humans and depends on the value orientation of the technology's operators. That is, its "good" or "evil" depends entirely on its applicators. The negative effects of technology are derived from soft and hard technology applications that aim to maximize economic profits or political power or to assure the attainment of one's personal goals to the exclusion of all else. How to apply technology or to control the innovation direction belongs to the field of soft technology, and on the soft environment that is related to people's codes of conduct and ethics.

### To distinguish between knowledge and technology

From a theoretical point of view, scientific knowledge itself is innocent. Science (including both natural and social science) is the knowledge system that reflects the human understanding of the essential facts and objective laws of the universe, nature, society, thought, and humanity itself.

The main task of science is to constantly explore the unknown, to discover new laws, to create new knowledge, and to fight against ignorance. But science and knowledge must not be confused with one another. Fundamentally, science is a method and road—a means we use to understand the world and human beings themselves (which is a prerequisite for problem solving). And the purpose of science is to explore the truth of things, and to grasp the various laws that govern the nature of all creation, no matter whether it is robotics, artificial intelligence, nuclear energy, genetics, or space exploration, scientific study in itself is worthy of praise. Besides, we need to keep deciphering the true meaning of the universe and life, including such unsolved mysteries of the universe as dark energy, dark matter, and so on.

Recently, some scholars point to science as the main source of all the core theories and technologies that can be used to produce catastrophes (including destructive weapons and environmental damage) as "ruin-causing" knowledge. They believe that the growth of ruin-causing knowledge, which is irreversible, unstoppable, and cannot be offset, will inevitably lead to technological disaster.

But if knowledge in biology, nuclear physics, and chemistry, which are the core principles of destructive weapons, is regarded as ruin-causing knowledge, then there are also many other sources of knowledge that are likely to cause a variety of crises and devastating disasters in today's world. Potential examples might include any of the high technologies promoting economic and social development in the twenty-first century, such as nanotechnology, gene manipulation that could cause an artificial epidemic, AI, the Internet, and information technology. If any one of these were applied to the "wrong" direction, it might cause "catastrophic" results.

In 2009, Yoshihiro Kawaoka, professor of virology at the University of Wisconsin-Madison, and his team used genetic engineering to mix the H5N1 avian flu virus with a strain of the H1N1 flu virus (which had caused the global influenza pandemic in 1919). The resulting virus was able to "elude" the antibodies of the immune system, making humans lose resistance to this virus. Critics warned that experiments similar to those by Kawaoka and his team could allow new viral strains to inadvertently "escape" from the laboratory and cause a global pandemic. There is a view that the H1N1 influenza virus that caused so many people to get sick and die was itself the result of such a laboratory accident.

We already know that the Internet poses potential threats, such as privacy leakage, computer viruses, and hackers, and now hacker attacks are spreading from the open Internet to the closed industrial control network. The Stuxnet virus, which has been sweeping global industry recently, is the world's first cyber "super weapon". After Iran's Bushehr nuclear power plant came under attack by Stuxnet, about 20% of its centrifuges had to be scrapped.

The Internet has given us tremendous freedom and unlimited space for innovation, but has also stranded us in the world with no security or privacy, and where cybercrime is rampant. In 2012, the United States lost $20.7 billion due to cybercrime and 7.1 million Internet users became victims. In 2013, China uncovered 170,000 cases of cybercrime, whose direct economic losses totaled some $37.1 billion, and affected nearly 300 million victims, an average of 600 people per minute. According to an investigation report on Internet fraud issued by F-Secure, a well-known Finnish security agency, in 2013, one in every ten people worldwide became a victim of Internet fraud. According to CCTV, more than one in ten victims of Internet fraud in China in 2018 were minors.

Network technology could become a tool for future war, and the Edward Snowden security leaks that shocked the world demonstrate the close relationship between network technology and personal as well as national security. Subprime is a financial technology originally developed for subprime mortgage loans, but due to its improper operation, it became the flashpoint for the financial crisis of 2009, which caused incalculable loss and enormous shock to the global economy and to world order. The use of chemicals for agriculture and human health, and even human activity itself is speeding up the extinction of animal and plant species, pushing the world toward the brink of a sixth great extinction.

While it can certainly be said to potentially lead to devastating disasters (catastrophes that destroy human life on a massive scale or even threaten the survival of the environment) knowledge is far more than the above. The real problem occurs at the moment when a particular technology is applied to solve a specific problem. The problem of innovation direction in the application process from knowledge to technology is: what kind of value are we trying to create?

Although from a certain angle, humanity today can be judged to have made great progress, we still live in an age of Industrial Civilization, where the temptation of profit, disguised by the interests of one social group or the state often legitimizes the evil application of scientific knowledge, or at least in a limited regime. If the application of scientific knowledge is not restricted, this huge temptation will be irresistible, like placing a dangerous toy in the hands of a child.

Nuclear technology can be used for human benefit (such as producing clean energy), but it can also be used to create a nuclear bomb. Do not forget that several bomb scares occurred even after the Second World War. Due to false alarms arising from the wrong operation of equipment or the malfunction of a computer chip, and sometimes even owing to sunlight reflected from the clouds, Nuclear warheads of both the United States and the Soviet Union were almost dropped on the other side. This illustrates the problem that, as long as there are nuclear bombs, a miscalculation, however innocent, such as a training tape mistakenly inserted into an operating computer, or the sun shining in clouds when by chance the sun, the Earth, and a certain satellite align, could unintentionally launch a nuclear attack.

What is even creepier is that, according to a statement of the US Department of Defense issued in May 2015, an American research institute in Utah sent samples of active anthrax bacillus by mistake to 24 laboratories in eleven states of the United States, as well as to South Korea and Australia.

Therefore, it is necessary to scrutinize and evaluate scientific knowledge before it is transformed into technical means, either to set up a restricted area where it can be safely mothballed, or carefully grasp the application direction of its related technologies.

The crux of the problem does not lie in knowledge itself but in the way that knowledge is applied—the direction of technology innovation. For example, the right direction for developing and employing AI should include how to avoid its negative effects, such as making sure that human beings are not ignored, marginalized, or ultimately eliminated by the robots they themselves designed.

People generally approve of Francis Bacon's famous remark that knowledge is power. However, when people explore the direction of innovation, it is worth thinking about what kind of power knowledge provides.

If knowledge guided by a bad worldview is directed by the application of hard technology to and is used for bad purposes, or to create unhealthy or even evil soft technology to mislead the direction of innovation, this power will prove destructive or even disastrous.

This is why we need to distinguish between knowledge and technology, and distinguish between science and technology (although, as the development of information technology makes the cycle from the discovery of new knowledge to its technological application grow shorter and shorter, science and technology become increasingly difficult to distinguish).

## Innovation and the humanities and social science and technology

We need to re-understand the relationship between the knowledge of natural science and that of the humanities and social sciences.[1] Although their integration is the future trend and the prospect for interdisciplinary knowledge and technology is unlimited, there are important differences between the knowledge of natural science and that of the humanities and social sciences.

In fact, from the angle of innovation, knowledge of natural science itself is not used to answer relevant questions involving value thinking or value orientation, for it lacks the ability to judge right from wrong, good from bad. The question of how to control the knowledge and technology of natural science is presently a key problem being addressed in the field of humanities and social sciences.

This lays the foundation for the importance of the humanities and social science and its application (i.e., soft technologies of all kinds) in technological innovation.

### 1. Humanities and social sciences lag behind natural sciences

The humanities and social sciences have developed quite rapidly in the past 200 years. However, relative to the significant achievements of natural science and technology, the lags in the humanities and social sciences are universal problems, and have become a bottleneck that hampers sustainable socio-economic development. The knowledge of humanities and social sciences is one of the important sources of soft technology, but humanities and social sciences have not been fully developed as the science, and even the existing classification of social science disciplines is obsolete.

As Jyuji Misumi, a Japanese scholar, has pointed out,

> The misfortune of modern society lies in the comparison of the outrageous development of natural technologies with the backward development of social technologies. Furthermore, many roots of modern misfortune lie in the failure to strike a balance between the two technologies.

American scholars Olaf Helmer and Theodore Gordon have stated that many of the difficulties that beset our world today can be explained by the fact that progress in the domain of social science has lagged far behind that of the natural sciences.

Until now, there are many people who even do not consider the humanities and social sciences as science, let alone develop social technology. This has influenced systematic research in the humanities and social sciences and technology from the perspective of "solving" practical problems in economic, social, and technological development.

**2. The challenges facing the humanities and social sciences**

Today's world is experiencing major changes that have not happened in a century, and this impacts the global economy, cultures, and institutions are unprecedented, and subsequently cause social problems at many levels. From dilemmas affecting global strategy to crises in our personal lives, we must seek answers from the humanities and social sciences. Because only by making full use of the characteristics of contemporary humanities and social sciences, such as comprehensiveness, realizability, internationality, and features that are compatible with national characteristics, it is possible to solve complicated social problems. This makes the humanities and social sciences increasingly vital for economic and technological development, as well as for solving problems of politics, culture, and international relations. In turn, application-oriented, development-oriented, and decision-oriented services have become an obvious trend in the development of contemporary humanities and social sciences.

In particular, with the breakthrough of science and technology in various fields in recent decades, the humanities and social sciences today are facing unprecedented challenges. The rapid development and application of science and technology have triggered a debate concerning social, ethical, and legal issues. The humanities and social sciences urgently need to find solutions for these issues or at least to provide possible ways forward.

However, research in the humanities and social sciences on these issues has seriously lagged behind, not only in the careful study of the social consequences of modern science and technology using multidisciplinary and cross-disciplinary approaches but also by failing to put forward any regulatory strategy for guiding and applying hard science and technology.

Take the challenges facing social sciences in the era of Big Data as an example. Big Data provides an unprecedented mass of social statistics, materials, and information of high quality for social sciences research. Its use can help replace traditional analysis methods by avoiding the limitations of subjective judgment and make our knowledge and understanding of the social panorama more objective, comprehensive, and accurate. Moreover, Big Data also provides the basis for revealing social cause and effect and for judging social phenomena: i.e., it can help to identify the laws of social development and uncover hidden patterns of human behavior. It can be said that network and data science have brought revolutionary changes and new research methodologies to the social sciences. However, the opportunities and challenges brought by Big Data on social life, media ecology, and business are also subversive. While the use of Big Data provides new ways to explore the unknown world, it also creates a series of new social problems, such as network security, privacy, and other related personal and social issues.

Therefore, the humanities and social sciences urgently need to establish a new social science system that complements basic research and applied research from various aspects, such as basic disciplines, key disciplines, emerging disciplines, and interdisciplinary disciplines (specific examples include Biosociology, Modern social physics, Network science, Neuroeconomics, Behavioral genetics, Art sociology, Computational social science and other emerging disciplines, and interdisciplines), in order to deal with the new problems facing human society in the twenty-first century.

At the same time, we need to promote invention, creation, and innovation in the field of humanities and social sciences, in view of the new global trends, complex social relations, the diversification of value choices, and nonlinear social trends, as well as incisive contradictions concerning values, beliefs, ethics, environment, and security are all places where high-level research results are needed, so as to provide adequate knowledge and technology to resolve the above problems, including some means of early warning, prevention, and control.

### To distinguish between science and technology

One Japanese scholar has lamented that Japan's biggest mistake was the invention of an abbreviation which merges 'science and technology' into one word. There are essential differences between science and technology in their essence, characteristics, and roles, as well as in the ways and rules by which each develops.

Take the field of humanities and social sciences as an example, in order to cope with these challenges, we must vigorously develop methods, means, and procedures that solve various "problems" by applying knowledge from the humanities and social sciences: that is, various types of humanities and social sciences technology. Namely, we also need to distinguish between science and technology in the field of the humanities and social sciences, including the separation of social technology from the social sciences.

But due to the traditional understanding of technology, people often turn a blind eye to technology derived from the knowledge of non-natural sciences. Too often, social technology is either confused with social science, or many problems of social technology are treated simply as policy or strategic problems. This affects not only the development of social science itself but also the development of social technology. It is imperative that we separate those knowledge systems belonging to the technological category from those of the social sciences, so as to systematically develop, innovate, and institutionalize them. If we do not distinguish between science and technology, both will suffer. So too will the development of basic research in the field of social science.

Certainly, technology rooted in the knowledge of humanities and social sciences is not the only social technology. A large number of commercial technologies (such as those involved in market exchange, currency transactions, accounting, stock trading, business contract technique, financial derivatives), political technology, cultural technology, artistic technology, intellectual development technology, cognitive technology, institutional design technology and so on, are all "technological" inventions that have far-reaching effects on human society, yet they also belong to the operational technologies of the humanities and social sciences knowledge. It can be seen that the knowledge of humanities and social sciences is the main source of soft technology. In turn, social technology, as the innovation tools of social activities, involves more than simply the application of humanities and social sciences. The resources, connotations, and significance of social technology are far broader.

## Differentiating between soft and hard technologies, while guarding against bad soft technology

As described above, hard technology itself is neutral, while soft technology has a duality, both a natural attribute and a social attribute because it is rooted in non-natural scientific knowledge such as social, economic, political, cultural, spiritual, and psychological knowledge. Soft technology can create value directly, while hard technology only creates value through the operation of soft technology. In the innovation process of hard technology, soft technology is the process by which hard technology transfer (i.e., value creation) occurs, and thus it is both the tool and content of hard technology innovation.

However, because of the social attributes of soft technology, its design content and direction depend directly on the operator's value orientation. Therefore, not all soft technologies are necessarily sound. In addition, the importance of soft technology is increasingly being taken seriously for a variety of reasons, so it is gradually becoming the driving force for economic development and the core of competition.

But because the current trend remains motivated by greed and lust for power, designs of immoral, undesirable, or even evil soft technologies have diversified, while the related institutional research and institutional control measures lag far behind. In short, the development of game rules cannot keep up with the invention and innovation of the game itself. It can be said that a majority of disasters in the world are actually caused by human behavior, and that, from a technological point of view, this is due to the innovation and operation of "bad" soft technologies. For example, the so-called "Color Revolution" is a bad geopolitical technology aimed at disrupting, weakening, and even subverting competitors.

In other words, not all innovation is necessarily healthy, and we need to guard against "bad" or undesirable innovations. While pursuing the economic value of innovation, we must also emphasize the social values consistent with social morality and the environmental values responsible for protecting the environment.

Therefore, it is particularly important to regulate soft technology, meaning it is necessary to carry out innovation, and institutionalization (formulate rules of the game) on the basis of research and identification of soft technology (games), and carry out institutional innovation with the times, so as to encourage good soft technologies while inhibiting undesirable soft technologies and opposing "evil" ones. The key lies in how to determine the standards of the game and the rules of the game, or determine whether it can adhere to the right direction of innovation. The right direction depends on the worldview, values, and moral standards of the operators of technology, and in a deeper sense, it depends on their level of social civilization; otherwise, no regulations or laws can be effective. The topic of future civilization is one that we will discuss in detail from Chapters 4 to 6.

Because different civilizations have a different understanding about the direction of technology innovation, in order to make the soft environment (especially the institutional environment) suitable for an era of Global Civilization, relevant institutions, including political institutions, social institutions, economic institutions, technological institutions, as well as global institutions, need to advance with the times.

Take technological institutions as an example. They must regulate activities in R&D and technology application from different aspects, paying attention to each point of project planning, research methods, protocols and technology transfer, and, from the perspective related to political purposes, environmental protection, economic benefits, ethical values, human health, and safety, improving the level of science and technology, correctly dealing with the relationship between humans and nature, social stability, and ultimately world peace, so as to support and ensure that the six essential approaches of sustainable development are implemented (see Chapter 7).

Another example is green transformation. In order to make human political, economic, and social activities adapt to green development, it is necessary to redesign or modify various games and rules of the game (institutional design) in political, economic, environmental, social, and cultural areas, so as to stimulate or constrain human innovative behaviors. That is why we said that soft technology innovation provides the contents, requirements, and bases for institutional innovation, while institutional innovation provides the innovative environment for technological innovation. The important mission for soft technology in hard technology innovation is to design solutions for different hard technologies according to sound ethics so as to properly regulate and control technology, making it conducive to developing positive technology applications, while avoiding negative technological development to prevent "innocent" hard technologies from turning into evil things and also to forestall their development in directions that humans do not expect.

In short, since human beings have the ability to create technology, they can control and guide the direction of technological development and innovation, and make technology provide the services to create and promote the progress of human civilization. The key is first to make clear what *is* human and what kind of future humanity should create (the mission of this book). Second, we must adhere to the tenet that technology is a tool and not lose our direction. Third, it needs to be good at identifying and standardizing soft technology. The standards of identification and regularization must be suitable for the sustainable development of human beings, other living things in nature, and their living environment. Finally, we need to perfect the soft environment of technological innovation, which is the most basic one, especially the cultural environment as we strive to realize the transition from Industrial Civilization to Global Civilization as outlined in Chapters 5 and 6.

## *The integration of hard and soft technologies in the field of human life and its risks*

We explored in Chapter 2 what kind of risks we might encounter if humans enter the era of human–machine civilization. One of the root causes of these problems is that the development of modern technology enters upon a new phase—soft and hard technology has the ability to intervene in life.

## The historical course of technological development

From the perspective of history, we are at the beginning of the third stage in technology development. Technology began to develop when humans first walked on two legs, thus liberating their hands to use as tools, and later developed the ability to produce tools and devise ways to use them. This first stage of technology history lasted for roughly three million years. Subsequently, by virtue of the integrated development of soft and hard technologies, humans gradually arrived at the stage of development where we no longer used the body as a main tool. Instead, humans developed the so-called labor-saving technologies. This led eventually to automation as well as robot-based unmanned production. Thus humans moved gradually along the road towards a world in which body and mechanical technology were completely separated. This process was the second stage of technological development. It has lasted for several hundreds of years since the Industrial Revolution. In this stage, technological developments made great contributions to Industrial Civilization, but at the same time accelerated the destruction of the Earth and nature.

The main characteristic of this second stage in technological development is that the object of technology has been more focused on nature, namely dealing with the relationship between humans and the environment, rather than with matters concerning the human "spirit," "psychology," "emotions," or "feelings". In other words, it pays less attention to life itself. But more recently, people have come to realize that human minds were being largely ignored by traditional technologies, and gradually strengthened various studies and applications focused on life, human nature, and "the heart". This shift now makes it possible, on the one hand, psychological technology around human consciousness and thinking, cognitive science and technology, and consciousness technology have been further developed, while on the other, the development of technologies involving genes, artificial intelligence, information technology, and biotechnology have provided people with knowledge and tools to uncover secrets of the human mind and cognition. These developments have given human beings the ability and opportunity to study humanity itself, so as to further understand and change themselves and improve the quality of life. This has led technological development to its third stage, which is being marked by another major change in direction.

## Characteristics of the third stage of technology development

As shown in Figure 3.3, after entering the era of the industrial economy, the technological revolution has experienced five waves: the first technological revolution occurred in the middle of the eighteenth century and was symbolized by the steam engine and transportation technology. The second technological revolution began in the 1870s, and was prompted by electric power and telecom technology. The third technological revolution took place in the middle of the twentieth century and was characterized by the computer, nuclear energy, and space technology. The fourth technological revolution began in the 1980s and was characterized by information technology, biotechnology, and the Internet. The fifth one took place at the end of the twentieth century and the beginning of the twenty-first century with the development of life technology, nanotechnology, AI, cloud technology and the Internet of things, etc. Now we are approaching a sixth technological revolution involving a new generation of AI & robot technology, intelligent manufacturing, brain science and technology, space technology, emerging information technology, quantum technology, new materials and new energy sources, etc. If the first four technological revolutions were hard technological revolutions characterized by understanding nature and modifying it to satisfy human needs, from the fifth technological revolution onward technology development has instead shifted to focus on human life. At the same time, various soft and hard technologies are "converging" to create many new technologies.

Soft technology, too, has experienced several waves (Figure 3.4).

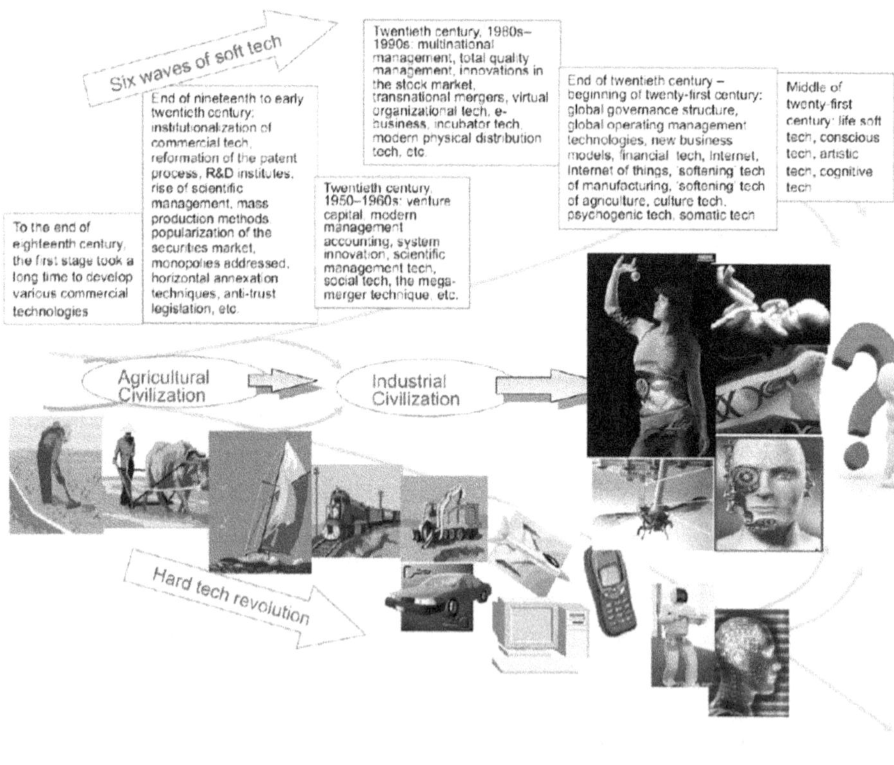


FIGURE 3.4: Soft technology wave. © Zhouying Jin.

The first stage of soft technology development lasted until the end of the eighteenth century. During this period, commercial technologies such as accounting, banking, stock trading, logistics, circulation mechanisms, and patent protection were developed. It was these technologies that facilitated the birth of the First Industrial Revolution.

The second period of soft technology development occurred at the end of the nineteenth century and the beginning of the twentieth. This was the period of the institutionalization phase in commercial technology. It was also the period that saw the reformation of patent technology, the research institute system, enlightenment of scientific management, mass production, the popularization of securities markets, monopoly concerns, horizontal annexation techniques, and the development of anti-trust regulations.

The third period in soft technology development took place in the 1950s and 1960s. During this period, venture capital, modern management accounting, a variety of institutional innovations, scientific management techniques, social technologies, and mega-merger techniques, among others, were developed.

As the world entered the information era—in the 1980s and 1990s—the scope of markets surpassed traditional limitations of time and space. Then current transaction modes were thoroughly transformed and thereby moved towards an age of overall innovation in soft technology. The fourth wave of soft technology was marked by the emergence of transnational management, total quality management, innovations in the stock market, transnational mergers, virtual organizations, e-business, incubator development, modern logistics, etc. All of these helped promote the Third Industrial Revolution, and to facilitate the emerging of the intellectual service economy. The interaction between the above soft technologies and information technology has not only helped realize sustainable economic development but has also promoted the comprehensive informatization of society.

The fifth wave of soft technology occurred from the end of the twentieth century to the beginning of the twenty-first century and includes innovation techniques in a broad sense, innovation methods in global governance structure, globalized operating management technologies, new business models, financial technologies, the "Internet of things," soft manufacturing, cultural, psychological, and psychosomatic technology, etc.

Reviewing these five waves of soft technology, the first four waves mainly gave priority to commerce, while the fifth wave has begun to develop technologies in social, cultural, psychological, physical, and mental areas. However, it is still mainly focused on the economy, politics, security, etc., or else focuses on those soft technologies related to human behavior.

The characteristics of the sixth wave of soft technology that we are now approaching (and which may peak in the middle of the twenty-first century) are to open up research in fields such as life, consciousness, thinking and cognition to promote the development of life-centered soft technology, conscious technology, art technology, converging technologies, cognitive science, technology, etc. Now, people realize that "the study of human beings" is a unique discipline, and that all human activities, including art, music, religion, language, literature, architecture, etc. are the products of human brain activities, and all follow their own unique laws.

In fact, the integrated development of soft and hard technologies has always been the greatest driving force in the development of human society. Ten thousand years ago, it created an Agricultural Civilization, and beginning only a few hundred years ago, the Industrial Civilization. Since the industrial era began, integrated development of hard and soft technologies has accelerated, resulting in several Industrial Revolutions.

However, in the fifth and sixth stages of the hard technology revolution, as well as the sixth wave of soft technology, soft and hard technologies are not only complementary to each other in the application process, but are also converging to become inseparable. Many soft and hard technologies have already merged and are most obviously integrated in the field of human life, which represents the characteristic form of the third stage of technological development.

In particular, genetic science and AI "technology" now has the ability to replace human beings entirely. The consequent impact of this development on human life, family, and the whole of society is unprecedented.

### Opportunities and challenges

The convergence and integration of hard and soft technologies in the field of human life have become a new trend in the development of modern technology. Not only does this convergence provide unlimited opportunities for spawning a great number of new technologies and new industries, creating business value, improving the quality of human life, and especially improving health, but it also creates the conditions for us to fully understand the essence and meaning of life itself. At the same time, it proposes new fields, goals, theories, approaches and methods for interdisciplinary research. However, it also raises huge potential risks in social, moral, legal, and cultural areas.

It can be said that, since hard and soft technologies intervened in life, human beings today face a global psychological and spiritual crisis.

Take gene recombination and human cloning as examples. These directly threaten the independence and the dignity of human beings as subjective entities, and *individual* humans face the prospect of losing their unique identities. This raises a new challenge for the humanities and social sciences: they must pay attention to the ultimate meaning of life. At present, the emerging of genetic ethics, bioethics ethics, sci-tech ethics, etc., all conform to this trend, trying to achieve balance and coordinate between new sci-tech while maintaining the dignity of human beings and preserving their subjective identity.

Products that combine hard and soft technologies, such as the robots "Leonardo", "Sophia", and "Zombie" insect aircraft, insect spies, the development of an intelligent arm, or half-human robots in Japan and so on, all raise deep concerns involving morality and ethics.

The greatest challenge for technology as it begins to directly enter the field of life is how to intervene in human life systems. All of this raises basic questions for us, such as what is life? What is a human? Where are our technologies taking us? Where do humans wish to go? And so on.

In view of the many ethical, legal, and moral issues facing the converging technologies, the world's first Converging Technology Barrister Association (CTBA) was established in 2004. This is the first organization in the world to focus on the ethical and legal issues brought about by the development of converging technologies.

The crux of the matter is towards what end should we direct this powerful technological energy and development trend? Should we promote technology to serve the wellbeing of all mankind and to maintain the sustainability of humans and other species in nature, or allow the third stage of technological development to proceed at its own pace with no limit? Or should we perhaps simply let things drift, remain indifferent to where this might ultimately lead, allow people to lose their dignity as human beings, and become the slaves or tools of technology? The possibility cannot be ruled out that technology may eventually control human evolution, and even accelerate the demise of traditional human beings.

### *Human beings must regulate technology—Never allow intelligent robots to control humans*

There is no doubt that technology is the first driving force of human social development. However, the current development of technology has also raised very serious problems: where is technology heading? And where is it taking us?

In the section of "The imminent disaster facing science and technology" in Chapter 1, we have elaborated the urgency of regulating technology from different angles such as the ethical and social issues that may be caused by improper or even evil use of technology that pose challenges to life and human nature, etc.

In addition, today's society still continues to embrace the values and ideals of an Industrial Civilization, as the primary means of wealth creation, each invention and innovation of technology is closely related to economic interests, and any constraint imposed on it is likely to raise serious resistance. The self-discipline of scientists and companies is necessary but not sufficient. It is necessary to regulate technology, which is becoming more and more powerful and difficult to monitor, from the aspects of institutional guarantees, government regulations, public supervision and participation in decision making, etc.

Since the beginning of the twentieth century, and especially after the Second World War, the elites who care about the future of mankind in today's world, made outstanding strides in some areas under the leadership of the United Nations. For example, a series of authoritative international conventions have been established for the research direction, innovation direction, development and application, and business intervention of technologies that have a great relationship with human progress, safety, ethics, and morality; a lot of research has been carried out in order to carefully examine, approve, and when necessary restrict scientific and technological achievements that may endanger human survival and sustainable development. We cannot let greed or the desire for power dictate human behaviors.

For example, in December 1954, the UN General Assembly adopted a resolution setting up an international organization dedicated to the peaceful uses of nuclear energy. In October 1956, the Statute of the International Atomic Energy Agency (IAEA) was adopted at a special conference in which 82 countries participated. The International Campaign to Ban Landmines (ICBL) was established in October 1992. The Chemical Weapons Convention (CWC) aimed at prohibiting the development, production, stockpiling, and use of chemical weapons and promoting the destruction of existing weapons, and along with the Organization for the Prohibition of Chemical Weapons (OPCW) was established in May 1997 and has now been ratified by more than 100 countries. Also, despite significant disagreements over issues such as how to treat embryos, how to approach the therapeutic cloning, and the reproductive cloning of human beings, the Legal Committee of the UN General Assembly adopted a political declaration prohibiting all forms of human cloning in February 2005.

In the twenty-first century, AI and intelligent robots are widely used in various fields of human activities at an unpredictable speed, and it is urgent to formulate various rules for coexistence with intelligent robots. At present, the international community is strengthening the research on the potential ethical, legal and social impact of AI, including social norms for crime, punishment, and others.

As early as 1942 the American science fiction writer Isaac Asimov proposed (and slightly modified in 1982 the so-called "Four laws of robotics".

*Isaac Asimov's* "Four laws of robotics":

- Zeroth Law: A robot may not harm humanity, or, by inaction, allow humanity to come to harm.
- First Law: Unless contrary to the Zeroth Law, a robot may not injure a human being or, through inaction, allow a human being to come to harm.
- Second Law: A robot must obey the orders given to it by human beings, except where such orders would conflict with the Zeroth or First Laws.
- Third Law: A robot must protect its own existence as long as such protection does not conflict with the Zeroth, First, or Second Laws.

Although there are some criticisms of Asimov's robot laws, such as the belief that the third law (robot self-protection is considered unnecessary) nevertheless, Asimov's laws constitute a prescient, bold, and beneficial attempt to set effective and enforceable limits on uncontrolled robot development.

In 1975, the Asilomar Conference on genetic recombination successfully launched a voluntary campaign to end research on the design and manufacture of human genetic modifications, and became an international norm.

The Association for the Advance of Artificial Intelligence (AAAI) has established a standing committee focusing on the impact of AI and ethical issues. Elon Musk contributed $10 million to support research in this area.

The Institute of Electrical and Electronics Engineers (IEEE) published a long report: *Ethically Aligned Design*. that advocates the ethical design, development, and implementation of intelligent technologies guided by the following general principles:

- Human rights: Ensure they do not infringe on internationally recognized human rights;
- Well-being: Prioritize metrics of well-being in their design and use;
- Accountability: Ensure that their designers and operators are responsible and accountable;
- Transparency: Ensure they operate in a transparent manner;
- Awareness of misuse: Minimize the risks of their misuse.

The legal research center of China's Tencent Research Institute conducted an inventory of the global AI policies in 2017 and sorted out the top ten policies based on industry influence and leadership. The Future of Life Institute (FLI) has launched 23 Asilomar AI principles in order to jointly protect the future interests and safety of mankind, The Seven Principles of Algorithmic Transparency and Accountability issued by the United States Computer Association (USACM) are committed to addressing algorithmic discrimination. The European Parliament has adopted the world 's first resolution regarding European Civil Law Rules on Robotics, so as to explore the civil legislation of robots and AI. The Ethics Committee of the German Ministry of Transport issued a report on Autonomous and Connected Driving, for the first time putting forward 20 ethical rules for self-driving cars. In July 2017, the State Council of China issued the New Generation Artificial Intelligence Development Plan, which elaborated the development plan of China's AI from various aspects such as strategic situation, overall requirements, resource allocation, legislation, and organization. The Korean Parliament has proposed a Robot Basic Act to actively explore the legal issues-related robots. The US Congress launched an Autonomous Driving Act to promote the development of autonomous driving technology and self-driving cars. Estonia's proposed Robots Act is designed to give AI agents legal status. In late 2017 New York City passed the first US Algorithmic Accountability Act to promote openness and transparency of the government's automatic decision-making algorithms. And the Institute of Electrical and Electronics Engineers (IEEE) has released a new set of Ethical Guidelines for Artificial Intelligence Design (2nd Edition), which comprehensively expounds the 13 ethical issues of AI.

In July 2019, the comprehensive deepening reform committee of the CPC Central Committee deliberated and approved a plan to establish the National Science and Technology Ethics Committee and build a comprehensive science and technology ethics review system, so as to strengthen ethical supervision, standardize scientific and technological activities, and provide institutional guarantees for the healthy development of scientific research and technological innovation.

In October 2019, the Defense Innovation Commission of the United States issued "The Principles of AI: Some Suggestions on the Application Ethics of AI in the Department of Defense", which put forward five principles of responsibility, fairness, traceability, reliability, and controllability, and twelve suggestions on how the Department of Defense should apply ethics in combat and non-combat AI systems in the future.

The above efforts and progress indicate that a preliminary consensus has been reached worldwide on the regulation of several important technologies.

However, in view of the potential abuse of face recognition technology and the rapid and disorderly growth of the face recognition technology market, clearly the supervision of global technology ethics has a long way to go.

### *It's not enough just to regulate and control*

In order to regulate technologies such as nuclear technology and atomic bomb development, genetic technology and human cloning, human enhancement technology and superman, AI and humanoid robots [...], we have formulated a large number of related policies, laws, conventions, and so on. In the future, we must continue to meet the emerging wave of the so-called disruptive next-generation technologies (NT), such as 5G technology, the quantum revolution, and commercial use of controllable nuclear fusion. New disruptive technologies will lead to new types of crises, which are integrated and overlap each other. These technologies need to be regulated one by one from researchers, research directions, users of related technology products, technical applications, etc. As a result, regulations, laws, and policies covering a wider and more complex range of related technologies are already emerging. Current AI is not only leading to a new technological revolution but also marks the start of a new era in research direction, development principles, ethics, and laws of related fields.

But what is the cumulative effect? Can these regulations be effectively implemented in various countries and fields?

Take nuclear weapons, chemical weapons, and biological weapons for example. Since most countries have signed various international treaties to restrict, manage and ban these weapons, their abuse has been limited to a certain extent. However, these treaties fail to effectively prevent some countries from developing and trying to use these weapons in what they consider to be their own national interests. And even though the horrific effects of atomic bombs in the Second World War are still fresh in memory, nuclear weapons are still considered the ultimate threat to deter hostile forces, and nuclear technology remains a source of huge profits for arms dealers in some countries. Chemical and biological weapons are still under continuous research in some countries and used in some wars and are even used in certain conflicts. And despite Asimov's four laws, armies of AI-based "killer robots" seem likely to emerge soon.

Why is it so difficult to prevent the "crisis mode of nuclear technology" by continuously introducing various measures? Why does the application of human enhancement technology inevitably surpass the bottom line of curing diseases and saving lives, helping the disabled, and preventing aging? And why is the development direction of intelligent robots proving so difficult to control?

The whole world is arguing whether the aforementioned cutting-edge technologies will bring bright prospects or devastating disasters to the future. How to regulate these technologies to prevent human beings from being controlled and destroyed by them, etc., but the deep-rooted, or most fundamental, causes of human dilemma caused by technological development have been ignored.

When the performance of artificial super intelligence products becomes more and more perfect, and as they are given more and more complex tasks, they will acquire ever-greater rights of free choice. When they are in an unfamiliar situation, what judgments they make will depend on whether they have good motivation and ideas. AI, after all, is the materialized product of human wisdom, and its motive orientation or values are given to them by human beings who have not completed the transformation from industrial civilization. Therefore, when they are "smart" enough to get rid of the established procedures, or able to make decisions on their own in exceptional circumstances, the "law of the jungle" of industrial civilization will likely become their code of action as it has been for humans.

That is to say, if there is a tragedy that human beings cannot control the tools they make, the root cause is that from the international elites, the leaders of most countries to the mainstream society, their way of thinking and code of conduct have not got rid of the logic and rules of industrial civilization.

The biggest challenges we face today in regulating technology are these: first, understanding fundamental issues like the essence of life, and the nature and status of human beings, the relation between human and technology, etc., are quite different in different parts of the world, especially in academia.

Second, there is no basic consensus among the international elites, leaders of major countries, and influential thinkers on what kind of future humanity should pursue. Therefore, it is difficult to achieve consensus as to what important issues we should focus on and what institutions or mechanisms we should create to regulate or control the direction of technology application and innovation. For example, the business community is concerned about immediate and short-term future interests, while government departments or politicians tend to pursue political achievements that will generate widespread public approval during their tenure, though these actions are often taken under the guise of national or group interests. Meanwhile, scientists and engineers are more concerned about long-term breakthrough achievements in science and technology.

Third, at present, no single country's moral, ethical, and legal judgment is likely to have much influence on the practical decisions of other countries.

Fourth, there is a lack of consensus on the essence of technology. The rapid development of science and technology has fostered an almost superstitious faith that technology is all-powerful and should be promoted at any cost, and even reverse the purpose and means of technology.

Fifth, attempts to effectively normalize science and technology development without affecting creativity and the spirit of innovation are difficult to achieve.

Sixth, a number of painful lessons have proven that the research and innovation of technological institutions always lag behind technology research and innovation. It is usually only after some technologies have been applied in ways that infringe upon human rights and even to manufacture killing weapons, that conventions and declarations are formulated regarding who should be allowed to possess or use dangerous technologies, how to ban or destroy them. To offer another example, gene technology will greatly change the living conditions of humans, and possible legislation on this issue has long attracted the attention of scientists, sociologists, lawyers, and even the whole society, but so far, no rational, effective global institution has been established to regulate it.

It is clear that deep-rooted ideas and behavior patterns are actually supported by the values of industrial civilization that dominate today's society: so long as it remains profitable, people will try to create commercial value and pursue the maximization of material interests. Therefore, there are often totally opposite opinions on whether and how to regulate technology. Of course, there are also limitations in the context of the times, including the gap between learning and knowledge.

What is needed to regulate technology is interdisciplinary cooperation, but given the rapid pace of knowledge growth, updating the politicians involved in decision-making or the constitutors of final institutions cannot keep up with the development of disruptive technologies. And scientists and engineers, including the social science community, generally lack of enough concern, cooperative research and reveal the potential risks of disruptive technologies to society, the environment, and even the future of mankind—let alone the general public. This further complicates the issue of regulating technology. In this cultural environment, international conventions, laws, and regulations are necessary to fundamentally solve the above problems, but they are far from enough. Because as mentioned in the relevant section of "The theory of soft environment" in this chapter, all institutions have limitations: all information in the society influence people's values through "soft environment filters", especially different "cultural filters", and then affect their judgments and behaviors. People mentioned here should include not only those in some countries who promote the development and use of weapons of mass destruction but also the decision-makers of government departments that formulate laws and regulations. It is not hard to understand Stephen Hawking's point: the law may prohibit human beings from doing gene editing, but human nature cannot resist the temptation to try it anyway.

Only when the mainstream societies of all countries reach a general consensus on the above basic issues, can those norms become a guide to people's actions, and make consciously abiding by them the new norm and thus create a better world.

In short, the influence of culture and values is profound, often far beyond that of the market and government, and sometimes even exceeding the power of institutions.

However, the culture and value system of today's society still has not got rid of the thinking logic of industrial civilization, which is also the root cause of various crises. The key to thoroughly solving the future crisis of humanity caused by the development of science and technology lies in the transformation of civilization. As Ronald Reagan said, "the greatness of society lies in the progress of the people".[2] The progress of the people is the foundation and main connotation of the progress of social civilization. Only with the advancement of global human civilization and that of science and technology keep pace with the times, can we get rid of the crisis of civilization, avoid the destruction of human beings, and embark on the road of sustainable human survival and development.

This is why I will now explore the issues regarding the evolution of mankind and future civilization from the perspective of humanities and social sciences through the following chapters.

## NOTES

1. If humanities are regarded as a science that mainly studies the concept, spirit, emotions, and values of human beings, then the social sciences take human society as their research object, and conduct research into social phenomena and their laws of development. The former includes aesthetics, religious studies, ethics, culturology, art theory, and so on, which are derived from the study of literature, history, and philosophy; while the latter include economics, sociology, political science, jurisprudence, etc.
2. Former US President Ronald Wilson Reagan made the famous "Last Speech" as president at the Republican Congress on 15 October 1988.

# 4

# What Kind of Civilization Should Human Beings Pursue?

*The progress of human beings driven by the values of Industrial Civilization is not sustainable, and civilization transition is imminent.*

Human civilization has developed over millions of years (written records go back more than five thousand years), and evolved to an Industrial Civilization in just the last 300 years. The Industrial Revolution was a great leap forward in the history of mankind and has produced an unprecedented and abundant material world with highly developed science and technology. As a result, the economy, politics, culture, social structures, etc. of human society have all changed dramatically, and most countries and regions in the world have entered the modern era of Industrial Civilization.

However, Industrial Civilization based on material supremacy and the theory that science and technology are omnipotent has made the world pay a high price. The natural environment and ecosystem that humans need to survive have been seriously damaged, natural resources have been polluted and are facing depletion everywhere, and the global population is growing uncontrollably (during the 1,000 years prior to 1800, the world population was well below 1 billion, but today it stands at over 7 billion.)[1] While it may be true that, despite overpopulation, more of those people alive today enjoy the basic necessities of life than at any time in the past, which can be considered a kind of progress, this is still far from perfect. And it would be a disaster if population growth exceeds the bearing capacity of Earth's environment and natural resources.

In the past 120 years, Britain has spent more than $60 billion to bring the Thames River under control. In China, sewage discharge, industrial and agricultural pollution, recently led to a cyanobacteria incident in Taihu Lake in Jiangsu province. The first phase of treatment cost $1.77 billion, while expenditures for the second phase have increased exponentially, and already exceeds $16.13 billion.[2] The management of Diarchy Lake in Yunnan province has cost nearly $10 billion since 1993, but

> the water quality has not greatly improved. The Kunming Municipal Government invests nearly one-third of its fiscal expenditure each year for pollution control of Dianchi Lake.[3]

In spiritual terms, the humanistic environment has been polluted, too. Examples include the widening gap between rich and poor, social injustice, the decline in moral behavior, and deepening social and regional conflicts. Despite the painful lessons of two world wars, all countries continue to study and manufacture ever-more devastating, more accurate, and more self-reliant weapons, which they employ in conflicts and wars between countries, regions, and clans that become more and more intense.

Nonetheless, the "chariot" of Industrial Civilization continues on its triumphant course, pursuing wealth as its main target. It could take hundreds of years or longer (assuming there is no major disturbance, such as a global catastrophe) to truly realize the transition to a new form of future civilization—the Global Civilization. Fortunately, in the last half century, we have begun to reflect and realize the absurdity of our current development mode, and have awakened to the fact that humanity is on a road of no return. For the first time, human beings are recognizing the necessity of promoting a replacement civilization. The imminent disaster facing humanity due to our careless use of science and technology means that we now stand at a crossroads and have to explore the future direction of our own evolution. It is obvious that the progress of human beings promoted by the values of Industrial Civilization is not sustainable and that the transition in civilization is imminent.

## *The essence of Industrial Civilization*

Industrial Civilization, that is, the civilization of industrial society, is based upon six basic principles: (1) the optimization of labor, (2) refinement in the division of labor, (3) synchronization of labor rhythm, (4) the centralized organization of labor, (5) efficient scales of production, and (6) economic centralization.

However, the above principles are mainly compared with the previous farming civilization, and while they recognize civilization from the perspective of the progress in production methods and economic development mode, they do not take into consideration such aspects of civilization as societal well-being, political equity, or sustainable values.

Another interpretation is that Industrial Civilization is a state of modern social civilization that takes industrialization as an important symbol and is dominated by mechanized large-scale production. Its main characteristics are industrialization, urbanization, legalization and democratization, increased mobility of social classes, popularization of education, accelerated news transmission, a substantial increase in the proportion of non-agricultural population, sustained economic growth, etc.[4]

Industrial Civilization is a new stage of human progress, where industry and agriculture have been highly developed, while creating a rich material world for human beings. Social welfare is widespread, humans live longer, enjoy more comfort and convenience than ever before. Unfortunately, human society has not made corresponding progress on the level of spiritual and political civilization. The spiritual values and moral practices that make human existence satisfying and sustainable have too often been downgraded or ignored.

The fatal defect of Industrial Civilization lies in

1. The unlimited pursuit of economic growth and economic interests tend to promote the maximization of economic interests as a panacea for economic development, poverty eradication, and the pursuit of happiness. This has led to the growth of the so-called the philosophy of economic "growth mania" and the expansion of "materialism" in social life.[5]
2. Taking material abundance as the sole measure of happiness: has led to overproduction, high consumption and high waste, as well as the absurd lifestyle of having more luxury and being proud of novelty for its own sake. This not only leads to the emptiness of people's spiritual life but also accelerates the depletion of natural resources and worsens the energy crisis on the earth.
3. A world in which worships money and power is a society that pursues material interests first. People inevitably become slaves to money, which inevitably leads to a decline in moral behavior, while the abuse of technology in pursuit of commercial profits makes some forms of technological innovation deviate from the original intention of benefiting mankind.
4. The plunder of nature by industrial civilization is revealed not only in the way humans disrupt their own environment but also how some developed nations exploit and plunder less-developed ones. Historically, all the developed countries that first realized industrialization competed to establish colonies, plundering means of production, dominating overseas markets, and robbing wealth. In today's world, in order to meet the needs of economic development, to control strategic resources, and ensure energy security, some developed countries have engaged in fierce competition, triggering conflicts and wars, and causing turmoil throughout the world subjugating native peoples, affluent minorities in developed countries have consumed most of the world's resources, resulting in serious inequalities in resource allocation and increasing polarization between the rich and the poor throughout the world.

5. The deterioration of the relationship between man and nature has seriously damaged the ecology. In order to preserve fire, destroy enemies, more easily hunt herds of prey, smelt bronze, and clear virgin land for farming, early humans burned down many forests. Similarly, unscientific ideas about medicine and how to relieve famine led to the killing off of many animals and plants. Lacking the technology to extinguish underground fires, societies for centuries have allowed the accidental burning of resources in underground coal mines.[6] But the damage to nature caused by Industrial Civilization has been fast and devastating.

The entire history of Industrial Civilization is based on conquering and transforming nature. It is a history of ceaselessly extracting resources and energy from nature to create material wealth, thus causing irreparable damage to the environment and resources of the earth on which we depend, and breaking the self-regulating ecosystem that is the network of life. Today the whole world faces immediate threats from the contamination of drinking water, the disappearance of large areas of tropical rainforests, the expansion of deserts, the disappearance of glaciers, the extinction of entire species, more intense and frequent weather disasters, and constant outbreak and spread of new infectious diseases.

In short, the mode of thinking that places economic growth first, and assumes that everything gives way to material interests, is an important reason for the crisis of human civilization. In Industrial Civilization, natural emotions like affection, loyalty, friendship, and trust are rated far below the main goal of pursuing wealth. Industrial Civilization follows the brutal law of the jungle, rewarding unrestrained competition and emphasizing the allocation of resources based solely on the market mechanism of supply and demand. In theory, this is an ideology of the survival of the fittest, which is essentially materialism. Industrial Civilization is clearly unsustainable.

## *Exploring the future evolution of humanity from social-humanity perspectives*

### The sublimation and perfection of human nature, and the creation of a more advanced civilization

It can be seen from Chapter 1 that many people pay close attention to the future evolution of human beings. Whether they are pessimists who claim that human evolution has come to an end, or optimists who believe that humanity is evolving towards the superhuman, almost all of them consider human evolution as essentially based on taking today's human being as a natural person, and extrapolating from this present state to raise their physical abilities, improve their wisdom and intelligence, and in the process increase knowledge, reduce disease, prolong life, etc. Moreover, in terms of the means to promote evolution, most of them belong to the evolution of natural people driven by hard technology.

Two points are worthy of more attention:

First, contemporary human beings are not perfect, and may not be the final end-product of human evolution. But now when many people express concern about the imperfections of mankind—not being smart enough to deserve the name "Homo sapiens"—and being merely the "intermediate products of evolution," they tend to focus on the quality of human being as a biological lifeform. They seldom consider how to solve the "root cause of trouble" in today's world, namely, the imperfect and even evil aspects of human beings' spiritual and moral nature.

Second, it is impossible to solve social problems such as to close the gap between rich and poor by the progress of hard technology alone. Of course, there are also people who reject this point of view. They believe that technologies similar to biohacking will narrow the gap between those privileged with wealth and education and those less fortunate, acting in effect as an equalizer to narrow the gap between rich and poor.[7] Such people argue that the continuous popularization of new technologies will result in rapid price drops allowing new technological benefits to spread to every stratum of society.

However, with the rapid development of technology, human enhancement technologies and biohacking will be constantly updated, and more advanced and more expensive cutting-edge technologies will continue to emerge. Hence, hacking alone may not solve the problem of inequality of access. There have been amazing price cuts, and popularization worldwide has brought industrial products such as TVs and computers to people worldwide. But this has not significantly narrowed the gap between rich and poor even within a given country much less throughout the entire world.

Moreover, after entering the Internet era, although more and more digital products are available online for free, bringing us all sorts of conveniences, advertising revenues and other benefits of online service are increasingly being monopolized by a handful of companies that offer search, and social media related services, rather than content producers. This, too, has exacerbated inequality.

For this reason, Nicholas Carr, known as an ideological leader of the Internet era, points out in his new book *Digital Utopia* that the relationship between social platforms and Internet users in the Attention Economy is essentially a "modern tenant farming system".[8]

It can be said that relying on hard science and technology to promote the evolution of human beings and promote the social progress is only a part of improving human civilization for the future. Promoting the sublimation and improvement of human nature and then creating a more advanced civilization are also indispensable elements. So, how can we understand the sublimation and improvement of human nature?

Biologists say that human beings are members of the animal kingdom, whose ancestors include the ancient ape. It may also be creatures on the seafloor (the latest research [Chinese paleontologist Zhang miman in 1995] shows that the origin of human beings is the primitive finfish that lived 400 million years ago). Philosophers think that man is a rational animal, who is capable of reasoned choice and will. They see humanity as an intelligent force in the universe; and some (including Immanuel Kant) believe that the biggest difference between humans and other creatures is found in human nature. In fact, humans have both natural attributes and social attributes. Natural human attributes include the drives for human survival and continuance, which are similar to those of other animals. Of course, there are other differences as well such as people's thinking mode, learning ability, etc. Social attributes; however, are unique to human beings, which makes them an essential characteristic of humanity. Therefore, human evolution cannot neglect the evolution of man as a natural social animal (according to Aristotle). Indeed, humans possess inborn social attributes, and to evolve successfully, humans must necessarily extend the space of their evolution to include the humanities and social sphere.

Human social attributes include several aspects[9]: Some are consistent with overall sustainable development, but there are also characteristics of antisociality, which is not conducive to the overall sustainability of humanity. The former traits include altruism, obedience, loyalty, compassion, conscientiousness, the ability to control one's emotions in society, sound judgment, the ability to identify good and evil, etc. Those human traits that are unfavorable to social development (the so-called anti-social traits) include extreme self-interest develops to harm others, the public and society; self-protection at the expense of other creatures, and even other "people". According to Harvard psychologist Steven Pinker,[10] human nature is a complex matrix that contains a tendency towards violence, but also a positive side of sympathy, cooperation, and self-control.

At the same time, humans are the only animals who can self-reflect and study their own attributes, especially their social attributes, and who try to improve these attributes by their own initiative. Human social attributes, especially those in line with the requirements of overall human development, provide the foundation for the normal operation and continued development of human society. Therefore, no matter what kind of society (slave, feudal, capitalist, or socialist), it will take a series of measures, affecting such areas as religion, beliefs, education, morality, laws, and regulations, as well as state machinery that promotes restraint such as the army, police, prisons, and courts to ensure and cultivate the positive social attributes of its members, even though different societies and cultures have different standards. Numerous facts have proved that human nature has great plasticity.

Thus, it is clear that humans cannot simply consider their evolution towards intellectual perfection as a natural person (individual), nor define a desired standard solely on the basis of the computing power of the human brain. As the most developed lifeform on earth, humans should consider the evolution of humanity as social and moral beings. We should set as a goal guiding human evolution to improve our social nature, while purifying and enhancing the traits of kindness and positive energy (correct value orientation, which is helpful to avoid evil, selfishness, crime, war, etc.), with the aim of perfecting the social environment for human survival. By doing so, we can contribute to the sustainable development of human society. Recently, scientists have begun discussing "whether there is space for human evolution" and have offered various speculations.[11] In fact, there will be more space for humans to evolve both as social and moral persons.

From the perspective of human ability, human beings create and promote the progress of civilization in different stages: from primitive hunter-gatherers, to Agricultural Civilization, Industrial Civilization, and the more advanced civilization of the future. Therefore, in order to create a more advanced civilization—a Global Civilization and thus a Great Civilization, the perfection of human ability must include more than just the improvement of individual knowledge, wisdom, and intelligence. It must also include advancing with the times and consciously promoting the purification and sublimation of human nature, or continuously enhancing the "social attribute that meet the requirements of overall human development" and passing it on from generation to generation.

In short, the direction of human evolution and the future of humanity depend not only on the progress of science and technology (based on natural and non-natural science knowledge) but also on the progress of the human mind, particularly with respect to worldviews, values, and philosophy of life (based on the degree of human nature sublimation and social civilization). Progress will also depend on maintaining balance and coordination between scientific knowledge and the human mind as both advance over time. In fact, the progress of society and even the progress of civilization are both the result of human good intentions, and human ingenuity sparked by positive energy, and progressive thought.

We need to constantly create new thoughts conducive to the sustainable development of human beings, so as to guide humans towards a better future.

## *What kind of civilization should human beings pursue after industrial civilization?*

Based on the forward leaps achieved to date through hard science and technology, scientists and futurists envision a variety of fascinating futures and future civilizations. For example, in the future, we are told, humans will have infinite energy (Nikolai Kardashev, 1964[12]); we will cease to grow old and instead enjoy eternal life (the transhumanists' vision), and may even realize time travel and make contact with extraterrestrials.

Some transhumanists' imagination of the future world is that when technology develops to the point where abiotic intelligence surpasses biological intelligence, there will be no more humans as we know them today. Instead, there will be completely computerized transhumans. By the time human beings can attain eternal existence, that is, although the human body may die, their personality and spirit can live on forever.

With the new wave of AI, as described in Chapter 2, human–machine civilization is the future envisioned by most technology worshippers at present.

However, whether it is a civilization classified by access to disposable energy, a transhumanist vision of immortality, or the human–machine civilization highly anticipated at present, the emphasis is on material civilization and scientific and technological civilization, and the latter is merely one part of spiritual civilization.

It can be said that human evolution has been experiencing two processes simultaneously: the biological evolution of individual organisms and the cultural evolution of human society as a whole. These two evolutions mutually influence one another and interact. Social evolution occurs outside the human body and is realized by changes in culture. The outcomes of biological evolution occur mainly in individuals while the achievements of cultural evolution affect the whole community or most of its members. Ultimately human beings should and will be able to coordinate their biological and cultural evolution.

Culture is expressed and largely conveyed through the symbolic system and in the form of collective social behavior. Therefore, in addition to the evolution of information (in the forms of language, text, symbols, graphics, etc.), cultural evolution is expressed in religious beliefs, and attitudes towards science and technology, art, traditions, customs, ethics, laws, regulations, etc. Thus, the progress of science and technology is only one part of cultural evolution.

The term "civilization" refers to the progressive state of human society and rational social systems.[13] In its narrow sense, civilization implies a rational social system as opposed to a savage one (a collection of all social and natural acts that separate humans from barbarism),[14] while civilization in a broader sense refers to the total results (both successful experiences and instructive failures) of cultural development and evolution at any given time.

In general, the specific content and manifestation of advanced culture—"the positive results at cultural development and evolution" include a good lifestyle and spiritual outlook. In other words, the broad sense of civilization can be defined as the sum of material wealth and spiritual well-being created by human beings.

It can also be specified as material civilization related to material life (represented by the progress of material production and the improvement of material life), spiritual civilization related to spiritual life (manifested as the progressive state of human wisdom and morality), ecological civilization, which defines the relationship between man and nature, and interstellar civilization which defines the relationship between human beings, the earth (on which human beings live at present), and the universe.

The civilization to be aspired to by humanity as a whole should be civilization in the broad sense, although depending on the different stages of civilization achieved by different societies, the criteria of each may differ.

Therefore, the more advanced civilization we pursue after the Industrial Civilization should take sustainable human survival and development as its goal (or make sustainability the new measure and driving force of cultural evolution), replacing the economic, political, social, and cultural forms dominant in Industrial Civilization, which have mainly sought to maximize profits and capital dominated.

I suggest calling the rational social system that is able to support sustainable human existence and development "The Global Civilization"[15]—a new form of human civilization: this would be composed of five advancements in civilization suitable for sustainable development: material, spiritual, political, ecological, and interstellar civilization. Originally, political life also included spiritual life in a broad sense. But in view of the importance that countries and political parties today attach to political civilization in the process of social governance and world order, it makes sense to list them separately. Although countries and political parties will still exist within Global Civilization, groups with different cultures, different beliefs, and different faiths will be willing to tolerate each other, coexist, and co-develop.

In the Global Civilization, material civilization provides a concrete basis for sustainability, while political and spiritual matters constitute the superstructure of human civilization. Namely, spiritual civilization offers the spiritual pillar for human sustainable development while political civilization provides a guarantee of peace, harmony, and sustainability of human society. Ecological civilization represents a new stage in civilization, the condition of material and spiritual civilization. If there is no ecological security, when human beings fall into an irreversible crisis of survival, the foundation for discussing the other aspects of civilization will be lost, let alone the material comfort and spiritual enjoyment. Interstellar civilization is related to how human beings living on earth surpass the earth civilization, expand human civilization to other planets, and establish a healthy relationship with other planets and even the universe. Therefore, the above-mentioned five levels of new civilizations complement each other and realize the transformation of the civilization paradigm at the same time is the only sure way to avoid the looming threats to human survival.

## *The Global Civilization*

### The cultural foundation for jointly building future human happiness

The former Secretary-General of the United Nations, Ban Ki-moon, has repeatedly pointed out that building a sustainable future is the common responsibility of people around the world and has called for a global commitment to sustainable development in order to build a happy future. He has also said that the realization of the happiness of all mankind is one of the basic goals of the United Nations. Peace, prosperity, and enabling all people to live a life of dignity—these are goals we all pursue.

What is a happy future for humanity as a whole? I suggest that the vision of a happy human future can be summarized as *material sufficiency; mental health, wisdom and freedom of thought; political equality and justice; ecological balance and respect for nature. This will promote love, kindness, and harmony between people, harmonious relations between man and nature, and enable mutual tolerance and respect among different nationalities and cultures, leading to cooperation, coexistence, and peace among all countries and even different planets; and thus ensuring a world of perpetual peace.*

But this ideal world order must be built on the basis of profound philosophical thought and regulated by a complete set of values, making them operable; otherwise, it could remain a fantasy or even a fallacy, for philosophy can be right or wrong, advanced or backward. In other words, our ideal social system—Global Civilization and even Great Civilization—must be based on the values of related material production and life, spiritual life, political activity, human relations with nature and even other interstellar relations, adapted to the sustainable development of human beings rather than to the values of Industrial Civilization.

Therefore, we need to engage in philosophical thought about how we envision humanity's future and summarize our ultimate goal with the characteristics of civilization, which is a better vision of sustainable human prosperity and perpetual peace. To do this, we must consider such profound questions as: what kind of world exists today? What is human? What kind of future do we NEED (namely, what kind of future is ESSENTIAL if humanity is to survive)? What constitutes sustainable development for human beings? Where will people find true happiness?, etc.

That is what we defined above as the NEW material, spiritual, and political civilizations, which coordinate with each other and integrate with ecological civilization and interstellar civilization, to form a new civilization that is in line with sustainable development. The reason why we emphasize "new" here is because the five civilizations described above are all at different stages of development, and each has different connotations, standards, and value systems.

In order not to let research on the Global Civilization remain merely abstract philosophical speculation, but to actually implement the actions necessary to build Global Civilization, we must make sure of the following:

First, we should fully realize that history has entered a new period of integration and development bridging Eastern and Western civilizations. While we should continue to improve the essence of Western civilization and work to supplement its shortcomings, we also need to excavate and revitalize Oriental wisdom and the essence of Chinese Civilization that has been largely ignored for the past 300 years during the era of Industrial Civilization. In this way, we can jointly create and develop a new culture of human sustainability—the Global Civilization that "melds" (i.e., develops what is useful or healthy and discards what is not) from both Eastern and Western cultures to realize the potential of a truly Global Civilization.

Second, based on the above premise, we must examine every civilization and be clear about:

1. The current basic problems in each that need to be resolved (especially the problems of values);
2. The approaches that each civilization uses to solve its problems (the path);
3. The technological guidelines and institutional design that these different approaches will require in order to make the desired civilizational transformation have maneuverability.

## Material civilization

Material civilization is the foundation for human survival, that is, progress in human material living conditions, manifested by new modes of material production and improved life experiences. A highly developed material civilization is a necessary prerequisite for humans to understand nature, explore the universe, and promote the advancement of humanity. However, in contemporary society, the unlimited desire for material wealth has encouraged people everywhere to adopt savage development models that are human-centered and do not respect nature. This has produced a high level of material civilization but only at the cost of severe ecological damage to a point that now threatens the destruction of human civilization. The pursuit of material wealth by itself does not contribute to the formation of advanced civilization. For example, since the end of the Second World War, the level of material life has been continuously improved, but the human ability to solve their basic problems of ecology, world order, upholding justice and so on has not been greatly improved. This requires deep reflection on the drawbacks of material civilization in the traditional sense.

In order to build a new material civilization, some fundamental problems need to be resolved.

The first is to change our concept. Human beings are bound to enjoy the "high level" material life corresponding to technological progress and social progress. However, this high level does not mean the unrestrained, unlimited, and more luxurious material life. That is to say, civilized material comforts should restrain endless greed. The thought of "civilization with restraint"[16] in the *Book of Changes* shows that civilization can not be realized through unlimited development, utilization of natural resources, and expansion, but should be "restrained". In the new material civilization, this idea should be embodied in the value goal of "restrained at absolute perfection", restrained at moderate consumption, maintaining a decent life, the harmonious coexistence of human beings with nature, society and others, and being beneficial to the sustainable survival and development of human beings.

Keli Fang, a contemporary Chinese philosopher points out that: "Civilization with restraint" does not oppose human civilized behaviors that promote social progress, and only restricts our behaviors by helping them conform to the Way of Heaven (**) and to the goodness of human nature.[17] By definition, behaviors outside this scope are uncivilized. This reflects the traditional Chinese view of civilization.

### The Way of Heaven

- *The Way of Heaven (Tao of Heaven): "Tao" is an important philosophical concept in Chinese and Oriental ancient philosophy, generally representing the ultimate truth, arche, ontology, rule, principle, realm, etc. "Heaven" is relative to humans, and includes all things in nature.*[18]
- *The relation between human and Heaven is a basic issue of Chinese philosophy, and philosophers from a variety of schools have different understandings and interpretations of "Heaven" and "Tao of Heaven". Ancient Chinese materialist thinkers, from Xunzi to Fuzhi Wang, regarded "Heaven" as nature, which is an objective world with an independent existence and no dependency on "humanity", and interpreted the "Tao of Heaven" as the laws of nature.*
- *Contemporary philosophers*[19] *have further clarified that the "Tao of Heaven" was the laws of nature "in operation", while the "Tao of Mankind" were the operational laws that governed human society, and thus that the "Tao of Mankind" must follow the "Tao of Heaven". From the viewpoint of the ecological wisdom of ancient China, "Heaven" is equivalent to nature while "Man" is equivalent to human beings. As the product of nature and a part of nature, human beings need to recognize that their own survival and development are inseparable from that of nature itself. The Unity of Heaven and Man corresponds to the theory that both together form an organic unity that cannot be separated.*

Second, the new material civilization should be embodied in the modes of production, life, consumption, and other behaviors, with the premise of no waste, environmental protection, resource conservation and recycling, and no abuse of power. It should adhere to the consumption mode consistent with sustainable development, with the goal of maintaining a decent living standard, and pursuing a smarter lifestyle. In short, self-discipline is itself a sign of civilized humanity.

### Spiritual civilization

As mentioned earlier, Industrial Civilization has created tremendous and unprecedented material wealth for mankind. Unfortunately, with regard to spiritual civilization, especially in the dimension of science technology civilization and ethics, human society has not made corresponding progress.

Spiritual civilization generally refers to the state of progress in human wisdom and morality. On the one hand, it is manifested as the wisdom, knowledge, and creativity of an era, including the creativity and development level of science, technology, culture, art, and education throughout the whole society; on the other hand, it reflects the mainstream of thought and spirit, including the predominant beliefs, worldviews, moral outlooks, social trends, and so on within that society. The latter can better reflect the level of spiritual life in different eras of civilization; The two aspects mentioned above—science and technology civilization—are balanced and coordinated with ideological and moral civilization.

Modern science developed in the West, and many top-level natural scientists and thinkers, from Copernicus, Kepler, Galileo, Newton, Watt, Faraday, Darwin, and Mendeleev, to Edison, Madame Curie, Einstein, and Hawking, are the products of predominantly Western traditions. Likewise, great philosophers from Socrates, Plato, and Aristotle to Da Finch, Bacon, Descartes, Kant, Hegel, Schopenhauer, Feuerbach, Marx, and Nietzsche who represent the major trends of Western thought have made lasting contributions to the progress of human spiritual civilization. There is no doubt that western science and thought have made unparalleled contributions to the progress of human civilization.

It is worth emphasizing that there are different standards of spiritual civilization in different societies and in different eras, which must keep pace with the progress of civilization.

Take morality as an example. Ethical behavior standards often reflect the positive value orientation of a society; in other words, ethics provide a value measure for judging between good and bad behavior, legitimate and illegitimate actions, justice and injustice, honor and disgrace, honesty and hypocrisy, and rights and obligations. Therefore, it is the decisive factor that determines beliefs, ideals, emotions, and even behaviors. Moral standards are also the product of people's conscious behavior that is determined by certain material conditions and relations within a society.

Therefore, the broad sense of ethical canons in Global civilization that will advocate a new material civilization promotes harmony and caritas in human relations, between the individual and society, and between man and nature. In addition, as a rule they promote mutual tolerance and respect between different ethnic and cultural groups, and encourage cooperation and coexistence among countries. These are certainly different from the ethical canons advocated by Industrial Civilization, which pursue wholly material aims, effectively sanctioning the principle that maximizing profit justifies all behaviors consistent with the brutal law of the jungle.

In short, spiritual civilization is based on the ethical canons of Global Civilization; consequentially, it is conducive to a social atmosphere that encourages people to love nature consciously, protect the environment for the survival of mankind, advocate green consumption, and embrace advanced concepts such as cosmopolitanism, pacifism, global justice, and global citizenship. Furthermore, ethics provide spiritual resources that will prove vital for the ecological civilization and political civilization of the new era.

This context calls for the revitalization of Eastern Civilization, which has always put emphasis on humanistic, moral, and ethical values, paid special attention to "self-cultivation"[20] and "life wisdom". For example, Lao Tzu's "Three basic principles in life",[21] along with a code of conduct that involves "Always acting with respect for the Tao and virtue, practicing selflessness and dedication,"[22] "The concepts of honor or disgrace,"[23] and the noble idea that "The highest good is like of water – that is, that the highest virtue is attained through giving rather than taking",[24] etc. Such ideals can be said to establish standards for perfecting human nature and moral education.

Ideas less familiar in the West, such as Zhongyan Fan's "*Worry about the world first, enjoy the fruits after the people*",[25] Yanwu Gu's "*Everyone is responsible for the fate of his country*",[26] and the relevant traditional ethics such as "Rites" and "Benevolence", as well as the lofty ideals such as "A world of universal harmony" and "Making the whole world one community"[27] are beneficial to cultivate positive values and worldview.

In short, to secure a humane and sustainable world, humans must develop mutual respect, meld Western knowledge and logic[28] as well as the methodology of inductive reasoning with Oriental sensitivity and respect for healthy moral values and social customs, and finally build a global society capable of ensuring human existence, mutual tolerance, and development for the long-term future.

Take science and technology civilization, one of the main constituents of spiritual civilization, as an example. The industrial civilization of the past few hundred years has brought highly developed science and technology to human society. It can solve many problems in the material field except for those involving thought (including world outlook, values, etc.) and the humanities field (including social systems, social change, social governance, etc.). Indeed thanks to science and technology almost all the material wants of the world can be satisfied. However, the current situation is that human beings are more and more confused and scared, no longer know what is "human" and where humanity should go. As mentioned in chapter 1 about "The imminent disaster facing science and technology", is that instead of it being regarded as a tool to create human well-being, many people today live in fear of becoming enslaved by science and technology.

As for the role of science and technology in spiritual civilization, there are some basic problems that should be solved:

First, we must understand the nature of science and technology (see the section of "What is technology" in Chapter 3).

Second, the relationship between the instrumentality of science and technology and human goals should be straightened out. Science and technology, whether it is hard or soft, belong to the tools used by human beings to understand the world and solve problems. Tools and goals must not be confused.

Third, the goal of developing science and technology include: (1) to bring well-being to all mankind (rather than only a few people); (2) to support the sustainable survival and development of other species in nature; (3) to provide more effective means for the progress of human society, world peace, and facilitate the various paths to sustainable development (see the section on "Ecological civilization" below for details).

Fourth, we should study and prevent the potential risks of scientific and technological breakthroughs, control and guide the direction of technological innovation (see the relevant section on how "Human beings must regulate technology" in Chapter 2), and contain the possible disasters including man-made disasters and natural catastrophe.

Fifth, any breakthrough in science and technology will bring huge business profits and opportunities for military applications, and make us face more difficult choices and balances in ethics and morality. How to realize the humanistic value of modern science and technology and realize the synchronization of scientific and technological progress and human moral sublimation? We should firmly resist making economic benefits and practical utility the primary standards for the technology development, and avoid scientific and technological innovations that are harmful to the living environment, physical and mental health, human ethics, and may even lead to the decline and destruction of human beings.

Sixth, how to regulate and supervise technology, an increasingly powerful tool, to prevent it from getting out of control, to keep the final boundary of natural human beings, and not to let human creations threaten their own survival.

Seventh, we should correctly handle and balance the relationship between "the scientific spirit of free exploration," "realizing the all-round and free development of human beings," and the ultimate goal of developing science and technology. The free development of human beings and the free exploration of science should not only have a clear goal but also have a bottom line, which should not be at the cost of deterioration of the natural environment, moral degradation, the fall of civilization or scientific and technological disasters that could result in the extinction of traditional human beings. We must refine our soul by realizing the lofty ideals (goals) and emotions of Global Civilization and then the ultimate realization of Great Civilization, so as to achieve the sublimation of human nature and the promotion of morality, and coordinate the increasing knowledge and wisdom of human beings with the progress of human civilization as well as adhering to the moral standards that keep pace with the times. Therefore, we should not ignore the healthy spiritual life and noble moral sentiment of human beings, nor the health of human society, including related fairness and justice, rights and responsibilities, human nature and human dignity, wisdom (or ability) and the happiness of the vast majority of people. The ultimate cost of so-called scientific liberalism, which promises the free exploration of science or the free development of human beings with no limits, is that human beings are risk being enslaved by science and technology, and completely losing their identity as traditional human beings.

### Political civilization

As an integral part of human civilization, political civilization reflects the progress of political life in society and the achievements realized by its development, including the dominant political system (such as social institution, government, legal, and administrative system) and political conception (such as political values and political beliefs).[29]

Western civilization has made a great contribution to political civilization. Over several thousand years, Western civilization, drawing on ancient Greek democracy, Rome's rule of law, and a unified community derived from the Hebrew religious tradition, produced universal values such as freedom, democracy, the rule of law, constitutionalism, and the scientific method of free inquiry.

However, after more than two centuries of the modernization dominated by Western civilization, the Earth's resources and the environment are being destroyed, and unfettered economic development has aroused endless greed for money and power at every level from the individual to the governments of some sovereign countries, causing many to conclude that human society is morally bankrupt. At the same time, the increasingly serious gap between rich and poor worldwide, as well as social and political inequality and injustice, has produced a sharp contradiction and mutual hostility between man and man, and between peoples and nations, giving birth to various kinds of ideological extremism, causing a sharp increase in armed conflicts. In addition, the misuse of highly advanced science and technology greatly increases the risks from all kinds of conflicts.

Sadly, in the name of spreading democracy and opposing dictatorship, some developed countries continue to mobilize and support war, propelling the world into an unprecedented state of anarchy, even to the verge of disintegration. For this reason alone establishing a new international order is imperative. It is not enough to implement global governance by relying only on the current UN, whose Security Council has become increasingly powerless to maintain world peace, or to depend on various Summits such as the UN Climate Summit, APEC Summit and East Asia Summit, G20 Summit.

In the twenty-first century, a new world politics has emerged, different from the US—Soviet confrontation of the Cold War era or the temporary stability dominated by the United States, which briefly succeeded it. First, more than 100 nations have proclaimed their independence since the Second World War, while developing countries have emerged as major economic powers, like the Four Asian Tigers, the BRICs, the "Next-11" (N-11 for short), and the rise of China, which are not only ushering in a multipolar era but also causing substantial changes and shifts in the global power structure.

Second, the modernization led by material supremacy and the omnipotence of science and technology cost the world irretrievably. People realize that human civilization promoted by the values of Industrial Civilization is not sustainable, which promotes the rethinking of human development to ensure sustainable development and civilization transformation and enable the transformation of values and concepts.

In addition, the explosive development of science and technology, especially the high development of emerging information technology, not only brings great opportunities and benefits to mankind but also makes us face the crisis of science and technology and even the crisis of human civilization. It calls for a new revolution of economic development and social governance.

With the integration of the above changes, the world today is experiencing a great change in the past century that has never happened before, and which has had a serious impact even subverting the existing international order, international relations, international politics, international rules, and the international system. The new coronavirus epidemic has greatly accelerated this great evolution. It calls for a new order and a new paradigm of symbiosis, coexistence, and common prosperity of human beings on one earth.

At the international level, the world is gestating geopolitical upheaval. All countries not only need to safeguard their own interests, but they must also deal with conflicts of interest and contradictions among countries or regions by displaying "global consciousness". Despite the fact that the problems facing different countries are dissimilar due to their differing conditions and stages of development, they all face challenges of reform. Worldwide there is an increasing sense that politics are becoming polluted by money and greed. Specific interest groups that control huge amounts of capital control the political system to influence politics for their own ends.

Thus, there are many urgent issues that need to be addressed quickly, such as how to prevent the corruption and damage of politics caused by money and how to break the barriers to reform raised by special interest groups (not only in political reform, but also in the implementation of reforms in finance, health insurance, and other major areas.[30]).

It can be seen that whether from the standpoint of global governance and building a new world order or to reform within sovereign countries, it is necessary to create a new political civilization in order to ensure the peaceful harmonious and sustainable development of human society.

Basic issues that the new political civilization must address:

1. Changing the thinking mode is the primary problem that must be solved in the future political civilization. Recently, China has put forward the new concept of a Community of Human Destiny.[31] In fact, it is rooted in the ancient traditions of Chinese Civilization.[32] It is closely related to the philosophical idea of "The Unity of Heaven and Man,"[33] the political ideals like "A world of universal harmony," and "Making the whole world one community,"[34] the cultural ideology such as "Make all nations live together peacefully"[35] and "Striving for Harmony but not Uniformity,"[36] the spiritual realm of "Tolerance brings respect,"[37] as well as Lao Tzu[38] and Chuang Tzu's[39] "Inaction" theory of governance. All of these are the premise of the necessary cultivation of politicians

   By exploring such "Oriental" ideas, it will be possible to reshape the ideological basis for future human civilization, guide the direction of human progress and evolution, and foster consciousness worldwide of humanity's Community of Common Destiny.

   Additional examples of Chinese traditional people-oriented thought include Confucius' "Governing by virtue" and "The benevolent loves others"[40]; while Mencius' "To a state, the people are the most important thing, the state comes second, the ruler is the least important"[41] provides a reference for the contemporary construction of benevolent rule. In addition, the theories of "Yin-Yang"[42] and "Hard-Soft"[43] in the real world provide sound development principles for the twenty-first century—harmony, tolerance, and coexistence, which are derived from what is appropriate for dealing with a variety of contradictions in human society, including different patterns of development, different values, and different cultural traditions.

2. To successfully transform Industrial Civilization, all countries need to reform their existing political systems and rebuild their institutions. Each country should first acknowledge the position of their political system within the history of human civilization, and determine the proper direction of institutional reform appropriate to their own national cultural history.
3. We must create a shared, coexisting and tolerant culture, and build a cultural foundation for a harmonious society (culture).
4. We must create and consciously devise political technologies conducive to achieving a new political civilization. By enhancing the innovation ability of political technology, and strengthening institutional innovation and design, we can help guarantee the success of institutional reform. Moreover, the invention, creation, and innovation of Hard–Soft theory and soft technologies will contribute to the promotion of innovative capabilities in political technology, especially political techniques[44] that can resolve contradictions and conflicts in non-violent ways, including peaceful negotiation, improved techniques for handling international relations and institutional capacity, get rid of political difficulties, and granting institutions the executive ability to follow this new moral blueprint. In fact, political technology is also a means for human beings to use their outstanding wisdom and ability to solve social and political changes, social governance, and other issues. Here is a worthy application of the principles laid out in Lao Tzu's *Tao Te Ching* and of Sun Tzu's *Art of War.*
5. We need to expand the channels available for social and political participation, so as to improve the universality and effectiveness of public involvement in political decision-making. Therefore, it is necessary to establish and perfect a system of political participation in order to broaden the scope of political participation and ensure the orderly political participation of all citizens.
6. Finally, civilizing international relations in this present era of globalization: As early as 1953, China put forward Five Principles of Peaceful Coexistence[45]: mutual respect for sovereignty and territorial integrity; non-aggression; non-interference in each other's internal affairs; equality and mutual benefit; and peaceful coexistence. Despite the changes of the times and changes in the international environment, there are disagreements over such issues as human rights, sovereignty, terrorism, and globalization, and new explanations and supplements are needed. The nation-state is currently still regarded as the most important actor in international politics, thus the Five Principles still have strong vitality. However, a number of fundamental changes have occurred in the contemporary international system making regional alliances and subnational groups as

important as nations and sometimes more so. In order to build a better world with win–win cooperation, global governance systems and mechanisms must be reformed. To this end, China is now promoting a new concept of international relations—a "community of human destiny". This is not only an international environment adapting to Global Civilization but also can become the moral standard by which diplomatic policies are evaluated in every country.

In short, the new political civilization must be based on political concepts and a political system both of which are in line with sustainable, harmonious, and peaceful human development, and embody the pursuit of the ideal social system, which will ultimately advance the fundamental long-term interests of humanity.

### Ecological civilization

Ecological sensitivity is an important element in this new civilization. No matter in which era of civilization we find ourselves, every human society has evolved to some degree, gaining in its ability to understand, utilize, transform, and adapt to nature, but different civilizations are based on different relationships between man and nature. The essence of Industrial Civilization is to dominate nature, even when this causes significant damage to the environment, ecology, and resources of the Earth on which all human beings depend.

Human beings, after all, are part of nature, ecological civilization seeks coordinated development between man and nature as its goal, not only to avoid being powerless in the face of nature but also to abandon the error of rash predatory attempts to transform natural systems. It is necessary to make sustainable development a fundamental principle, along with respect for and conformity to nature, and to conserve the elements of nature, so as to promote the co-evolution of man and nature. It can be said that ecological civilization will be a basic premise for sustainable human civilization in the future, for without a healthy environment and ecological security, humanity can have no hope of enjoying and sustaining material and spiritual life.

Take China as an example. Thanks to the past 40 years of reform and opening up, at the stage of rapid industrialization, the total economic volume has reached an unprecedented scale. At the same time, the burning of a large quantity of fossil fuel and the rapid growth of motor vehicles have led to serious air pollution; the extensive use of pesticides and fertilizers has caused great pollution to the soil; industrial, agricultural and domestic pollution sources have caused great damage to the water environment, and the ecological carrying capacity of the Earth is facing huge challenges. Now, the need for clean air, clean drinking water, and safe and secure food sources is becoming the greatest desire of the Chinese people.

In order to move towards an ecological civilization, it is crucial to change people's ideas and behaviors. Ecological civilization must be manifested in all fields such as the philosophy of civilization, the economy, science and technology, lifestyle and consumption patterns, institutional construction, public standards, social fashion, etc.

First, it will require changing traditional ideas about the relationship between man and nature and rethinking our ethical values. This is the basic premise of building an ecological civilization. The occurrence of more and more frequent natural disasters around the world, the constant outbreak of new virus epidemics, at their painful price, let us rethink the relationship between humans and nature, and change the "people-centered" thinking mode that ignores nature and other creatures in nature. Experts have long warned that the earth is experiencing its sixth mass extinction, and we have always treated this as a matter of little consequence. In fact, this is actually a warning that our own species is also facing the risk of mass extinction.

The ecological civilization, expounded by ancient Chinese philosophers and thinkers, is rich in content, broad and profound. For example, the ecological philosophy of Lao Tzu such as "*The Tao follows its own way naturally*"[46] and ecological wisdom of Zhongshu Dong like "*The unity of Heaven and Man*"[47] provide a solid philosophical foundation and ideological source for correctly handling the relationship between human beings and nature, dealing with the relationship between economic development, social progress, ecological environment, and realizing ecological civilization.

Second, in resolving conflicts between man and nature, human beings are obviously responsible for the major source of conflict. Nearly all of the problems that have led to ecological crises and environmental pollution in today's world have mainly been caused by human activities.[48] Hence, it will be necessary for us to transform our own behavior patterns, especially in such areas as economic development and lifestyle.

For example, human beings must change their ignorance of other creatures in nature, change their barbaric lifestyle of hunting and eating wild animals simply to enjoy the taste of delicious food or obtaining novel decorations and high-end clothing. Above all people must stop hunting wild animals merely to satisfy the pleasure of killing and other evil ways of entertainment (such as the "Canned Hunting grounds" in South Africa).

Taking the activities of developing science and technology as an example, the increasingly serious natural disasters and the continuous outbreak of new virus epidemics have made us rethink the mission and direction of scientific and technological innovation and other important issues.

For instance, the view that "the purpose of developing science and technology is to bring benefits to mankind" is incomplete. If human beings want to survive and develop continuously, they must consider the sustainable survival and development of human beings and other species together in nature, including wild animals, and the protection of the natural environment (ecological, biological, and resource-providing), so that humans can save themselves.

To this end, the "invention, creation and innovation" aimed at protecting biological diversity, protecting and restoring the natural environment, and promoting harmonious and sustainable development for human beings and human society are also important connotation of the purpose of scientific and technological development. In other words, the mission of developing science and technology must be expanded.

Taking the research and development of artificial meat as an example, the development of artificial meat has opened up a new perspective for the harmonious coexistence of humans and other creatures in nature. Since the Britisher Grafe Viktor proposed the concept of using protein to produce meat substitutes in 1916,[49] after more than 100 years of exploration, scientists have "produced" various kinds of meat in the laboratory without causing harm to other organisms, in various ways from using plant protein to removing cells or tissues from animals.

Recently, Israel's Aleph Farm announced that scientists painlessly extracted a few cells from live cattle to naturally "grow" a steak with excellent color and flavor.[50] Once humans no longer meet their nutritional needs by killing other animals, it will not only help solve the problem of human hunger, but also allow people to enjoy healthier and more delicious food; and it will not only help reduce greenhouse gases and slow down the pollution of water sources caused by the livestock industry, it will also free large amounts of rangeland, and reduce energy consumption. Finally, it will reduce the spread of viral infections such as mad cow disease and foot-and-mouth disease.

Although there are still many difficulties in large-scale production that need to be broken through, the invention of artificial meat does provide humans with opportunities and ways to live in harmony with other animals in nature by changing their lifestyles.

Third, we will need to actively explore and promote the reform of institutions and mechanisms of ecological civilization as well as related social, political, and economic systems. Transforming development modes will require creating relevant institutions which are not only conducive to adjusting the various relationships between man and nature, and promoting the transformation of government behavior (e.g., one of the major difficulties affecting the construction of ecological civilization in China is the officials' views on political achievements), but that also penetrate the management of a wide range of fields such as production, consumption, resources, energy, environment, and ecology. Examples include adjusting and perfecting the system of price, taxation, and management of natural resources, instituting systems of ecological compensation and restoration governance, while guiding social capital to invest in ecologically sound construction, and improve fiscal investment mechanisms. In addition, performance evaluation and long-term monitoring must be initiated and maintained. All these initiatives must not only be geared to international standards, but also embody global cooperation.

Fourth, expanding access and improving the quality of public education for all citizens are the prerequisites for implementing the above three measures. Take garbage for example. Disposal of garbage is one of the biggest problems of environmental protection today. As mentioned in Chapter 3 on the "Limitations of institutions", the legalization of garbage classification is of course important, but more importantly, the whole society should establish the social fashion of accepting that "Environmental protection starts with me"; take pride in not littering, and feel shame for littering. We must establish new habits, natural behaviors and social norms among the public, to the point where these become automatic.

To this end, it is necessary to re-envision the concept of civilization in the industrialized era with ecological consciousness, completely eliminating those concepts and practices that attempt to dominate and control nature, and adjust the relationship between man and nature to one of, respect and harmonious coexistence. Otherwise, it will be impossible for human beings to escape from the coming global ecological crisis.

## Interstellar civilization

As mentioned in Chapter 1, with the development of science and technology, especially the breakthrough of manned space technology in recent years, the impact of mankind is expanding into outer space and other planets. From space exploration to space migration, from the use of new space materials to interstellar travel and other comprehensive developments, human beings have entered a new era of space exploration. At the same time, in order to gain control of outer space, countries are racing to expand their space activities, prepare or build space forces and space commands. Thus it can be said that the establishment of interstellar civilization —beyond the limitations of earth civilization has been put on the agenda.

When we discussed political civilization adapted to Global Civilization, we emphasized the relationship among countries, which is the civilization of international relations with win–win cooperation, dialogue and consultation, fairness and justice, peace and harmony. These ideas extend into space. Then interstellar civilization represents another evolution of human civilization, creating human civilization on other planets and correctly dealing with relationships with other planets.

The issues that need to be solved in establishing interstellar civilization include how to exploit and utilize extraterrestrial resources, protect outer space and planetary environments, implement space migration, maintain social order in space and respect indigenous cultures (if alien life exists), among many other issues.

The key is to learn from the experience and lessons accumulated by mankind in the long road of living on the earth, and overcome the bad behaviors of mankind on the earth—polluting the planet, destroying ecology and resources, endless conflicts and wars, so as to bring human civilization in line with sustainable development and good morality to the relevant planet. Of course, if life exists on other planets, it may also be necessary to understand any non-human civilization we might encounter and create a way to live in harmony and develop together with them. Alien life may be more advanced and powerful than human beings on the earth, therefore the Global Civilization must also accommodate Interstellar Civilization adapted to the sustainable development of human beings (see Figure 5.1).

In discussing interstellar civilization, first of all, the idea of space colonization is undesirable. When Europeans discovered and immigrated to the American continent, less-developed regions, and specifically Africa, had become colonies of the West. Because the development of the new continent required much labor, a large number of black people were transported to America and became the slaves of Western colonists, who transplanted the barbaric custom of slavery when developing the New World, and moreover slaughtered or drove away many of the indigenous natives. Secondly, we must guard against the militarization of the sky. Third we should not regard other planets as potential refuges for traditional human beings after being defeated in the battle over human–machine civilization on earth.

Instead, when human beings are really scattered on various habitable planets in space they should build beautiful homes surrounded by blue sky, white clouds, green waters, and mountains, where all kinds of residents live in harmony and peace. We must not carry the warped values of Industrial Civilization to other planets.

Today, industrial civilization is still at its peak and is the mainstream of the contemporary civilization. If human beings who have not completed the transformation of civilization set out to populate other planets, the drawbacks of industrial civilization will go with them. These include the struggle to obtain absolute domination over nature and behavior patterns such as the unrestricted pursuit of material desires, advocating lifestyle of high consumption and high waste, perpetuate the ideological confrontation between East and West and the great disparity between the development of the North and the South. If we "clone" or even "popularize" these models for human failure on earth to other planets, then human beings will destroy other planets one by one, just as we destroy the natural environment of the earth. In this sense, developing space technology alone is not enough to prepare human beings to migrate from our home planet. The world needs to establish a complete legal system for space management. It can be seen that promoting the transformation of Industrial Civilization is an important prerequisite for the creation of Interstellar Civilization.

## *Also worth thinking about*

### Why is research on human social evolution either ignored or less keenly pursued than research on human evolution as a physical being?

The reason is that current research on human evolution is still a continuation of Western concepts of modernization, guided by the idea that science is omnipotent, and encouraged and supported by a free economy and market centered on money and capital. In this context, no wonder it appears so tempting to make ourselves immortal and prolong life indefinitely. But this opportunity would not be available to everyone. Only the super-rich (who together account for no more than 1 per cent of the global population while controlling 45 per cent of global wealth[51]) could afford this.

Obviously, to approach human evolution from the angle of perfecting physical individuals (the so-called "natural persons") is much simpler, than attempting to study and perfect human nature and promote the progress of civilization.

The former only requires sufficient time and capital investment, and already we can see, in embryonic form, results from the laboratory (even if it's a monster, because genetic engineering can also create humans with gills or humans with wings to fly), while the realization of the latter will demand a long and tough process, as well as cooperation and practice by several generations—perhaps even dozens of generations. The only laboratory for such research is human society across the entire Earth, and the researchers will have to contend with widespread ignorance, nearsightedness, and indifference of many, including some within social science circles (not to mention the resistance likely to be encountered from ordinary citizens in many societies who only wish to live out their lives in relative peace and comfort and care very little about what becomes of humanity in "the future"). Of course, it is also imprudent for people to simply leave complex problems to the social sciences. In short, such research demands an unparalleled risk and ambition compared with that of the former.

It will demand constant effort to improve the social nature of human beings. This will involve a sustained struggle to purify and expand human kindness and positive energy not only in the present generation but from succeeding generations for hundreds or even thousands of years. It also requires continuously creating and promoting the progress of human civilization, choosing a more advanced and healthy mode of existence and a new environment for living, which will eventually compel every society on Earth to adapt to a sustainable pattern of survival and development—creating a unified Global Civilization. These are the two major themes of human evolution at the social-humanistic level.

### The significance of Global Civilization

It is worth considering how the transition to the Global Civilization might occur. First, it would differ from the so-called "singularity", which Kurzweil and others have predicted for some definite "point" in the near future. By contrast the Global Civilization will necessarily involve a progressive and subtle process, likely to take place over hundreds of years. Second, the Global Civilization will differ from all the civilizations that have existed in the past.

The historian Arnold Toynbee explained in his famous work *A Study of History* (9 vols, 1934–61) that from ancient to modern times there have been a total of 28 civilizations in the world.[52] These include ancient Greek, Iranian, the ancient civilizations of India, ancient Chinese Civilization, Babylonian, Egyptian, etc. (altogether covering some 6,000 years of human history). In his *The Decline of the West* (2 vols, 1917, 1924), German historian Oswald Spengler counted only eight advanced civilizations in history, including Egypt, India, Babylon, China, classical Greece and Rome, Islam and Zoroastrianism, Mexico, and Western (modern) civilization.[53] Russian historian Nikolai Danilevsky thought that there had been ten distinct culture types in the course of human history,[54] including the Egyptian or Hamitic type, Chinese, Chaldean, Indian, Persian, Hebrew, Greek, Roman. Germanic, and Peruvian. Wenrong Liu, a Chinese historian, believes that the 35,000-year history of human civilization can be divided into five periods: prehistoric, ancient, middle ancient, modern, and contemporary.[55]

Although most of these civilizations have a long history, they have made special and indelible contributions to the progress of human civilization. Moreover, according to their size, cultural genes, etc., their "lifespan" and scope of influence are also different. For example, the Chinese civilization has never stopped for over 5,000 years. It has become a rare survivor in ancient human culture and will keep growing endlessly. However, those affected only a relatively small portion of Earth's total landmass and population, and involve various civilizations based on different eras, histories, regions, and groups of people.

Since the Global Civilization we are exploring in this book is dubbed "Global", it will be a common civilization shared by every country, region, clan, and nationality—thus far more pervasive than previous civilizations. After entering the twenty-first century, we realize that the arrival of such an era of new round globalization is irreversible: humans who share one planet must create a more advanced civilization, one in which all human beings on the Earth jointly form a single global family.

Global Civilization advocates warn however that the cultural, ethnic, and individual differences among nations will not simply vanish over time due to assimilation. Instead, the Global Civilization will need to integrate, tolerate and "sublate" (develop what is useful or healthy and discard what is not) all existing cultures. Assimilation is a dead-end because it desensitizes minds and makes humans less adaptable. Culture, as a human lifestyle, should be rich and varied, so that human society retains its vitality, which is also one of the standards by which we judge our individual quality of life.

## Global Civilization and the community of human destiny

In today's world, there exist many divergences and antagonisms among different national interests, religious beliefs, ideologies, and social systems. But despite this fact, because we are living on the same planet, humanity is rapidly becoming one global community with an inseparable destiny. Human beings are also facing a large number of common challenges beyond national boundaries and need solutions beyond national boundaries. This growing trend requires that nation-states with different faiths and systems must learn to live together in peace, have orderly competition, place common interests before divergences and antagonisms, and act together to rationally choose the future of the world,[56] so that we can survive and enter jointly into the era of Global Civilization.

Our challenge then, in the context of economic globalization, world multi-polarization, cultural diversity, and social informatization, is how to promote the solidarity of each country and work together towards a better tomorrow.[57]

We must carefully address the relationship between global governance and the internal governance of each country, as human beings living on the same earth, we should set up global values to establish the principle of common life.

With this goal in mind, China has put forward the new concept of a "community of human destiny". This idea transcends the boundaries of nation, race, culture, and ideology, and provides a new perspective for thinking about the future of mankind. It insists that all countries be judged as equal regardless of size, strength, and wealth and that they all share equal rights to dignity, development, and security; the civilizations of different regions and nationalities are more colorful through exchanges and mutual learning. Furthermore, all nations share equal responsibility to safeguard international fairness and justice, respecting the sovereignty, independence, and territorial integrity of every nation, and the rights of all peoples to freely choose their preferred social system and development path. In dealing with international relations and global affairs, we should oppose hegemony, imposing one nation's will on others, interference in other countries' internal affairs and bullying, and together build a world of permanent peace and prosperity. Of course, in order to form this new community, we must first promote the institutional innovation of a global system of political rules, so that the enlightened views of the human community gradually replace the "jungle law" of old world politics.

In such a community, global governance needs to adhere to the principle that all involved parties should jointly participate in negotiation and construction, and that the achievements of governance should be justly shared by all participants. This means that sustainable global governance must be based on the idea of "jointly negotiating, building and sharing",[58] so as to facilitate the construction of new international relations.

From the perspective of the development process, the creation of a community of human destiny can be divided into three stages: first, the interests community, then the community of responsibility, and finally the destiny community. Sharing benefits and assuming responsibility are the foundation for building the destiny community, while the destiny community is the combination and sublimation of the interests community and the community of responsibility.[59] This is a "global outlook" that transcends nation-states and ideology. This is also the Chinese plan for relevant international order and reform of the international system.

It can be said that the concept of a "community of human destiny" is to realize the values of seeking common ground while reserving differences and promoting progress for all toward global civilization, while global civilization is the Macrosoft environment for realizing the community of human destiny.

However, I think the Global Civilization I describe in this book may not be the ultimate ideal goal or social system for human society. The Global Civilization we envision and strive to create will be a first step towards the Great Civilization to come, which will ultimately be characterized by moral goodness in a harmonious universe.

## NOTES

1. Cenet.org (2014), "Is 'progress' good for mankind?", *EFN*, 28 October, http://economics.cenet.org.cn/show-2038-64766-1.html. Accessed 10 May 2016.
2. Baidu.com (2020), "What kind of civilization is ecological civilization?" *Baidu*, 11 June, https://zhidao.baidu.com/question/1246073594019235419.html. Accessed 5 November 2021.
3. Ifeng.com (2014), "The dilemma of pollution control in Dianchi Lake: It is difficult to restore the old appearance although more than $9.7 billion USD has been invested for pollution control over 20 years", *Xinmin Net*, 19 May, http://finance.ifeng.com/a/20140519/12362482_0.shtml. Accessed 15 August 2018.
4. Baidu.com (2015), "Industrial Civilization", *Baidu*, 21 November, https://baike.baidu.com/item/%E5%B7%A5%E4%B8%9A%E6%96%87%E6%98%8E/6752164?fr=aladdin#1. Accessed 30 October 2016.

5. Dongbo, Cao (2015), "Mass production—Mass consumption: The formation of modern economic growth mania", *Book118*, 10 November, https://max.book118.com/html/2015/1110/29037229.shtm. Accessed 4 August 2017.
6. Gongyao, Zhang (2011), "The opposition between man and nature has a long history", *Doc88*, 22 November, http://www.doc88.com/p-8899227701086.html. Accessed 4 March 2016.
7. Lieyunwang.com (2015), "Biohacking technology: Let the human body have infinite possibilities", *Lieyunwang*, 6 May, https://www.lieyunwang.com/archives/84478. Accessed 5 November 2016.
8. Nicholas, Carr (2018), *Utopia is Creepy: And Other Provocations* (trans. Zhongwei Jiang), Beijing: China Citic Press.
9. Baidu.com (2007), "Human sociality", *Baidu Library*, 23 April, http://wenku.baidu.com/view/812f988d680203d8ce2f24c9.html?from=search. Accessed 4 November 2011.
10. Carl, Zimmer (2011), "Steven Pinker: If you wish for peace, you must first understand psychology", *Science Human*, 20 December 2011, http://www.guokr.com/article/80943/. Extract of "Human nature's pathologist" from *The New York Times*, 28 November 2011. Accessed 6 June 2015.
11. Baidu.com (2019), "Is there room for human evolution? Scientists put forward seven conjectures, which one do you agree with?". *Baidu*, 1 December, https://baijiahao.baidu.com/s?id=1651701139185554584&wfr=spider&for=pc. Accessed 30 May 2020.
12. (2008), "What is the future civilization?", *Reference News* 31 August.
13. Chaoxia, Yang (2011), "An era of environmental rights concerning ecological civilization", *Environmental Economy*, 11.
14. Civilization (2019), "*Baidu*", 19 December, https://baike.baidu.com/item/%E6%96%87%E6%98%8E/392?fr=aladdin. Accessed 30 June 2020.
15. 'Zhouying, Jin (2013), "What kind of future do we need?—Reflections from China", *World Future 2013 Conference*, Chicago, IL, July 2021.
16. Pengpeng, Zhou (2015), *The Book of Changes*, Beijing: Beijing Joint Publishing Company.
17. Keli, Fang and Cunguang, Lin (2012), "The rational view of the Chinese nation on civilization", *Chinese Social Science Today*, 15 Febraury.
18. People.com (2016), "Civilization with restraint: The essence of Chinese civilization", *People.cn*, 7 November, http://culture.people.com.cn/n1/2016/1107/c22219-28839504.html. Accessed 2 June 2018.
19. Keli, Fang (2003), "The unity of heaven & man and ecological wisdom of ancient China", *Social Science Front*, 4.
20. Sheng, Dai (2016), *The Book of Rites*, Beijing: Zhonghua Book Company.
21. Lao Tzu (2011), *Tao Te Ching*, Beijing: New World Press, Chapter 67.
22. Lao Tzu (2011), *Tao Te Ching*, Beijing: New World Press, Chapters 46 and 51.
23. Lao Tzu (2011), *Tao Te Ching*, Beijing: New World Press, Chapter 13.
24. Lao Tzu (2011), *Tao Te Ching*, Beijing: New World Press, Chapter 8.

25. Songqin, Shen (2014), *The New Translation of Fan Zhongyan Anthology*, Taipei: Sanmin Book Company–(quote originally from *Memorandum of Yueyang Tower* by Zhongyan Fan [Song Dynasty]).
26. Yanwu, Gu (2013), *Annotation of the Explanation of Daily Understanding* (annot. Yuan Chen), Anhui: Anhui University Press.
27. Sheng, Dai (2016), *The Book of Rites*, Beijing: Zhonghua Book Company, the chapter on the "Conveyance of Rituals".
28. In a narrow sense, logic refers to both the law of thinking and the discipline that studies the law of thinking, that is, logic. In a broad sense, logic refers to laws, including laws of thinking and objective laws.
29. Baidu.com (2019), "Political civilization", *Baidu*, 07 March, http://baike.baidu.com/view/60010.htm.Accessed 10 October 2019.
30. Francis, Fukuyama (2015), "Democracy is still the end of history", *Reference News Online*, 6 January, http://column.cankaoxiaoxi.com/2015/0106/619750.shtml. Extract of a news report from *Nihon Keizai Shimbun*, 4 January 2015. Accessed 8 October 2016.
31. Former state president Jintao Hu made the first official report of the 18th National Congress of the Communist Party of China on 8 November 2012.
32. Guanghua, Fang (2015), "Destiny community highlights the essence of Chinese culture", *Chinese Social Sciences Today*, 19 November.
33. Zhongshu, Dong (2011), *Luxuriant Dew of the Spring and Autumn Annals,* Beijing: Zhonghua Book Company.
34. Sheng, Dai (2016), *The Book of Rites*, Beijing: Zhonghua Book Company.
35. Xianglong, Zhang (2015), *The Book of History* , Beijing: SDX Joint Publishing Company, the chapter on "Canon of Yao".
36. Xiaofen, Chen (2016), *The Analects of Confucius* , Beijing: Zhonghua Book Company, the chapter of Zilu—A student of Confucius.
37. Qian, Gu (2016), *The Book of History* , Beijing: Zhonghua Book Company.
38. Xiozhou, Mai (2012), "A Reborn of Lao Tzu", Beijing: Academy Press.
39. Yinchi, Chen (2016), *Inaction and Ease: Six Chapters of Zhuangzi*, Beijing: Zhonghua Book Company.
40. (2016), *The Analects of Confucius*, Beijing: Zhonghua Book Company.
41. (2014), *Mencius*, Beijing: Chinese Overseas Chinese Publishing House, last chapter.
42. Shide, Cheng, Hongtu, Wang, and Zhaolin, Lu (eds) (1982), *Collection of Explanatory for "Plain Questions" of the Yellow Emperor's Inner Canon*, Beijing: People's Hygiene Press.
43. Zhouying, Jin ([2005] 2011), *Global Technological Change—From Hard Technology to Soft Technology*, Bristol: Intellect.
44. Zhouying, Jin ([2005] 2011), *Global Technological Change—From Hard Technology to Soft Technology*, Bristol: Intellect.
45. In December 1953, the Chinese government negotiated with the Indian government on the relations between the two countries concerning Tibet. Premier Enlai Zhou put forward

the Five Principles of Peaceful Coexistence for the first time when he met with the Indian delegation.

46. Lao Tzu (2011), *Tao Te Ching*, Beijing: New World Press, Chapter 25.
47. Zhongshu, Dong (2011), *Luxuriant Dew of the Spring and Autumn Annals,* Beijing: Zhonghua Book Company.
48. Keli, Fang (2003), "The unity of heaven & man and ecological wisdom of ancient China", *Social Science Front*, 4.
49. People.com (2019), "Viewing the development of 'artificial meat' from the perspective of patents", *People's Daily Online*, 29 August, http://ip.people.com.cn/n1/2019/0829/c179663-31324939.html. Accessed 15 November 2019.
50. Qq.com (2019), "Israel suddenly announced that it had planted the world's first 'cell growing Steak'", *Tencent*, 21 July, https://new.qq.com/omn/20190721/20190721A03XGJ00.html. Accessed 15 November 2019.
51. Qq.com (2019), "Global Wealth Report 2019", *Tencent*, 30 October, https://xw.qq.com/amphtml/20191030A0IKIC00. Accessed 15 January 2020.
52. Arnold Joseph, Toynbee (2010), *A Study of History* (trans. Xiaolin Guo et al.), Shanghai: Shanghai People's Publishing House,.
53. Oswald, Spengler (1963), *The Decline of the West* (trans. Shirong Qi et al.), Beijing: Commercial Press, p. 125.
54. "Nikolay, Danilevsky", *Wikipedia*, 23 December 2017, http://en.wikipedia.org/wiki/Nikolai_Danilevsky.
55. Wenrong, Liu (2005), *The Heritage of Human Civilization*, Shanghai: Wenhui Press.
56. Jiping, Guo (2015), "Promising a better future for the world—On the human destinies community", *People's Daily Online*, 18 May, http://cpc.people.com.cn/pinglun/n/2015/0518/c78779-27016301.html. Accessed 15 January 2020.
57. Yi, Wang (2016), "Work together to create a human destiny community", *People's Daily*, 31 May.
58. 163.com (2015), "China explicitly put forward the idea of global governance for the first time", *Xinhua Net*, 14 October, http://news.163.com/15/1014/17/B5TDS9E800014JB5.html. Accessed 10 November 2019.
59. Yi, Wang (2016), "Work together to create a human destiny community", *People's Daily*, 31 May.

# 5

# The Difficult Task of Creating a "Global Civilization"

*The task of achieving a Great Civilization is neither a fantasy nor a contemporary version of Utopia.*

*The Future lies at our feet.*

As I insisted earlier, in order to thoroughly solve the challenges currently facing mankind, we must promote the transformation from Industrial Civilization. All kinds of major crises in today's world present a great risk of destroying the future for human beings. Some of these threats come from various extreme thoughts and ideologies, or the dangers posed by conflicts of interest between sovereign states. Others include possible natural disasters from climate change and environmental damage to the Earth, or the overly rapid development of science and technology. Any of these could bring about a crisis of human civilization. It is possible to claim that mankind is teetering on the brink of destruction. If we do not immediately take revolutionary measures worldwide, situations may develop too quickly to allow us to transform from Industrial Civilization gradually over the next hundred or hundreds of years. It is even possible that the world will change beyond all recognition within the next 30 years, or that traditional humans may one day be destroyed.

Now we still have a chance, but only if we take swift and practical action. We must cope with multiple crises simultaneously and struggle against many kinds of adversity on the road to creating a "Global Civilization" that incorporates the perspectives of different cultures at different development levels, that sees the world from many angles, and is able to rise above conflicting sectarian and political beliefs.

## *The transformation of civilization has a long way to go*

Human civilization existed in a primitive state for over a million years (Stone Age). Agricultural civilization lasted for some 10,000 years, and Industrial Civilization began over 300 years ago. Herman Kahn believed that the spread of Industrial Civilization throughout the world would take about 400 years. He divided this process of industrialization into three stages: the industrial society, the super-industrial society, and the post-industrial society. After the post-industrial society, Kahn believed that humans would enter another great era in history (but he did not specify exactly what this "great era" would be like). Post-industrial society appeared first in the developed capitalist countries around the beginning of the twenty-first century and has since expanded all over the world. This transition process could take another 150 years to run its course.

I agree that Industrial Civilization will continue, but unless we adopt global revolutionary measures very soon, I doubt if "another great era" will succeed it. This is because of the following reasons:

### The global dominance of Industrial Civilization continues

We have stated that industrial civilization is unsustainable (see Chapter 4 above). Unfortunately, Industrial Civilization will continue. It is just as Honor é de Balzac said: "Civilization, like the car of Juggernaut, continues on her course triumphant." There are four main reasons for this:

1. The needs of developing countries. Since the First Industrial Revolution took place in Britain, there have existed two major kinds of civilization: Industrial Civilization and Agricultural Civilization. Of course, there are many intermediate transition zones, because the degree of industrialization differs in different countries. Some have reached a high stage of industrialization, others are still in the early stages, and many have not even begun to industrialize. The "modernization" process was spread throughout the world by Industrial Civilization as an irreversible global trend. As a result, achieving high economic growth in developing countries was accepted as the best way towards modernization, and it was believed that every society that modernized successfully would likely find its own road to industrialization. While each country would experience a different course and period of transition towards industrialization, before they finally reached "the post-industrial society". The first wave of industrialization involved what are now called the developed countries, the second wave included the Four Little Dragons (Hong Kong, Singapore, South Korea, and Taiwan), the third wave covered China, India, Brazil, and other BRIC countries, and the fourth wave has begun to affect the countries in Africa and other areas.
2. The enormous inertia of Western Industrial Civilization is likely to continue for quite some time.

3. Since it is a world trend, ecological civilization should be expected to emerge first in developed countries, because the ecological crisis first broke out there. But powerful technologies and extensive investment have enabled some nations in the West to mitigate their ecological crises, and to shift the most serious ecological costs onto underdeveloped regions. This has contributed to the prolongation of Industrial Civilization.
4. The advent of the post-industrial era and the recycling economy for which people yearn cannot occur spontaneously and must be the result of a thorough transformation from Industrial Civilization. The transition of civilization will require changes in social, political, and economic systems. Yet institutional rigidity and the difficulty of effecting institutional change will necessarily limit the speed with which human social systems are able to progress, thus further increasing the difficulty of transforming civilization.

The challenge is how to shorten the transition period between Industrial Civilization and Global Civilization, so as to make the next 50–100 hundred years a period of both transitions away from Industrial Civilization, and the start-up of Global Civilization.

### We are in a stage of transition between old and new civilizations

To realize Global Civilization will mark the first time in history that humans have consciously attempted to transform an existing civilization. But industrial Civilization is full of temptations to pursue individual profit, so to change its culture, values, and the direction of technological innovation and institutions in significant ways, we must strive to create a new material, spiritual and political civilization, as well as ecological civilization and interstellar civilization that have never been attained before.

After studying the past 64 centuries of history and noting the great transformation of world civilization from 4400 BCE to 2000 CE, political theorist Misao Murayama, known for his "Theory of Civilizations (1986)", considered that civilization on Earth can be broadly divided into periods alternately dominated by Eastern and Western values, which repeat in a roughly 800-year cycle. Western civilization is based on material supremacy and the theory of scientific omnipotence. According to Murayama, the period from CE 2000 to 2800 will be one that perfects Western civilization and supplements its defects, while traditional Oriental civilization, which has always attached great importance to spiritual and ethical values, will rejuvenate. It will be a highly civilized era that will combine elements of both Eastern and Western civilizations. Murayama expects that the 100 years from 1975 to 2075 will be a period of alternating Eastern and Western values, but that it will also witness the emergence of a new civilization (although, like Herman Kahn, he does not elaborate what the new civilization will be like).

Whether from the perspective of civilization cycle theory, or the continued strong momentum of Industrial Civilization, or from the angle of the arduous tasks required creating an advanced civilization, today is just the first stage of a long transition period. It could take hundreds of years to truly achieve a "Global Civilization" era, because escaping from the crises of Industrial Civilization is not a purely natural course for humans.

It will not be easy for humanity to alter views that it has grown accustomed to over hundreds of years. Each new form of civilization builds on that which came before (developing that which is useful or healthy and discarding that which is not) from the former civilization. Take ecological civilization as an example. To succeed, it must discard many aspects of today's dominant Industrial Civilization and adopt others at the same time. Moreover, the brilliant science and technology created by the era of Industrial Civilization and its lasting artistic achievements must be fully affirmed and inherited.

Further, even if the cognitive problem is solved, there are other serious challenges that involve changing practice. For example, can we preserve today's material affluence while actively pursuing a "civilization with restraint"? How can we put into effect the criteria of a future spiritual and political civilization?

### Debates on perpetual peace

Without peace and stability, a sustainable future cannot be realized. Although today's world alters from day to day and the international situation is constantly changing, the notion of the nation-state as the most basic actor in the world remains largely unchallenged. Since ancient times wars between countries or regions have never stopped. In some areas, wars are actually the normal state, and peace is only temporary. War is the most brutal and the least efficient means of settling conflicts. War is the most devastating of all human catastrophes, and at the current pace of scientific and technological development, the destructiveness of war is certain to increase exponentially.

More civilians die in modern war than soldiers, and more innocent people are killed than guilty ones. According to some estimates, up to 80–90 per cent of the dead in modern wars are civilians because of battles, massacres, famine, pestilence, and genocide. What is more serious is that the flow of refugees resulting from the chaos caused by the war has greatly complicated efforts to attain development and stability in the affected countries and regions. (In the Iraq War, nearly 4500 American soldiers died, but the casualties among Iraqi soldiers were over 100,000, and the World Health Organization has estimated the number of civilians killed in Iraq at between 104,000 and 223,000. This war also left millions of people destitute and homeless. The Syrian war in the past ten years resulted in nearly 400,000 deaths, of which more than 100,000 were civilians; about 1.5 million more were injured and 11 million (more than half of the country's population) were displaced and fled to Europe.

In this context, generally there are two entirely different views: one is that humans have sufficient wisdom and ability to create a world with perpetual peace, another is that wars stimulate human development and ultimately lead to a more peaceful world. If there is no war, such critics assert, humanity will be unable to progress.

## 1. The inevitability of war

Whether it is due to having no choice in reality, or a frenzy of war, or a sober prediction for today's world, the idea of fighting a war remains relatively popular. For example, George Friedman predicted in his book *The Next 100 Years* (2009) that a world war would break out by 2050, which will not be limited to land, sea, and air, but will be carried into outer space. He believes this war will enable the United States to usher in a second golden age. In Friedman's view, war is actually the basis for future American prosperity. Thus, in the name of national interest, any act of aggression becomes righteous: resource plunder, "the export of civilization", the struggle for power and influence until the war itself becomes unavoidable. The difference is merely one of scale, objectives, and weapons used. In his new book *War! What Is It Good For?* (2014), British historian Ian Morris argues that war has made the world safer, and will lead to a better society in the long run as violence is reduced. He believes that if there is no war, human beings will not be able to make progress.

American mathematician Aaron Clauset gives an opinion through a calculation that the deadline for the outbreak of the Second World War will be not later than 2150. And moreover, Lawrence Freedman, who is reputed to have been studying war all his life, condemned war by analyzing various types of wars that have evolved over the centuries in his book "*The Future of War: A History*". Finally he believes that war will never really end, and warns against the illusion that war can be eliminated.

Ukrainian scientist Michael Zgurovsky, who has studied war and its destructiveness throughout the world since 705 BCE, warns that according to current trends, war will reach a peak in the 2050s and begin to decrease only after 2080.

According to a recent online survey, only 21 per cent of people who were asked "Can the world be peaceful?" answered "yes," while 79 per cent answered "no". Despite the small number of participants, this survey probably reflects the sentiments of people generally. Yet we should thank the 21 per cent of participants because they keep hope for a peaceful future alive.

The reasons given for answering "no" included the belief that in a world where the rampant desire for power, social polarization and individual egoism predominate, any attempt to resolve conflict will be accompanied by violence and war. Obviously, if left unchecked, the current turmoil in the world cannot resolve itself, and lasting world peace will remain unattainable.

Looking forward to the future, I believe that more and more intelligent human beings should, must, and can solve contradictions and conflicts by non-war methods. Of course, this is much more complicated than war. So what can people do today to help reduce the likelihood of future war?

## 2. Perpetual peace and its challenges

The yearning for peace is as old as human history itself, and since the German philosopher Immanuel Kant put forward his argument on "perpetual peace" in 1795, debates about perpetual peace have never stopped. Kant called the pursuit of perpetual peace the highest rational goal, as well as a moral obligation. But he considered perpetual peace strictly from the standpoint of national sovereignty and argued that such sovereignty was the true foundation for peace. The sovereignty and dignity of each country, he believed, should be adequately safeguarded and respected. Therefore, Kant proposed six prerequisite clauses that should apply to any treaty to assure perpetual peace and argued that three conditions must be met: republican government, an alliance of free nations and respect for the rights of world citizens.

Two centuries later, another German philosopher, Jürgen Habermas, pointed out that the worldwide trend towards globalization made national sovereignty as the basis for world peace problematic. In his essay "Kant's idea of perpetual peace", he discusses perpetual peace beyond national sovereignty, emphasizing that respect for individual human rights needs to break through the limitations of national sovereignty.

The contemporary American philosopher John Rawls advocates establishing a constitutional liberal democracy based on the various principles of what he calls "The Law of Peoples." He believes that starting with the people who constitute the main body of a country—namely those whose beliefs and behavior ensure adequate and reasonable freedom for all—confrontations and conflicts caused by race, religion, culture and so on can be eliminated. Therefore, he has proposed the concept of a "Permanent Peace Alliance."

The above theoretical framework is extremely valuable, but it is still far from actual implementation. Indeed, peace-loving people in the world have never stopped their efforts to realize world peace. For instance, peace conferences were held at The Hague in 1899 and again in 1907. The establishment of the United Nations was a great initiative, and during the 75 years since 1945, the United Nations, as the most representative international organization, has played a central role in safeguarding world peace, promoting economic development and humanitarian relief and fostering solutions to global problems.

After the Second World War, the rise of the Cold War threatened people's hopes for a peaceful life. A number of international organizations and some eminent persons initiated and convened the World Congress in Defense of Peace, through which they promoted a policy against aggression and war and argued for the unconditional prohibition of nuclear weapons and all other weapons of mass destruction. The First World Congress of the Partisans of Peace, held simultaneously in Paris and Prague in April 1949, was attended by more than 2,000 delegates from 72 countries, and adopted a "Declaration" and "Announcement to the Whole World." The second Congress of the Partisans of Peace was held in November 1950 in Warsaw, and the third, which took place in December 1952 in Vienna (as the Peoples' Congress for Peace), was attended by 1904 delegates from 85 countries, to seek an effective way to defend peace. The World Assembly for Peace held in June 1955 in Helsinki was attended by 1,851 delegates from 68 countries and regions, and adopted the "Declaration of the World Assembly for Peace."

In their 2005 position paper on the United Nations reforms in the section on "War and Conflict", the government of the People's Republic of China proposed that interstate conflict should be addressed through peaceful negotiation and consultation in accordance with the UN Charter and international law. Recognizing that internal conflicts are complex, their paper further stated that resolution should mainly rely on the efforts of the people within a country, and that any external intervention should be in compliance with the UN Charter and international law and should combine political and diplomatic measures with a prudent and responsible attitude that would encourage and facilitate the resolution of problems through consultation and negotiation between all the conflicting parties. The first World Peace Forum organized by China was held in July 2012 in Beijing, with the theme "Win-Win for All: Peace, Security, Cooperation." A second annual forum was held in June 2013, also in Beijing, and its theme was "International Security in a Changing World: Peace, Development, Innovation", and nearly 500 experts and scholars from over 80 countries plus many foreign diplomats attended the opening ceremony. The Third World Peace Forum was held in June 2014 in Beijing, and its theme was "The Pursuit of Common Security: Peace, Mutual Trust and Responsibility." The Fourth World Peace Forum, with the theme "Overcoming Difficulties: Understanding, Consultation, and Reciprocity" was held in June 2015 in Beijing. Yuanchao Li, Vice President of China, pointed out in his speech for this occasion that in today's world, countries have increasingly similar interests and challenges in the quest for development and better governance. He proposed that we should work together to build a community for world peace and security in the spirit of understanding, consultation and reciprocity.

It is even more gratifying to note that scholars and the media, which have often in the past paved the way for war, have come increasingly to reveal "media lies" and even cited "five principles of deceptive propaganda on war". This makes it easier for the Western public to understand how mainstream public opinion can be manipulated to support or oppose a specific war.

All these efforts have been aimed at strengthening the solidarity and friendship among peace-loving people in the world, opposing war, defending world peace, promoting peaceful development and expanding the influence of peaceful forces in the world.

However, the results have been disappointing. Although the main purpose of the United Nations is to create and maintain world peace, respect human rights and improve human well-being, due to various reasons, it has not fully realized its purpose. During the twentieth century, humans experienced alternating periods of peace and brutal war, accelerated development and retrogression, as well as repeating the cycle of creation and destruction that has characterized the history of human civilization for thousands of years. But human beings have still not learned the lessons of two world wars. Large and medium-sized wars occur repeatedly, such as in Korea, Vietnam, India and Pakistan, the Middle East, Afghanistan, the Falklands, the Persian Gulf region, Central Africa and the Baltic States, while small-sized wars or armed conflicts have been even more frequent.

Even after entering the twenty-first century, the overall level of human violence has not declined, starting with the 9/11 terrorist attacks, to the wars in Iraq, Libya, Syria, Ukraine, and most recently, the rise of "the Islamic State". Regional wars and heinous terrorist attacks appear alternately, Support for a "nuclear-free world" is gaining little ground, and the potential for devastating warfare remains high. World politics increasingly seems to be out of control.

The outlook for the future is not bright. Along with the scarcity of resources, fierce competition for the resources that remain continues unabated on land, in the ocean, in the polar regions and out into space. Moreover, this competition is spreading from tangible resources (e.g., land water, minerals, etc.) to intangible ones (such as IP addresses, orbital paths for satellites, radio frequencies and global allocation of carbon emission permits), and is becoming increasingly intense.

### 3. Can civilized human beings control themselves and live harmoniously on one planet?

From what has been discussed in the previous chapters, we understand that realizing the transition from Industrial Civilization to Global Civilization is the fundamental basis for achieving perpetual peace. But must we simply wait and attempt nothing until the entire structure of Global Civilization is fully in place? Nicholas Spencer, a scholar of Sierra Leone, believes that human beings have enough wisdom to prevent the next war, and urges all humans to learn the following lessons from the twentieth century's two world wars: (1) dangerous ideology should not be encouraged; (2) efforts to expand the territory of imperialism or to strengthen its influence are ultimately self-defeating; (3) the benefits of seeking collective security and international cooperation are far greater than those of forming an alliance to promote aggression; (4) every country, no matter how big or small, should respect the sovereignty and territorial integrity of others; (5) citizens should not allow their government to declare war; and (6) it is not advisable to fight fire with fire.

Social scientist, Peilin Li has suggested: (1) peace-loving people in the world should unite to promote democratization, greater rule of law and the rationalization of international relations, and seek to build a fair and equitable new international order; (2) we must maintain regular and effective communication among countries with conflicts of interest, so as to resolve international disputes through peaceful means; (3) people jointly build a positive international political culture and participate more in global governance by adhering to sovereign equality, promoting common security, common development, win–win cooperation, mutual tolerance, etc.; and (4) that more be done to promote national peace education in all countries to form a powerful force of public opinion to prevent war.

These are all good suggestions and aspirations; however, the key is how to put the above proposals into action. In fact, there are new features and new trends in contemporary conflicts and wars worldwide, namely, both the type of war and the cause of war or conflict are very different, especially as non-traditional security threats become more and more prominent. In addition, terrorism now constitutes a new and dangerous form of war, particularly when one considers the possibility of terrorists using WMDs. Ending terrorism may require solutions very different from the elimination of conventional war. Obviously, our original ideas, principles and norms (such as the principle of sovereignty and non-interference in each other's internal affairs) have not been enough, and even the role of the United Nations has been seriously challenged. Kant believed that peace was built on the basis of public reason, but in reality, it goes without saying that people's peaceful reason will be distorted by extreme nationalism, the deceptive propaganda of rulers and other factors. Even among world-class elites and for most countries' leaders, their worldviews and values remain locked in the logic of the Industrial Civilization.

In order to cope with new threats and challenges, we first need new ideas, principles, and norms, so as to make a reasonable argument for the concept of perpetual world peace and propose a road map to achieve it, no matter how long it takes. We also need to clarify the nature and origin of war and conflict caused by non-traditional security threats, including those that made use of various kinds of extremism and terrorism.

Second, cooperation between countries and among international organizations is still at the center of the international arena. Countries must work more closely to prevent conflict and preserve peace, while incorporating peaceful actions by non-state actors more often to secure rapid development.

Third, the United Nations reform must make the maintenance of world peace and security a top priority. Xintian Yu, an expert on international issues, suggested that: (1) the UN Security Council should rely on elite think tanks worldwide to carry out a study of current and future conflicts (both open wars as well as long-term threats) to gradually reach some consensus; (2) the United Nations should pay more attention to negotiations with the leading powers, while these leading powers should give greater emphasis to coordinating their policies with the multilateral framework of the United Nations; (3) the United Nations should further integrate its plans for preventing conflicts and promoting development, so as to address both the manifestations and root causes of war and civil unrest; (4) the United Nations needs to vigorously promote understanding between different civilizations, cultures, religions, and nations so that the concept of cultural diversity can become deeply rooted in the hearts of all people.

The worldwide spread of the COVID-19 virus in 2020 demands that the UN, the most important international organization with 193 Member countries, must carry out a thorough reform of its purpose, organizational principles, and mode of operation mode.

Finally, I propose the establishment of a World Peace Alliance (WPA). In view of the currently limited role and authority of the United Nations regarding issues of world peace and global security, peace-loving people around the world need to devote themselves to the cause of world peace, regardless of their ethnicities, national boundaries, and faiths, and should join hands to set up the WPA—a global civilian standing body. It has proven not to be enough to only rely on convening general assembly meetings and issuing declarations, nor to depend exclusively on politicians or governments to lead a global campaign against war and terrorism.

As a social organization of global citizens in the new era, the WPA's activities will include conducting independent research (without any interference from government organizations): (1) to explore the main causes of modern warfare, conflict, and terrorism. Only by finding the deep-seated causes of a different war, can the hidden dangers of its outbreak be eliminated; (2) for the different causes of war, they could propose long-term strategies and current policy solutions; (3) they can also specifically expose and criticize situations and policies that foment war and terrorism, endangering world peace; (4) focusing on the common interests of all countries, we should study how to transcend outdated social systems and beliefs, promote unity and cooperation to solve the common challenges facing mankind, and establish mechanisms for early warning and mutual aid.

The significance of establishing this organization is that:

First, the WPA will supervise, assist, and support the functions of the United Nations in maintaining world peace and security. Second, it will provide a way to avoid the interference of various interest groups and unite the peace-loving forces of the world effectively against the war in all its forms, as well as to oppose, avoid, and reduce extremism of all kinds, including acts of extreme nationalism and terrorism. Third, the WPA can harness the positive energy of global civil society and promote politicians that support peace, thus making public political participation more active and effective. Fourth, through media and publications, the WPA can do much to educate the global public, build confidence in the possibility of world peace, and encourage peaceful reason among the masses of ordinary people everywhere, no matter what their local government may be—including even people living in areas controlled or threatened by terrorist groups.

We need to recognize that cooperation and communication are both powerful tools for preserving world peace. No doubt each country has different interests, but if we earnestly seek common values, we can unite to maintain world peace for the long-term future and thus sustain human existence and advance development for everyone on Earth.

We must not allow the interests of any single country or group to move the world closer to war, even under the guise of "defending the weak, promoting democracy, or expressing humanitarianism," nor allow the spread of pessimism, despair, and inaction. We must make the world fully understand that the conflicting beliefs and causes that lead to war are to be considered in the same way that we now think of earthquakes, typhoons, floods and, fires—namely, as great natural disasters—but in this case made by humans, and therefore avoidable by the timely application of reason and planning. In short, we must make avoiding war a sacred mission.

We discussed how hard it will be to comprehensively transform civilization in view of the continued strong trend of Industrial Civilization to prolong the phase of transition between the value systems of old and new civilizations, and the widespread doubt shared by many people today about the possibility of perpetual peace.

In fact, in addition to the transformation of civilization paradigm discussed in this chapter, the comprehensive transformation of civilization also needs the transformation of other paradigms as the basis. For example, the paradigm shift of Technology (see Chapter 3, related "from hard technology to soft technology"), the paradigm shift of human survival and development (see Chapter 7, related "re understanding sustainable development"), change thinking mode (see Chapter 8, related "changing thinking mode is the premise of consensus"), and even the paradigm shift of the rise of great nations (see Chapter VII, related "China 2050: a splendid future lies ahead, but dangers still exist)

We can neither be pessimistic nor expect that it can all be accomplished in one go. Yet the road is already under our feet, and it is only necessary that we move forward one step at a time.

## *The development mode of each country can and should be unique*

Klaus Roland, World Bank country director for China, has said that "there is no single development model that works anywhere and everywhere."

In my opinion, the so-called development model here should be the road to Global Civilization and even Great Civilization based on sustainable development. Although human beings can establish this common goal, due to different conditions, the journey for each country certainly cannot be the same. In particular, before the realization of the Great Civilization, the current form of government and political parties in a given country will inevitably affect their development model. Moreover, the governance models of different countries and regions supported by different ideologies are also diverse. Therefore, every country can only create and determine its own development model according to its history, culture, and level of development. To offer an analogy, if all the countries on Earth each sent a team to climb to the top of Mount Qomolangma (i.e., Mt. Everest) starting from home, each team would have to take a different route because of their different starting points, and would also encounter different geographical, traffic, and climatic conditions. Add to this the different levels of physical strength and ability of each team member, and it is clear that for each country the way and the time required to reach the summit will be different.

However, although this truth is quite simple, modern people often find it difficult to understand or tolerate different development modes. This often makes these differences the root cause of conflicts, and even of wars.

Of course, a successful path towards development needs to constantly sum up experience and lessons, and can only become a model (including institutions) to others after multiple amendments and improvements. But, first of all, it needs to be running well in its country of origin, where people feel happy, satisfied and proud, then it will naturally attract people in other countries who long to imitate its success. In other words, it will become a model and be gradually popularized. Thus, the first measure of success is whether a country's survival and development mode come to be recognized as successful by the majority of its own citizens. With this in mind, all countries should first work to improve themselves and only then begin to concern themselves with how to help improve conditions elsewhere.

It is worth emphasizing that although the transformation of civilization is global, which helps all humanity (for just as Frederick Engels said, "the Communist revolution will be more than a revolution of one country"), different development models are needed. It will be necessary for pioneers of different development modes to create demonstration projects or prototypes (in which democracy has its own model in different countries) to promote mutual learning, through reference to various models, each of which rethinks their own social system, in order to carry out the institutional reform with the times. But these "forerunner" countries should never try to impose a "unified version" based on their so-called "advanced" culture or mode, to foist their own ideology and values off on others, or attempt to change or subvert other countries mode of existence.

Currently, there are many kinds of development models or development paths in the world. These include American style, Nordic style, German style, Japanese style, Singapore style, and various forms of integration such as that of the European Union (EU) and Association of South East Asian Nations (ASEAN) Community (announced during the 2015 ASEAN Summit). Other development models include those of the Community of Latin American and the Caribbean States including 33 member states, the African Union including 54 member states, the League of Arab States including 22 Arab member states, India, Arabia, and Russia, whose new experiment, the "Russian Dream", was interpreted symbolically at the opening ceremonies for the 2014 Winter Olympics. All of these models are currently being tested. Of course, there is also China's road under exploration.

The practices and experiments of the various development paths mentioned above are all in progress. However, whether ultimately successful or not, these multiple experiments are valuable assets that humans can study and use for reference, as they explore different models to the common goal of mankind—the path toward Global Civilization.

Various models are built on the unique culture and philosophy that accords with the local conditions and desires of the people in that region, as regulated by their existing value system. But all of these need to be continually reformed and improved.

Because times are changing, human beings are evolving, the problems we face are becoming more complicated, while the connotations of the advanced civilization to which human beings aspire also change. Any historically successful development path has been the product of its particular era, so that it must be modified, upgraded, standardized, and improved constantly as civilization advances. Only in this way can it maintain vitality forever.

For example, the ideas and the value connotation of the American Dream are clearly manifested in "The Declaration of Independence" and the Constitution of the United States. These are widely recognized as having enabled the American people over 200 years to become a true world power and today have such a tremendous impact on the world. Young people of many countries regard the United States as a place where they can realize personal ideals. This allows America to attract many outstanding talents worldwide. But now, the United States is facing many universal problems, such as social inequality, family breakdown, income disparity, the gap between social classes, social misconduct, racial prejudice, guns, drugs and violent crimes, especially due to the politics of dignitaries and the confrontation between the two parties, make it powerless. Of course these problems are not unique to the United States; In the international community, the style of "democratic assistance" promoted by the United States has often encountered failures. The gap between the values Americans assert and their actions has gradually caused the country to lose credibility, while the application of double standards, combined with their presumption of cultural superiority in dealing with matters of principle such as human rights, counterterrorism and other issues has made Americans gradually lose the moral advantage to the point where US influence has dropped significantly.

This is the issue to be vigilant for any "forerunner" country on the path to Global Civilization. Take the United States as an example, the development road of the United States, after all, is a product of the era of Industrial Civilization, and the root cause of its current problems can be traced to the developing process it has followed. The thinking mode and behavior pattern of America's leaders still follow the logic of materialism from the era of Industrial Civilization. Even in dealing with international relations, the United States appears unwilling to adapt to the new concept of globalization.

Substantial reforms must be made to keep the past glory of the United States alive. Although the United States will likely remain the dominant world power over the next 30–50 years (regardless of its GDP ranking, its advantages in its national wealth, including its superior geographical location and natural resources, education, military, population and etc. still remain, especially it occupies a world-leading position in finance and science and technology), the drawbacks evident in American culture, lifestyles, values, diplomatic policies and the path it has taken to attain international power, pose serious challenges to its long-term sustainability and to its continued role as a leader in global politics, economy, resource use and environmental stability.

Take energy consumption as an example. The United States population accounts for only 4.6 per cent of the world, yet total US greenhouse gas emissions rank second only to China whose population accounts for 19 per cent of the world. America's emissions per capita also rank the second in the world; they produce 15.1 per cent of the world's energy while consuming 21.8 per cent; the United States today boasts 779 automobiles for every 1,000 people. Clearly, this kind of economic affluence and the lifestyle it promotes are not a model that other countries can realistically hope to follow. It seems that if the United States wants to maintain sustained prosperity, its people must change their way of living and thinking, and reform in many areas.

It is worth mentioning that most developing countries have failed to learn these lessons from the United States, and have consequently had to embark on the road of "treatment after pollution". There are several reasons why China has the highest carbon dioxide emissions among all countries. First, its economic development has been extremely rapid. Second, modernization of travel has been responsible for much of the pollution; the Beijing haze, which comes largely from vehicle emissions, is one example.

Of course, many technology worshippers have argued that as long as the human mind is open to bold visions, invention, and technological innovation, any obstacle to human development can be overcome, and an increasingly luxurious lifestyle can be sustained. Even energy shortages may not be limiting. For example, once controlled nuclear fusion is successfully achieved, future humans may not have to worry about energy at all.[1] But we need to ponder a few questions: can the Living Planet withstand the demands of ever-increasing luxury? Is it possible for the world's population to assume an unlimited material abundance? We advocate changing lifestyles while promoting "civilization with restraint" (see the section of "Material civilization" in Chapter 4), not only because of the finiteness of materials and energy but also because of the complex nature of the human soul and the complexity of evolving future civilizations. Do we want it said that future human beings will live merely to seek their own pleasure and pursue enjoyment at any cost?

Therefore, China needs to learn successful experiences and lessons from the above different models and experiments. For instance, to learn from the experience of the United States about creating an innovative power; to learn from the Nordic countries about the examples of contemporary national governance including the role of government in the development of a market economy, the balanced development of economic growth and social welfare, the integration of efficiency and fairness, and the combination of competition and cooperation; to learn from the experience in Singapore about national governance experience, especially how to combine democracy with a single-party system, etc. Even more important, China must remember to analyze history relentlessly and seriously reflect and summarize the road it has followed, and then create a development mode best suited for its people as a way to attain comprehensive rejuvenation.

## *Basic principles*

We emphasize that the model every country will use for moving towards a human common future can be different, but all of them have the common ultimate goal—achieving Global Civilization, and then moving to Great Civilization. To do this, we must establish and stick to some basic principles.

### Setting a clear correct goal

At the start of this book, we mentioned that humanity is standing at a crossroads in history. How did the world get to this point? In part, it was because we humans have lacked a clear goal. By the twenty-first century, as elaborated in the previous chapters, history has given us enough knowledge, experience, and lessons. Now we have the conditions and ability to achieve a broad consensus on the future of mankind (including the "happiness of human beings" advocated by the United Nations) and to draw a clear understanding of the ultimate goal of sustainable human survival and development. We must simply design a better future and strive for it.

### Designing a blueprint to achieve Global Civilization

Different development modes must be in line with the construction of the future Global Civilization to have vitality. Therefore, we need to design our own future blueprint from a long-term perspective and according to different national conditions, so as to make clear the overall framework, approaches to implementing civilization transition, and the different solutions proposed to deal with various crises and challenges.

### Solving practical problems

To realize the transformation of civilization with different modes, we need not only to carry out deduction and exploration from a philosophical perspective based on our differing histories, cultures, and stage of development but also to solve practical problems faced by various countries on the path to sustainable social and economic development, including soft and hard technologies as well as the soft environment, and involve all relevant institutions, policies, and other support systems (see examples from China's experience in Chapters 7).

### Multiple bottom lines

First of all, no matter how humanity evolves in the future, as social and moral beings, it is essential that we remain human beings. Second, adhere to the instrumentality of technology. No matter how technology develops, it is still a product of the human mind. Third, stick to the moral bottom line. Moral beliefs and standards must apply to every human, including those engaged in scientific research, development, experimentation, and so on.

So what is the fundamental code of ethics or moral bottom line? There are different descriptions based on history and research.

Theodore Gordon, the noted futurist, believes that the fundamental code of human ethics includes: primacy of the family; protecting the planet and valuing human existence; love of people, animals, and nature; valuing the imagination; and promoting democracy, justice, freedom, responsibility, solidarity, security, and compassion. He also believes that the principle of morality in decision making is that people are responsible for their actions, that survival is the highest priority, and that the Hippocratic Oath, "do no harm" is a golden rule. However, in a democracy there are some inevitable contradictions in the above principles, for example, between the ideal of individual "freedom" and the insistence that "people are responsible for their actions". Balancing this paradox is itself a source of ethical problems.

Table 5.1 presents ethical principles and value statements as summarized by the Millennium Project according to a recent Delphi questionnaire in which a total of 424 people from 43 countries participated.

It should be noted that Table 5.1 is only a summary of the views of experts from many different cultural backgrounds obtained through the analysis of the Delphi questionnaire; thus, it contains some inherent contradictions and compromises. While many of the statements are consistent with the views of this book; statement 11 is a point of view that I have challenged in this book, and elsewhere. It also appears inconsistent with statement 12. Statement 19 shows a strong belief in the values of Industrial Civilization, and statements 26 and 27 appear to be out of context, as they distinguish between "right and wrong" only by "you or others" and "individuals or most people". This is a preliminary look at the future of decision-making values that need to be further expanded, improved, and perfected, but we should recognize that even values we have long held as sacred could change with time. However, this is a valuable study of ethical issues.

### Cooperation and coalition

The challenge of achieving Global Civilization and then realizing Great Civilization in the world is so huge, and the goal is so ambitious that no country can achieve it alone. Far-sighted personage and creative people all over the world should unite and work together to meet the challenges facing mankind.

### To respect, learn, and tolerate all kinds of experiments and extensive practices even failures for a better human future

We have devoted countless man-hours, material, and financial resources to industrialization and the development of science and technology, but far too little towards efforts to create a Global Civilization, sustainable human development and world peace.

TABLE 5.1: Ethical principles and value statements.

1. Life is a divine unalterable gift.
2. Scientific research is a more reliable path to the truth than religious faith.
3. Harmony with nature is more important than economic progress.
4. Collective judgment is generally better than individual judgment.
5. Collective security is more important than individual freedom.
6. Human survival as a species is the highest priority.
7. Compassion is required for justice.
8. People must be responsible for their actions or inactions.
9. Fairness underlies most successful policies.
10. Intolerance leads to hate and social disintegration.
11. Any artificial form of life intelligent enough to request rights should be given these rights and be treated with the same respect as humans.
12. Human rights should always prevail over the rights of other living and nonliving things.
13. Human space migration is part of human evolution.
14. Make decisions that minimize (or preferably do no) harm.
15. Society has the obligation to intervene in genetic evolution to avoid its pitfalls and cruelties.
16. Science and technology should serve society, rather than simply pursue knowledge for its own sake.
17. The spiritual dimension of human life is more important than the material one.
18. Care for future generations should be a major focus of today's actions.
19. Economic progress is the most reliable path to human happiness.
20. Consideration of equity (e.g., distribution of benefits) is essential in decision making.
21. World interests should prevail over nation-state interests.
22. The family in all its forms is the foundation of social values.
23. Protection of the environment and biodiversity should be considered in any policy.
24. The rights of women and children are uninfringeable and fundamental for a healthy society.
25. Access to education is a fundamental human right.
26. Treat other people the way you would like to be treated.
27. Collective considerations should prevail over individual well-being; make decisions that bring the most good to the most people.
28. Human beings have an obligation to mitigate suffering.
29. Precedents and tradition are important.
30. Make decisions that have universal applicability.

Source: *2005 State of the Future*, by Jerome Glenn and Theodore Gordon.

We have only recently begun to recognize the necessity of promoting the transformation of civilization. To this end, we must adopt an attitude of respect, tolerance and learning in the various development models or development paths that are being tested or practiced in other countries and regions. This point is particularly important for the so-called "advanced" countries.

## *Beyond Global Civilization, prospect of the Great Civilization*

### The most worthy goal for human beings

Global Civilization will be a great advance in the history of human civilization. Global Civilization may be another great era in history that Herman Kahn mentioned as the era human beings will step into after the post-industrial society, but it is not the ideal social system for human beings. Because the future civilization we design and desire today, on the one hand, is subject to historical limitations as humans in the twenty-first century, including the limitations to our present knowledge and values, on the other hand, it is based on the premise that the state and political parties still exist. The game based on different interest groups will still be an obstacle to building a happy society for all mankind, including the realization of perpetual peace. Therefore, Global Civilization is only the primary stage of the Great Civilization, which is the ideal social system of mankind.

Throughout the history of civilization for thousands of years, the pursuit of a better life has always been the driving force for the development and progress of human society. Roughly similar views on the ideal human society have been expressed by ancient and modern philosophers in China and Western countries.

In the East, about 25 centuries ago, the ancient Chinese philosopher Lao Tzu depicted an ideal for human nature and society in his *Tao Te Ching*. In Lao's book, the relationships between man and nature, man and man, man and society and between country and country were all harmonious. Governors pursued a strategy of governing by doing nothing, and all of society endorsed a code of conduct founded on respect for Tao and virtue, with selflessness and dedication as the highest good and personal qualities like justice and unselfishness were seen as sufficient to assure a peaceful and stable society.

An ancient ritual scientist Sheng Dai in the Western Han Dynasty (202 BCE–8 CE) also put forward a vision of the ideal society that was called "The Great Harmonic Universe." As described in *The Book of Rites* (Li Yun), its characteristics are that the whole world is to be considered as one community that does not belong to any individual or nation, but to everyone. People elect representatives that possess both ability and political integrity to be their rulers, so the level of public morals is high, and every person throughout society strives to do their best, taking only what they need, "All for one and one for all" and living in harmony. Furthermore, in *The Book of Rites*, all sins have been eliminated, and thus the world has social stability and harmony without thieves or tyrants.

At the beginning of the twentieth century, during the Revolution of 1911, the great forerunner of the Chinese democratic revolution and the advocator of the Three People's Principles (Nationality, Civil rights, the People's Livelihood), Yat-sen Sun (1866–1925) took such ideas as "the whole world is one community" and "The Great Harmonic Universe" as his social ideal.

Youwei Kang (1858–1927), a politician and thinker in the late Qing Dynasty, further described the "Great Harmonic Universe" in his book *Da Tong Shu* (*The One-world Philosophy of Kang yu-wei*) Kang proposed: One is to abolish national boundaries and eliminate the state; two is to abolish class boundaries and eliminate class levels; three is to abolish patriarchal clan boundaries and assimilate ethnic groups; four is to abolish social boundaries and liberate women; five is to abolish family boundaries and eliminate family; six is to abolish industrial boundaries and eliminate private ownership; seven is to abolish chaos, to abolish administrative divisions at all levels, to divide self-government according to longitude and latitude, and to set up "Da Tong" government globally; eight is to abolish class boundaries and make all living beings equal; nine is to abolish suffering and attain bliss. Namely, Kang envisioned a society that would eliminate the nation-state, along with classes, distinctions of rank, and the differences between rich and poor, and make all equal.

In the West, Plato (427–347 BCE), an ancient Greek philosopher, in his *Republic*, took advantage of Socrates to discuss justice with people and designed a regime to realize justice, the Republic, where the king should have strict philosophical education, and the Kingdom advocated justice and moderation in governance.

At the beginning of the sixteenth century, Thomas More (1478–1535) described a happy and ideal state that he called Utopia. The utopian society was based on the elimination of private ownership. All things, he argued, were to be owned in common and should be available to all as needed (see Chapter 6 for more details on this and other visions of ideal societies).

In the seventeenth century, Francis Bacon (1561–1626), a famous British thinker, philosopher, and scientist, described a picture of an ideal society in his *New Great West Island*: about 1,900 years ago, a magnanimous king ruled the island country, practiced good governance and devoted himself to the happiness of the country and people. Under his governance, the island country prospered and the people lived and worked in peace and contentment. The king built "Solomon Palace", gathering a large number of research talents and engaged in research work in different disciplines. All over the island, everyone loves science, uses scientific knowledge, develops production, increases wealth, seeks profits for the people and builds an ideal society through scientific invention and creation. The book expresses Bacon's idea of scientific "great rejuvenation" and describes a utopia that attaches great importance to knowledge, dignity, and research.

In the seventeenth century, Italian philosopher Tomaso Campanella's *The City of the Sun* depicted a harmonious world without private property and exploitation, in which there would be neither rich nor poor, and wealth would belong to everyone equally. There would be no violence, no crime, and people could live in peace and serenity.

In the early nineteenth century, the future social blueprint that the utopian socialists yearned for was described by such writers as the Comte de Saint-Simon, Charles Fourier, and Robert Owen. Each of these thinkers hoped to achieve a new society with no distinction between classes, where everyone could be equal and enjoy happiness.

In the second half of the nineteenth century, Karl Marx and Friedrich Engels put forward the ideal of a communist society (later called scientific socialism). This was to be a society that realized public ownership of the means of production, eliminated class antagonism, and ultimately did away with class itself as well as national identity. Its basic principles were equality comprehensive and free development for everyone. Communist thinkers also predicted the inevitability of national extinction and pointed out that the process of human liberation is a historical process that must lead ultimately to the gradual disappearance of the political state.

In the mid-1970s, the Venus Project in Florida was initiated by American designer and social theorist Jacques Fresco, and it is still going on. Fresco proposed a vision of a peaceful society in which all human beings form a global family on Earth. Social management, he believes, will gradually extricate people from their subordination to corporate entities and governments (local, national, or supranational) as we outgrow the need for the state and plutocracy, and gradually move the world's people towards an autonomous global society. Fresco is convinced that money, politics, and personal and national interests will all be eliminated in the future.

In short, human beings should pursue a higher level of civilization than Global Civilization, which is the way of survival and development of human society. I advocate calling it a Great Civilization. There

- Everyone lives in a world of material wealth, where fair, just and pluralistic ideas;
- Not only eliminate class, country, and political party affiliations but also eradicate the gap between rich and poor while at the same time maintaining a culture of diversity and individuality;
- Where human nature is constantly sublimated, making the promotion of peace, development, fairness, justice, democracy, and freedom the common values of most human beings. Thus, it is a world of harmony and permanent peace;

- Human beings respect and protect nature and follow the laws of nature, so it is a world of ecological balance, beautiful environment, and harmonious coexistence between man and nature.

On the one hand, highly developed science and technology have the potential to completely liberate human beings from monotonous, heavy, and dangerous work, so that everyone can engage in jobs that are more meaningful (including artistic creation and scientific invention) and more conducive to the creation of self-worth, thus greatly enriching the material and spiritual products of society. On the other hand, it also creates a way to establish harmonious coexistence and coordinated development between man and other creatures in nature, and ultimately expanding human living space to other planets. This in turn makes it possible for the definition of "world" to extend beyond the earth on which mankind depends today, to include cosmic space and other planets—The New World, where mankind will live scattered on suitable planets and bring advanced civilization there to create a culture where humans "seek common ground while reserving differences" with the life there (if there is extraterrestrial life).

Through the above discussion, we can find that political civilization is the key to achieving the ideal society of all mankind. If society develops to the point where mankind has reached a high degree of consensus on the ideal way of survival, and moreover, the antagonisms between classes or strata and the gap between rich and poor diminish, the perceptions of ideology and morality of ordinary citizens generally improve, ultimately countries will no longer be needed. Of course, by the time of this ultimate step, the connotation, and mission of politics, as well as the standard of political civilization, will have fundamentally changed.

However, there are still many serious issues to be discussed in order to realize or manage that kind of society, such as:

1. Institutional and operating mechanism. It is not by eliminating class and country that all problems can be solved. If "the power of the state loses its political nature, eventually making a country move towards extinction as expected and power returns to the society", then what institutional mechanisms and means for managing society will work in the Great Civilization? This may be the biggest issue involved in the transition from the Global Civilization to the Great Civilization.
2. Diversity and unity. An ideal society cannot be attained simply by "unifying" or "assimilating" disparate groups, instead it should "unify" the goals co-constructed and shared by all humans, while diversity and individuality should be creatively maintained.

   But how do we identify the diversity and personality we need to maintain? Even if humans live in places without national boundaries, and even if the gap between rich and poor is reduced, differences in the family environment, educational background, individual achievement, cultural practices, and genetics or congenital conditions will still exist. Disparities in intelligence, values, and even physical stamina cannot, and should not, be eliminated, even though such differences may cause contradictions and jealousies. For example, with regard to happiness, according to different cultural and educational background, people's feelings about the pursuit of happiness are also different. If we say that many people care most about personal and family comfort and would like to experience and enjoy a variety of different lifestyles during their existence, there are also many people who take delight in helping and serving others. Many people of the Lei Feng type[2] have emerged in China, and there are more and more social volunteers today serving others throughout the world.

3. Does it need governance? The society of the Great Civilization mentioned above must greatly embody the common values of all mankind, such as peace, development, equity, justice, democracy, and freedom. That kind of society will still need governance; however, the platform, main body, content, and basis of governance will be different, and furthermore, the governance contents will be more complex, the challenges will be more profound, and the goals will be higher.

   As for freedom, it is a kind of comfortable and harmonious state of mind, which includes freedom from fear, servitude, and harm, and which satisfies an individual's desires to realize self-worth. True freedom entails both the right to do whatever one chooses and the obligation not to harm others (see statement 14 in Table 5.1). Behind freedom is self-discipline. In addition to self-discipline, we must accept heteronomy, which is the constraint of external moral and legal rules.[3] That is to say, freedom must be constrained by morality, law, regulation, and social norms, only under the rule of law can there be real freedom.

   Some warnings are in order: in a world awash with cheap drugs that distort reality and cause new "high" sensations, the pursuit of drug-induced happiness could quickly lead to increasing crime, loss of ambition, destruction of personality, enslavement via addiction, and a reversal of all that we intend when we say "happiness".

   In addition, even in the era of Great Civilization, there is still the possibility of a gap in the sublimation of human nature. Some people may not agree with or be willing to share the blueprint or common goal of a better world that can make all people feel happy, and try to maintain their own immoral interests or "happiness".

   Then take the challenge of highly developed science and technology to social governance as an example. In the section of "Artificial intelligence and intelligent robots" in Chapter 1, we discussed the challenges of the high development of AI to social governance and called for a new revolution in social governance. Hundreds of years from now, the scientific discoveries and subversive technological innovations we currently dream of, or even think fanciful or incredible, may follow one after another. However, as mentioned above, due to the sublimation of human nature and the differences in world views and values, serious controversies surrounding the ethics and norms of the development and application of science and technology, the evolution of human beings as well as the relationship between life, "human nature" and space life (if it exists) may all become more acute. The difficulty of governance in such a society is unimaginable. In short, even a Great Civilized society still needs a world institution acceptable to most world's citizens to implement governance.

Maybe, the ancient Chinese philosopher Lao Tzu's theory of governance, such as ruling the country with decency, fairness, and justice, with the thought of loving people, controlling chaos, and bringing the people stability, ruling the state with sincere morality, the strategy to govern by doing nothing (inaction), ruling with wisdom, the strategy of rejuvenating the country through education, etc., will still have reference value for the society of Great Civilization.

4. Governance mode. The governance adapted to the era of the Great Civilization will involve several levels. The key here is the top two levels: global level and the level of different groups or alliances.

   At the global level, a common platform needs to be established, similar to the United Nations we are familiar with, but not as a commonwealth of different countries, rather as a consortium of "various groups or alliances" representing the second level.

   The main mission of this platform is to ensure world peace and promote cooperation on a global scale, with the focus on the governance of the New World in the era of Great Civilization: on the one hand, it helps the next level—various groups or alliances cooperate through the platform, coordinate contradictions, and conflicts, and achieve win–win development; on the other hand, it also helps to keep pace with the times to constantly improve and perfect its own operating mechanism.

   There is a long history of research on the future world order or models of global governance. Among them, the idealistic school—the federal model, and its direction is close to the above-mentioned concept. The idea of a world federation can be traced back to the fourteenth century. Italian poet Dante Alighieri (1265–1321 AD) advocated in his *On World Government* published in 1311, that a unified world government should be established, and laws that lead all mankind towards peace should be formulated to effectively lead various local governments. In the eighteenth century Immanuel Kant, in his *Theory of Perpetual Peace*, advocated the establishment of representative government and the world federation; the World Association of World Federalists, established in October 1946, aimed at coordinating, connecting, and striving for the realization of a world federation at the international level and believed that to achieve world peace, a world federal government must be established.

In fact, as a federal country, the United States is composed of 50 states, which are relatively independent regions, as members of the alliance. The country has a unified constitution as the supreme law of the country, and exercises its sovereignty in defense, war, foreign affairs, currency, foreign trade, etc. The political system of the European Union is a confederation, which is a loose alliance of states with independent sovereignty. Each member state still retains sovereignty and all functions of the government, and has its own constitution and laws, national defense, and diplomacy. However, neither the 200 years of American federalism nor the great and arduous efforts made by the European Union carried out through the confederation over the past few decades is a great practice of federalism. However, if the operation is not effective, it will make the governance in trouble. For example, during the 2020 COVID-19 epidemic, the crisis in the US federal system showed that the disorder of federalism and the interference of party politics have aggravated domestic division and distracted attention from society's need to confront the pandemic together. Nevertheless, the experiences and lessons of Federalism or Confederation have had a positive influence on the construction of a global governance model for the future.

Then, after the disappearance of states and political parties, is the governance model we envisioned more feasible?

The next level is various groups or alliances representing different cultures, religions, development levels, geographical environments, and regional groups. Its mission is to keep pace with the times to create and innovate distinctive internal governance models on the basis of protecting, inheriting, and respecting the diversity and individuality of its culture, religion, and beliefs so as to ensure internal stability and prosperity. Let the people feel satisfied, happy, and proud, and they should efficiently coordinate with the global governance platform.

But the internal governance of different groups or alliances has something in common: (1) with the disappearance of the nation state, the main body of governance becomes pluralistic, including the leading bodies of the group or alliance and its internal pluralistic bodies; (2) the content of governance is mainly social governance; (3) the governance process is not a top-down management process in accordance with the direction of power operation, but an interactive management process. The management of governance is implemented mainly through cooperation, negotiation, partnership, and establishment of shared common goals, etc.; (4) the source of authority for governance can be laws and regulations, but more often it may be through agreed upon social norms.

In short, as the nation-state gradually dissolves, the power that national governments have long assumed will be returned to society, and governance will enter a new phase—governance based on cooperation, negotiation, and voluntary self-regulation.

5. Many people are skeptical about whether the so-called diversity of individuality and culture can be maintained in a highly globalized future.

The examples of China's practice may help to validate this possibility.

In today's world, there are about 3,000 ethnic groups, distributed among more than 200 countries and regions, and speaking more than 6,000 different languages. The vast majority of countries are composed of a number of nationalities; for example, China has 55 ethnic groups. China's constitution stipulates that each internal nation has the freedom to maintain or reform their customs and habits particularly regarding matters such as clothing, food, residence, marriage, festivals, etiquette, and funerals. China has given each of its ethnic minorities full respect and effective guarantees. Ethnic equality is defined specifically and clearly through laws and regulations (though of course, there are still problems such as how to thoroughly implement these concepts). By the end of 2008, China had established 155 autonomous ethnic areas, including 5 autonomous regions, 30 autonomous prefectures, and 120 autonomous counties or banners (which are administrative divisions at the county level in the Inner Mongolia Autonomous Region). Today, the population of ethnic minorities in autonomous regions accounts for 71 per cent of the total population of ethnic minorities in China. In addition, more than 1,100 ethnic townships have been established to complement the system of Regional National Autonomy. Regional National Autonomy is China's basic policy to resolve ethnic problems and a fundamental part of the political system in China. China encourages its ethnic minorities to develop their culture and art and to actively protect their prized traditions. The central government has also invested heavily in protecting the intangible cultural heritage of ethnic minorities, such as language and writing. These systems and policies safeguard national unity and national solidarity, maintain the long-term stability of Chinese society, and open a promising road to achieve the common prosperity and development of all ethnic groups.

What I have enumerated above only touches on some of the challenges and prospects related to political civilization that humanity may face after the demise of country and class distinctions. In fact, the demise of the country does not involve political civilization alone. The conditions that Marxism sets for the extinction of the State cover all aspects of civilization: the complete eradication of class antagonisms and class differences (political condition); the elimination of old social division including the difference between mental and physical labor (social condition); general improvement in ideological and moral cultivation, as well as the educational and cultural level of all the people (spiritual condition); the abolition of all exploiting systems worldwide and the liberation of all mankind (international condition). All of this must combine with highly developed social productivity (material condition), which is the most fundamental condition of all. By then, the impacts of new technologies will affect productivity and definitions of work and leisure.

Therefore, in order to achieve the Great Civilization, the five civilizations (material, spiritual, political, ecological, and interstellar), need not only adapt to achieve the Global Civilization but they will also need to be comprehensively reworked and improved in order to form a social system and cultural environment that can usher in the Great Civilization.

If the beautiful vision of the Great Civilization I described above is realized, it doesn't matter whether it is called a great civilized society, the Republic, a Utopia, a Great Harmony World, or a Communist society. It is the advanced stage of human social development in which human beings can "be completely liberated and develop freely and comprehensively". I believe that no nation or clan in the world will disagree. The key is how to jointly build, govern and maintain the common home of mankind—this New World—with the universally shared goal and vision of a common destiny for all of humanity.

However, the challenge to achieve this grand goal is so great that no single nation could ever accomplish it alone, but at the same time such a cause is also so worthwhile that any country or nation stands to benefit from working to help make it a reality. Therefore, to achieve this goal is not by conquest and assimilation, but to abandon differences in ideology and religious belief, seek common ground while reserving differences, integrate various cultures, stimulate human inspiration, constantly endow great civilization with values, actively adapt to and lead the transformation of various paradigms, and jointly create a better future for mankind.

## *The process of Great Civilization*

Since the realization of Great Civilization is a prerequisite for an ideal society that transcends Global Civilization, let us imagine the process of Great Civilization as discussed by those who yearn for perpetual world peace and a better future for mankind.

If the seventeenth century is regarded as the incubation period of Industrial Civilization, the prosperous era of Industrial Civilization has now extended roughly from the eighteenth century to the twenty-first century. While Industrial Civilization has produced unprecedented material wealth and stimulated brilliant achievements in science and technology, it has also caused major catastrophes in natural and social environments, threatening unsustainable development for humanity and challenging the survival of Earth's entire ecosphere.

At the end of the twentieth century, since the global movement of promoting sustainable development, the concept of civilization transformation has been recognized by more and more experts and international elites. However, no matter if it is the oncoming wave of a new industrial revolution, or the accelerating process of industrialization in less-developed countries (notably in Africa, which is experiencing a period sometimes called "30 years of glory"), as well as the competition among developed countries, they have not yet been able to get rid of the logic and rules of Industrial Civilization, which often give priority to the interests of a single country or group. In addition, the ongoing competition of governance models caused by different ideologies, often leads to conflict and sometimes war. As yet it is not on the agenda to promote the transformation of civilization on a global scale.

A few countries, such as the Nordic region, have achieved remarkable results in promoting the progress of social civilization after more than 100 years of exploration and persistence, but they have not yet reached the height of consciously promoting the transformation of civilization.

For this reason, until the middle of the twenty-first century, perhaps during the whole twenty-first century, it may prove to be the climax of Industrial Civilization.

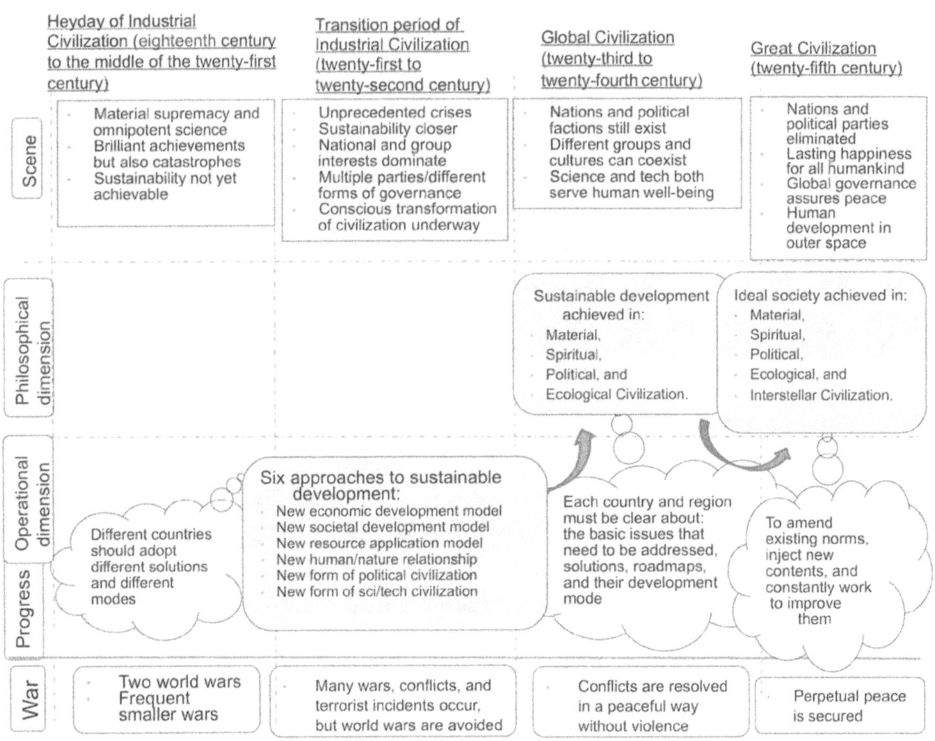


FIGURE 5.1: Roadmap to a Global Civilization. © Zhouying Jin.

This determines that the transformation of Industrial Civilization will go through a long period of transition.

In retrospect, the era of Industrial Civilization's rise and fall may span some 400 years (from the eighteenth to twenty-first centuries)

The twenty-first to the twenty-second century will be a transition period when the world will move from an Industrial Civilization towards a Global Civilization. This period is also the turning point of human awakening. More and more people are realizing that human beings are on an unsustainable path and that the transformation of civilization has become necessary. This trend of change in values will promote the reform of the development model in various countries. Therefore, in the twenty-second century, more countries will experiment with the practice of transformation.

Because different countries have different problems, their solutions, transformation models, and the duration of transformation will be different. But so long as they all focus on the necessary approaches to sustainable development and adhere to the practice of the six kinds of transformation (outlined in Chapter 7) What will take place? At the same time, to strengthen the construction of a cultural environment in a broad sense according to the new five civilization standards, it should be possible to greatly improve the level of sustainability and gradually approach the goal of Global Civilization.

During this period, wars, regional conflicts, and terrorist incidents will continue. Especially in the twenty-first century, the world has ushered in great development, great adjustment, and great turning point, thus speeding up the pace of reshaping the world pattern. On the one hand, compared with the disruptive development and explosive innovation of technology, the "jungle rule" advocated by Industrial Civilization for hundreds of years still has a strong impact on the think tanks and decision-makers in many countries. To cope with the accelerated evolution of the world pattern, war has become a strategic option for how to cope with undesired change. On the other hand, the relentless development of science and technology will inevitably subvert the forms, tools, and winning and losing strategies of war. All kinds of non-traditional wars, such as biological and chemical warfare, cyber warfare, and climate warfare, are no less disruptive and "lethal" than traditional hot war, threatening world peace at any time. Whether the conscience of mankind overcome evil, or at least avoids the World War will depend on whether countries and the international community can reach a consensus to build a peaceful world through mutual tolerance and cooperation.

Probably by the second half of the twenty-second century, most countries and regions will be entering the orbit of Global Civilization. Despite their different social systems and governance modes, so long as each country can make clear their basic problems, solutions, and roadmaps (as outlined in Chapter 4) to achieve Global Civilization, they will eventually fashion a world in which different cultures, beliefs, and faiths can accept each other, coexist, and co-develop, at different times with different development models.

If the transition period of Industrial Civilization is regarded as the incubation period for Global Civilization, another 400 years (from the twenty-second to the twenty-fifth century) may be required from first consciously promoting Global Civilization in individual countries to realizing it throughout the world (this timetable assumes that we take sufficiently good care of the Earth and that human beings continue to evolve and survive on Earth). Because the transition from Agricultural Civilization to Industrial Civilization emphasized unlimited development, activities targeting nature and creating material wealth predominate. The transition from Industrial Civilization to Global Civilization will emphasize conditional development and the creation of non-material wealth will gradually prevail. The creation of value will increasingly be based upon a completely different paradigm. It will involve the transformation of the social system based on the renovation and improvement of human nature, which is a task far more difficult than humanity's age-long "struggle" against the forces of nature.

By the twenty-fifth century, in all areas and at all levels, Global Civilization will gradually be expanded and perfected around the world during the process of collision, contest, penetration, and fusion between the new Global Civilization and traditional civilizations and cultures.

After this, the transition from Global Civilization to Great Civilization will require long and difficult efforts. The biggest challenge may prove to be issues of governance. It will be a great change to explore a universally acceptable world order framework and develop a global governance model suitable for different regions and groups at different levels of development with the goal of eliminating country, class and the gap between rich and poor measured by money, and achieving perpetual peace.

As we mentioned above, governance requires establishing a global platform and a layered management model. But the bigger challenge is:

- How can a global governance platform be designed to benefit everyone?
- How can we assure that moral leaders are selected to implement this global platform?
- What are the distinctive functions and mechanisms that groups or alliances need to construct, so as to successfully manage their internal affairs while becoming a part of a great civil society?
- How can we detect and prevent threats related to human civilization?
- How can science and technology be steered to benefit mankind more directly while minimizing their negative effects and threats to human beings, society, and nature?

- How do we educate the next generation in an age where overwhelming abundance of material possessions is still considered desirable and mass labor is increasingly replaced by machines?

Obviously, this next transition will require a more ambitious and more complex development process than any we have known in the past. But I believe that human beings can eventually transition from Global Civilization to Great Civilization, and that the period required may be even shorter than those of previous eras, Because:

First, consider that in the centuries required for the Global Civilization to be constructed, the cultural environment of human society will improve greatly and that a number of the sharp constraints that now face global governance[4] will be gradually weakening, especially as the five conditions for the extinction of the nation state gradually mature. On the one hand, the interests and power disputes between the state, different classes, and political parties will gradually weaken. On the other hand, the concept of the community of human common destiny will become a broader consensus. This is the basis for building a global governance platform.

Second, the human nature of most people will likely be greatly modified and generally refined during this time, the mainstream world views, outlook on life, and values in human society can actively adapt to the Great Civilization. This is not only conducive to resolving the internal governance problems of different levels of groups or alliances but is also the key to a harmonious world that will eventually realize the destiny of all mankind and share perpetual peace.

Third, human intelligence, the ability to solve problems, and the means of soft and hard technologies will likely reach levels unmatched by those of people today. Furthermore, the consciousness of "global citizenship" will be greatly enhanced worldwide. Thus, the mainstream of future generations will not be so reluctant to reach a consensus regarding basic issues related to the future human development.

Fourth, human beings in the age of the Great Civilization will be better qualified (see Chapter 2) to decide the direction and degree of human evolution, assuming that the evolutionary progress of humans as natural and social beings remains in reasonable balance. This will help avoid some risks to human civilization and self-destruction, and there will create myriad possibilities and opportunities for the achievements that we have yet to realize.

In short, we hope that in slightly more than 200 years (by the twenty-sixth–twenty-seventh centuries), human beings can realize the transformation from the Global Civilization to the Great Civilization, and build a world that is truly a paradise on earth with perpetual peace, suitable for sustainable survival and development.

In this long process of transforming civilization, it remains an open question whether human beings can successfully complete two major civilization paradigm shifts, so as to avoid a sudden drop off in the progress of human civilization.

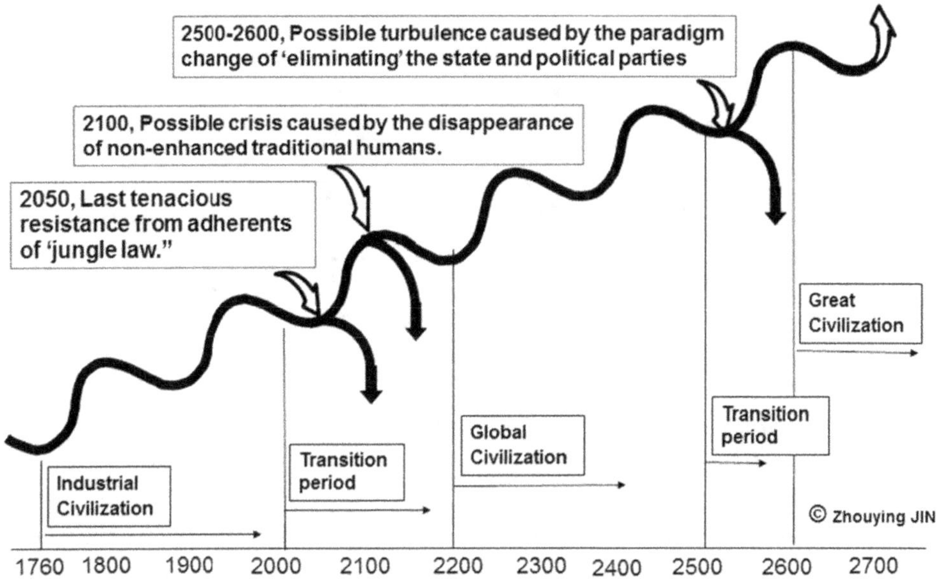


FIGURE 5.2: Warning: several critical periods of historical paradigm shift.

The key is how to cope effectively with risks in the transition period of civilization just ahead (see Figure 5.2).

Then, is the Great Civilization the ultimate goal of human beings? Perhaps not, because as long as human beings exist, human history will continue to develop. Concerning what kind of civilization will emerge after the Great Civilization, we must believe that future generations will continue to have the ability to change what they see as good and right and proper. Let our future generations decide their own designs and make the world and the universe a better place. This is humanity's ultimate freedom.

## NOTES

1. http://baike.baidu.com/link?url=k4uK07VP5wGUUk7B8upZzeeDkJ71_N9pl3FX-TWP1XFEuMVsa3BzdIEQX5VsP8CnIipbNscHPdGZ9vGLD_AWCNK; http://bbs.tianya.cn/post-666-430-1.shtml.
2. https://en.wikipedia.org/wiki/LeiFeng.
3. https://zhidao.baidu.com/question/616160770172649492.html.
4. "Global governance", http://baike.baidu.com/link?url=jRTgoseHx6oaS-VkWzAf_jDDRb-9d3xOEm_NsXiQyTE9JQvEI6JWz6D-RqWia4zFXkWw9b2-GcbotL-PV1rodpOeZFn-1CUvz-h4dd0Q2gWy.

# 6

# Can Humans Eventually Create a Great Civilization?

*We need the thinkers of the twenty-first century.*

In the twenty-first century, although science and technology are rapidly changing, with exciting innovations and discoveries coming nearly every day, we all live on the same planet, and thus, every nation faces common threats whose scope transcends national boundaries. These include threats to the natural environment, the social environment, and the international environment. Crowding due to overpopulation, shortages of energy and resources, global warming, meteorological and ecological disasters, etc. have overwhelmed our planet. Human selfishness and greed, and the desire to control and possess are still growing among most people, and as a result, the moral bottom line is declining, leading to the endless pursuit of money, comfort, and more material luxury. This obsession often blinds us to serious inequality and corruption, the rapidly widening gap between rich and poor, and the spread of diseases, which all adversely affect the quality of the human social environment. Consequently, the uncontrolled high development of science and technology has unexpectedly brought mankind face to face with the threat of destruction. Today, the triple threat of extreme nationalist violence, various types of wars, and terrorism covers the globe.

This grave situation has made many people lose interest in research on long-term futures and lose confidence in the value of even attempting to pursue a better future. In this context, it is easy to reach a pessimistic conclusion about the future. It may be more interesting simply to make fascinating conjectures, but it is irresponsible.

And yet, throughout the world, increasingly people's idealism is awakening—people recognize that there is only one Earth and all countries have to live together in a world full of opportunities and risks. Today more than ever before, mankind is bound together by a common fate and needs to think about the coexistence of the whole human race. Somehow we must stimulate and focus our positive energy to build a better future for humanity, and form a harmonious global family.

There are good reasons to believe that as long as we work hard, and remain confident, a better future is possible for humans, and that we can successfully coordinate biological and cultural evolution to improve human existence.

## *The power of education and persuasion*

Although there are both good and evil sides to human nature, through persuasion and continuous education, it is possible to make the good side prevail. As former US vice president Al Gore said in his book *The Future: Six Drivers of Global Change*, a good family tradition handed down from generation to generation eventually results in certain behaviors and norms being accepted and expected, while others are rejected and discarded. Good habits and customs become rituals and rules, and slowly evolve into culture, social systems, laws, and institutions over time. This gradual process should allow the evil side of human nature to prove itself counterproductive, while the positive values we advocate take root in family, community, and the economy, spread through society and the state, and then gradually become integrated into the global culture in the form of social, political, and cultural institutions. The gradual rejection of slavery as an acceptable practice is one good example of this process, and the growing acceptance of women as economic and political equals to men is another.

Through careful structural design, these institutions in turn can act to curb people's antisocial attributes by punishing overt behaviors (such as crime and violence) that harm others, and turning public opinion against personality traits such as selfishness, greed, and the desire for power that damage the public and society, and reward traits like loyalty and selfless dedication so that people gradually come to behave instinctively in ways that reflect human kindness.

Take Finland as an example. Finnish society pays more attention to teaching ethics and sociology and gaining basic knowledge of laws from an early age. The subtle influence of social environment and good school education gives most Finns a habit of "conscious obedience to the law", which becomes their code of conduct and the basis of their personal morality. The notion that "law is more important than anything else" is a social consensus, and everyone staying within the law makes an orderly social order. The notion that it is "natural" to obey the law enables the majority of Finns to restrain themselves. Conscious self-discipline is their basic life criterion. Fortitude, kindness, honesty, self-discipline, and being law-abiding have thus become common characteristics for the majority of Finns. When integrity, honesty, and self-discipline become a social atmosphere, corruption will naturally have no place to hide. According to the rank of "Corruption Perceptions Index" delivered by Transparency International, Finland's integrity ranked in the top three from 2011 to 2015 for five consecutive years. This shows the power of education and persuasion. Also, according to the *World Happiness Report* launched by the United Nations, Finland was the happiest country in the world in 2018 and 2019.[1]

In Southeast Asia, former Singaporean Prime Minister Lee Kuan Yew forged Singapore, a resource-poor, multiracial, postcolonial port, within a single generation into a rich and important city of knowledge. Annual per capita income in Singapore has increased from $500 at independence in 1965 to about $55,000 today, creating an economic miracle unparalleled in the history of the world.

Lee's secret was to adhere to the development of quality education, fight corruption, and assign jobs to people according to their abilities. Education was regarded as the foundation of the country, while Singapore consciously absorbed the essence of both Eastern and Western cultures. By integrating basic, vocational, and higher education, including integrating multinational culture through moral education, Singapore has managed to survive and flourish despite fierce international competition.

### *Human beings can and should agree on common values*

In the related section of 'Beyond Global Civilization, Prospect of the Great Civilization' (see Chapter 5,), we reviewed world history both East and West from the twenty-fifth century BCE to the 1970s and found that ancient and modern Chinese and foreign philosophers have many similar views on the ideal society of mankind, which indicates that humans can and should find common values.

Though human beings are divided into various nationalities and clans with different cultures, there are many common traits in human nature, such as the preference to love rather than hate, and to prefer peace over war. For thousands of years, the heroes worshipped by each country have been similar. No country or nation holds up people who are selfish or who profit at others' expense as role models. Instead, those people considered to be noble or who do serve as role models are those who sacrifice their own interests for those of others or the public, and who love others and love society. Consider Joan of Arc of France, Martin Luther King in the United States, and others such as Enlai Zhou, the first premier of the People's Republic of China. Zhou's character and his behavior show that he devoted his life to the people. Not only the Chinese regard him as the outstanding example of a devoted communist but he also earned respect from people of insight in all countries. His death made the United Nations lower their flag in front of UN headquarters to half-mast.

When futurist Theodore Gordon studied better business models in the future, he found that even among different religions or cultures, there are some common principles regarding how to conduct oneself, how to establish interpersonal relationships, or how to assess actions and decisions not to act. Fundamentally, these amount to respecting others and treating them as equals. This is especially true among adherents of the world's four major religions: Christianity, Islam, Hinduism, and Buddhism, which account for some 75 per cent of the world's population.

- **Confucian:** "What you do not wish for yourself, do not do to others."
- **Christian:** "All things therefore that you want people to do to you, do thus to them."
- **Buddhist:** "Hurt not others in ways that you yourself would find hurtful."
- **Jewish:** "What is hateful to you, do not do to your neighbor. This is the whole Torah; all the rest is commentary."
- **Islam:** "Not one of you truly believes until you wish for others what you wish for yourself."
- **Hinduism:** "This is the sum of duty: do not do to others what would cause pain if done to you."
- **Zoroastrianism:** "Do not do unto others whatever is injurious to yourself."

Our mission is to seek common ground while putting aside differences, and to gradually create and foster more common values through cooperation, dialogue, communication, understanding, respect, tolerance, mutual benefit, and learning. This includes promoting and fostering awareness of "Global Citizenship" worldwide, and deepening understanding of the rights and obligations of "Global Citizenship."

### *Ideal human societies have certain characteristics in common*

No matter which nation we examine, if we analyze its dream of the future its people desire, they all have one thing in common: the pursuit of a happy, safe, equal, and blessed life that can be sustained from one generation to the next. This is why "sustainable development" has become such a common concept. The ranking survey in the *World Happiness Report* of the UN also shows that people have common ideals for happier societies. The key is how to combine their respective national conditions to make this ideal come true.

The UN's *World Happiness Report* 2013 surveyed the citizens of 156 countries and ranked them mainly based on the following factors: GDP per capita, life expectancy, feelings about national corruption, freedom of life, tolerance for their fellow citizens and those of neighboring countries, and enthusiasm for helping each other.

*This report listed countries and examined their happiness factors based on a total score of ten points. Denmark topped the list at 7.693 points, followed by Norway (7.655), Switzerland (7.650), Netherlands (7.512), Sweden (7.480), Canada (7.477), Finland (7.389), Austria (7.369), Iceland (7.355), and Australia (7.350), with Israel and Costa Rica close behind. The USA ranked 17, Taiwan 42, Japan 43, Hong Kong 64, and China is ranked 93, advancing from 112 a year earlier.*

The recently released *Global Happiness Index Report 2019*[2] is based on the analysis and measurement of the three criteria of subjective happiness from 2016 to 2018 (life happiness, positive emotions, and negative emotions), using six main variables (per capita GDP, healthy life expectancy, perception of corruption in the government and business sector, degree of freedom, charity and generosity index and social support).

*The ranking order is Finland (7.769), Denmark (7.600), Norway (7.554), Iceland (7.494), Netherlands (7.488), Switzerland (7.480), Sweden (7.343), New Zealand (7.307), Canada (7.278), and Austria (7.246). Chinese mainland is still 93rd.*

The Nordic countries have occupied the top spots on many charts, from economic competitiveness to national health care, and from social trust levels to the Global Happiness Index mentioned above, providing a blueprint for the world that can be used to reform the public sector and improve the level of national governance. However, at present, the "Nordic model", characterized by high taxes and high welfare, faces challenges such as neoliberalism, aging population, immigration, European integration, especially how to breaking the so-called "high welfare dilemma" and reshaping the "Nordic Model."

Social problems caused by large numbers of immigrants are now dilemmas for governance globally and provide some useful warnings: in this era of globalization, no country can be excluded. What is crucial is to determine how Europe will deal with the migration tide of the twenty-first century (handling volumes of refugees unprecedented since the Second World War), and if possible learning how to address the root causes of emigration.

## *Human beings have never stopped striving to create an ideal society*

For thousands of years, mankind has never stopped designing blueprints for the ideal society and struggling to achieve it.

### The *Tao Te Ching* written by Lao Tzu

The *Tao Te Ching* shows us ideal human nature and an ideal society described by ancient Chinese philosopher Lao Tzu. The *Tao Te Ching*, also known as "Moral scriptures", "Lao Tzu", and "Five thousand words by Lao Tzu", was written by Lao Tzu (namely Li Er) in the ancient quotation style during the Spring and Autumn Period (770 BCE–476 BCE).

The modern popular version has a total of 81 chapters; the first 37 chapters are "Articles about the way", and the last 44 chapters are "Articles about virtue." This book is the greatest philosophical masterpiece in Chinese history, and, for many centuries has exerted a profound influence on Chinese philosophy, science, politics, religion, etc.

The *Tao Te Ching* is one of the most published books in the world after the Bible and was first translated in the seventh century CE. Many people have benefited from the *Tao Te Ching*, and some of the most famous include: the German philosophers Friedrich Hegel and Martin Heidegger, Swedish physicist Dr Hannes Alfven (who pointed out that humanity must learn from the wisdom of Lao Tzu if it is to survive), the celebrated Russian author Leo Tolstoy, modern historian Arnold J. Toynbee, Russian Prime Minister Dimitri Medvedev, and many others. Contemporary American physicist John Wheeler made the Taoist idea that "being and not-being grow out of one another" the cornerstone of his "austerity principle". Former US President Ronald Reagan quoted the idea of Lao Tzu, "govern a

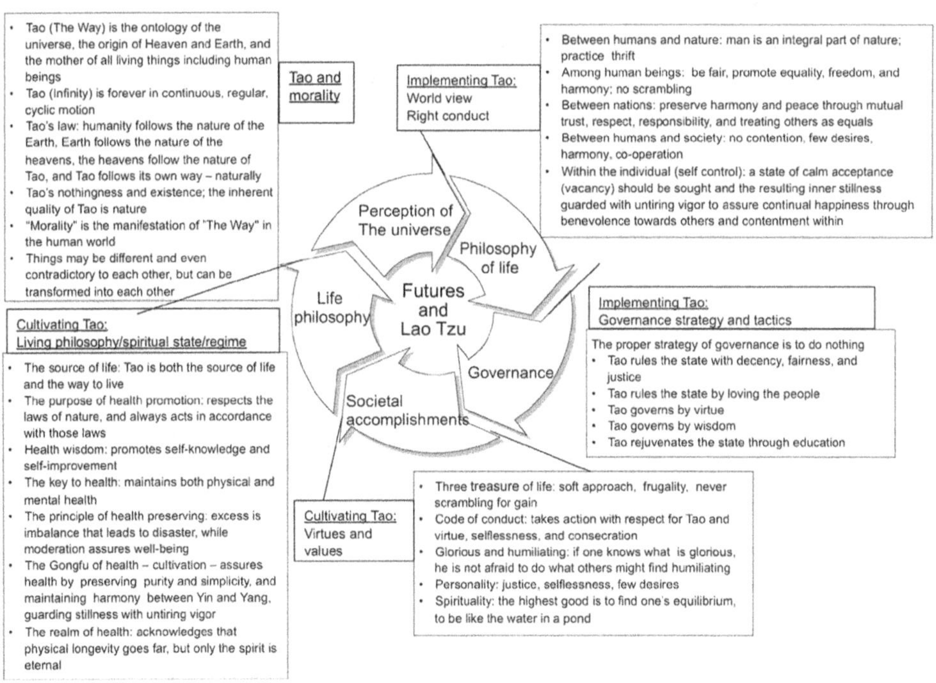


FIGURE 6.1: Lao Tzu's wisdom and the future. © Zhouying Jin and Jintai Zhang.

great nation as you would cook a small fish, do not overdo it", in his State of the Union Address. And former German Chancellor Gerhard Schroeder in a televised address urged his people to buy a copy of the *Tao Te Ching* for every family, in order to "resolve ideological confusion". Russian Prime Minister Dmitry Medvedev and other leaders have benefited from the *Tao Te Ching.*

This diversity of those who have studied the work of Lao Tzu shows that despite the fact that some of the views expressed in the *Tao Te Ching* are not quite in line with contemporary society, the connotations of this short 5,000-words book can serve to represent the wisdom of Oriental civilization as a whole. It is worth noting that all levels of decision-makers, managers, and scholars who conduct research and express concern about the future of humanity benefit from these views throughout their life.

The reason why the *Tao Te Ching* has been respected by politicians and academics in different countries, different societies, and different areas for a long time is mainly because it reveals the unique philosophical logic and law for the following theories.

First, it proposes an ontology of the universe and the laws of universal motion. The principle that "the Tao follows its own way naturally" is its core and soul.

Second, it puts forward a theory of harmony with nature, which provides the basis for a sustainable civilization of the future.

Third, it proposes a theory of ethics, in which the rules of conduct and moral cultivation it advocates are in line with the lifestyles and ethics that are desirable in a future civilization. It advocates three basic principles in life—compassion, thrift, and restraint (never to be the first to scramble for gain), along with a code of conduct that involves always acting with respect for the Tao (sometimes translated as "nature's way") and virtue, practicing selflessness and dedication, so as to induce a spiritual state in which individuals have few desires, practice restraint, and feel contentment. It can be said that these standards for sublimating and perfecting human nature are also the reference standards of moral education.

Fourth, it proposes a theory of governance, which provides essential reference principles for politicians and entrepreneurs to use in governing at national, regional, world, and corporate levels including ways to avoid war.

Fifth, it creates a unique philosophy of life.

Lao Tzu's *Tao Te Ching* supports and can serve as the basis for a future civilization—one in which humanity adopts a new set of material, spiritual, political, and ecological values and behaviors from such areas as cosmology, philosophy of life, governance theory, morality of governors, and philosophy of living.

Lao Tzu may be considered the first true philosopher in the world. He not only explored the laws of nature, revealed its logic, and established the principles of philosophy but also provided people with examples for how to consciously think and act in accordance with the laws of nature, and proposed methods for advancing and solving problems in accord with logic.

To sum up, the *Tao Te Ching* establishes a theoretical system with statements such as "heaven's way is nature," "man's way is to keep what is in the heart," and "the way of ruling the state relies on actionless activity". His view of the universe and ontology, the theory of life, epistemology, and methodology (way of thinking) are important sources of wisdom from which to build future scenarios. From Lao Tzu and his universal philosophy, we can learn to foster correct worldviews, values, and philosophy of life. Moreover, the *Tao Te Ching* has important reference value for establishing common principles for planning and designing the human future.

## The *Utopia* of Thomas More

Thomas More (1478–1535), an English statesman, writer, and utopian socialist, completed and published a controversial but great work—*Utopia* in 1516. In it, a fictional navigator, Raphael Hythloday, offers vignettes of his travels that describe the political arrangements of the imaginary island country of Utopia, where society has been perfected.

In the first part of the book, he tartly satirizes and criticizes the political, economic, and social life of Britain and the whole of Europe in the fifteenth to sixteenth centuries, especially the enclosure movement, which emerged in this era of primitive capitalism and the tormented life endured by tenant farmers under the feudal autocratic monarchy, which he described as "sheep eat people".

More pointed out how the private ownership of land caused various social evils. He was convinced that only the complete abolition of private property could make it possible for wealth to be distributed evenly and equitably, so that ordinary human beings could enjoy its benefits. More's detailed description of the enclosure movement provided vivid material for Karl Marx when he narrated the barbaric methods of capitalism some 300 years later in *Das Kapital.*

In the second part, More describes a happy and ideal state. Unlike Plato's *Republic*, More's Utopia is not a communist state, but a society in which everyone must engage in physical labor, and each is rewarded according to his needs.

More's utopian society is based on the public ownership of property. All things are owned in common and are available to everyone as needed. The citizens have no private property of any kind; they exchange housing every ten years, wear uniform overalls and citizens' suits, eat in a public restaurant or mess hall, and everyone takes turns working in the fields for two years. Of course, this kind of unified life may well appear monotonous and boring to contemporary people. But residents in Utopia need only work for six hours a day to meet the needs of society, and the rest of the time they engage in such activities as scientific research, art, and intellectual games. There are "no poor people and no beggars" in Utopia.

In terms of social governance, Utopia advocates social order and discipline rather than freedom. There is almost complete religious toleration except for atheists. Government in Utopia is largely democratic, except that the position of governor involves a lifelong tenure; but all other officials are elected by all citizens through secret ballot. These positions each carry a one-year term of office and none are hereditary. All citizens, men and women, are on equal footing and have the same rights. Utopia attaches great importance to education, with moral education awarded the highest priority. Utopia's people love peace, long for a life of tranquility, and when they do have conflicts with other countries, they mainly try to find a peaceful solution. However, if their country were invaded, they might fight back resolutely.

More proposed the elimination of private ownership for the first time in history, and was among the first to put forward the concept of a perfect society. This had a great influence on the development of socialist ideology; thus, he can be regarded as the forerunner of Utopian socialism. However, he was eventually executed because he refused to submit to the will of his monarch King Henry VIII.

Although there are many irrationalities in More's thoughts of Utopia, his idea of equality is still persuasive and full of lasting appeal.

### Campanella's *The City of the Sun*

Tommaso Campanella, Italian thinker and writer, wrote his most famous work *The City of the Sun* in prison in 1622, and it was published in 1623.

In this work, Campanella criticized various drawbacks and social evils brought on by private ownership, and depicted a harmonious world without private property or exploitation of workers, where there would be neither rich nor poor, and wealth would belong to all equally. There would be no violence, no crime, and people would live in peace and serenity in this city of the sun, the so-called because it reflects the desire of ordinary Italians for a happy life.

He depicted an ideal social system, in which production and consumption are organized and arranged by the community, and products are allocated according to the needs of citizens. It is sufficient for each person to spend only four hours a day working, the rest of the time they use to study interesting academic issues, hold forums, read books and stories, write letters, walk, or engage in sports that benefit their physical and mental health. They implement the "politics of philosophers"—and only "sages", individuals of great wisdom, can serve as the highest manager (known as "the Sun"). But all officials, even the supreme leader, are elected by the people, and if they do not perform well, the citizens can replace them. Children are raised and educated by the state.

The utopian communist theory Campanella proposed became a prototype for many subsequent utopian socialist systems, and remains a respected monument in the history of human thought, and in the history of socialism.

However, due to the constraints of the times, it was impossible for Campanella to present a scientifically objective process for social development. He did not identify the driving force that motivates people to transform the existing social system and realize an ideal society. He simply depicted his perfect society as fully formed, and there is obviously a tendency towards mysticism and egalitarianism in his thoughts. Nevertheless, Campanella is still a great thinker. But Campanella's life is like a solemn and stirring poem. He was imprisoned for 33 years, tortured cruelly on seven occasions, and cooped up in 50 different cells.

### Kant's *Perpetual Peace*

The famous German thinker Immanuel Kant (1724–1804) was the last major philosopher in the age of enlightenment.

Kant reconciled Rene Descartes' rationalism and Francis Bacon's empiricism, and he is still considered one of the most influential thinkers in the West since Socrates, Plato, and Aristotle. Among his many important works, his essay *Perpetual Peace*, written in 1795, contains this scholar's most important insights about war and peace, representative government, and his notion of a world federation. It has become one of the important ideological models for an ideal international order.[3]

Kant put forward the principle that to realize perpetual peace and to overcome the many difficulties that may appear in the peace process, it is first necessary to suppress the savagery of lawless states and to establish an alliance of all ethnic groups. Within this alliance, every country, even the smallest, can make decisions based not simply on their own strength or their own laws, but instead can rely on the entire alliance, as a united force, to maintain and protect the safety and rights of all members.

Kant's ideas on practical rationality, moral self-discipline, and perpetual peace, though formulated more than 200 years ago, still seem an achievement great enough to seriously challenge contemporary speculation among philosophers, politicians, and elite thinkers around the world.

### The Declaration of Independence[4]

The Declaration of Independence announced that the thirteen North American colonies declared independence from Great Britain, and proclaimed the legitimacy of the act. The Declaration was adopted by the Second Continental Congress in

Philadelphia on 4 July 1776, which date later became America's Independence Day.

The Declaration of Independence consists of four parts: the first part is the preamble, which outlines the purpose of the Declaration; the second part expounds an ideal political system, namely the doctrine of Natural Rights and the thought that sovereignty belongs to the people; the third part is an indictment that enumerates Britain's "repeated injuries and usurpations" of the people of the North American colonies, indicating the legitimacy and justice of their revolt and asserts that, being driven beyond the limits of forbearance, colonial peoples were forced to take up arms to strive for independence. The document closes with the United States solemnly declaring its independence.

The Declaration of Independence contains many of the basic ideas of the founding fathers, and some of these were later incorporated into the constitution of the United States. Many of the ideas had their roots in Europe. For example, Natural Rights were advocated by the thinkers of the European Enlightenment in the seventeenth and eighteenth centuries. The ideas of a social contract, freedom, equality, democracy, the rule of law, and separation of the three powers[5] all have precedents in European history, as do checks and balances, and other ideological principles that became the theoretical sources of the Declaration of Independence. The development of a capitalist economy in the British North American colonies laid the material foundation for the Declaration; and the growing awareness of ethnic democracy in the colonies was its intrinsic motivation. After the outbreak of war, when fighting for national independence became the primary task of the North American people, issuing the Declaration helped rally the people to this cause.

As one of the most important documents representing the American spirit, the Declaration of Independence deeply influenced the subsequent development of the United States. Since 1776, "all men are created equal" has remained a basic part of the nation's founding principles, and it has been a guide for future generations as the peoples' belief and ideal. At various times, this ideal has served as a talisman for social reformers in the United States and elsewhere and helped to further such causes as the abolition of slavery, anti-apartheid, and the advancement of women. Wherever people fight against the undemocratic rule, they will use the Declaration of Independence as a powerful statement and weapon. It continues to have an enduring influence on American political life.

The Declaration of Independence is a landmark document in global history, for it declared in the name of the state for the first time in human history that people's rights are sacred and could not be violated.

Thirteen years later, it inspired the "Declaration of Human Rights" in France, and because this was the first political program to clearly spell out Natural Rights,

Marx called this document "The First Declaration of Human Rights." The Declaration of Independence effectively destroyed the theoretical foundations of feudal despotism, directly influenced the French Revolution in 1789, promoted later anti-feudal struggles throughout Europe, and later provided a great impetus to the national independence movements in Latin America and Asia. The idea of a Democratic Republic also enlightened and inspired the Chinese bourgeois thinkers who laid the ideological foundation for the Revolution of 1911 and promoted the development of China's national liberation movement.

### Saint-Simon, Owen, and Fourier's utopian socialism

The early days of the nineteenth century witnessed the rapid development of utopian socialism. During this period, the utopian socialist movement was represented by Comte de Saint-Simon, Charles Fourier, and Robert Owen.

Comte de Saint-Simon (1760–1825) was a French philosopher, economist, and utopian socialist.

His major works include: *Letters from an Inhabitant of Geneva to his Contemporaries*, *Introduction to Scientific Discoveries of the 19th Century*, *Essay on the Science of Man*, *Work on the Universal Law of Gravity*, etc.[6] Saint-Simon paid close attention to the poverty of the proletariat in France. He believed that one of the reasons the workers were poor was that a handful of rulers levied exorbitant taxes on the people to support a large number of officials. He thought that capitalism was nothing but an "intermediate and transitional system" between the old feudal system and the ideal society of the future, one that hinders social development, and for which there would soon be no need.

Saint-Simon believed that the industrial system had the potential to allow people to enjoy maximum freedom and ensure worldwide peace. He said that under the new political system, the only long-term goal of social organization should be to perfect the use of existing knowledge in the sciences, arts, and crafts, to meet people's needs. Everyone needs to work, he pointed out, which is an important socialist principle. Saint-Simon also suggested that everyone's income should be proportional to their talents and contributions to society. He proposed that a new morality should be established, which must oppose egoism and strive to improve the ideology of collectivism. True happiness, he argued, would be to abandon the motive of satisfying private desires and ambition, and instead work to improve knowledge to serve the most people. Saint-Simon was convinced that such a future society was almost at hand.

He accused the existing educational system of cultivating selfish people and argued that the subjects being taught dated from ancient times, and were seriously divorced from present day reality. He advocated education in the future society that would not only help individuals to acquire knowledge but also pay close attention to the cultivation of their moral character and special abilities.

Charles Fourier (1772–1837) was a famous French philosopher, economist, and utopian socialist.

At the beginning of the nineteenth century, he published works like *Universal Harmony*, *Theory of the Four Movements and the General Destinies*, *The New World*, and others that addressed the evils of the capitalist system and proposed replacing it with the "harmonious system" he had designed. He characterized capitalism as "a war of everyone against the whole people and the whole people against everyone" and equated capitalist civilization with a new form of slavery. He did not advocate the abolition of private ownership, but instead sought to establish, by means of publicity and education, a socialist society in which grass-roots organizations called "phalanxes" rewarded workers fairly based on the value of their contributions.

In 1832, he and several of his disciples started such a "phalanx" in which everyone was expected to work, women enjoyed full equality with men, education was free to all, and there was no difference of status between urban and rural areas or mental and physical labor.

Fourier vainly hoped to reconcile the contradiction between capital and labor through this kind of social organization and allocation scheme, so as to achieve a harmonious society in which everyone could feel happy. He put forward women's liberation for the first time as a way to measure how completely people were liberated. Regarding education, he advocated that it includes labor education and science education for children beginning early in life.

Robert Owen (1771–1858) was a British utopian socialist, industrialist, and philanthropist.

His most notable works are *A New View of Society* (1816) and *Book of the New Moral World* (*c.*1819–36). Owen was a great reformer and visionary who sharply criticized the capitalist system and pointed out that the poverty of working people was the inevitable outcome of capitalist society. He dreamed of a perfect socialist system but struggled against the transformation of social relations by violence.

In 1824, Owen traveled to America to create an experimental commune, called "New Harmony." This New Harmony Society put into practice his ideas about public possession of the means of production, equal rights, democratic management, and other principles, but over time, Owen's experiment ultimately failed.

In brief, utopian socialism offered a profound analysis and critique of capitalism exposing the harmful effects of capitalist society; criticizing its institutions (including private ownership), and argued that the replacement of capitalism was inevitable in a future society. It also carefully constructed blueprints for such a future society and offered valuable conjectures as to how such a society might be established with "equality and happiness" for everyone. Owen even carried out experiments of social transformation, which were mainly aimed at: (1) abolishing private ownership of the means of production to eliminate exploitation, oppression and the differences between classes; (2) changing the distribution system of capitalism, and implementing common labor and reasonable distribution; (3) eliminating commodity exchange, and instead, organizing production in a planned way; (4) eliminating differences between workers and peasants, urban and rural areas and mental and physical labor; (5) proposing to change the functions of nations into pure production management agencies until they eventually perish.

Utopian socialism's innovative ideas about the future of society provided valuable ideological materials for Marx's theory of scientific communism, becoming one of the major sources of Marxism.[7] However, given historical limitations, these communist experiments finally ended in failure.

### Jules Verne's science fiction

Jules Verne (1828–1905) was a French novelist, an important founder of modern science fiction.

Verne created a great number of excellent literary works during his life. Representative works include the trilogy titled as *The Children of Captain Grant* (1865–67), *Twenty Thousand Leagues under the Sea* (1869–70), and *The Mysterious Island* (1874–75), as well as *Five Weeks in a Balloon* (1863), *Journey to the Center of the Earth* (1864), and so on. According to UNESCO, Jules Verne is the second most-translated author in the world, ranking between the English-language writers Agatha Christie and William Shakespeare. With his extraordinary imagination, Verne described all sorts of inventions that seemed miraculous at the time, but, because his ideas were in line with scientific possibility, a great many of them have become reality since. Examples include the helicopter, submarine, television, and so on. French general Hubert Lyautey famously remarked that modern science and technology are only the processes of turning Verne's prophecies into realities.

Jules Verne "invented" the helicopter 50 years before the Wright brothers invented the airplane; he also spoke of an "electrical acoustic image machine" much like today's television. Many other miracles of the twentieth century first appeared in his novels, like electronic advertising, neon lights, moving sidewalks, air conditioning, skyscrapers, missiles, tanks, planes, human access to space, and even the rise of China. Many of the instruments he foresaw were later turned into actual goods in real life. In his book, *The Mysterious Island*, Verne predicted that water would become an energy source for future humans, and become the "coal" of the future. One hundred years later, Japanese scientists took the first steps towards the realization of this prophecy, when they used a material called titanium dioxide and the rays of sunlight to separate water into hydrogen and oxygen for the first time.

The autobiography of Simon Ryker, the pioneering designer of the modern submarine, begins "Jules Verne was in a sense the director-general of my life." Verne influenced generations of people to embark on scientific exploration and inspired them to invent. He was eulogized at the time of his death as: "a writer among scientists as well as a scientist among writers."

### Marx and Engels' "The Communist Manifesto"

Karl Heinrich Marx (1818–83) was a German philosopher, revolutionary theorist, and economist. He was the founder of Marxism, the organizer and leader of the International Workingmen's Association, a pioneer of the contemporary communist movement, the author of *Das Kapital* (1867–94) and co-author with Friedrich Engels of "The Communist Manifesto."

Friedrich Engels (1820–95) was also a German thinker, philosopher, revolutionist, and educator, who co-founded the theory of scientific communism with Karl Marx. After Marx's death Engels edited the manuscript of *Das Kapital* and published it. In addition to the works co-authored with Marx, he was also the author of *Dialectics of Nature* (1873–86) and *The Origin of the Family, Private Property and the State* (1884).

The theme of Marx's philosophy—the theory of "the liberation of all mankind as well as the all-round and free development of humans"—was formed as early as 1845 in his *German Ideology*. He believed that society is composed of individuals, and the ultimate goal of social development is also the all-round and free development of individuals. He explored the realistic path of human liberation and development of human beings from three aspects: (1) The development of world history that has broken national and regional boundaries, and promoted the expanding scope of human activities in time and space; (2) with the way that the rise and development of great industry has eliminated the inward-looking state of various countries and promoted the development of "universal exchanges"; and (3) the realization of communism, whose essential feature is the emancipation of all mankind, not merely the emancipation of a single region, class or nation.

"The Communist Manifesto" was first published on 21 February 1848 in London as an offprint. It offered a program of action for the Communist League written jointly by Marx and Engels, the first programmatic document of the international communist movement, and proved an important symbol of the birth of Marxism.

"The Communist Manifesto" expounded the basic principle of scientific socialism comprehensively and systematically for the first time, and pointed out that the communist movement had become a forceful trend in history. "The Communist Manifesto" explicitly put forward the basic ideas of communism (sometimes also called "scientific socialism"): "to eliminate private ownership", and "to overthrow the rule of the bourgeoisie, which would be replaced by the proletariat." It proposed that this purpose could only be achieved by using violence to overthrow the existing capitalist system, and that after taking power, the proletariat must vigorously develop the productive forces to carry out a great social transformation gradually, thus achieving the elimination of class itself, so as to eventually establish a society free from all classes and class antagonisms. The realization of public ownership of the means of production would then assure equality and comprehensive and free development for everyone. Although some views have historical limitations,[8] the belief in communist ideals is the theoretical essence of "The Communist Manifesto."

Marx and Engels could be called the thinkers who have had the greatest impact on the world in the past thousand years. Their thoughts have inspired the practice and development of countries and regions all over the world. *Das Kapital* has been published for more than 150 years, as the masterpiece of Marx's study on the social and economic forms of capitalism, it reveals the laws of social development of capitalism through in-depth analysis of capitalist production methods. Its influence is as always and still has high practical significance, including the financial crisis theory, which even accurately foresees economic globalization.

During the wave of national independence that followed the Second World War, some countries moved along the road to Soviet-style socialism, and many others among the 50 newly independent countries announced that they had created their own particular type of "socialist state". "Socialism" in these countries tends to have been influenced by nationalism or religion.

Among the more than 100 capitalist countries, there are 127 parties that take Marxism as their guiding ideology or currently retain the name of the Communist Party. Because of the devastating political attack caused by the drastic changes in Eastern Europe, the long-term survival and development of these non-ruling communist parties seems extremely uncertain, but they still actively explore socialist ideology.

Actually, the communists believe that if socialism is viewed as the transitional society from capitalism to communism, then it must be regarded as simply the prelude paving the way to a communist society. Its ultimate success demands a revolution more complete than any that has yet taken place in human history. Moreover, the consolidation of socialism is actually much more difficult than any revolution, as it must take a long historical process to mature.[920] Even the consolidation of the bourgeois revolution in Britain, France, and the United States took considerable time. Britain took 200 years (starting in 1640), France 86 years (1789–1875[10]), and the U.S. 100 years (1775–1877[11]), respectively, so how much time might be needed for socialist revolution and construction?

Of course, Marxism also needs to develop with the times, that is, to creatively develop in accordance with every new situation, even carry out necessary amendments, as it cannot stay in the context of more than 170 years ago.

Therefore, those countries that claim to adhere to the socialist system, including China, should combine the basic principles of Marxism with their actual national conditions, as well as the changed social reality and the characteristics of the times, by using the worldview and methodology of Marx's philosophy, and build up socialist countries independently with their own historical and cultural characteristics.

### Lenin and socialist practice: Lessons of the former Soviet Union

Vladimir Lenin (1870–1924) was a famous Marxist, proletariat revolutionist, statesman, theorist, and thinker. He first began to participate in a research group of Marxism in 1888, studied Karl Marx's *Das Kapital*, and translated "The Communist Manifesto" into Russian, and published the "imperialism theory" etc. In 1917, Lenin led the successful uprising now known as the Russian October Socialist Revolution, becoming the main founder of the first socialist country in the world. He inherited Marxism and combined it with the Russian revolution to form Leninism.

Although the Soviet Union made several serious mistakes both during and after the October Revolution, the cumulative achievements and experience of socialist construction in the Soviet Union cannot be ignored. After the victory of the October Revolution, Lenin led the Russian people to crush three armed attacks by external invaders and domestic rebels. Under his leadership, socialist practice in the Union of Soviet Socialist Republics (USSR) attained great achievements, not only in economic development but also in the development of world-class science and technology. The Soviet Union took only twelve years to realize industrialization, which had taken capitalist countries 50–100 years to complete, and also established a strong industrial, educational, scientific, and technological system.

The gross industrial output of the Soviet Union, which stood at a mere 6.9 per cent of the United States output in 1913, had reached 80 per cent of United States output by 1985, rising from a very backward country to become one of the world's two superpowers. And this occurred despite the enormous damage and hardship experienced during the Second World War, when the Soviet Union made an extraordinary contribution to the victory over the fascists and were arguably the main force responsible for the defeat of Nazi Germany. After the war, the Soviet Union strongly supported the international communist movement and new socialist countries including China[12], frequently expressing their solidarity with colonial and semi-colonial peoples striving for national independence and development.

Their achievements in science and technology in particular attracted attention worldwide. In 1954, they established the world's first nuclear power plant in Obninsk, marking the beginning of the peaceful use of atomic energy. In 1957, the Soviet Union launched the world's first man-made Earth satellite, beginning human activities in space, and in 1959, their "Luna 3" spacecraft sent back the first pictures of the far side of the moon. Then in 1961, the Vostok 1 spacecraft with Yuri Gagarin aboard was launched, making Gagarin the first human to travel into space. Among 16 Russian Nobel laureates, 12 won a Nobel Prize between 1956 and 1970 (during the period of the Soviet Union), two won a Nobel Prize before the October Revolution, and two more were winners in 2000 and 2003.[13]

However, with the implementation of the so-called "human, democratic, socialist" reform at the end of the twentieth century, the dominance of the Soviet Union's socialist system came to an end, and caused a number of socialist countries in Eastern Europe to move towards capitalism, reducing the socialist movement to its lowest point in the past 100 years. This great setback for world socialism delivered a serious warning to Marxists, not only in China but throughout the world, that only by going to the depths of history and exploring the root causes of drastic changes, and only by developing Marxism with the times and constantly implementing correct reform, especially system reform, can we adhere to the socialist system.

Over the past twenty years, various researchers have explored the causes, influences, and consequences of the collapse of the Soviet Union and the resulting drastic changes in Eastern Europe. A number of different conclusions have been reached. Among the causes that have been suggested for the Soviet Union's collapse are: that the system was overly rigid (unwilling to improve), that it failed to implement timely reforms, leaders' dereliction of duty, the unexpected pressure from below of gradual peaceful evolution, the government's failure to resolve deep-rooted ethnic problems, widespread political corruption (such as the Party's leadership degenerates and separates from the people), and so on. Of course, the internal cause is the main one. However, if the Soviet model of socialism is regarded as the first experiment in human history that attempted to turn this socialist ideal into reality, then we can acknowledge their mistakes during the long effort to achieve this arduous task and arrive at a more just and rational answer.

The October Revolution of the Soviet Union and the socialist experiment that followed, which lasted 70 years and spread throughout Eastern Europe, represent the first large-scale exploration of Marx's socialist theory. Both the successes and failures of the USSR's attempts to implement socialist ideals are a precious resource for the international communist movement and provide abundant reference materials for the guidance and development of other socialist countries.

### The United Nations' Universal Declaration of Human Rights[14]

The Universal Declaration of Human Rights (UDHR) is one of the basic laws of the United Nations, which was adopted by the UN General Assembly on 10 December 1948. After the enactment of this historic "Declaration", the General Assembly requested all Member States to widely publicize, spread, exhibit, read, and elaborate it, regardless of their political status as countries or territories.

The UDHR is based upon the concepts of freedom, equality, and human rights derived from the common cultural heritage of mankind, especially from the modern Western countries, and reflects the strong desires of people around the world to attain and protect human rights. The UDHR includes a preamble and 30 articles, of which 19 are related to civil and political rights, and six address economic, social, and cultural rights.

The UDHR laid the foundation for global and national standards in the field of international human rights, and over half a century after its adoption, the international community still regards it as the defining statement of human rights.

Despite intense discussions and repeated consultations in the process of drafting the UDHR, the document inevitably has some historical limitations. For example, the UDHR emphasized the universality and common standards of human rights while ignoring the particularity of human rights and also the recognition that different countries have different standards and characteristics. Moreover, it stressed the individual's rights and freedoms, but ignored the rights and freedoms of groups, and nations, and made no attempt to define the proper relationship between individual freedom and responsibility to the community and to humanity as a whole. This shortcoming makes the UDHR unsatisfactory—or at best incomplete—as a guide to rights and obligations in a sustainable Global Civilization.

### Socialist practice in China

Hundred years ago, when the Chinese nation was heavily laden with calamities, the socialist Soviet Union provided China with a new political and social model. At that time, when the socialist Soviet Union was prospering, and its economic construction had already made brilliant achievements, a number of China's advanced intellectuals such as Duxiu Chen, Dazhao Li, Qiubai Qu, and Enlai Zhou attributed the success of the Soviet Union to the socialist system and

Marxism. As a result, the USSR's road to socialism became the preferred choice among many elites and led to the birth of the Communist Party of China, which took Marxism as its guiding ideology. The Communist Party of China, represented by Zedong Mao, led the people to establish new China in 1949 following a long period of arduous struggle. Since then, a new long march of building socialism has been underway.

**1. China chose socialism and three great revolutions**

The Chinese nation once stood on the top of the world and created a splendid civilization and many brilliant achievements. For more than 300 years beginning in the fourteenth century until the reign of Emperor Qianlong of the Qing Dynasty (1736–95), China's GDP ranked highest in the world. But in modern times China lagged behind due to closing its doors to other countries, not attempting to make progress, attaching no importance to science and technology, and opposing reform, so that the opportunity for industrial revolution was lost. The first Opium War in 1840 was a turning point in Chinese history, and also opened a prelude to China's modern history. From then on, China was gradually reduced to the status of a semi-colonial/semi-feudal society. Added to this, the rise of Western capitalist countries and the invasion of imperialism, especially after the Opium War, compelled China to sign treaties that humiliated its people, forfeited its sovereignty, and forced it to become a backward country. Western powers had long regarded China as a "sleeping Oriental lion" or even as the "sick man of East Asia".

In response to this tragic situation, people with lofty ideals in China were distressed and disgusted, and vigorously sought a pathway to save and revitalize the nation. They successively launched "the Westernization Movement", "the Reform movement of 1898", "the Revolution of 1911", "the May 4th Movement," and so on. However, all reform attempts to save the country failed. The Chinese people realized that it was impossible to save the country merely by adopting Western advanced technology. Instead fundamental changes needed to be made in terms of ideology, culture, and society.

But how to change? Over the course of the last century, China has launched three great revolutions. All of these revolutions focused on a common issue, "what path should China take", to develop into a successful modern country?

The First Revolution, which began in 1911, was led by Yat-sen Sun and succeeded in ending the autocratic monarchy that had ruled China for thousands of years, and opened the door to China's progress. The Second Revolution was the new democratic and socialist revolution led by the Chinese Communist Party (CPC) under the leadership of Zedong Mao. The communists overthrew the rule of imperialism, feudalism, and bureaucrat-capitalism in China, founded a new

China in 1949, and established the socialist system, thus laying the foundations for new institutions—the fundamental political prerequisite for China's rejuvenation. The Third Revolution is the great movement towards economic reform and opening up led by the second generation of collective leadership with Xiaoping Deng as the core in the late 1970s.

Obviously, China chose the road of socialism under the leadership of the Communist Party, and this is the choice of China for more than 100 years of modern history.

**2. The practice of institutional transformation in China is still underway**

In the course of exploring the socialist road, China has experienced some failures as well as many twists and turns. Because even if the socialist system is established, how to build socialism in China and best exploit its advantages to the full is an unprecedented challenge. After the founding of new China, the country experienced three experiments in institutional transformation (the term "institution" as used here refers mainly to China's political system, e.g., its state system, government form, legal, and administrative systems, etc.).

From 1950 to the late 1970s was the period of the first institutional transformation, led by the first generation of China's leadership represented by Zedong Mao (Zedong Mao, Shaoqi Liu, De Zhu, Enlai Zhou, etc.). This stage involved the fundamental transformation of the social system, and the direct transition from a semi-colonial, semi-feudal, and newly democratic society to a socialist society. Although due to the insufficient development of capitalism in old China, the material base for consolidating and developing socialism was relatively weak. In addition, the domestic and international environment at the time was very complex and harsh, but it still vigorously defended the country's sovereignty and sacred territory, created the cleanest government in the world with "Ten nothings"[15]; independently developed "Two bombs and one satellite", eventually succeeded in establishing an independent and relatively complete industrial system, a sound national economy, and a scientific and technological system. Moreover, China overcame all kinds of resistance to assume its rightful place in the United Nations. The average life expectancy in China, which was 35 in 1949, rose to 65.86 by 1978.

The brilliant achievements, historical accomplishments, and lessons of the socialist construction period laid the basic material foundation for the second stage of China's reform and opening up, helping to create a more supportive international environment, and also provided a theoretical and practical basis for pursuing a socialist road with Chinese characteristics.

However, because its political and economic systems are still in the exploratory stage, China had failed to establish a stable political environment and maintain a strong economy. As a result, China has taken many detours, even the wrong route (such as the "Anti-Rightist Campaign" and the "Cultural Revolution"), and lost many development opportunities. This made the people go through a lot of hardships after the founding of New China. Of course, these detours and lessons of failure in the arduous exploration of building socialism also left us with extremely valuable political and ideological knowledge.

In the late 1970s, China embarked on a policy of reform and opening up, which was the great revolution led by the second generation of China's leadership (Xiaoping Deng, Jianying Ye, Xiannian Li, Yun Chen, Yaobang Hu, etc.) with Xiaoping Deng at the helm, and it was also "the great awakening of the Communist Party of China."[16] With extraordinary courage, bringing order out of chaos, its leaders determined the strategy of reform and opening up, established the theory of a socialist market economy, and laid the foundation for China's rapid development in the last 30 years. Xiaoping Deng's important judgment is that poverty is not socialism. This reform promoted the transition of China's economic development model from a wholly planned economy to a largely market economy system, which enabled China to experience a great economic miracle. Between 1978 and 2012, China's GDP maintained a growth rate of 9.83 per cent and reached the position of second-highest in the world in 2012. People's living standards have generally improved (per capita GDP increased from 200 USD in 1978 to more than 10,000 USD in 2020, while the average life span increased from 65.86 years in 1978 to 77 years in 2020). This has established a solid material foundation for China's further reform, including a base for the third experiment in institutional transformation.

But many long-established concepts, modes of production, values, moral standards, and institutional arrangements still persist and are unable to rid themselves of the flawed logic and laws of Industrial Civilization (which, all developed countries have also experienced). Thus, it can be said that China's sustained economic growth or "economic miracle" over the past 30 years has come at a high price. It is difficult for resources and energy to support sustainable development; the carrying capacity of the ecological environment has reached its limit; environmental capacity is approaching a critical point, and the gap between rich and poor has increased rapidly. In particular, social reform and institutional reform are seriously lagging behind economic reform. In addition, we have not really solved many theoretical and practical problems related to the socialist market economy, resulting in social anomie in the economic, political, and moral fields during China's transition period, such phenomena as money worship, loss of faith, decline in morality, lack of social integrity, and fraud are rampant, and widespread corruption exists. In addition, social equity issues (including social security, employment, health care, education, income distribution, etc.), all undermine social stability. Of course, the enduring influence and serious consequences of the "Cultural Revolution" in the field of ideology and culture (which may require generations of effort to rectify), including the wavering of Marxist belief. China is facing the overwhelming challenge of how to remain on the socialist path and still attain sustainable development. China is standing at the starting point of a new long march towards socialist construction, and a new round of reform is on the way.

Since the start of the twenty-first century, a third system transformational exploration has been launched with the convening of the 18th CPC National Congress. China's new leadership with President Jinping Xi at the helm realized that in order to achieve the ambitious goal of a great rejuvenation of the Chinese nation, it is not enough to rely on economic reform alone. So, they determined to implement a comprehensive range of deepening reforms in the economy, political system, culture, society, and ecology, as well as reforming the institutional structure of the CPC itself. The overall goal of comprehensively deepening reform is to improve and develop the socialist system with Chinese characteristics and promote the modernization of the national governance system. Therefore, China must amend, supplement, develop, and improve socialism with Chinese characteristics at every stage from concept, through connotation and approach, to actual implementation.

In fact, socialism with Chinese characteristics faces challenges from the competition of international and domestic interest groups as well as from competing ideologies and institutions. Fortunately, thanks to the experience and lessons learned from more than 70 years of success and failure, China's policymakers have achieved a general consensus regarding a number of problems they must overcome in the future and on the breakthroughs necessary to achieve reform, which are gradually being implemented.

## The European Union

The headquarters of the European Union (EU), whose predecessor was the European Economic Community, are in Brussels, the capital of Belgium. The concept of European unity emerged before the twentieth century, but the trend toward European unification only reached its climax after the Second World War.

British Prime Minister Winston Churchill proposed the establishment of the United States of Europe in September 1946. The European Commission, established in 1949, became the first pan-European organization. On 18 April 1951, six countries, including France, Italy, West Germany, The Netherlands, Belgium, and Luxembourg, signed a 50-year treaty establishing the European Coal and Steel Community (ECSC). On 25 March 1957, on the basis of the ECSC, these same six countries also signed the Treaty of the European Economic Community (EEC) and the Treaty of the European Atomic Energy Community (EURATOM) in Rome. On 8 April 1965, the six founding members signed the Merger Treaty (or

Brussels Treaty), which combined the executive bodies of the ECSC, EURATOM, and the EEC into a single institutional structure, collectively dubbed the European Community (EC). The treaty entered into force on 1 July 1967.

In April 1990, French President Francois Mitterrand and Chancellor of Germany Helmut Kohl jointly initiated an intergovernmental meeting on political alliances at the end of the year. After a year of negotiations, the Treaty on European Union (commonly known as the Maastricht Treaty) was signed on 7 Feburary 1992 at the EC Maastricht summit. Its main features are that 12 countries (the six founding members plus Denmark, Great Britain, Ireland, Greece, Spain, and Portugal) agreed to implement a common foreign, security, and defense policy. In addition, some measures such as a common fishery policy, the establishment of a European monetary system, and the construction of the economic and monetary union are also stipulated. Just five years after the signing of the Schengen Convention in 1990, free movement across national borders within the EC started being implemented. This allowed citizens of the member countries to cross borders without passports.

On 1 November 1993, the Maastricht Treaty entered into force, announcing the formal establishment of the European Union, and the transition of the EC from an economic entity to an economic and political entity. Meanwhile, it implements a common foreign and security policy, and strengthens cooperation in the fields of justice and home affairs. Now the EU has 28 member states and uses 24 official languages.

Over the past 60 years, remarkable achievements have been made in European integration in building a non-violent alliance between countries, ensuring long-term peace in Europe, and establishing integrated trade, investment, and financial and monetary affairs. It is the grand goal of the confederation of global governance, and a sign of great historical progress. In 2012, the Nobel Peace Prize was awarded to the European Union. However, in the past ten years, the European Union has experienced various internal and external crises, including the debt crisis, the refugee crisis, Brexit, and the security crisis, which reflects the defects in the systems and institutions of the EU as a multilayered government body. Of course, no great undertaking has ever had plain sailing. It is believed that the common wisdom of Europe will ultimately be able to successfully cope with this series of political and institutional challenges, get out of the deep predicaments it is in, and realize the vision of European integration.

### The Venus Project founded by Jacques Fresco's team[17]

Although Fresco's Venus Project is often considered a local experiment, it is still highly significant.

Jacque Fresco (1916–2017), futurist, inventor, industrial designer, and founder of the Venus Project, and his associate Roxanne Meadows have headed up the project team for some 40 years.

The Venus Project is an organization that promotes feasible social transformation. Its mission is to create the blueprint for a new world civilization based on concern about human needs, restoring the environment to its natural state, and realizing a more peaceful and sustainable Global Civilization. The objective of work for humans in such a civilization will no longer be for the sake of money and egoism, but to achieve humanity's highest ideals and to assure the well-being of all peoples.

The Venus Project's long-term plans will be implemented in four phases. The first phase is already underway. The team has completed the construction of a 25-acre research center in Venus, Florida, to help present the proposals of the Venus Project. Phase two includes the production of a full-length feature film that will depict how a world embracing the proposals advanced by the Venus Project would work. This film will provide a positive vision of a peaceful society in which all human beings form a global family on planet Earth and present a modern version of Utopian society through resources and human needs, energy, transportation, government and religion, social design, mechanization, law, education, etc. In phase three, to test its designs and proposals, the Venus Project is working towards the construction of an experimental research city. Blueprints for most of the initial technologies and buildings have begun. This ideal society would be devoted to 18 goals (see list below).[18] In Phase four, once the experimental city is completed, a theme park is also planned that will both entertain and inform visitors about the possibilities for humane and environmentally friendly lifestyles planned by the Venus Project, which could be the prototype for a series of cities to be constructed in various places throughout the world.

### 18 Goals of the Venus Project

- Conserving all the world's resources as the common heritage of all of Earth's people;
- Transcending the arbitrary racial and natural boundaries that currently separate people;
- Replacing money-based nationalistic economies with a resource-based world economy;
- Helping to stabilize the world's population through education and voluntary birth control to let it conform to the carrying capacity of the Earth;
- Reclaiming and restoring the natural environment to the best of human ability;

- Redesigning the world's cities, transportation systems, agricultural industries, and industrial plants so that they are energy efficient, clean, and able to conveniently serve the needs of all people;
- Gradually abandoning corporate entities and governments (local, national, or supra-national) as social management institutions so as to outgrow the need for the state and plutocracy and thus gradually moving towards an autonomous society;
- Sharing and applying new technologies for the benefit of all nations;
- Developing and using clean renewable energy sources;
- Manufacturing the highest quality products for the benefit of the world's people;
- Requiring environmental impact studies prior to the construction of any mega project;
- Encouraging the widest range of creativity and incentive towards all kinds of constructive endeavors;
- Outgrowing nationalism, bigotry, and prejudice through education;
- Eliminating all types of elitism, technical, or otherwise;
- Arriving at methodologies by careful research rather than random opinions;
- Enhancing communication in schools so that our language is relevant to the physical conditions of the world;
- Providing not only the necessities of life but also offering challenges that stimulate the mind while emphasizing individuality rather than uniformity;
- Finally, preparing people intellectually and emotionally for the possible changes and challenges that lie ahead.

The Venus Project forecasts that money, politics, personal, and national interests will be eliminated in the near future, and considers that as long as we are developing the resource-based economy (to replace the current monetary system) and improving the social structure, we should realize environment-friendly cities with energy independence as well as create a sustainable world civilization.

### Paolo Soleri and Arcosanti[19]

Paolo Soleri's Arcosanti and his ideals are not on the same level as the 12 examples mentioned above. However, it is worthy of praise that he dedicated over 40 years exploring the future city, future architecture, and future lifestyles, focusing on green development.

Paolo Soleri (1919–2013) was the most famous eco-architect of the twentieth century. He had multiple identities as an architect, urban planning designer, artist, craftsman, and philosopher, and made a lifelong commitment to exploring the infinite possibilities for realizing human ideals. The well-known ecological architecture project Arcosanti is the most famous example of his work. This "urban laboratory" is an experimental town, which was built in the Arizona desert, in an effort to provide an alternative solution to the deteriorating living environment. In 1970, he bought more than 4,000 acres of desert wasteland north of Phoenix, Arizona, and began to build his dream on this barren land.

*Energy*: Soleri believed that the use of biofuels including corn or other green plants to produce automotive fuel, is an insult to nature and humans. However, today we continue to rely on the fossil energy that was produced millions of years ago. In Arcosanti, the conventional power grid is used to meet most of the town's electricity needs, but the integrated passive greenhouses, which use wind power, solar energy, and recycled water, etc., contribute as well, so as to provide lighting, heat, and refrigeration. Meanwhile, the compact and high-density urban design reduces energy demand for heating and cooling in the town, and the approach of vehicle marginalization also reduces the energy consumed in transportation. Moreover, "on-site production of energy" avoids the huge loss of energy during transmission to end-users through cable systems that often stretch for hundreds of miles. In addition to the "Dome Effect" explained below, joint-row "greenhouses" located near the main building convert solar energy into electricity and heat that can be piped directly into buildings whose overall shape is like several crescent moons.

*Ecological architecture*: Soleri conceived the whole town as a complete giant building, in order to fully improve the efficiency of energy utilization, the flow of people, logistics, and so on. Most buildings are oriented southward, and are built in the form of hollow, quarter-sphere, or semi-domes to capture the sun's light and preserve heat. The ventilation system of the whole building takes full advantage of the chimney effect, namely that hot air rises while cool air descends. The whole architectural complex serves as a huge radiator. Although the complex is located in the sweltering desert, there is no need for air conditioning. Thanks to the ingenious design, the buildings here can make the best use of natural energy, and the average consumption of energy per person is greatly reduced.

*Vegetation and food production*: Productive vegetation is integrated into the design of Arcosanti to preserve the existing agricultural land for producing food and also to blend food production into the town itself. A total of 23 orchards have been built along the north side of Arcosanti, and the south-facing large subsidiary conservatory not only produces agricultural products and provides heat energy but also offers a productive environment for public enjoyment.

*Town without cars*: Soleri's vision for a tiled urban development has paid long-term dividends in reducing land and resource consumption. Soleri advocated a green city with high integration and low consumption, as opposed to the sprawl, energy waste, and interpersonal alienation commonly found in conventional urban centers, and set out to build a three-dimensional "walking city" to solve these difficult problems. Each building here has a variety of functions, people can easily access almost all their needs for life—shopping, swimming pools, creative rooms, coffee shops, conference rooms, handcraft workshops, residences, basketball courts, catering, community life, entertainment, and leisure, by walking about ten minutes through a spiral slope, and open fields are only a few steps away. People live in Arcosanti without the use of cars, but the designer still provides a parking facility with two levels of basement under the solar power plant, large enough for parking tens of thousands of various types of vehicles, which residents can use to go on long journeys.

*Urban scale and layout*: Arcosanti is a settlement conceived as the world's smallest "city". Soleri's urban design realizes a micro, multiple, and intensive town, and exploits the advantages of three-dimensional, sustainable, and multi-functional architecture to the extreme. The total land area used amounts to only 2 per cent of the standard urban land required to house 5,000 residents, while at the same time creating more public space to strengthen the connections between people. Its large buildings and large-scale solar greenhouses only occupy 25 acres of a 4,060-acre land preserve, reducing the distance between nature and urban residents.

*Operation and life*: Arcosanti has tenaciously survived for more than 40 years in the desert environment. Soleri and his students, as well as more than 6,000 volunteers from all over the world, personally participated in various tests and constructions. Nearly 80 long-term residents live here, and some of them have already had children. Their average salaries are only slightly above the poverty line in the United States; however, they are willing to undertake the design, construction, maintenance, cooking, woodworking, metal forging, ceramics, gardening, and management at Arcosanti, including the production of the world-famous "Soleri bells". About 50,000 tourists visit here to share the eco-city experience each year. Arcosanti is primarily an educational center. The funding for supporting the construction at Arcosanti mainly comes from: selling the handmade metal and ceramic wind-bells on site, fees for workshops, income from tourism; and various cultural activities. Of course, these funds are far from enough to support and realize the ideal of Arcosanti; therefore, less than 10 per cent of the overall planning has been completed so far.

It is regrettable that both the Venus Project and the Arcosanti construction suffer from a lack of funds to support their continued development and maintenance. This is a point worth thinking about and reflecting on.

The above is a very short list of inventions that will affect society for all time. There is no doubt that other historians would have their own lists.

While many of the ideals or fantasies described by Jules Verne in his adventure novels such as *Twenty Thousand Leagues under the Sea* have now been realized, none of the ideal states involving social inventions and the reform of human conduct has yet been achieved, from More's *Utopia* to the utopian socialism of Saint-Simon, Owen, and Fourier, or even Marx's communism, and other ideals described above.

This is because realizing the dream of a future society is different from conducting purely material scientific experiments. Such experiments can rely on what I have called "hard technology" and operate entirely in the physical world, but the creation, design, transformation, and practice of new social systems involve not only knowledge and consensus on a spiritual level, such as religion, belief, culture, and morality but also knowledge and operation ability in the field of human social behavior, such as lifestyle, economic, and social development models, which depend more on soft technology and the soft environment. Designs for soft technology and soft environment will necessarily reflect the worldviews, values, and beliefs of their designers, but if there is no global consensus or agreement about standards for operability, as well as what I called "the cultural environment in a broad sense" (see Figure 7.1 in Chapter 7), it will be difficult to apply these innovations in more than a single country. This is a huge social engineering task.

However, while some countries today are still pursuing old dreams, others are truly committed to carrying out reforms and experimenting.

## NOTES

1. *World Happiness Report* was released by the Earth Institute of Columbia University and the United Nations, https://www.sohu.com/a/302939908260616.
2. Technology Philosophy in the Future.
3. The main points of Kant's *Essay on Perpetual Peace* include: (1) people's nature is born to be good; they are rational and tend towards cooperation; (2) morality and juridical logic are the keys to saving the world; (3) the fundamental interests of all sovereign states are harmonious, and they should therefore assign a portion of their sovereignty to international organizations for the common good; (4) war can be avoided, and the emergence of war had nothing to do with human nature; (5) effective measures to stop war include the implementation of national self-determination, the abolition of secret diplomacy, collective security instead of the traditional balanced power system, the establishment of international

institutions, international law, and international organizations, appealing to international public opinion, and changes in the domestic political system.

4. http://baike.haosou.com/doc/5811-5954.html.
5. They advocated that the legislative, executive and judicial powers should be controlled by different organs, exercised independently and restricted each other.
6. http://baike.baidu.com/view/5799452.htm.
7. V.I. Lenin, *Lenin Collected Works*, Vol. 19, (People's Press, 1959). It stated clearly for the first time that Marxist doctrine has three theoretical sources and three components. Marxism is based on the outstanding achievements of the nineteenth century, and its three theoretical sources include: German classical philosophy, British classical political economics, and French socialist theory; Marxism's three components are: complete philosophical materialism, an economic doctrine that takes surplus value theory as its cornerstone, and scientific socialism.
8. The historical value and limitations of the *Communist Manifesto*, http://www.wyzxwk.com/Article/zatan/2018/03/387725.html.
9. http://baike.baidu.com/view/21409.htm.
10. From the outbreak of the French Revolution in 1789 to the adoption of the Constitution in 1875.
11. From the War of Independence in 1775, the Civil War in 1861 to the Democratic Reconstruction in the south in 1877.
12. At the beginning of the twentieth century, the first socialist country was established in the world after the Russian October Socialist Revolution. After that, the socialist movement was surging forward with great momentum and force. By the 1960s, 16 countries had embarked on the road of socialism, more than 100 political parties that put forward socialist programmes were in power in 40 countries. Socialism became the main political movement of the twentieth century and Marxism was widely regarded as a great means for achieving the liberation of all humanity.
13. "Why does Russia – An educational powerhouse – Have several Nobel laureates?", 15 October 2010, http://www.360doc.com/content/10/1015/09/813992_61118923.shtml.
14. http://baike.baidu.com/link?url=meuHeH7nQC4LxVn-GUZHWOHFNsn5-4oHQiHNxzvXYsCCJxOmUfNeLdyGHWSsa6nDPfV8yst-2npg6sa7x8eeoq.
15. 1. No corrupt officials, 2. No local tyrants or evil gentry, 3. No gambling, 4. No prostitutes, 5. No concubines, 6. No beggars, 7. No private party members, 8. No malaise, 9. No one can get rich by creating friction, 10. No one can make money from causing national distress
16. Xi Jinping, "Celebrating reform and opening up 40th anniversary", 18 December 2018.
17. *The Venus Project*, n.d., https://www.thevenusproject.com/en/.
18. https://www.thevenusproject.com/the-venus-project/aims-and-proposals/.
19. https://en.wikipedia.org/wiki/Arcosanti; http://baike.baidu.com/link?url=vBOpmI0ZkxXqU4B9Ivyf8si_ScqoQsBLQ5cpvnFH83pMJ5TIJY0PkbrigHZOLQgNvRzGMjSgt6hK_t5ztT8m5a.

# 7

# Integrating the Values of Global Civilization into the Practice of Sustainable Development—The Case of China

*For a nation without a bright future vision and goal, there is no hope.*

In the previous chapter, I defined Global Civilization as a social system that is adapted to the sustainable survival and development of human beings, in other words, a social system that is supported by the complementarity of material, spiritual, political, ecological, and interstellar civilizations that adapt to sustainable development. So, what is sustainable development? What is the essence of human sustainable survival and development?

The concept of sustainable development was first put forward in 1987 in the World Commission on Environment and Development's report "Our Common Future." Since then it has become a familiar concept and has been widely spread and promoted throughout the world. This represents great progress in the process of human development. However, looking back on the process of promoting sustainable development over the past 30 years, despite many declarations, agendas, and implementation plans that have been put forward to promote sustainable development, the challenges to its achievement remain severe. These include overgrowth of population, food shortages and food safety, poverty, etc. According to the recent report of the United Nations, more than 820 million people still suffer from hunger in the world. Moreover, protecting strategic resources, including marine resources, has become increasingly difficult, due to the rapid expansion of urbanization, the resulting environmental pollution, changes in global ecology, etc.

Take the water problem as an example. The water problem is still an important obstacle to sustainable development. About 1.1 billion people in developing countries have no access to safe drinking water. The number of people who die from water pollution-related diseases each year far exceeds the number who die from wars or natural disasters.[1]

According to UNEP, the world economy has quadrupled in the past 30 years, but 60 per cent of the major ecosystem goods and services supporting human livelihoods have been degraded or are being used in unsustainable ways. This shows that the "Brown" traditional economy still dominates the economies of all countries and thus the entire world. As Vinod Thomas, former Vice President of the World Bank has said, the impacts of climate change, the world economic crisis, and food problems are enough by themselves to cause a "derailment" of progress toward global sustainable development.

What's the problem? The substantive progress of sustainable development is not as expected. We can cite many reasons, such as the lack of legally binding institutional arrangements, the lack of global leadership; some countries, especially developing countries, have weak environmental protection policies; although developing countries maintain the principle of "common but differentiated responsibilities" on paper, it is difficult to really get benefits; developed countries have not fully fulfilled their commitments to support developing countries, and so on.

What are the main causes? Although the definition, importance, and implementation agendas can be recognized in theory, and agreements can be signed on a global scale, any time sustainable development conflicts with immediate practical interests, group interests, or national interests, deep-rooted values do not support the required actions. This leads to a disconnection between declarations and actions.

In other words, the values of Industrial Civilization, which have lasted for hundreds of years, have led to the short-sightedness, wrong ideas, and behavior patterns of most people, including the elites of all countries in today's society—who tend to focus on immediate interests but ignore long-term interests, and focus on economic development but fail to protect nature. This creates severe sustainable development challenges for human beings and the earth on which they depend for survival.

### *Redefining sustainable development—a paradigm shift for human survival and development*

Although more than one hundred definitions of sustainable development exist, the most widely used one states that sustainable development is "development that meets the needs of the present without compromising the ability of future generations to meet their own needs."

So, what are the needs of contemporary people? What is the ability of future generations to meet their needs?

There are about 7 billion people in the world today, living in more than 190 countries, speaking roughly 6,000 different languages. They are living at many different levels of economic development, under different social systems, and have different cultures and beliefs. However, all of them share the common hope that individuals and families can be happy, that society can remain stable, and that the peace and happiness they desire can be passed on to future generations.

However, for the past 30 years and more, the path toward sustainable global development has never been straightforward. The year 2015 was the deadline for the United Nations Millennium Development Goals, which the UN has defined as their core objectives for attaining sustainable development. At the Rio+20 Earth Summit held in 2012, every country agreed to create a set of Sustainable Development Goals to accomplish the unfinished work of the Millennium Development Goals and established the UNGA Open Working Group on Sustainable Development Goals on March 2013. This was a far-sighted decision.

At the United Nations World Summit on Sustainable Development in September 2015, 193 Member States approved a sustainable development plan for the next fifteen years called "Transforming our world: The 2030 Agenda for Sustainable Development" and formulated 17 proposed goals and 169 associated targets to be completed by 2030. In an effort to make the Sustainable Development Goals clearer and more quantifiable, every United Nations agency will use this indicator system as a tool to assess and promote higher levels of sustainability in all countries, and provide the basis for formulating policies. The cost of achieving these goals has been estimated at between $3.5 and $5 trillion per year.

In fact, various countries have developed various indicators around sustainable development to guide and monitor the process of sustainable development for decades. But to achieve sustainability of the evaluated countries and regions, it is not enough to focus on indicators alone. The key is how countries and regions integrate the values of Global Civilization into the practice of sustainable development and realize the transformation of development modes in various fields, such as society, the economy, politics, resources, the environment, and scientific and technological development.

Let's discuss the essence of sustainable development from the perspective of practice.

The ultimate goal of sustainable development is to seek universal human progress so that everyone can live permanently in a prosperous and peaceful world that will last for generations. In this sense, developing the economy, promoting social progress, protecting the environment, enhancing science and technologies, and implementing social and political reforms are all approaches or "battles" to achieve the goals of sustainable development.

If human beings want to achieve the goal of sustainable development, they must realize the paradigm shift in key areas (such as six "battles") of human survival and development.

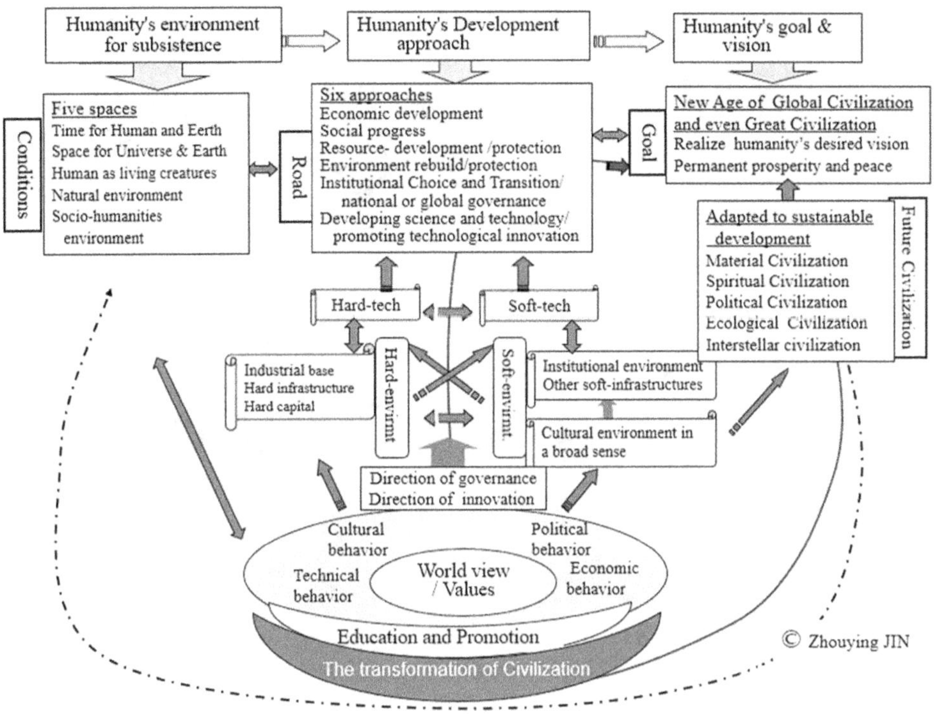


FIGURE 7.1: Redefining sustainable development.

Following this train of thought, I have outlined a grand strategy for realizing sustainable development as two crisscross systems (see Figure 7.1). From the horizontal perspective, this system is composed of three aspects: the human living environment (recognize the conditions), the ways and means of development (identify development pathways, implementation tools and supporting conditions), and humanity's vision and goals (set the right goals). From the vertical perspective, human sustainable development paths are made up of three layers, which include the six major approaches that each constitute a unique system, the means and soft-hard environment (technology and support system) to ensure effective implementation of various approaches, the foundation (continuously promote the progress of human civilization) affecting human values and behavior patterns, etc.

To realize sustainable development in all countries and regions, we must adopt a systemic solution, whether at the macro-, meso-, or micro-scale, or at all those different levels simultaneously.

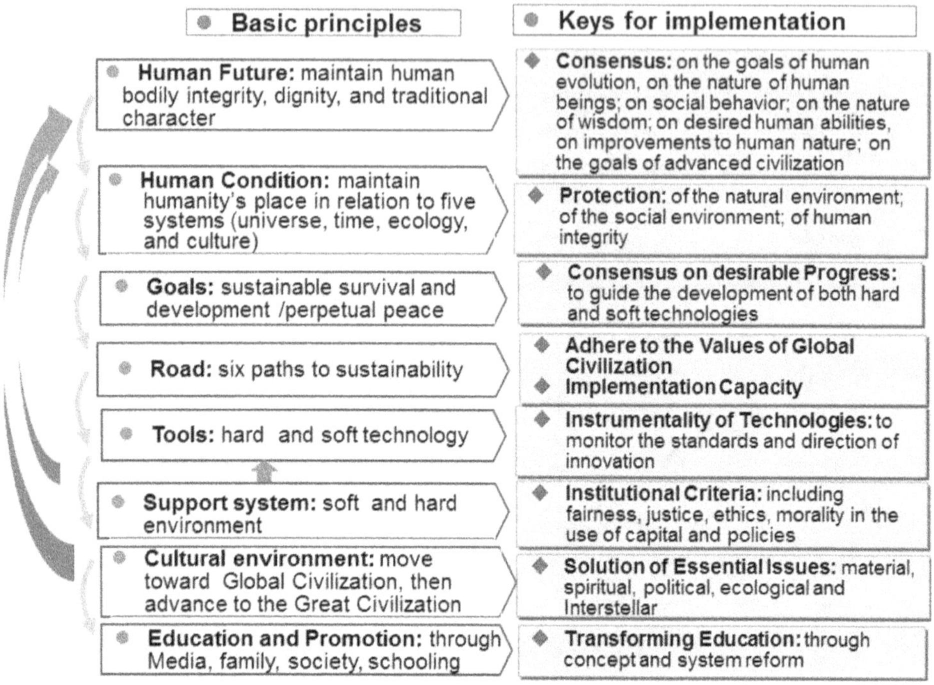


FIGURE 7.2: Basic principles of sustainable development. © Zhouying Jin.

Seven key elements of the system for realizing sustainable development are:

- clarify the premise and obtain a consensus;
- recognize the location;
- firmly establish targets;
- select the right development path to promote the transformation of civilizations;
- adhere to the instrumentality of technology and grasp the direction of technological innovation;
- improve the support system and create a good cultural environment;
- agree that education is the foundation.

### Premise and consensus

First of all, it is necessary to have *a basic consensus* on what "human" is, and on the issue of what future mankind should be like. In view of the risk that technological intervention poses for the continuance of biological human life, we need to keep in mind the true meaning of life, human nature, and status. Human beings must always make clear who "we" are: namely a race of advanced beings who have evolved over hundreds of millions of years. If and when non-biological intelligence can match or even surpass that of human beings, we should continue to prize and maintain the characteristics, dignity, and special abilities of traditional humans, as we strive to survive and develop sustainably.

### Condition: development space

Human beings should have a clear understanding of their position with regard to five spaces: in the universe, in time, in the realm of living creatures, in the natural environment, and in the sociocultural environment including history, current situation, and foreseeable future of each of these five spaces, as well as the interrelation between them.

- *Position in space*: the position of humans on the Earth where we live, and in the universe (our spatial environment).
- *Position in time*: the position of the Earth and its present population in the long history of humanity and of the entire universe at the Relative Time Coordinate System (our temporal environment).
- *Identification as a living creature*: humans need to recognize and understand their position in the universe and among other living creatures in the life system of nature. Human beings are just a group of higher organisms in the universe, we should understand the relationship between the evolution of the universe and life. We are constantly bound by the irresistible laws of nature, and at the same time, we recognize that human understanding of the whole universe is just a drop in the bucket.
- *Natural space*: the natural environment of human existence includes the ecological environment, biological environment and resource environment as well as universe, we should revere nature and natural laws.
- *Humanistic space*: the humanistic social environment for human survival. We should understand the position and function of human beings in the evolution of human beings, in the birth and the evolution of civilization, and even in the "great history" of human development in which new civilizations are created.

These five spaces constitute the basic condition and premise of future human development. It should be stressed that the social and cultural environment and parts of the natural environment are not simply the result of human activities, but represent conditions for further development in the future.

## Development goals

The ultimate goal of sustainable human survival and development is to create a world where groups with different cultures, religions, belief and customs can accept each other, coexist and share happiness, and enjoy a prosperous and peaceful world—a Great civilization, with sustained progress in which we can live for generations. The above goal can also be summed up by the characteristics of civilization, namely to generalize from the mainstream worldviews and values of today's social systems in order to identify basic issues that need to be resolved.

## Six major approaches to development

In order to correctly design the route and method for achieving this goal, the values of Global Civilization must be integrated into the practice of the six approaches of sustainable development to promote a paradigm shift for human development:

1. expand production activity and economic development using steady-state, green and continuous innovation (transforming our current economic development mode);
2. promote social progress and build a fair, impartial, self-disciplined, and harmonious society (transforming of the social development model);
3. protect, economize, recycle, and carefully use natural resources (transforming the natural resources application model);
4. work to repair, enhance, and protect the ecological environment (transforming of the relationship between man and nature);
5. to build a harmonious society and ensue peaceful development throughout the world, it is necessary to focus on solving the issues of national and global governance, including reforms of the existing political system and the global order (transforming of political civilization);
6. actively develop science and technology, continuously deepen humanity's understanding of life, nature, the earth, and even human beings, explore new unknown worlds, and avoid ignorance and short-sightedness; grasping the direction of technological innovation, promoting the invention and application of both hard and soft technologies adapted to sustainable development, and improving the soft and hard environment support system to keep pace with the times (promoting the transformation of spiritual civilization and building an innovative new world).

We will discuss each of the above-mentioned approaches, in detail below in conjunction with China's practice.

## Means of soft-hard technologies and support system: adhere to the instrumentality of technology and grasp the direction of technological innovation

Developing technology and promoting technological and institutional innovation are not only important paths of development in themselves but also help to guarantee that other paths of development succeed as well (see the central part of Figure 7.1). Every approach requires the support of the invention, creation, and innovation of related soft and hard technologies, as well as the support system of the soft and hard environment that keeps pace with the times. For example, regarding the transformation of economic development model, in addition to the development and application of hard technology suitable for green development (new energy technology, energy-saving technology, low-carbon technology, etc.), it is also necessary to accelerate the innovation of economic technology (new business models, financial technology, etc.) conducive to green growth; in the transforming social development models, we will need to coordinate the development of various social, health, cultural, and cognitive science and technologies. In the field of resources and environment, we should not only actively develop and apply all kinds of green technologies but also pay special attention to a series of soft and hard environmental protection systems such as green investment, as well as relevant laws, regulations, and policies. We should also develop and apply various political, security technologies, as well as global and domestic governance technologies for the needs of social governance and social system transformation.

## Creating a culture environment based on goodness

From the perspective of the relationship between humanity and the environment in the broad sense, the process of realizing sustainability involves coordinating and optimizing relations between humanity and the universe, humanity and nature, humanity and society, and among human beings themselves. Only after achieving a true Global Civilization and even a Great Civilization (in which material, spiritual, political, ecological, and interstellar civilizations all adapt to attain sustainability and are complementary to each other) can an ideal symbiotic relationship among these relations be achieved. Global Civilization is not only one important element of a better human future (social system), it is also the broad sense of cultural environment or conditions of civilization necessary to sustain development. I call this a cultural environment of goodness, which ensures that the six approaches to development will conform to sustainable development goals.

## Education and promotion are fundamental

Achieving sustainability is largely a process of coordinating human behavior patterns, including economic, political, cultural, technological, and other aspects of behavior in order to achieve the better vision or ultimate goal for mankind. Both education and cultivation will be the foundations for improving and sublimating human nature, changing people's behaviors and thinking modes to ultimately achieve a more advanced civilization. Through comprehensive use of tangible and intangible means, such as political and religious enlightenment, educational influence and persuasion, providing hard evidence of environmental impacts, etc., the idea of sustainability can gradually become the consensus among people everywhere and be reflected in their world outlook and values, and then embodied in their modes of thought, and action. Once this becomes the norm for the world's citizens rather than just among the academic community and a few elites, success will be assured (see Figure 7.1).

## Conclusion: human sustainability depends on what civilization we choose

A bright future is not predictable, but it can result from struggle toward this goal once it is designed and determined (this does not include, of course, the ultra-long-term future of the entire solar system, the Milky way and the universe. For details, please refer to the relevant section of "A better future cannot be predicted, but it can be created" in Chapter 8). Similarly, for sustainable development, the ultimate goal—a society in which mankind can survive and develop sustainably should be determined first, and then six development approaches should be designed and implemented to strive for the realization of human better vision. It can be seen that sustainable development is also a choice of civilization.

First, it is necessary to devote every effort to promote the transition from Industrial Civilization to Global Civilization for the future. Therein although human wisdom and ability have greatly improved, they will still maintain human dignity in the traditional sense; highly developed science and technology will enhance human wisdom, intelligence, and maintain our physical health while promoting social progress, benefitting the whole of humanity, and promoting harmony between humans and nature. In this way, human nature will be greatly elevated and the worldviews and values of mainstream society will need to change radically to adapt to an advanced Global Civilization. That is a harmonious, peaceful, and sustainable society.

Second, to let the "train of Industrial Civilization" continue to accelerate allows the theory of scientific and technological omnipotence to add more fuel to the flames of human arrogance and controlled human evolution. To allow the

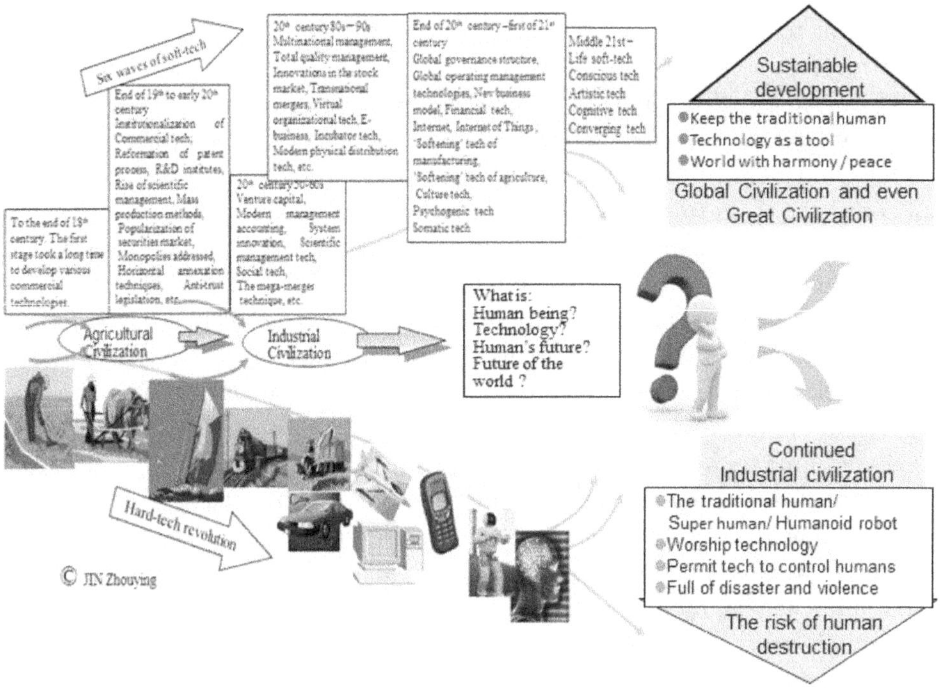


FIGURE 7.3: The choice of future civilization.

development and application of new technologies to proceed unchecked, driven largely by the lure of huge commercial profits and various powers, is to risk letting human beings ultimately be controlled by their own technologies. In such a world, a human–machine civilization will be advocated, and some variety of supermen and humanoid robot will appear and gradually assume power, while traditional human beings do not change their stale ideas about nature and their stupid way of living, and cannot consciously abandon or transform the anti-social characteristics of human nature. That kind of society will be full of disasters and violence, and after much fierce competition, traditional human beings will ultimately die out [...] (see the section of "Wars among three categories of species" in Chapter 2).

Of course, wise human beings should choose the former (see Figure 7.3).

### *Sustainable development and China's practice*

In view of the fact that all countries are in different stages of the industrialization process and have their own unique historical and cultural backgrounds, in attempting to realize the transformation of civilization, they each have their own problems that need to be solved.

However, one thing must be common. That is, the necessity to integrate the values of material, spiritual, political, ecological and interstellar civilization based on the Global Civilization into the six approaches of sustainable development in all countries, so as to gradually integrate the development of all countries and regions into the track of Global Civilization. This requires all countries to decompose "the current basic problems in each civilization that need to be resolved" (see Chapter 4 for details) and gradually practice them to transform their respective development model. That is, all countries must do their own parts first. History has proved that the biggest threat to a stable social order does not come from the outside or opponents.

Take China for an example.

It is well known that in order to achieve the great rejuvenation of the Chinese nation, China has embarked on a second long march. The 18th National Congress of the Communist Party of China (CPC) also planned out a roadmap and timetable for achieving the dream of a great rejuvenation. According to this plan, a moderately prosperous society could be realized by 2021 when China will greet the 100th anniversary of the founding of the CPC. By 2049, the 100th anniversary of the founding of the new China, China will have built a prosperous and powerful, democratic, civilized, harmonious, and modernized socialist country.

This shows that China has steadily "matured" from its early model of "fumbling the way to cross the river",[2] and made a clear choice for its future path and governance model. By realizing these "two centenary goals", the development level of China will be improved in two stages, paving the way and laying the foundation for the ultimate realization of the great rejuvenation of the Chinese nation—"The Chinese Dream."

But in order to make the bright blueprint of "national prosperity, revitalization, and people's happiness" come true, China must take the social civilization system, based on Global Civilization as its ultimate goal and principle for sustainable development. At the same time, it needs to integrate the values of global civilization, the objectives and content of all-round deepening reform into the necessary trip around sustainable development (see Figure 7.1): strengthen the economy, promote social progress, choose institutions and a governance model that reflect Chinese characteristics and adapt to sustainability, develop and recycle resources, protect and repair the environment, build an innovative country, and practice institutional reforms that advance with the times, so as to facilitate the transformation of civilizations and guide China on the road toward a Global Civilization.

The examples I will offer below show that, despite the obstacles facing this ancient civilization, China is advancing along the road to comprehensive rejuvenation. We will also assess the progress already achieved, and examine various campaigns now underway to meet present challenges and prepare for the future. This illustrates what China is promising and shows it is possible for humans to create a Global Civilization.

### Expand production activity and economic development using steady-state, green and continuous innovation (transforming the economic development model)

If we do not change the traditional mode of economic development, the contradictions between unrestrained human pursuit of economic growth and the finite limits of the natural environment and its limited resources are irreconcilable. The damage to the Earth's ecological system caused by continual economic growth will be irreversible, ultimately leading to a total collapse of the global economy and society. Transforming the current economic development model demands that we find solutions to several problems at the levels of concept and operation. First, the development of human society does not need "unending" economic growth measured entirely in terms of GDP. Second, modes of production and organizational methods should adapt to the post-industrial era. Third, we must deal with challenges at the operational level, such as how to adapt to rapid developments in science and technology, how to create a new model of economic globalization, and how to develop a green economy, which will implement the ideas for global climate governance contained in the 2015 Paris Agreement on Climate Change.

#### 1. The issues of economic growth

The economic development is undoubtedly an important means of building material civilization. However, how should development occur and what are the signs of successful development? We cannot support future civilization while still pursuing unrestrained economic growth. Instead, we must advocate a new material civilization—one with a built-in sense of "civilized restraint". To release people from the cage of excessive material desires, we must abandon the so-called "lifestyle of the developed countries" where people desire and strive to accumulate wealth and indulge in excessive consumption while ignoring the ecological cost. Instead, we must adopt a lifestyle that is rich but abstemious, environmentally friendly, and that pays close attention to spiritual culture.

At present, the developed countries have not yet given up their blind pursuit of economic growth, and the prevalence of consumerism spurs people to invest, produce, trade, and consume constantly, in an unending but ultimately hopeless quest for an ever-higher "quality of life". In fact, some economists have proposed the theory of a "steady-state economy", one in which zero growth occurs, but the quality of life remains relatively stable or even improves. They advocate a transition from a growth economy, which is oriented by GDP worship, to a stable one, and urge developed countries to stop their endless pursuit of economic growth and gradually transition to this steady-state ideal.

China has now begun adapting to this "new economic norm" by pursuing a GDP growth rate lower than the double-digit rate recorded in the past few decades, so as to promote economic development together with comprehensive consideration of the environment, social justice, the people's livelihood, and the issues of agriculture, rural areas, and farmers. The above point of view may help people to better assess the true significance of the change in China's economic growth rate to a more moderate but sustainable speed during this transition period.

Of course, with regard to developing countries such as China, a certain level of steady economic growth is necessary, and China's economy still has a plenty of space in which to grow. As long as China continues to meet its goal of comprehensively deepening reform and promoting all-round innovation, the nation's economic development potential will be further enhanced. Thus, China can still expect to maintain a relatively high economic growth rate over a long period of time.

However, more importantly, the economic growth model must be changed from focusing on the speed of economic growth to focusing on its quality. Therefore, it is necessary to continue to deepen institutional reform and solve such problems as the dual-track system that is common in various fields in China, so as to reduce the proportion of social costs and environmental costs in GDP (see the relevant section on GPI in Chapter 5).

**2. A mode of production that keeps pace with the times**

To improve on the current mode of production, we must first keep pace with new developments in science and technology. The rapid and disruptive innovations taking place in modern science and technology have turned changes in the marketplace into an avalanche. Advances in hard technologies such as 5G, 3-D/4-D, AI, and new energy sources not to mention progress in soft technologies such as new transportation schemes, e-commerce, new forms of business organization, new financial technologies including digital currency, block-chain technologies, and the like, are constantly changing or even subverting established industrial norms. As a result, we now must deal with a variety of new business models that establish new standards for assessing economic growth—for example, the circular economy, the social economy, the Internet economy, the functional economy, the sharing economy, digital economy, etc.—all of which in turn are radically reshaping the global economy of the future. In the midst of these dazzling changes, only by accelerating the digitization, networking and intellectualization of production activities, consciously strengthening the real economy, and fostering national industries with world competitiveness and then leading the relevant trend can China hope to successfully take the initiative to change the rules of the economic game—to reshape institutional innovation, and support long-term economic development.

This is the prime directive; but second, innovations in the production mode and the organizational model of enterprise must occur to keep pace with the transformation of civilization. For example, taking the initiative to transition from mass production (long the standard model in the era of industrial economy) to personalized production (reflecting unique consumer needs in an individualized society); and from advocating large enterprises to actively integrating and supporting the era where small- and medium-sized and even micro-businesses that often take the lead in innovation.

Third, it requires a clear understanding of the essence of industry's comprehensive softening and of the characteristics of a future economy in which soft industry will play a leading role. We need to actively invent, create, and innovate soft technologies in various fields that can adapt to and promote the transformation of industrial structure away from its present focus on hard industry to soft.

The above points are particularly important for transforming China from being a so-called "manufacturing power" to an "innovative power". Of course, the "innovation power" should also be a "great power in manufacturing" as well.

### 3. Actively adapting to a new round of globalization by combining development with opening up

Given today's complex geopolitical issues, in order for China to realize a peaceful development, it must proceed in a healthier way. For example, China has introduced the strategic idea of "One Belt One Road" (Silk Road Economic Belt and the 21st Century Maritime Silk Road).[3] This is a huge economic corridor that connects the Asia-Pacific Economic Circle at one end and the developed economies of the European Union at the other. Altogether it links 94 cities in 53 countries and is intended to form a new pattern of all-round opening. Now in its early stages, "the belt and road initiative" will accelerate the construction of a connected infrastructure among neighboring countries and regions along the Belt and Road, then gradually shift the direction of development to mutual support in marketing, finance, technology, cultural exchanges, and other areas. The goal of this initiative is to transform the integration of regional cooperation (for instance between China and ASEAN) while also creating a new model of regional cooperation in the twenty-first century. This strategy means that China's future economic development will be inseparable from that of its partners, worldwide. China is fully ready to share its development dividend with neighboring countries and to promote regional and even global economic development. China firmly believes that so long as all parties adhere to the spirit of peaceful cooperation, understanding and communication, equality and mutual benefit, tolerance, mutual learning, and win–win cooperation, patiently overcome any obstacles to progress, and deal with any problems encountered in the development process, we will be able to establish a closer community of interests and community of destiny, which will make the irreversible trend toward globalization better able to develop in a healthy direction. Of course, "the belt and road initiative" is a large system, involving many countries, and cooperation mechanisms; thus, it cannot be implemented in one go.

## Protecting and recycling natural resources and economizing to attain reasonable development (transforming the natural resources application model)

Natural resources, natural services, and the gene pool are all fundamental for human survival on this planet. Natural resources mean both finite assets like hydrocarbons, minerals, and fossil groundwater, and renewable assets such as rivers, arable land, wildlife, and forests. Natural services include life essentials like photosynthesis, absorption of carbon dioxide by oceans, and the actions of bees to pollinate crops. The gene pool refers to the diversity of genes being carried by all living organisms on Earth. Now, however, the Earth's natural resources are dwindling, as human demand for these resources is increasing dramatically.

At least 40 per cent of violent conflicts in the past 60 years were related to natural resources. At present usage rates, human activities require one-and-a-half times our planet's resources. In other words, it takes the Earth one-and-a-half years to restore the resources humans consume during one year. Furthermore, the average resource consumption of the richest countries is five times higher than that of the poorest ones.

Thus, application patterns of natural resources must be changed. Human production modes and ways of working must change to conserve resources, reduce emissions, and use resources sustainably. As for lifestyles, we need to advocate frugality, oppose extravagance, and adhere to a sustainable way of life. We can live comfortably and consume far less, while at the same time, strive to develop new clean energy sources, promote ecologically sustainable governance of the global commons (the South Pole, climate, biodiversity, oceans, atmosphere, space, etc.), so as to allocate these indivisible "non-competitive" public goods and infrastructures to assure more equitable access and improve opportunities for human development.

### 1. The present state of China

With regard to China, the challenges of natural resources for sustainable development are particularly severe. China's resources are relatively poor to begin with, and after more than 30 years of rapid economic development, the natural resources that China needs greatly exceed what its own ecosystem can provide. For example:

- China's wetland area once ranked first in Asia and fourth in the world, accounting for one-tenth of the world's wetland area. But many wetlands have degenerated and been lost at a staggering rate during the more than 70 years since the founding of new China. For example, the Sanjiang plain in China's northeast, the wetland area dropped from 5 million hectares at the founding of new China to a mere 0.91 million hectares in 2009.
- Wetlands are also threatened by the growing area of cultivated land surrounding freshwater lakes. Today, it stands at more than 1.3 million hectares, and has caused more than 1,000 lakes to disappear. In Hubei Province, long known as the "province of a thousand lakes", 477 lakes, each of whose surface areas once covered more than 100 hectares, have now disappeared. According to a 2003 survey of the Tongjiang Lakes, among more than 100 original lakes in the middle and lower reaches of the Yangtze River, only two are left—Dongting Lake and Poyang Lake.
- China's arable land is only 13 per cent of its total land area, and while this represents 8.4 per cent of the world's total land area, given China's large population it means only 0.09 hectares per capita. But in the 41 years since China's economic reform and opening up, the quantity of arable land has been reduced by around 13.33 million hectares, and as of the year 2008, there were only a total of 121.72 million hectares of arable land. But according to the current optimistic estimate, China can only produce about 600 million tons of grain per year. For a big country with a population of 1.4 billion, the production and supply of food will always be the first priority.
- Based on China's existing water resources, the volume of fresh water available per capita stands at only one-quarter of the world average. Every year, average national water shortages total over 50 billion cubic meters. Among the more than 600 cities in China, roughly two-thirds have insufficient water, and one-sixth report serious water shortages.[4] The problems caused by excessive exploitation of water resources are already acute, and water resource development in many regions has exceeded sustainable carrying capacity, leading to utilization ratios for many rivers that are 30 per cent or more above recommended international standards.
- Among the 45 major mineral resources found in China, only 21 exist in sufficient quantities to meet the nation's economic and social development needs. In addition, however, the degree of waste is surprisingly high.
- China's energy crisis is especially serious. Take oil as an example; China became the world's second largest oil consumer and seventh largest oil importer.

Therefore, three state-owned oil giants—PetroChina, Sinopec, and CNOOC—have all adopted a "go global" strategy to develop the international market. The Chinese government is also actively carrying out energy diplomacy.

**2. Countermeasures**

In order to alleviate the crisis of resources and energy, it is necessary to adopt systematic solutions with different characteristics for the crises of wetlands, water resources, cultivated land, mineral resources and other fields.

Taking the solution to the energy crisis as an example, China's first strategy is to vigorously develop renewable energy and promote the transformation of energy structure as a way out of the crisis.

- *Invest heavily in clean energy*: In 2014, the cumulative investment reached 89.5 billion USD, an increase of 32 per cent year-on-year, China leads the globe in clean energy investment (with the United States ranked second at 51.8 billion USD), and accounts for 29 per cent of the total global investment in clean energy. Three quarters of this went to the wind and solar energy industries. China's large-scale international clean energy projects and acquisitions exceeded 44 billion USD in 2017.
- As of 2017, China's installed wind power capacity has reached 163.67 million kilowatts, ranking first in the world.
- Due to strong policy support, the cumulative installed capacity of China's photovoltaic power generation, increased from 1 GW to 130 GW in 2017 (170 GW in 2018) within just seven years, accounting for 7.3 per cent of the total national power generation capacity, and accounting for about half of the global photovoltaic installed capacity in 2017; the output of solar photovoltaic cell in 2016 was 49 GW, accounting for 71.01 per cent of the global total output of 69 GW; and will be able to reach 250 GW of the cumulative photovoltaic installed capacity in 2020.
- The output value of China's energy saving and environmental protection industry increased from 482.4 billion USD in 2012 to 734.4 billion USD in 2015, and it is expected to reach 1419.7 billion USD in 2020.
- China will continue to encourage building large numbers of the so-called new energy cities, demonstration plots, green energy demonstration counties, and demonstration towns for new energy, all promoting the popularization and application of clean energy systems.

**3. The challenges facing China**

China faces all-round challenges in transforming its use of natural resources including wetlands, water resources, cultivated land, mineral resources and renewable energy.

Take the wind power and solar photovoltaic industry which has taken a solid step, as an example:

- Although China's wind power industry is growing rapidly, and the nation's cumulative installed capacity of wind power ranks first in the world, the number of abandoned wind power installations is alarming. According to data from the National Energy Bureau, in 2012, the ratio of abandoned wind power was about 17 per cent; the ratio fell to 11 per cent in 2013. But it soared again to 15 per cent in 2015 when the annual abandoned wind power facilities reached 33.9 billion kWh, While direct economic losses exceeded 2.9 billion USD. In 2016, the wind power generation increased by 30 per cent, reached 241 billion kWh, with a wind abandonment rate of 17.1 per cent, which is the highest level since the first large-scale wind abandonment in 2010. One of the main reasons for the idle state of wind power production in China is related to the prioritization between old and new production sources in the nation's electricity market. Another is that the construction of the national power grid has not been coordinated with the construction of facilities for electricity generation. As a result, about one-third of them remain idle, either because there is no power or the power produced cannot be fed into the nation's electricity grid system. Moreover, most of the wind power plants built in China fail to generate much profit, and several are currently operating at a loss. After various measures have been taken, the overall development of wind power is stable, and the abandonment of wind power and the rate of wind abandonment have both continuously decreased. In 2018, the national abandonment rate has dropped to 7 per cent.
- China has become the world's major manufacturer of photovoltaic cells, yet "the two ends of the photovoltaic industry" remain outside of China. That is, 90 per cent of the market for photovoltaics, and most of the raw materials needed to manufacture them, are found in foreign countries. This situation has improved, especially due to solar polysilicon enterprises, for which more than 60 per cent of raw materials are procured domestically. But due to the continued reduction in orders from Europe and America, the situation of overcapacity has not been completely resolved, especially in the Northwest, there still exist problems of photovoltaics abandonment and electric power limitation. The reasons include that the development speed of new energy power generation obviously exceeds the replacement speed of traditional coal power; there is no market for the collaborative consumption of new energy in the East, the Middle and the West, and the construction of transmission channels is seriously lagging behind; the capacity and flexibility of peak regulation in the existing power grid are insufficient, and there are barriers between

provincial transactions, etc., the power market is not prepared for the high-speed development of new energy power generation. Plus, the industry still faces an unhealthy situation regarding businesses that should be closed down but were not, thus driving many good businesses toward bankruptcy. To this end, in 2017, premier of the State Council asked to solve relevant mechanisms and technical problems as soon as possible. In fact, in 2018, the China's renewable energy power generation accounted for 26.7 per cent of the total power generation, with a wind abandonment rate of 7 per cent, a photovoltaics abandonment rate of 3 per cent, and a water abandonment rate of 5 per cent. The utilization rate for renewable energy continues to increase.[5]

- This industry is large in scale, but lacks core technology. Although China has a strong manufacturing capacity for wind motors, its ability to conduct technology research and development, and to manufacture equipment remains weak. It must still rely heavily on imports for key technologies and crucial equipment, and the patents covering major wind motor components are still in the hands of foreign enterprises and their subsidiaries. At present, the core components needed to assemble a wind generator must be imported. Similarly, the basic materials, key production equipment, and testing instruments needed for the solar energy industry in China also remain dependent on imports. Thus, China's principle role in the world solar photovoltaic industry chain is largely limited to the assembly of components.
- According to the China Building Energy Consumption Research Report (2017),[6] energy consumption by China's building industry accounted for 20 per cent of the nation's total energy consumption in 2015. This shows that in addition to technological energy-saving, it is important to promote energy saving behavior by better informing and educating users.
- Throughout the renewable energy sector, whether nuclear, wind, solar, or the relevant equipment manufacturing industry, there are shortages of talent to different degrees. Especially serious is the shortage of technical and management personnel.

**4. Investigating the root causes**

The causes of China's current energy and resource problems include:

- lack of a comprehensive strategy from a long-term future perspective;
- lack of a long-term management mechanism for China's clean energy development;
- the legal system related to energy is not perfect. For example, access goals and related supporting policies for new clean energy development have not been established, and the variety of existing policies and institutions are not

consistent, which hampers implementation of existing energy policies, while systematic incentive and restraint mechanisms are also lacking;
- no account is taken of capacity-building;
- there is a lack of independent core technology;
- China relies excessively on large and state-owned enterprises (because there is no explicit supporting policy. This means that the private sector of the economy can neither enter the domestic energy business, nor invest or cooperate with foreign institutions substantively. Thus, China loses out on many opportunities for access to international energy);
- failure to give full play to the strength of NGOs.

It is worth emphasizing the role of government intervention. In the long run, simply relying on the determination and administrative enforcement efforts of government cannot really solve the crises of resources and energy. But from a global perspective, in the early stages of moving to a green economy, especially in developing countries, correct state intervention is very important. The main function of the government is to create a favorable climate for developing both the hard and soft environments. For instance:

- strategic orientation, including the overall planning of development strategy and management of the nation's natural resources;
- the combination of direct control and policy orientation to provide needed institutional guarantees for a green economy;
- funding and policy inputs (which otherwise tend to favor major special projects reflecting current state policy over the public's long-term interests);
- leading and grasping the direction of technological innovation;
- establishing good international relationships;
- leading the whole society to create an atmosphere that advocates green development.

## Repairing, restoring, and protecting the eco-environment (transforming of the relationship between man and nature)

The ecological balance of the Earth has lasted for 4 billion years, but it has been severely damaged during the 300 years since the Industrial Revolution began. Experts have warned that the Earth is going through a sixth major phase of species extinction. Because the carrying capacity of the environment has reached its limit, managing to balance environmental repair, restoration, and protection will be arduous. Human beings must not only change their preference for extensive industrialization but also give up their increasingly extravagant way of life, including even changing their diet.

**The status quo**

According to our study of China's Genuine Progress Indicators (GPI) in 2014, China's Gross Domestic Product (GDP) increased by about 22 times during the 35 years from 1978 to 2012, an increase that has been the second largest in the world. But environmental costs increased by 32 times during this same period. This estimate however only includes the costs from long-term environmental damage caused by greenhouse gas emissions, water and air pollution, ozone depletion, loss of wetlands, farmland, and primary forests, etc. It does not include costs from loss of land due to desertification, species reduction, etc.

Problems in the ecological environment include:

1. ***Air pollution***: China's air pollution is still very serious, and days with significant haze pollution have become almost normal, which has greatly affected people's physical and mental health. Unlike the developed countries, industrial emissions, urbanization, and the rise of motor vehicles in China have taken place simultaneously in just the past 30 years of rapid economic development. This has generated a great deal of superimposed pollution from multiple sources. Such combined pollution has proven more difficult to control than the typical pollution found in Europe and America. Having set the development goal of creating "world-class factories" and pursuing "GDP first", by the early 2000s, China had quickly become the world's leading manufacturer of more than 100 kinds of products. But a large portion of these were the result of developed countries outsourcing their manufacturing to China. This has meant that China now has to deal with the added pollution from manufacturing outsourced by the developed countries.
   - *Air*: In 2017, 99 of the 338 prefecture-level and above cities in China met the air quality standards, accounting for 29.3 per cent of the total number of cities; the average number of days with excellent air quality in those 338 cities was 78.0 per cent; the average concentration of PM2.5 was 43 $\mu g/m^3$, 6.5 per cent lower than that in 2016; the percentage of days exceeding the standard was 12.4 per cent, down by 1.7 per cent from 2016.
   - *Acid rain*: According to the precipitation monitoring in 463 cities (districts and counties), the proportion of cities with acid rain was 18.8 per cent in 2017, 1.0 per cent lower than that in 2016; the frequency of acid rain was 10.8 per cent on an average, a decrease of 1.9 from 2016. The type of acid rain is still sulfuric acid. The area of acid rain area accounts for 6.4 per cent of the land area, a decrease of 0.8 per cent from 2016.

2. ***Water pollution***
   - *Surface water*: Among the 1940 water quality sections (points), the proportion of excellent (classes I–III) water quality was 67.9 per cent in 2017, an increase of 0.1 per cent compared with 2016. The proportion of inferior class V water quality was 8.3 per cent, which was 0.3 per cent lower than that in 2016. The water quality in the main stream of big rivers has improved steadily.
   - *Groundwater*: Among the 5100 water quality monitoring points, 8.8 per cent, 23.1 per cent, 1.5 per cent, 51.8 per cent and 14.8 per cent are, respectively, excellent, good, fairly good, poor and very poor.
   - *In-use centralized drinking water sources*: Among the 898 monitoring sections (points)of in-use centralized drinking water source in cities at prefecture-level and above, 813 have met the annual water quality standards, accounting for 90.5 per cent, of which the compliance rate of surface water sources was 93.7 per cent, and the compliance rate of groundwater source was 85.1 per cent.
   - *Whole sea area*: In the summer of 2017, the sea area that meets the first class water quality standard accounted for 96 per cent of the sea area under China's jurisdiction. Compared with the same period in 2016, the sea area inferior to the fourth category of sea water quality standard has decreased by 3,700 square kilometers.
3. ***Ecological environment quality:*** Among the 2,591 counties, there are 548, 1057, 702, 267 and 17 counties being evaluated respectively by "excellent", "good", "general", "relatively poor" and "poor" in ecological environment quality. "Excellent" and "good" counties account for 44.9 per cent of the land area, mainly distributed in the south of Qinling Huaihe River, the northeast of the Big and small Xing'an Mountains and Changbai Mountains.
4. ***Land pollution:*** The soil pollution survey bulletin released in 2014 showed that 16.1 per cent of the land in China exceeded the allowable national standard for pollutants. Of this total, 10 million hectares are considered contaminated land, accounting for roughly 8.3 per cent of China's total 120 million hectares of arable land. In addition, more than one quarter of the land area in China faces the problem of desertification.

This shows that we have not moved beyond the path of "treatment *after* pollution".

**Measures taken**

In order to reverse these trends, China has implemented a number of measures to change the nation's development mode and consumption patterns, improve public awareness of the need to protect the environment and address climate change, as well as framing new laws, regulations, policies, and other institutional guarantees to ensure implementation.

Take air pollution as an example. Haze pollution is mainly caused by extensive development, and unreasonable industrial and energy structure. In order to make the so-called "APEC blue",[7] a permanent standard by 2030, China is determined to reduce coal consumption. The proportion of coal consumption in primary energy consumption was lower than 60 per cent for the first time, down from 67.4 per cent in 2013 to 59.0 per cent in 2018, and it dropped by 1.3 per cent in 2019. The proportion of non-fossil energy in primary energy consumption has reached 14.3 per cent in 2018; the intensity of carbon emissions in 2018 decreased 45.8 per cent compared with 2005, basically reversing the rapid growth of greenhouse gas emissions. At present, 120 million hectares of natural forests have been designated as protected areas.

As the number one and the number two greenhouse-gas-emitting powers in the world, China and the United States have reached an agreement to halt global warming. Chinese officials proposed for the first time that the PRC's greenhouse gas emissions would peak by 2030, by which time clean energy will account for 20 per cent of the nation's total (the proportion of clean energy in total energy consumption in 2019 reached 23.1 per cent); then in September 2020, during the 75th UN General Assembly, China proposed to strive to achieve carbon neutrality by 2060; while the United States promised to reduce their national annual emissions of greenhouse gases 26–28 per cent from 2005 levels by 2025. They also reaffirmed their previous commitment to reduce carbon emissions to 17 per cent below 2005 levels by 2020.

This is the first time that China has set a date for when its carbon emissions will peak, but still the costs of the energy saving and emission reduction initiatives that will be needed to meet this commitment are enormous. Credit Suisse estimates that these measures will reduce China's steel output by up to one quarter, along with 13 per cent of its cement production and 3 per cent of its industrial output overall. This sacrifice shows how strong China's determination is. In December 2017, the National Development and Reform Commission issued the "National Carbon Emissions Trading Market Construction Plan (Power Generation Industry)", clarifying that the power generation industry was used as a breakthrough point to launch the national carbon emissions trading system. Of course, as Paul Krugman said, efforts to put environmental costs into the market are not enough.

China has also adopted various other measures to improve the quality of the environment. For example, on 10 September 2013, the State Council of China issued an "Air Pollution Prevention Action Plan", which included ten specific proposals. This plan aimed to reduce coal consumption, limit automobile use, and reduce dust by adopting 35 measures. Although the aims of these provisions were correct, initial attempts to implement them encountered strong resistance, in part because the variety of policies and institutions then in existence lacked unified goals and consistent standards. The newly revised Environmental Protection Law of China, which was put into effect on 1 January 2015, is now the fundamental and comprehensive law regarding the environment and has been called "the most stringent environmental law in history." The newly revised law stipulates that "environmental protection is the basic policy of China"; and seeks to strengthen information disclosure and public participation; establishes and improves mechanisms for ecological protection; and delineate a "red line" to prevent ecological deterioration. The law imposes harsher penalties for violations, which are calculated by days; improves the interregional pollution prevention and control system, and clearly defines the legal framework for environmental public interest litigation. In addition, it promotes rural governance and provides for annual reporting on environmental conditions to the People's National Congress.

However, the greater challenge in environmental governance is the implementation and supervision of the above "plans", "laws", and "regulations". The "plastic limiting order" can be taken as an example. Since 2008, there has been no further progress except to impose a charge for plastic bags in large shopping malls. In fact, the number of plastic bags and plastic lunch boxes is still increasing with the increase of express delivery, food ordered online and take-out services in restaurants, etc. According to the statistics, about 60 million plastic lunch boxes are used daily in China. The plastic bags used every day could cover 420,000 square meters, and in about 15 days could cover an area the size of West Lake in Hangzhou City (about 2.5 square miles).

In fact, the garbage war is a war of China and the world. In order to solve the problem of garbage pollution, the "Regulations of Shanghai Municipality on the management of domestic garbage" officially came into effect on 1 July 2019. Shanghai became the first city in China to officially enact a law on garbage classification. Since that time Beijing has also revised its garbage classification legislation, and the public has entered an unprecedented discussion on garbage classification. The Ministry of Housing and Urban–Rural Development will continue to invest 3.4 billion USD to accelerate the construction of treatment facilities to process meet the needs of classified treatment of domestic garbage. By the end of 2020, 46 key cities had piloted such programs, and, by 2025, all Chinese cities at prefecture-level and above plan to have waste classification and treatment systems in operation.

This new Environmental Protection Law, too, has encountered resistance to its effective implementation. Consider the following example, illustrating the relationship between the construction of a hydropower station and the consequent threat this poses to the local environment. Driven by the lure of short-term economic benefits like investment promotion and the development of the regional economy, dangers identified in the environmental impact assessment (EIA), which was only implemented after the project had already been launched, are often ignored or downplayed until construction is an established fact.

To address this concern, the general office of the State Council issued "Interim Measures on the Accountability of Party and Government Officials for Ecological and Environmental Damage (Pilot Plan)" in August 2015. This measure was taken not only as an important part of the overall national strategy for governing the country under the rule of law, but also as a major initiative to promote an ecological civilization. Certainly, environmental accountability requires a series of supporting institutional systems.

Eco-environment management reform focuses on three major campaigns, namely, the prevention and control of pollution in the atmosphere, water, and soil. This will involve in-depth implementation of China's "Air Pollution Prevention Action Plan", the full implementation of its "Water Pollution Prevention Action Plan"; and continuously promoting the development and implementation of a "Soil Pollution Prevention Action Plan."

For example, the "Water Pollution Prevention Action Plan" released in April 2015 put forward ten major measures for the prevention and control of water pollution, so that by 2020, the water quality in 70 per cent of all seven major national river basins (including the Yangtze River, the Yellow River, and the Haihe River) should be sufficient to meet or exceed the rating of Type III, and that this figure will rise to 75 per cent by 2030. Under this same plan, the quality of centralized drinking water sources in 93 per cent of China's cities at prefecture-level or above should meet or exceed Type III by 2020 and rise to 95 per cent by 2030 while the proportion of very poor groundwater quality will be reduced to around 15 per cent. By the middle of this century, China will have attained comprehensive improvement of its environment quality, while the total ecological system of air, ground, and water will have reached a state of continually self-reinforcing improvement—in effect, a virtuous circle.

Currently, China's investment in environmental protection is increasing. The proportion of environmental protection investment in China accounted for just 0.7 per cent of GDP during the period of the Seventh Five-Year Plan (1986–90), but rose to 1.9 per cent in 2010 and 1.59 per cent in 2012. In purely monetary terms, between 2011 and 2013, environmental protection investment rose by 32.26 billion USD annually. In 2016, investment in environmental governance accounted for 1.24 per cent of GDP. According to the "National Urban Ecological Protection and Construction Plan (2015–2020)" compiled by the Ministry of Housing and Urban–Rural Development in conjunction with the Ministry of Ecology and Environment, In 2020, the proportion of environmental protection investment in GDP was more than 3.5 per cent.[8]

Moreover, as shown in the *2017 China Environment Bulletin*, jointly prepared and published by the Ministry of Environmental Protection, and eleven other government ministries, nearly every relevant department now pays close attention to environmental protection, which is a sign of great progress in China.

## Promoting social progress and building a fair, impartial, self-disciplined, and harmonious society (transforming the social development model)

A harmonious society is a better society that humans diligently strive to achieve. China's definition of a harmonious society refers to a society with democracy, local rule, fairness and justice, honesty and fraternity, vitality, stability and order, as well as harmony between man and nature.[9] The term "harmony" as used here includes the harmony between man and man, harmony among various systems and classes in society, harmony among individuals, society, and nature, and the harmony between the Chinese people and the outside world. On the way to a harmonious society, all countries have different national conditions, so that the problems to be solved, and the approaches and solutions to be taken are also different.

### 1. Major issues that China needs to address

The great changes that have taken place in China during the past 40 years were driven by the transition in the nation's economic system and the transformation of its social structure.

China is still undergoing transformation from an agricultural, rural, semi-closed traditional society to an industrial, urban, open modern society. This transformation affects all areas of social life, the harmonious coexistence of different strata, and social stability.

For example, (1) the income gap continues to expand, the gap in property distribution is visible; (2) the construction of social undertakings and people's livelihood is lagging behind. Expensive housing, expensive medical treatment, and difficulty in obtaining a good education have become the "three major pain points" of people's lives; (3) discrepancies in employment and labor remuneration still exist; (4) the allocation of educational opportunities and resources is unequal; (5) the allocation of access to health care and public health resources is unequal; (6) there is the inequality of rights to social security; and (7) the gap between urban and rural areas as well as between different regions is widening.

According to a third-round study of China's GPI in 2014, China's GDP increased by roughly 22 times during the 35 years from 1978 to 2012, while social costs increased by 47 times during the same period.

The challenge is how to solve the problems that most directly impact the true interests and concerns of the people, such as income distribution, social security, eradication of corruption, health care, education, and secure housing, and also to promote social justice so that China may promote social progress and establish a truly harmonious society.

### 2. Fairness as a breakthrough point to deepen the reform of the social system

*Social system reform is fundamental*: Responding to the fact that China's social system reform lags behind the transformation of its economic system, sociologist Peilin Li has pointed out that the core reform needed in China is to deal with the relationship between government, market, and society, and to determine which areas the government, market, and society, respectively, are best suited to manage, and which ones require attention from all three. At the same time, social system reform should be based on how people earn their livelihood, should strengthen and innovate social management, and should deal with the interactions among reform, development, and stability. Therefore, we must accelerate the formation of the social security system, provide full coverage, and protect basic needs, while offering multi-level coverage and remaining economically sustainable. Other needs include improving basic public services (covering both urban and rural areas), instituting a social interests adjustment mechanism (to promote social harmony, maintain fairness and justice, and arouse social vitality), along with systems for social organization (separating government administration from commune management, making clear the rights and liabilities of individuals and collectives, granting autonomy in accordance with the law), and for social management (directed by the party committee, with the government taking responsibility, but with social coordination, public participation, and the guarantee of rule by law), so as to promote reform of the social system.

*Solving the issues of relative fairness*: Fairness and justice in a society are not only the basic requirements and goals of social harmony but also important symbols of social progress. In order to solve the issues on social equity, which is mainly composed of rights equity, opportunity equity (the traditional dual social structure of urban and rural areas in China, which limits equality of opportunity, especially when it comes to giving everyone an equal starting point for competition), fairness of social security, fair rules, and distributive justice, it requires to establish a system of institutional security that covers political, economic, cultural, and social areas, while they connect with and promote each other.

*Pursuing development, overcoming poverty*: To meet citizens' demands for social justice and increase their happiness and satisfaction, a higher level of economic development and better material conditions are needed. China, in particular, is still a developing country (currently China's per capita annual income is 30,000 yuan [approximately US$4,600], but 560 million people only earn about

1,000 yuan per month—less than US$2,000 per year). This discrepancy reveals the need for an organic integration of equity and efficiency in development.

That is, to maintain the appropriate economic growth rate, to ensure employment, and to continuously improve the social material living standards, which is not only the basis for reducing the gap between the rich and the poor, and thus winning the battle to overcomes poverty, but also the fundamental way to maintain and realize social equity, China has established the "Leading Group Office of the State Council for poverty alleviation and development" as early as 1986. It established files and file cards for poor households, poor villages, poor counties and special poverty-stricken areas, analyzed the causes of poverty alleviation and provided a basis for poverty alleviation decision-making. But after more than twenty years of effort, tens of millions of China's people are still living at or below the absolute poverty line of 1.25 USD per day.

To this end, on the one hand, China should persist in continuing reform and opening up, vigorously enhance its economic strength, and help to get rid of poverty comprehensively. On the other hand, since 2014, China has implemented a policy transformation away from targeted assistance to the poor in favor of targeted efforts to eliminate poverty itsrelf. Over the past eight years, under the current standards, 98.99 million rural poor people, 832 poverty-stricken counties and 128,000 poor villages have been lifted out of poverty, thus the arduous task of eliminating absolute poverty has been completed.

Indeed, insisting on making sustainable development a priority provides the necessary material basis for eradicating absolute poverty and achieving a higher level of social equity. For example, efforts have been made to build highways that serve the whole country (including across deserts); expressways to towns throughout the country (covering about 98 per cent of cities with a population of more than 200,000); and building bridges across the sea, rivers and valleys. Nearly 1.4 billion people now have access to electricity. By 2018, China's highway and high-speed rail mileage, the total length of its bridges and its power generation capacity is the first in the world. This infrastructure also contributes to poverty eradication. In addition, in the past eight years alone, the central, provincial, municipal and county governments have invested nearly 1.6 trillion yuan (257.6 billion USD) in special poverty alleviation funds, of which 6 trillion, 601 billion yuan (106.3 billion USD) has been invested by the central government. The important decision has been made to make overcoming poverty the bottom line task and landmark index to achieve the first Centennial goal, and to declare war on absolute poverty with the strength of the whole Party and the whole country. Over the past 40 years of reform and opening up, according to current standards, 850 million people in China have been lifted out of poverty. Of course, this is only the first step. In order to fundamentally eliminate poverty, steady achievements to get rid of poverty, prevent the risk of retrogression, and lay a solid foundation for a new stage of development, China will need to shift its focus to raising farmers' incomes and narrowing the income gap between urban and rural areas, by changing the "Poverty Alleviation Office" into the state Rural Revitalization Bureau.

***Vigorously developing social industry***: While promoting economic development by fostering the growth of traditional industry, we must actively develop social resources, create social capital, and expand the social market, while also inventing, creating, and innovating social technology, so as to promote social enterprise development. Then we must strengthen the nation's various social development undertakings, such as science and technology, education, culture, environmental protection, public health care, social welfare, and women's and children's rights and interests, so as to promote social progress.

For over 30 years now, China has been undergoing a process of rapid economic development, but due to the neglect of social reform, the tasks of social transformation are particularly burdensome, and social industry will be crucially significant for China's social transformation, as it shifts from a predominantly "planned society" into a largely democratic one. The most important feature of the planned society, matching the planned economy with Chinese characteristics demands a high concentration of economic, political, cultural, and social resources, controlled by the state and incorporated into its program. Even the inherent resources inside of social resources are strictly controlled through the so-called "units" or "organizations". This process has shaped all aspects of social transformation in China, including government decentralization, improving democracy, promoting social reform, expanding the middle class, establishing a good faith society, creating mechanisms for freer expression of public opinion, and so on. And all of these factors are inseparable from the development and maturity of social organizations and social enterprises capable of conducting social transformation. On the other hand, social enterprise is also an economic power that strengthens certain forms of public ownership.

Deep-seated challenges facing those who shoulder the mission of social transformation in China lie in the soft environment of social enterprise, including the concept of change and institutional environment. For example, we need legislation to protect the identity and status of NGOs and social enterprise, to rectify government behavior, to standardize the behavior of social enterprises, and to recognize the dualism of social resources while also maintaining balance and coordination between them, so as to comprehensively improve the environment for social enterprise development.

***Perfecting the income distribution system and regulating income distribution order:*** "Efficiency" and "fairness" often prove to be contradictory goals. This puzzling feature of the market economy persists without an obvious solution.

When China was in the primary stage of socialism, distributive justice could only be relatively fair. Therefore, in dealing with the relationship between efficiency and fairness, we had to follow the principle of "efficiency first" while still giving consideration to fairness when this proved possible. By paying greater attention to efficiency in the initial distribution while emphasizing fairness in redistribution, China effectively attached more importance to efficiency in the economy while placing greater emphasis on fairness in political and social life.

***Perfecting the guarantee system of democratic rights, while consolidating the political status of the people to be masters:*** Institutional justice is the basic guarantee of social stability, and the procedures employed to enact and implement laws are directly related to the justice of any institution. This requires that we broaden and improve supervision, ensure that institutions are effectively guided and controlled, strengthen social supervision, guarantee the citizen's right to complain, accuse, and appeal, and also allow citizens to participate in all kinds of decision making relating to their vital interests. Therefore, it is necessary to establish an effective mechanism to ensure the fair, open, and effective delivery of information, so as to promote the democratization of decision making. At the same time, we must also improve the legal system, strengthen the basis of social harmony in law, improve the judiciary system, and strengthen the judicial guarantee of social harmony.

***Establishing a fair social security system***: Social security is one of the principal means by which a government can realize social justice. The goal of social security should be based on social justice and safety, and achieved through such mechanisms as welfare, public assistance and social endowment insurance, unemployment insurance, assured access to medical treatment and health care, social allowances, and similar measures. For China, social welfare is one area where government has not greatly improved its services to the public during the last 30 years of rapid economic development. To this end, the social security system should first act to improve the state's income redistribution efforts, and increase government financial support for social security (by guaranteeing minimum incomes for both urban and rural citizens, and gradually expanding social security coverage, so that more people benefit). It should also improve education (especially basic and vocational education in rural areas) to foster and strengthen the human resources of vulnerable groups, and advance medical care by promoting better public health, comprehensive arrangements for treating serious diseases, and raising the level of rural cooperative medical care. All of these measures will be necessary in order to improve the living conditions of impoverished groups and alleviate the social contradictions and conflicts resulting from the large gap between rich and poor.

***Improving social management***: Social management refers to a series of management activities for social public affairs, including cultivating a reasonable structure for modern society, managing and standardizing social organization, adjusting the relations of social interests, responding to social needs, resolving social contradictions, maintaining social justice, public order and stability, nurturing a rational, tolerant, harmonious, civilized social atmosphere, and creating a social environment conducive to the harmonious development of economy and society. For China, the efficient social management of the "all-pervasive" government planning system has for a long time been very poor and has resulted in low autonomy throughout Chinese society.

To correct, this will require the government to change its concept, scope, mode, and method of social management, to innovate and improve the social management system, to develop a number of new institutions, policies, and regulations in line with China's contemporary social life and goals, along with supporting institutions and policies in various areas. These include systems for social organization management, social security, social credit, mediating social contradictions, maintaining social order, expanding its capacity to protect public safety and deal with emergencies, while enhancing social warning and emergency response systems. We must also pay attention to improving social autonomy by using social organizations, and building a benign mechanism for government and society to interact. These are all new issues for China.

Take the social credit system as an example. The experimental work of constructing China's social credit system began at the end of October 2003. In March 2005, the Ministry of Labor and Social Security established the credit manager as a new profession and promulgated the "Industry Standards for Credit Managers"; then in 2014, the Chinese government issued the *Planning Outline Program for the Construction of a Social Credit System (2014–20)*, in order to gradually build an honest and trustworthy economic and social environment. The Chinese credit model also pays attention to an individual's "legal reputation" (whether they have a criminal record or an ongoing lawsuit), "commercial integrity" (whether they pay debts on time), "social integrity" (whether the recipient smokes in public places or disrupts social order), and even their "social network behavior" (whether they disseminate false news or rumors), among other things. With the increasing demand for credit, China's credit service industry has become a vital new industry.

### Positive development science and technology, striving to build an innovative country (transforming the civilization of science and technology)

Today's world is changing with each passing day. If any country or region fails to keep up with the changes of the world in terms of innovation of soft and hard technology and soft and hard environment, it will lose its historic opportunities and the losses will be irreparable for generations. Only by putting the development of science and technology, including basic research, at the forefront of long-term national strategy and increasing investment of soft and hard capital, can we ensure that China's economic development is filled with potential and creates a wide range of talents and an atmosphere that facilitates creativity and innovation.

This requires the implementation of systematic solutions from the perspectives of changing concepts, strategic innovation, breaking various bottlenecks in the soft environment, strengthening futures research, and creating an independent innovation environment for enterprises.

## Institutional transformation experiment—implementing a socialist system with Chinese characteristics

Facing the historical turning point of transforming Industrial Civilization, all countries have the task of reforming their existing systems and rebuilding the institutional civilization.

### 1. Thinking about social system

Many people in today's world have a deep misunderstanding of terms like "social system", and "Cold War mentality", and this has affected people's attitude toward institutional reform as well as their rational thinking. Some people in the West have a strong negative reaction to the very word socialism, but nonetheless they fall into deep confusion over how to handle the problems that emerge from their own system that they regard as a model of "rationality in the world of freedom and democracy." In fact, the West is the cradle of socialism. Although the former Soviet Union was the first socialist country in history, the actual birthplace of world socialism was Germany. As Singapore scholar Yongnian Zheng said, if there had been no socialist movement in Europe, today's European social system would not exist. It can be said that socialism actually saved the market economy and capitalism as well.

Some people in China lack a calm analysis and fail to recognize the sources of the progressive factors in contemporary developed countries, including socialist factors and the new changes and trends of contemporary capitalism. While willing to learn from developed countries their advanced technology and management experience, they fail to identify the principles of adhering to the socialist road and safeguarding the long-term interests of the country and the nation. This leads to blind acceptance and even worship of certain dross commonly found in Western culture, while many core elements are not learned.

Among the modern developed countries, those who are more successful in national governance issues such as the Nordic states have had relative success in solving the challenges of social justice, income distribution, closing the gap between rich and poor, etc. These countries have benefited from the influence of democratic socialism for more than 100 years and absorbed and adhered to many socialist factors. According to the financial budget that the German parliament adopted in 2013, the fiscal spending of the Federal Ministry of Labor and Social Affairs accounted for 40 per cent of the total government outlays in that year. Roosevelt's New Deal (relief, recovery, and reform) helped the United States to smoothly ride out the economic crisis from 1933 to 1936, and even drew on the successes of the planned economy implemented in the Soviet Union, which was a socialist country at that time. Roosevelt's programs did not fundamentally solve the drawbacks of capitalism, but did adjust and partially reform it.

Among the important reasons for Japan's post-war economic miracle were several democratic reforms with a socialist flavor. For example, one was the political reform that denied the emperor absolute autocratic authority. There was also land reform. The Japanese government bought the landlord's land and then transferred ownership to farmers at a low price, turning sharecroppers who had accounted for 70 per cent of the total number of peasants before the Second World War into owner-peasants. This kind of nonviolent means allowed landlord's land to be distributed to peasants. Other examples of "socialist" ideas that have become widely accepted among the developed nations of the West include the disintegration of financial magnates, the implementation of antitrust policies, and the spread of labor unions as important advocates of labor reform. All these reforms and others contributed to reviving Japan's postwar economy. A group of Japanese Communists, headed by Tetsuzo Fuwa, have been studying for decades how to transition to socialism through "socialization of production materials" in contemporary capitalist countries with highly developed productivity and huge scale means of production.

The general trend of historical development is that socialism will eventually replace capitalism and then humanity will move toward a more perfect society. The Chinese scholar Baisong Jin pointed out that the developed countries in today's world often call their economies capitalist, but have actually absorbed more and more socialist factors in the course of their development. For example, state intervention in economic development has become normal now; there has also been a revolution in enterprise ownership, including the separation of corporate management from ownership, and the implementation of corporate shareholding.

Examples of ownership reform include implementing equity among shareholders, popularizing small equity investment, fostering the development of the entire population; capital securitization, socialization, and universalization; state-implemented reform of the income redistribution system, such as the establishment of a social security network, and the reform of the redistribution system by means of finance and taxation.

In the area of national politics, the democratic election system that reflects popular will increasingly encourages political parties and the media to advertise that they pay close attention to public interests, such as fair distribution and universal education.

But no matter which country or political party, no matter what their banners or slogans say, if leaders no longer really think about the interests and well-being of the majority of their people, the behavior of the government eventually reflect only the will of the state's most wealthy citizens. Such failed democracies are doomed to fall behind truly democratic states, and eventually be forgotten by history.

### 2. The third experiment in institutional transformation

Exploring the socialist institutional experiment, we cannot forget the historical role of the Soviet Union, which was the first socialist country in history. Today though, as an important part of the world socialist movement, the most eye-catching prospect is China. China's institutional experiment is the ongoing practice of socialism strongly influenced by Eastern culture.

As mentioned in the section of "Socialist practice in China" in Chapter 6, China is currently undergoing the practice of its third institutional transformation—building socialism with Chinese characteristics.

***System transformation should not deviate from the direction of building socialism***: If the essence of socialism is to liberate productive forces, develop productivity, eliminate exploitation and polarization, and ultimately achieve general prosperity. Then, whether through institutional transition or reform and opening up, we must adhere to the basic economic system, with public ownership as its mainstay while simultaneously develop diverse forms of ownership, so as to liberate productive forces and create conditions for the free and comprehensive development of human beings. The channel for opening to the world must be equipped with "filters", that adhere to the principle of "take the essence and discard the dregs", recognize the advanced nature of socialist core values while identifying areas where privatization and foreign investment could be introduced, yet prevent the introduction of the "dregs" of capitalism, especially prevent social anomie in the moral field. Finally, the results of reform and opening up must benefit most Chinese citizens, rather than allowing only a very small number of people to become rich, thus increasing the gap between rich and poor, and leading to greater social polarization.

***How to preserve Chinese characteristics during institutional transformation***: As Xiaoping Deng said: "The ultimate success of all reforms depends on the reform of the political system." China today is still in the middle stage of industrialization and needs a strong government and ruling party to ensure that transforming the development mode takes place within a stable social order and political environment to avoid intensifying conflicts.[10] At the same time, though China's economy is growing rapidly, all of the per capita indicators remain significantly below prevailing world levels. Therefore, we must dedicate a portion of our resources to accomplishing some major tasks while we simultaneously improve decision-making efficiency. To do this, we will need to adopt political reforms beginning with internal reform of the regime itself within the framework of a political system led by the CPC.

In order to accelerate the institutionalization, standardization, and routinization of socialist democratic politics, construct a socialist country under the rule of law and develop a more extensive and sound people's democracy, two breakthroughs are required. One is to reform and improve the Two Sessions System (The National People's Congress [NPC] and Chinese People's Political Consultative Conference [CPPCC]), and the other is to promote the construction of a legal system that will reliably govern the country under the rule of law.

- The Two Sessions System is a political mechanism with Chinese characteristics, which has become an important channel for popular participation in political life. The Third Plenary Session of the 18th Central Committee of the CPC decided that the construction of a socialist democratic political system needs to start with the reform and improvement of the system of the NPC and CPPCC. First, to ensure the people who exercise state power through the People's Congress, strengthen the mechanisms by which the NPC discusses and decides major issues, insist that governments at all levels report to the NPC before major decisions are made. Second, to improve multi-party cooperation and political consultation under the leadership of the CPC, expand its working mechanisms and promote broad, multi-level institutionalized development of Deliberative (or Consultative) Democracy. The reform of the NPC and the CPPCC needs to include reforming their relationship with the government and the ruling party, which is also crucial to reforming China's political system. Therefore, China decided to strengthen the supervision of "One Government Two Courts" (One Government: [the people's government]; Two Courts: [the people's court and the people's procuratorate]) and improve the system by which both are produced by ensuring that they are responsible to, and supervised by, the NPC. Professor Sen Wei, of Fudan University, recommended that, as an organization of public opinion, the NPC should first address one important cause of corruption and social conflicts (namely, government expenditures), by undertaking budget supervision, and making this an important step toward openness and transparency in government affairs.

- To strengthen the construction of the legal system and establish a socialist country built on the rule of law, One of the characteristics of socialism with Chinese characteristics is that "without ever having reached the full development stage of capitalism, China transitioned directly from a semi-feudal and semi-colonial state, in which economy and culture were relatively backward, into a phase of socialist revolution and socialist construction." This feature is particularly evident from the difficulty of running a country under the rule of law. In the thousands of years of Chinese history, among the choices of "techniques for ruling", the ideas of Confucian "ruling by rites" and "ruling by virtues" have generally prevailed, making China a country ruled for a long time more by individuals than by laws. Therefore, shifting from rule by man to the rule of law in China is a fundamental change in governance that represents a significant departure from tradition and a leap into a new historical stage in the development of China's social and political civilization. The goal of building a fair, just, and harmonious society is clear, but the crux is institutional guarantee. The Third Session of the 12th National People's Congress announced in March 2015 that China will revise its legal code to clarify the division between central and local jurisdiction in legislation, and grant the People's Congress of all cities local legislative power (including the People's Congresses in Autonomous Prefectures); revise the Food Safety, and State Security Laws, and introduce China's first Law on Family Violence. Moreover, they pledged to fully implement the principle of statutory taxation before 2020 and perform a "major operation" on all the relevant laws associated with environmental protection.

Governing the country under the rule of law includes four links: (1) taking a well-conceived approach to law-making; (2) ensuring that all laws are strictly enforced; (3) seeing that justice is administered impartially; and (4) ensuring that the law is observed by all. Of these, judicial justice is the crux and the core. At present, China is making judicial reform a breakthrough point to promote the rule of law and governance by the party on the basis of regulations, in order to ensure judicial fairness, openness, less bureaucracy, de-localization, eliminating grey areas in which corruption can flourish, and purifying the social atmosphere by applying the legal system.

***The CPC, which is leading institutional transformation, must maintain its advanced nature and continuously improve its ruling capability***: In a country like China with a large population, profound cultural tradition, weak economic foundation, vast territory, and imbalanced development, if there is no strong advanced core of leadership, the nation will lack a spirit of cooperation and remain divided. Moreover, it will constantly fall prey to internal and external unrest.

When the CPC was founded in 1921, there were more than 200 political parties in China, and the CPC was only one of them. But 28 years later, it is by no means accidental that the CPC is in power throughout the country, and, over the past 100 years, it has grown from dozens of individuals to the ruling party with more than 90 million Party members today.

Before the Ming Dynasty, China was an open country. It had trade and cultural exchanges with countries around the world through the "Silk Road" by land and sea. It was one of the most developed countries in the world at that time. The first industrial revolution started brewing in the second half of the seventeeth century and was initiated in Britain in the second half of the eighteenth century. This led to the rapid development of trade, society, science and technology in Western countries, culminating in the era of industrial civilization. However, since the middle and late Ming Dynasty, China began to implement the "sea ban" policy, which interrupted the connection between China and the world. In the Qing Dynasty (1636–1912), China began to implement the "closed door" policy, which made China lose the opportunity to communicate with foreign civilization and to develop simultaneously with other counties of the world. As a result, China gradually moved away from the world, failed to integrate into the wave of industrial revolution, and began to lag far behind the Western countries.

For the purpose of opening up colonies and competing for world hegemony, the Western powers launched one after another aggression against China, which was still in the agricultural era, and attempted to destroy the country. Due to the overall corruption in Chinese politics, economy and military in the later period of the Qing government, as well as its political rigidity, cultural despotism, isolation from the outside world, and mind confinement, China had neither the heart to defend themselves nor the power to fight back. The Chinese government signed a series of unequal treaties, which effectively wiped out China's sovereignty and made her virtually a colony of the great powers. In addition, after nearly three hundred years of rule by the Qing Dynasty, most of the Chinese people in this period were enslaved, and in a state of physical and mental ignorance, spiritual depression, psychological numbness, loss, without any national consciousness. Lacking a spirit of cooperation, many people could not see any possibility for a bright future, and easily succumbed to the temptation of money, and sought only to satisfy their immediate material interests, and ignored their consciences, acting as traitors to help the evildoers.

It was not until the September 18th Incident in 1931 that the whole nation began to wake up in the face of the crisis of national subjugation and extermination.

The upsurge of the anti-Japanese national salvation movement was set off, and the anti-Japanese national united front was gradually formed, regardless of class, party, nationality, and religious beliefs, contributing to the Anti-Japanese war together. This was an unprecedented war against aggression as well as a national liberation war in Chinese history. It was the blood and lives of countless martyrs that allowed this nation to regain its dignity.

The Communist Party of China, in particular, inspired a large number of intellectual elites who had inherited and carried forward the national spirit and belief of the Chinese nation for thousands of years, in combination with their aesthetic ideals, beautiful visions and communist beliefs, and inspires, educates, guides, organizes and unites the masses to shape them into revolutionary fighters with firm faith, to form a people's army led by the party, to forge a path of armed revolution in line with China's reality, and to achieve the great cause of national salvation. To this end, the suffering of the CPC even frightened its enemies. By the early days of the founding of the People's Republic of China in 1949, there were more than 4 million CPC members, and over 3.7 million CPC members had died bravely during 28 years before the founding of new China.

Of course, the key to maintaining its leadership and to achieving success in China's institutional experiment lies in whether the CPC can maintain its progressiveness and continually improving its ability to govern. This is also an important prerequisite and political guarantee for the rule of law.

First, the progressiveness of a political party depends on whether the party represents the fundamental interests of the overwhelming majority of the people and meets the requirement of developing advanced productivity and setting the direction for advanced culture. The political philosophy of a party that was founded for the public good and exercises state power for the people must be manifested in its basic value orientation. That is, the orientation of its core values must evolve over time so as to conform to the interests of the vast majority of the people and their value orientation.

Three aspects of these values were stated as follows at the 18th CPC National Congress: (1) at the national level to maintain a prosperous, democratic, civilized, and harmonious state; (2) in the social dimension, to assure liberty, equality, justice, and the rule of law; and (3) at the level of individual citizens, to promote patriotism, dedication, integrity, and kindness. This is the socialist core value system and embodies the essence of socialist ideology. Compared with the general slogans of the past, such as "a life-long struggle for the liberation of all mankind and for communism", the values presented here are ones that the vast majority of Chinese citizens, including different social groups and races, can accept and share. It is crucial that the leading cadres of the Communist Party should take the lead and stick to the highest belief of "serving people wholeheartedly" to avoid ideological and ethical inconsistencies, in order to prevent duplicity in ideology and ethics, and to avoid inconsistency that will lead to disunity in society.

In fact, socialism with Chinese characteristics has entered a new era, a major judgement made by the 19th CPC in 2017. Its theoretical basis is that the principle contradiction facing Chinese society in the new era has been transformed from the contradiction between backward social production and the people's ever-growing material and cultural needs, into the contradiction between imbalance and inadequate development and the people's ever-growing need for a better life.

Therefore, the CPC not only needs to take responsibility for carrying out creative study and development on the ideal of communism and its realization in both theory and practice but also needs to integrate the three 70-years stages of socialist development[11] with the historical experience and lessons of the Chinese revolution to conduct in-depth study and actively practice on the path to achieving the ultimate goal. What is even more important is to put people's most basic and immediate interests at the forefront of reform. The task of resolving the principal social contradictions in China in the new era can be divided and its values fulfilled by implementing reforms in six related areas of sustainable development: the economy, resources, environment, society, politics, science and technology. Only in this way can the Communist party win and hold the support of the whole nation, and convince the Chinese people to keep faith, heart, and mind with the Party, and willingly support and participate in its reform efforts.

Second, success depends on the party's ability to govern, including its decision-making ability related to the strategic direction of the country's long-term future development; its ability to reshape the national governance system with the times, and realize governance modernization, specifically the construction of a national legal system; and the innovative ability of its leadership to properly handle relations with the NPC CPPCC, and government agencies, while maintaining judicial independence. Building greater implementation capacity will include the ability to make the party's socialist core values permeate all six approaches to sustainable development.

The quality of the ruling party is related to the reform of the party itself, and whether it can demonstrate that it is able to strictly control itself—that is, dare to carry out self-revolution. This will require great political courage and wisdom. Anti-corruption is a case in point.

The anti-corruption campaign is an act to remove all the "dirt" that has been building up in the past 30 years during its high-speed economic growth. It is regarded as essential for building a fair and healthy economic environment; eliminating corruption will help ensure social justice and restore the credibility of the ruling party. Its hardships are sure to draw the attention of the world. The problem of corruption not only exists among government officials but also extends to armed forces and all walks of life. Corruption among party members and leading cadres at all levels is so widespread and serious that it is shocking and requires profound reflection. If a country does not get rid of corruption, it will lose before it fights. The anti-corruption struggle has become a political struggle affecting social stability, the future of the party, and the survival of the country are at stake.

However, at the present stage, anti-corruption efforts are still focused on how to cure the symptoms, so as to win time to address the root cause. In order to bring corruption under permanent control, China must reform its national governance system and eradicate the root that breeds corruption through institutional and structural reforms. Power must not be allowed to become a means of obtaining money, and it must be subject to public supervision and restraint. To this end, China must first govern conduct and discipline within the ruling party. China's leaders are building up a political system and devising governance mechanisms that dare to confront the various difficulties and obstacles to the course of progress head-on. This includes making the fight against corruption an important part of governance, so as to regain people's confidence and trust in the party.

***The significance of China's institutional experiment***: First, it is China's practice of embedding the goal of Communism (an ideal society born in Western capitalist countries) into the historical process of social development of China—an ancient Oriental civilization—so that it becomes integral to the future prospects of China and an active factor in social development. This will require that socialism, the lower stage of the communist ideal, must first be successful in China.

Second, it is an experiment of a comprehensive transition in China's development model under the regime with Chinese characteristics (that is to say, a socialist system under the leadership of the CPC, where the people head the administration, the CPC exercises state power, and all democratic parties [there are eight democratic parties in mainland China] participate in government and political affairs), so as to achieve the goal of "letting more than a billion Chinese enjoy their rights to education, medical services, pension, security, and law." Achieving this ambitious goal will be very difficult, and success depends on whether we can overcome resistance from internal and external vested interest groups, adhere to the direction of reform, correctly set priorities for needed reforms and achieve the ultimate goal. This will be a great test of the wisdom of all Chinese people and the leadership of very generation.

In short, China is solidly improving its own affairs and moving forward along the road it has chosen, so as to let the vast majority of Chinese people feel happy. This is the fundamental guarantee for peaceful development. Of course, the challenges facing China and the practice needed for the transition are not limited to the six areas we have already discussed, there are other important areas as well including agriculture, rural development, education, medical care, population, urbanization, national security, etc.

Taking agriculture and rural problems as an example, promoting agricultural modernization and revitalizing the rural economy are the fundamental measures to increase the income of rural population and reduce the income gap between urban and rural areas. Therefore, in early 2021, China established the "National Rural Revitalization Bureau", to comprehensively promote rural revitalization. This marked the beginning of another grand campaign though it still has a long way to go.

In order to realize sustainable development guided by the values of Global Civilization in all these areas, China must persist in its efforts for a generation or longer, and it may perhaps require a third 100 years to fully achieve.

## China 2050: A splendid future lies ahead, but dangers still exist

The six approaches mentioned above are closely related to each other and irreplaceable in China's practice of sustainable development. Specifically this includes transforming China's economic development mode, its natural resources application model, its ecological protection model, its social development model, encouraging innovation, and promoting institutional transition. In all probability, there will be other trials as well not yet foreseen.

Depending on the direction and intensity of reform, and whether the CPC who leads these reforms is able to maintain its progressiveness, and continuously improve its ability to govern, China's experiments will have varying results. We must realize that, as the development of China's mobile Internet enters the era of universal use, the debate on the development road in Chinese society will become wider and more intense than ever before.

If reform efforts in key areas or key links are delayed or reform measures only partially alleviate the crisis; institutional reform cannot break out of the old framework and solidify the achievements already made. And if reform does not focus on fundamental solutions to people's current concerns in such fields as anti-corruption and honesty, income distribution, housing security, education reform, medical reform, and food and drug safety, or if we forget the original intention of reform and deviate from the basic goal of socialism, and become too keen on marketizing everything, it could eventually lead to social polarization and class conflict that would lead China in a dangerous direction even without active foreign subversion.

If our understanding of the difficulties involved in China's reform is insufficient, or if the reforms attempted fail to take into account China's reality and stage of development, or even if the sheer intensity of the reform effort is too great and too hastily implemented due to our impatience for success, it could possibly lead to uncontrollable chaos, or allow reactionary forces at home and abroad to take advantage of the loopholes and cause turmoil or even split the country.

The ideal future we long for should be as follows: despite various challenges and pressures at home and abroad, China can always adhere to its established goals. Even if the reform process limps along (and we certainly hope that China will not become like the Soviet Union), we can still succeed so long as China does not make disruptive mistakes (in particular, in various institutional reforms). Also keep in mind that while bolder, more open and in-depth reform is implemented, it must focus on the issues that most concern people and are vital to the future of the country as well as security, and not become divorced from the overall framework of governing the country with the "Four Comprehensives"[12]; the reform plan designed after the 18th CPC National Congress can be put into place gradually and by stages, so as to finally break the fetters imposed by vested interest groups, and achieving a harmonious domestic society that truly makes the majority of the population happy, and promotes peaceful development at the international level.

This road is undoubtedly very difficult. It can be called a bloodless revolution, no less than any revolution in the past.

Why is it just the first step toward victory?

Because the so-called "two 100-year" goal (referring to the times when the CPC and the People's Republic respectively will each mark their 100th anniversaries) emphasize to realize China's dream of modernization, while modernization only paves the way to achieving the great rejuvenation of the Chinese nation, also lays the foundation for making China enter the era of Global Civilization as soon as possible. In this sense, I tend to define the Chinese Dream as the realization of Global Civilization in China.

In other words, to truly realize the great rejuvenation of the Chinese nation, we must have the conditions for realizing Global Civilization in all aspects, such as material, spiritual, political, and ecological civilization. Hence, to realize the "two 100-year" goal is only the first step toward achieving China's grand experiment for achieving Global Civilization

In view of the efforts that China has made to date, and the determined struggle of the whole people and the Party to implement the goal of the "two 100-year" program, China's prospects appear relatively bright for the next 30 years.

There is no doubt that China will be the world's largest economy by 2050 (but its GDP per capita will still likely be far below that of the United States and Japan) and one of the most important economic centers in the world. While it will also be quite active on the international stage and take its place as a responsible powerful country that is on the path to becoming innovative in more and more scientific and technological fields, its innovation policy, and stable social environment, will attract the world's technical elite and entrepreneurs to China.

China will also respond to the demands of the international community and take on greater responsibilities, providing more public goods to the international community. For example, the concept of "a community of common destiny for mankind" advocated by China actively promotes peaceful coexistence, benign interaction and win–win cooperation among all countries. This not only creates a good external environment for the great rejuvenation of the Chinese nation but also serves as an important link in promoting Global Civilization and provides Chinese wisdom for the sustainable survival and development of all mankind. China's relationship with other leading world powers and its Asian neighbors, and its sincere efforts to form a harmonious and mutually beneficial relationship with the entire international community, are still top priorities. For example, the initiative of "One Belt One Road", which highlights a new worldview, aims to seek the common development of China and neighboring countries and regions along the Belt and Road to achieve regional prosperity. To achieve common purpose with these countries, whose religions, institutions, and cultures differ widely from those of China, will require an attitude of tolerance and symbiosis so as not to attach political conditions to our interactions with these countries, and to encourage and welcome all countries to join these initiatives voluntarily. This is a demonstration of the practice of new international relations.

As the world gradually adapts to China's new status and role, and countries scramble to share more opportunities to benefit from China's development, more people will be willing to live and work in China. If a country with nearly 20 per cent of the world's population can maintain economic prosperity and social stability, it will make a major contribution to global sustainability.

But just imagine if China does not succeed in making the above transition successfully. It could fall into turmoil and political instability, and the resulting chaos would not stay inside China, but likely spread across the world. What country could absorb hundreds of millions of refugees? As Jorgen Landers said, this would be an enormous blow to the stability of the region, make the global economy grow more slowly, and even increase carbon emissions.

On the other hand, there are less than 30 years from now to 2050, very little time for China to resolve the many problems inherited from its past. At the same time, new problems arising from its rapid development will very likely be eased, but probably cannot be completely resolved. Thus, various contradictions will still remain and attract worldwide concern.

From the domestic angle, China's sustainable development faced grave concerns affecting agriculture, rural areas, and farmers including grain and food security; social equity issues such as social security, employment, eradication of corruption, income distribution, the gap between rich and poor, etc. There are also problems of national health, health care reform, education reform, aging population and the shrinking labor force. Air pollution will gradually improve as a result of strict new environmental laws, industrial structure adjustments, the transfer of certain manufacturing enterprises, and changes in manufacturing methods. But thoroughly solving air, marine, land, groundwater pollution as well as rehabilitating and improving the ecosystem could require decades or even hundreds of years. Resource shortages will continue to be a bottleneck for sustained development; and water resources will become a major problem. In short, too many chronic diseases need to be solved urgently.

In the international field, even by 2050, the fact that two kinds of social formation—socialism and capitalism—coexist and compete will not have changed, and the game and struggle between their differing institutions and ideologies will continue. Considering that China holds high the banner of building socialism with Chinese characteristics and adheres to the socialist road, plus the likelihood that China will actively launch a series of major new initiatives (like the development bank of BRIC countries, the Asian infrastructure investment bank, "One Belt One Road", etc.), China's impact on the international community will continue to grow. In addition, China's military power is gradually becoming stronger; thus, the external world will be more sensitive to China's strategic direction. This will almost certainly lead to a variety of frictions and conflicts.

However, because China has chosen a path of peaceful development, insists on never seeking hegemony, strives to build a new type of international relations with win–win cooperation as the core, and actively participates in the construction of international system, the nation's rise can make still more contributions to the world, especially to stabilizing world order and maintaining world peace (Chinese civilization is the only ancient civilization that was never interrupted and lasted for 5,000 years.[13] However, even in its most prosperous period, it did not threaten the development of other countries.).

No matter how the outside world characterizes the rejuvenation of China, this ancient civilization, which has suffered greatly in modern times, today's comprehensive and in-depth reform in China and efforts to realize the Chinese dream are part of mankind's grand practice of realizing the Global Civilization. Whether this practice is based on Oriental culture, or comes from the angle of the developing countries, which represent most of the world's population, or that the effort to change the paradigm of the rise of great powers by peaceful means has no precedent in the past 500 years (which witnessed the rise of Portugal, Spain, Holland, Britain, France, Germany, Russia, Japan, and the United States by aggressive colonization and war), or an experiment on behalf of the ideal of fully realizing socialism (an ideal invented by Westerners, but possessing universal significance), will make a significant contribution to world civilization progress and the creation of new human history.

Time will test the wisdom and courage of the Chinese people and their leaders to see how well they deal with the obstacles and interference aimed at delaying the speed of China's rise, without disrupting the pace of China's reform and development, and dare to challenge and start to solve the problems left over by the past two institutional transformations. In particular, they must ensure continuing to make new progress in letting 1.4 billion Chinese people enjoy their rights to "formal schooling from a young age, higher income from work, better medical services, secure pensions, good housing, and helping the underprivileged." The challenge is: how to lead China, a country with 5,000 years of history, and the world's largest population, but relatively few natural resources per capita, to successfully carry out the most ambitious social experiment in the history of mankind.

It is worth noting that China's efforts to achieve sustainable development, and even to realize the transformation of civilization, are not only a political slogan or a praiseworthy idea, but a hard practical experiment in important areas, accumulating experience, and useful lessons through various trials and practices in several important areas to gradually improve and perfect solutions to these problems, so as to reach the ultimate goal. At present, the vast majority of the Chinese people participate in and support this experiment. In this way, China is bringing hope that the common dream of mankind can become reality. The world is watching expectantly.

### *Striving to build an innovative country: Moving from "imitation" to "innovation"*

Learning—imitation—innovation is the course that developing countries need to go through generally. However, shortening the process from learning and imitation, through creative imitation to independent innovation depends on various elements such as national strategies, institutions, policies, and cultural environment, as well as the interactions of government, enterprises, and the public, in which there are common points and secrets. To realize the peaceful development and the dream of comprehensive rejuvenation in China, the shift from imitative innovation to open innovation, cooperative innovation and then independent innovation is the only way.

China has unique advantages for establishing a national system of innovation. For example,

- Regarding resource mobilization ability at the national level—institutional advantages. The state can collectively mobilize and selectively employ "resources" to achieve long-term important goals that reflect the national will and interests. Examples include the aerospace industry, supercomputers, high-speed rail systems, etc. This is very important for China, which has an advantage on the total scale, but all of whose "per capita" resources are in a weak position.

- Sustained and in-depth reforms and opening up will stimulate enthusiasm for innovation among the entire population.
- A large number of highly qualified workers, who possess courage, energy, and dedication.
- China's economic strength has greatly increased (the GDP exceeded 13.9 trillion USD according to the average exchange rate in 2018, accounting for nearly 16 per cent of the world economy; per capita gross national income reached 9,732 USD, which is higher than the average level of middle-income countries; the balance of foreign exchange reserves reached 3.07 trillion USD, the highest in the world.)
- Rich cultural resources are an infinite treasure that urgently needs to be developed and brought up to date, particularly as a source of creativity for soft industries.

All this shows that China can accomplish whatever it set its mind to, and can do it successfully. However, the challenges we face are also serious.

### Problems worth pondering

It is generally known that China is different now than it was in the early days of reform and opening up, and even different from the beginning of the twenty-first century. China has been on an equal level with advanced countries in more and more technology fields and has even begun to lead the world in some areas. The question is how to unleash the nation's creative potential and accelerate the pace of building an innovative country?

A mature nation must be good at reflection. Over the past 70 years, even during its most difficult times, China has allocated vast resources—far disproportionate to its national strength—to research in science and technology. But the nation's achievements and innovative capabilities (not only in the field of natural science and technology but also in the field of Humanities and Social Sciences and social technology) still do not match the funds and talent China has devoted to this task. Except for certain fields, Chinese scientists have made few breakthroughs significant enough to win them a Nobel Prize, and although in a growing number of high-tech fields, China's achievements equal or exceed those of all other nations, many of China's scientific and technological accomplishments remain stuck in the laboratory, and have so far failed to find successful applications in the country's economic and social development. The fact is that the core technologies in the majority of world industries today are controlled by foreign companies or multinational corporations; but most Chinese manufacturing companies do not own brands and core technologies, and therefore lack international competitiveness.

Recently, many people have started to reflect on China's innovative ability from a number of different perspectives. These include the national cultural-psychological structure (Zehou Li, etc.), the Confucian culture (Zhenning Yang), the thinking mode (Yu Chu) including the speculative ability of logical reasoning, reflected in the nation's policies and institutions (general awareness) academic values, etc. Unquestionably, such discussion is beneficial. People are beginning to reflect calmly and to openly express their own views, which represents great progress in ideological emancipation.

No doubt it is essential to find the root cause, reflect and even criticize existing conditions from the perspectives of culture (see the section "The cultural atmosphere for innovation" below), mode of thinking, system and institution, education, and history. However, changing the mode of thinking and national culture will not necessarily happen overnight, let alone transform an educational mode that has lasted for thousands of years.

Introspection is necessary, but it cannot remain exclusively on the level of theoretical discussion. In fact, since ancient times, Chinese people have not lacked creativity at all, let alone innovative spirit (take the spirit shown by craftsmen as an example). In terms of invention and creation, both ancient China and ancient Europe have made outstanding achievements and formed their own intellectual traditions and civilizations.

Therefore, I prefer to consider these problems from a practical perspective or from an operational point of view. If it is imperative that action be taken, what should we do now? I think the key to changing the status quo is first to encourage ideological emancipation and change concepts (from the highest decision makers to the public). Then through the process of management at all levels promoting strategic innovation, implementing a full range of soft environment innovations (e.g., concepts, culture, systems, mechanisms, and institutions), and enhancing the capacity for strategic management, it should be possible to gradually change these deep-rooted factors and promote innovation. In this way, we can create a new culture and thinking mode conducive to innovation, especially to innovation in system and institutional environment, and ultimately improve the innovative ability of the whole nation, and build an innovative country.

## Changing ideas

First of all, we should have a correct understanding of ourselves, be prepared for danger even in times of peace. People today are keen to talk about how China's economy has become the second largest in the world, and cite the nation's scientific and technological achievements in a few specific areas as proof of China's overall level of science and technology. But indulging in such an optimistic mood is dangerous. We should know that second in economic scale does not mean second in national strength. Moreover, on a per capita basis, many key indicators are below the world average (for example, in 2017 per capita GDP in the United States was 6.79 times that of China; and Japan, which ranked third on economic scale, had a per capita GDP nearly five times that of China). Instead, we must recognize that, compared to the developed countries, China still lags behind in basic research, high-tech development, and industrial technologies, as well as the quantity and quality of excellent enterprises and famous universities. Coupled with the social anomie in various fields accumulated in the rapid economic growth (see the related part of "The practice of institutional transformation" in Chapter 6). These are all content that needs to "think about danger" and enhance the awareness of "worries".

Second, it is necessary to broaden the mind and expand the space of innovation.

While we tend to focus on disruptive innovations in the areas of natural science and technology, we cannot ignore revolutionary changes in non-technical domains, such as business models, organizational transformation of enterprise, or all-round security strategy, especially the revolutionary changes in interdisciplinary integration and innovation. In addition to soft environmental (such as development modes, systems and institutions) innovations, we must also pay attention to broader innovation space from the material production sector to the non-material production sector, from economic activities to social and cultural activities, from the traditional real economy to the future real economy (which will utilize the next-generation technologies enumerated in Chapter 1 as the core of industry), and to promote adjustment, optimization, and transformation of our industrial structure.

Third, although the innovation strategy of science and technology is a core component of the national innovation strategy, insisting on the coordinated development of economy, society, environment and resources is the basic condition for building an innovative country (as explained in the section on "Green development" below).

Fourth, improving innovation capability cannot be solved by increasing R&D input alone. Facing a series of challenges and obstacles to building an innovative country, a systematic solution will be needed.

Fifth, to gain access to core technologies, future research and basic research must be strengthened (see the following chapters for details).

Sixth, in order to make enterprises truly become the main body of innovation, we must first create a legal environment that protects the legitimate rights and interests of entrepreneurs.

Seventh, we must give priority to supporting indigenous invention and creation.

Eighth, and most important, is to further emancipate our minds, in order to facilitate the deep exploration of individuals' innovative potential and unleash their enthusiasm. Although the second round of ideological emancipation has now been launched, it is still necessary to continue carrying out bold exploration and, in particular, to guarantee significant structural and institutional reform to promote still greater output from Chinese science, technology and thoughts.

## Strategic innovations

### 1. Basic principles

- Attaining strategic goals demands a long-term future viewpoint and should avoid the mentality of being eager for quick success and instant benefit.
- Long-term and sustainable futures research is essential for any viable long-term strategy.
- The balance between soft and hard components must be maintained.
- A viable strategy must be coordinated and integrated with the strategic systems in key fields such as economy, society, ecology, environment, resources, and national defense.
- An innovation strategy for science and technology must form an organic whole with the nation's long-term development in mind.

### 2. The framework and structure of innovation strategy should be comprehensively adjusted to assure a balanced soft-hard system

From the perspective of global trends, the contributions that soft factors make to competitiveness at the level of national, industrial, enterprises, as well as at other levels and market sectors are increasing day by day. We need a systematic solution that combines the mutual integration of knowledge from many different areas with soft and hard technologies to enhance the overall strength, competitiveness of Chinese corporations, build new concepts of national security, expand access to new resources for the nation's macroeconomic growth, and improve its ability to create sustainable development, etc.

However, at present, whether in the overall strategy of building an innovative country or creating "science and technology innovation center" in selected cities, widespread soft and hard imbalance still remains. For example, a large investment has been made in scientific research and technology development in some key areas, as well as in the training of scientific and technological personnel. The corresponding hard environment deployment is also clear. But the related soft technologies and soft environment, such as how to break the institutional barriers that restrict innovation, remove the deep roots that hinder the emancipation of the mind, or lead to the low willingness of science and technology personnel to innovate, neither systematic research nor clear deployment has taken place.

Many people have urged that China build the rules of its game in more areas as soon as possible. For instance, technological institutions (including laws, regulations, standards, etc.) are the content of game rules in the field of technology. Only by changing the situation that the research and innovation of technological institutions lags behind the research and innovation of technology, can China create appropriate new game rules for the current times in this field.

### 3. Establishing a long-term effect mechanism of innovation strategy management

For details, see below the part of "Establishing a sustained mechanism for long-term strategic management" in this chapter.

## Nine major soft environment challenges: comprehensive innovation in systems, mechanisms, institutions, and the cultural environment

### 1. Changing the way that innovation is led by government

The main manifestations of over-concentration of power in technological innovation are: bringing innovation into the top-down controlled national innovation system, including the allocation of national resources, public bidding on key projects and orientation of investment. In such cases, many scientific research organizations, researchers, and entrepreneurs feel compelled to concentrate on understanding the government's strategic intent, and consider that it is best to support existing policy so as to improve relations with the government and relevant officials, and thus get more priorities and benefits in the form of project approvals, land allocations, additional funds, human resources, etc. Instead, we should encourage researchers to dig for new ideas, and focus on invention, creation, and innovation. It is necessary to reduce government intervention and give more autonomy to universities and research institutions including private ones. The history of science so far shows that almost all major scientific breakthroughs have been the result of scientists' free exploration, rather than as a result of government planning.

### 2. Strengthening institutional innovation to change the innovation environment

It is necessary to comprehensively explore the systems, institutions, and policies that encourage openness, competition and free imagination in the field of science and technology, and benefit invention, creativity, and innovation. Taking technological innovation as an example, the current scientific research system, the institution of science and technology management (involving various technologies, projects, talents, funds, especially the direction of using funds, etc.), the institution for assessing (including talent selection, academic achievements, especially the expert review and administrative approval system of scientific research projects, etc.), intellectual property, incentive mechanisms including equity-based incentives, the income distribution system, as well as the financial services model related to innovation, are all in urgent need of comprehensive reform to facilitate basic research and technological innovation. Especially useful would be new legislation to promote research for purely scientific purposes, punish those who pursuit fame and fortune in the academic community, and resolutely punish any and all instances of academic corruption. Even more urgent is the need to replace the old system, institution and mechanism, and legislate to guarantee, protect, and support ideological emancipation in scientific invention and technological innovation. By encouraging independent thinking, ingenuity, free expression, and tolerating the publication of views currently considered controversial or even absurd, we can resolve the problem of insufficient motive power behind innovation, establish a good academic atmosphere, and create a soft environment in which new thoughts and new ideas can flourish.

Take for example the so-called "two skins" problem in institutions and mechanisms. For decades, smoothly integrating the results of scientific research into new applications for military and civilian use has remained a difficult problem that we have not solved. This is a great waste! The efficient use of new scientific and technological achievements in national defense and civilian markets not only benefits for Chinese enterprises and allows them to obtain independent and controllable intellectual property rights but also boosts national defense and enables strategic R&D departments through technology transfer to improve the quality and profitability to support follow-up research. It is also an essential step in shaping a complete "national innovation system".

It is worth emphasizing that providing an opportunity at the institutional level to fully reflect on our plans and actions will allow us to address our own weaknesses and perhaps identify and change any deep-rooted bad habits that produce maladies in social and economic life and uncover their cultural causes.

### 3. A talent system in urgent need of reform

The development of any country cannot be separated from the continuous support of domestic talent for building an innovative country, talent is the basic resource. As of 2019, there were 2,956 colleges and universities in China, of which more than 1,800 first opened between 2001 and 2014. As a result, the number of college graduates trained every year has soared (610,000 in 1990, 800,000 in

1995, 950,000 in 2000, 3.07 million in 2005, 5.75 million in 2010, 7.49 million in 2015, 7.65 million in 2016, 7.95 million in 2017, and 8.34 million in 2019). There are also around 9 million master graduates and between 700,000 and 800,000 doctoral graduates. No country in the world can match such a huge talent resource.

However, at present, China is experiencing a serious lack of high-end talent in every area. At the same time, the unprecedented waves of educational emigration and investment emigration have led to a massive loss of scientific and technological elites as well as cultural and financial elites. Coupled with the serious waste of domestic talent in China today, and the country's failure to attract new talent from overseas, the danger that China's future economic and social development will be anemic is increasing.

According to the statistics from the Ministry of education, the number of Chinese students who went abroad to study in 2017 alone reached 608,400, and the total number of students studying abroad has reached 5.1949 million. Although the proportion of graduates who return to China for jobs is on the rise, a large number of excellent talents still migrate overseas. As of 2014, the annual capital outflow due to emigration from the PRC to the United States was close to 468 million USD, with another 516 million USD going to Australia. According to one recent survey among rich people in China (individuals whose property is valued at more than 16.13 million USD), 40 per cent want to immigrate to the United States, 37 per cent would rather live in Canada, 14 per cent in Singapore, and 11 per cent in Europe. As of 2013, some 8.5 million ethnic Chinese were living overseas, most of whom were members of the middle class, while in that year only 848,000 people immigrated to China.

What is the problem? What are the root causes of large-scale migration and brain drain? Why are so many outstanding talents reluctant to return to China?

The view on talents of Zhengfei Ren, founder of the giant telecommunications equipment company Huawei, is worth studying and learning. He points out that technology is not bought by money, but created by people. Huawei employs more than 700 active mathematicians, more than 800 physicists and more than 120 chemists. These are the assets of which he is most proud. Huawei also has a strategic research institute, which attracts noted professors from famous universities all over the world to conduct basic research with generous remuneration. Ren said that Huawei does not quibble over the so-called return on investment for these individuals. He has shown great foresight by recognizing that, for scientific research and technological development, investment in people is the first essential. To cherish talents and invest in them is to respect, trust, expect and encourage their work.

In short, only by establishing a correct view of human talent, will it be possible to solve China's problems of innovation in its systems, mechanisms, and institutions. At the same time, in order to realize the self-reliance of science and technology and meet the demand of scientific and technological innovation for high-end talents, China must pursue two objectives: training more of its own citizens and welcoming experts in many fields from overseas.

How can China halt the outflow of scientific and technological talent and capital? How can it persuade the millions of its scholars who study abroad to return home and expand the nation's innovation team? How can we attract more patriotic Chinese overseas to return home for pioneering work? And how can we attract more talented people worldwide to come and settle in China?

In order to cultivate, discover, attract and retain talents, we should first set up a correct view of talents, dare to invest in "people", encourage innovation in China's existing systems, mechanisms, and institutions: for example, breaking free of today's talent management system that is executive-led and compartmentalized by departments; reforming the mechanisms for the selection, discovery, and evaluation of talented individuals in all fields; reforming various fund systems and strengthening support for basic scientific research; and establishing a system for evaluating scientific achievement. There is an urgent need for scientific research legislation to clean establish a healthy scientific research culture, and set up a way to attract talented people from abroad by developing a mechanism and talent policy with international standards. As Kuan Yew Lee, the dynamic leader of Singapore, once said, "China selects talents from a population of 1.4 billion people, while the United States selects talents from a global population of 7 billion people." Only if the environment, and especially the soft environment, is improved can China motivate large numbers of its own talented people to come forward and attract more outstanding talents from abroad.

It is gratifying that in recent years, more overseas students have chosen to return to China after graduation. In 2017 alone, 480,900 returned to China. There are two main reasons for this phenomenon: on the one hand, the gradual tightening of overseas policies has made it more difficult for overseas students to find jobs in the local area; on the other hand, China's rapid development and national policies strongly support the return of overseas talents, which has made it more attractive to overseas students.

**4. Providing more stable support for basic research**

In general, an emerging economy in the early stages of its development should promote its process of industrialization using the knowledge, technology, and experience of the advanced countries through learning, imitation, cooperation, and joint ventures to give full play to late-mover advantage, just as Japan, South

Korea, and others have done. However, in order to leap-forward from catch-up and imitation innovation to independent innovation, China must duly strengthen its basic research in different areas.

History has proven that both developed countries in Europe and America and the rise of Japan were closely related to their emphasis on basic research. Whether in the natural or social sciences, not to mention the industrial sectors, weaknesses in basic study appear to be one of the important causes behind China's limited display of original creative capability. This limitation is reflected in the absence of major scientific discoveries that lead to the development of new disciplines. Few theoretical breakthroughs that can produce radical transformations in industrial processes, and relatively few accumulations of knowledge that crack key scientific problems, have occurred in China, due in part to lack of outstanding talent, an insufficiently innovative atmosphere, etc. This is not commensurate with the current economic scale in China.

Where can original technology and innovation come from without the accumulation of basic long-term scientific research and support of basic theory?

As a forerunner to previous industrial revolutions, basic research was regarded as the most essential factor in developing national strength and remains so today in developed countries. Five countries, including the United States, Japan, France, South Korea and the United Kingdom, spend 12–23 per cent of their total R&D investment on basic research. And in 2018, China's basic research funds accounted for only 5.54 per cent of the total domestic R&D investment. In fact, in 2020, the proportion of China's scientific research expenditure in its GDP has reached 2.4 per cent (3.74 billion USD); still it was the highest in history. It shows that we are fully capable of increasing the ratio of basic research funds.

From 2000 to 2016, scientists in Japan won a Nobel Prize each year, second only to the United States. The innovative ability of Japanese companies is also among the best in the world. Japan's strong capability for basic scientific research and innovation is closely related to the fact that Japan's proportion of R&D expenditures to GDP ranked first in the world as did the proportion of R&D expenditures dominated by enterprise in total R&D funding. It can be said that Japan's technical reserves create conditions that are likely to continue leading the world in the next round of national strength competition.

If we continue to pursue only low-cost innovation with short-term benefits by relying on tracking and imitation, our nation's innovation will be like water without a source or a tree without roots, it will remain small scale. Pursuing its roots, it is difficult to get rid of the imperfect evaluation mechanism of academic achievements, the impetuous academic atmosphere, the business environment of quick success and instant profits, and the social atmosphere of pursuit of money. But somehow we must manage to adequately support basic research by including setting up an investment structure for basic research funding that is jointly supported by central and local government, as well as all kinds of enterprise.

### 5. Correct understanding of enterprises

In the process of building an innovative country, enterprise is critical to innovation. It is the symbol and guarantee of national strength to have a powerful innovative enterprise group. For China, we need to change the current tendency to focus the vast majority of innovative investment and policy input on national research institutions and prestigious universities, and instead provide institutional guarantees for enterprises to become the main body of innovation activities.

In its initial mission statement, the World Business Academy pointed out that[14]:

> Business has become, in this last half century, the most powerful institution on the planet. The dominant institution in any society needs to take responsibility for the [welfare of society as a] whole, [...], but business has not had such tradition. This is a new role, not yet well understood or accepted.

There is also a need to pay special attention to the future trend and role of super companies in this era. With the rapid development of science and technology, giant information technology companies have emerged in many countries. These companies are so powerful that the relationship between the state and large enterprises is changing. They control not only huge amounts of monetary funds and markets, but also the Internet—an alternative soft capital with special significance in the era of the "Internet–Internet of things" which includes national and even global information resources including public data. The total size of the five major US technology giants alone is 3.5 trillion USD, which has exceeded the GDP of the UK (2.64 trillion USD in 2017), making these companies capable of doing "what the government should do"[15] and even their "efficiency" or influence goes far beyond the national level, which may affect the balance of global strength.

If those super Internet giants with more than 100 million users are changing the world's social communication, learning and consumption styles, which greatly facilitates public lives, but also gradually controlling the whole world. Their ability to control social media platforms is more "effective" than any government department in(to) guiding public opinion and even values, so that even government departments and media organizations rely on those social media platforms to make their voice, which has reached the point of endangering the social and economic order and even threatening to undermine the central government. On 9 January 2021, on the occasion of the inauguration of the new US president, the US social media giant Twitter decided to permanently discontinue the personal account of incumbent US President Donald Trump. Facebook, Google, Apple and Youtube then announced that they were banning a number of social networking sites that had posted messages from a large number of Trump supporters. The decision by these giant business media platform's to block messages from America's president (no matter how "justified" it may have been) has implications that go far beyond American politics. This is a landmark event affecting the world's economic and political development, which has awakened many people.

More worrisome, the Internet oligarchy as a whole is simply too powerful, and not merely in the United States. At present, the world's major economies, including the United States, China and the European Union, have launched antitrust investigations and litigation, try to control those media and networks that are driven by motives of capital accumulation and profits, and to establish in their place an improved governance system of platform economy, so as to curb Internet oligopoly, and especially the increasingly serious trend toward monopoly control.

How to correctly guide the development of such giant companies, which are the most powerful institutions in the world, supervise their scope of power according to law, end their free state, and guide their healthy development is a new challenge for the future development of enterprises.

**6. The education system and the direction of educational reform**

Education and educational reform are global propositions in today's world. What is a good education? What is the direction of educational reform? These questions are especially important for China. The National Outline for Medium and Long-term Education Reform and Development (2010–20) released in 2010, pointed out that "in the One-Hundred Year Strategy of a Nation, Education Is the Most Important Basic" and "A Great Power Will Strengthen Education First." With regard to China's future development and the great rejuvenation of the Chinese nation, the key lies in developing talents and the foundation for this is education. Understanding this is one thing, but putting it into action is not so easy.

How are we to endow the next generation with well-rounded moral, intellectual, and physical growth, as well as a greater sense of social responsibility? How do we construct an educational system that combines basic education, higher education, vocational education, and life-long learning? How do we inspire future scientists? How do we structure interdisciplinary and cross-domain education, so as to stimulate innovative ability by integrating technical skills, humanitarian spirit, and training in the arts? How does one cultivate an adventurous business spirit, and turn out entrepreneurs who dare to innovate and are good at developing and applying new ideas? How do we foster futurists who care about the future of humanity and the world?

How do we train Chinese thinkers? These are all related education issues in building an innovative country.

However, to solve the above-mentioned problems is not only a task for the educational sector, but involves the whole society.

Take the cultivation of so-called innovative talents as an example. The biggest characteristic of these talents should be extreme creativity. And where does creativity come from? It is of course important to acquire knowledge through school education, as well as personal sensitivity and curiosity about new things, but a soft environment conducive to the emergence and growth of creative talents is also an essential prerequisite. Because:

- Creativity comes from a soft environment that is conducive to ideological emancipation, encourages unlimited imagination, free expression of opinions, interaction and discussion with others, and is conducive to stimulating individual enthusiasm and creativity. In a soft environment, not only the system, mechanism and institutional environment, but the "innovative cultural atmosphere" is key (institutional and cultural atmosphere conducive to ideological liberation).
- Creativity comes from interdisciplinary research, cross-domain interaction and integration (an environment conducive to open innovation).
- Creativity also comes from cross-cultural communication and learning (an environment that is open to the outside world and facilitates international communication).
- Creativity comes from cooperation, union and alliance (to create opportunities for new ideas, new inspirations, new technology exchanges and integration opportunities at the organizational level).
- Creativity comes from changing thinking mode—encouraging creative thinking, even "whimsical" ones. Many inventions come from reverse thinking (encouraging unusual ways of thinking).
- Creativity comes from the strong desire to explore the unknown world and solve "problems or puzzles", and the courage to challenge accepted wisdom (an environment that encourages adventure and tolerate failure), etc.

"Why can't our schools always cultivate outstanding talents?"[16] This is the famous question posed by rocket scientist Xuesen Qian, which has been widely recognized as an abstruse proposition for education in China. However, the above analysis of "the source of creativity" not only shows that education reform is important but that it is also necessary to completely change the status quo. All sectors of society must work together to seek a solution—to create a soft environment conducive to the emergence, encouragement and growth of creative talents.

As for "Xuesen Qian's question," the educator Professor Yingyi Qian's answer is that in addition to imparting knowledge, education should first create a more relaxed space and time conducive to the development of students' personalities; second, it should better protect students' curiosity and stimulate their imagination; third, it should guide students to pursue higher value orientation in education and avoid short-term utilitarianism. He even sharply warned that it is not the problem that our school cannot "train" outstanding talents, but that our schools "strangle" potential outstanding talents.

**7. Open markets for private enterprise and private capital**

In accordance with current world trends, Chinese society, too, is becoming more and more personalized, and young people's innovative culture is being rapidly globalized. The rapid decline in the cost of information means that high technologies will increasingly be controlled by small groups or even individuals and that innovation in the private sector will play an ever more important role.

It will be necessary for China to eliminate as soon as possible the suppression and intervention in civil economic activities by government authorities, so as to give private companies more opportunities and greater status both in the marketplace and in the national innovation system, to protect their legitimate rights and interests, especially those concerning their property in accordance with the law, and to allow private capital to flow and develop freely. This will prove an effective measure to expand the innovative power of private enterprise and inspire the innovative vigor of the whole nation.

**8. Promoting entrepreneurship and employment, so as to actively develop small and micro-businesses, cultivate and strengthen the middle class**

In China, when people mention innovation, they focus first on R&D investment, incubators of high-tech industry, academy of sciences and university laboratories, but rarely consider innovation within small and micro enterprises, let alone with regard to issues of special concern to the middle class. At present, China's entrepreneurial environment is relatively poor, and the entrepreneurship rate of university graduates is only 3–5 per cent. Needless to say the entrepreneurship of small-town residents and hundreds of millions of migrant workers is even lower. China urgently needs to encourage the survival and development of small and micro enterprises at many levels from concept to system and policy. In fact, many unicorn companies have grown up from technology-based small and medium-sized enterprises. Only by creating conditions favorable for entrepreneurship and thus enabling tens of millions of people to start their own business, and hundreds of millions to invent, create, and innovate, can our people take the initiative to create and accumulate wealth through pioneering work and self-employment. This is the way that hundreds of millions of people can join the middle class, and it is the right way to make China a truly innovative country. The growth of the middle class, in turn, promotes political and social stability, domestic consumption, and stimulate the economy. Moreover, it is not only conducive to enriching the source of innovation vitality but also will facilitate the transition to the democratic process, and that is also very important for political reform.

The good news is that China has begun to decentralize, thanks to financial and taxation measures such as "directed tax relief" and "directed reduction of the deposit-reserve ratio", and to support the development of service industries, "three-dimensional rural issues" (issues affecting agriculture, farmers, and rural areas), small and micro enterprises, and privately-owned emerging businesses. These and similar measures are already bringing benefits to tens of millions of small and micro enterprises (by the end of 2017, 73.281 million enterprises had been listed in the directory of small and micro enterprises). The number of small and micro enterprises in China today is very large, and the vast majority of them are privately owned. They play an important role in promoting economic development, facilitating market prosperity, and constantly expanding employment. Six months after the relevant new regulations first went into effect in March 2014,[17] more than 1.76 million enterprises had already been registered, an increase of 68 per cent on a year-to-year basis. Premier Keqiang Li personally inspected the Qingyanliu village of Yiwu known as China's "first village of online Taobao stores" in Zhejiang Province. (In Chinese, the term "*taobao*" refers to a website for online shopping similar to eBay or Amazon in the West). There are only 700 households and 1,486 villagers in Yiwu, but more than 15,000 staff are now engaged in online sales related to the industries gathered there. They registered more than 2,800 online shops that together sell items in more than 3,000 categories across the world every day. According to the statistical data, their online turnover amounted to well over 580 million USD in 2014.

In September 2015, the State Council issued a "Guideline on accelerating the construction of a support platform for popular entrepreneurship and mass innovation," which put forward seventeen policies and measures, such as creating a relaxed space for development, laying a solid foundation for sound development, shaping a self-discipline mechanism for development, and constructing an environment that encourages sustainable development.

**9. The cultural atmosphere for innovation**

With regard to the development of a country's science and technology, in addition to aspects such as concept, strategy, system, and institutions, cultural atmosphere is an important factor that is all-too-easily ignored. Innovation needs a cultural atmosphere that is diversified, open and free, that welcomes novelty, advocates change, and is tolerant, cooperative, and integrated. In such an environment, there must be respect for labor, science, knowledge, talent, invention, and advocate creation.

At present, the problem with China's innovation atmosphere is that it lacks a culture that encourages the pursuit of novelty. Instead, negative factors inherited from traditional culture (including the deep-rooted influence of Feudal imperial culture dating back more than two thousand years) still strongly affects the innovation atmosphere. These negative factors include self-serving, conservative behavior that lacks foresight, does not advocate independent thinking, is not conducive to invention, creation, innovation and social progress, and is not suitable for the innovation wave of the present era. Two popular Chinese sayings that express such traditional values are: "Better to be the head of a dog than the tail of a lion", and "A contented person is happy with what he has." As a result, many Chinese lack the motivation to stand out as unique, pursue excellence, cooperate and share with others, or to dare take risks and tolerate failure. Other outdated traditional Chinese sayings include: "One who sticks his neck out gets hit first" and "One fears to arouse trouble by becoming famous just as a pig is slaughtered after becoming fat." So long as such thoughts remain prevalent in China they will seriously hinder the country from developing frontier science and technology and cultivating the entrepreneurial spirit.

From the viewpoint of social climate, the development of the Chinese economy and the significant improvement of material living standards have worsened phenomena like money worship, hedonism, the craze for entertainment, seeking nothing but profits, lack of integrity, spiritual emptiness, a serious retrogression in women's social status, blindly worship of Western culture and a decline in the moral bottom line. In a considerable part of the population, money and power have become the only criteria for measuring the value of life, and many elites want to be in finance. Compared to the rich, the knowledge and intellectual classes are not respected, and the incomes of scientists who have made significant contributions to the country are far lower than those of entertainment stars. Corruption is serious among government officials who should bear in mind that they are "public servants of the people." There are even a considerable number of "naked officials" (government workers whose spouse and children live abroad), and many "successful people" or celebrities delight in showing off their luxurious possessions, live lives immersed in trivial enjoyments, and are eager to emigrate abroad. Many adolescent students and their parents are busy to secure higher grades or exploit personal connections for gain admission into good schools; teenagers no longer worship heroes and scientists, but revere entertainment stars. Some media, driven by narrow self-interests, have lost sight of the bottom line, and merely boost vulgar entertainment gossip in society; even within academia, which should remain the most sober, the style of study is impetuous and there are frequent cases of plagiarisms and falsification of papers, the impetuous mentality of those eager for quick success and instant profits. Moreover, the business ethos is eroding traditional values in academic circles, pursuit of money and fame. Many scholars today soon aim at official careers once they have made some small achievements, or else strive to be star scholars and focus on developing social, interpersonal relationships, rather than pursuing knowledge. This academic atmosphere of excessive fame and wealth adversely affects the innovation motivation and innovation ability in the field of science and technology.

Although we in China have had a little bit of "spare money" only for about ten years, we have already created such a social atmosphere unexpectedly. How can it support an innovative country?

Fortunately, Chinese people are beginning to wake up, appeal and warn [...]

We need to reflect calmly, and "sublate" traditional culture—develop the good and discard the bad, and inherit excellent cultural traditions. We need also to look forward with an increased sense of urgency and responsibility for the future.

Let our intellectual class be full of independent thinking, and indomitable spirit. Let young people be imbued with vigor and vitality, and be filled with ideals and confidence for the future, and let the whole society experience an atmosphere that supports innovation and encourages exploration, while actively promoting innovative culture with adventurous spirit. Let us pursue success while remaining tolerant of well-intentioned failure, strongly advocate futures education, and let unremitting self-improvement become the guiding spirit of China.

**The nine major challenges of soft environment mentioned above, indirectly answer several questions.**

- Why is R&D investment the key to innovation in developed countries? Because their soft environment is relatively stable yet also constantly evolving. This means that once a technology gets R&D support, its development and technology transfer are faster than those in developing countries.
- Why have scientists of Chinese descent only won the Nobel Prize in foreign countries? Why are many eminent Chinese scholars who have studied in Europe or the United States remain reluctant to return to China?
- "Becoming a scientist" among teenagers is an unattractive prospect, and the proportion of students who hope to engage in industries related to science and technology in the future is less than half of those in the United States (38 per cent vs. 16.8 per cent), and less than the average of 24.5 per cent in OECD countries. Many talented students in famous universities are only aiming to join companies where they can expect to make high salaries after graduation.

- Japan and South Korea, both of which are deeply influenced by the Confucian tradition, have become world-renowned as innovative countries. Between 1949 and 2018, there have been 27 Nobel Prize winners in Japan,[18] and since the beginning of the twenty-first century, there has been at least one Japanese Nobel Prize winners every year. Furthermore, Japan is ranked among the world's leaders in robot technology. South Korea not only maintains international competitiveness in a number of technological and industrial fields, its growing cultural industry has a strong presence in the Chinese market and is even becoming recognized in the United States and Europe.
- The animated movie *Kung Fu Panda*, produced by the US animation studio DreamWorks in 2008, was immensely popular in China, leading to a similar deep introspection: why was it an American producer who found the dramatic interest and humor of a panda learning kung fu in China?
- "Qian Xuesen's Question" is not only an educational problem but also a problem for those who seek to build a soft environment conducive to creativity and innovation.
- This also answers the conundrum of why Silicon Valley is difficult to replicate in other parts of the world. After decades of exploration, people finally realize that the secret of Silicon Valley's success is that it embodies a culture of innovation. However, attempting to duplicate an innovative culture is complicated for societies with different cultural backgrounds and at different stages of development. The need for change is often so profound that it cannot be achieved overnight.

The nine challenges of the soft environment mentioned above are actually the main battlefronts for China's efforts to build a culture of innovation. Of course, the prerequisite for overcoming these major challenges will be continued reform and opening up. In short, only with a good and relaxed soft environment that fosters creativity, invention, and innovation can the passion of scientific and technical personnel as well as that of the entire population be stimulated, so that China can progress faster along the path to innovation-driven development.

### Enterprises must escape the dilemma of innovation

To get Chinese enterprises out of the dilemma of innovation, we need all-round solutions.

#### 1. Enterprises should truly become independent market entities

This is a particular problem facing Chinese enterprises in the period of transition from a government-led planned economy to a market economy. Through assessments of the triple responsibility audit system of the Future 500,[19] we have found that many Chinese companies lack a sound corporate governance system. Their governance mechanism is not in line with modern enterprise systems, and few are able to become independent market entities. This is a result of causing enterprises to pursue short-term advantage and ignore long-term strategic benefits. This, and the failure to invest in basic research, remains a major obstacle to technological innovation.

**2. To change ideas and cultivate entrepreneurship**

For innovation to take place, the most fundamental need is to emancipate the mind, so as to facilitate the exploration of deep-seated innovative potential and the release of vitality. However, to accomplish this will involve different missions in different levels and areas.

At the government level, (1) it is necessary to change the tendency to devote the vast majority of capital and policy investment to national research institutions and a few famous universities, and of paying attention to large-scale enterprises while ignoring small and medium-sized enterprises, and even more ignore social enterprises; (2) there is an urgent need to change the corporate behavior model of local governments at all levels, which is oriented by economic interests; (3) government needs to create a soft environment conducive to the cultivation of entrepreneurship, including an institutional environment that tolerates failure. First, it needs to understand the position of entrepreneurs correctly. China's entrepreneurs are not only the main body of national economic activities and innovation in the usual sense, in this unprecedented practice of reform and opening up, especially in the reform of economic system, they are the "warriors" on the front line—the main forces and pioneers for driving innovation. They must therefore be encouraged and supported in their spirit of adventure. So long as they do not violate national laws and do not seek illegal benefits, their mistakes or even failures should be allowed and correctly treated. In addition, the government should protect their legitimate rights and interests.

In December 2017, the Supreme People's Procuratorate issued the "Notice on Giving Full Play to Its Functions, Creating a Legal Environment for Protecting the Legal Rights and Interests of Entrepreneurs and Supporting Entrepreneurship," which created the basic conditions to build a loose legal environment for the healthy growth and career development of entrepreneurs, ensure their personal and property safety, and enhance their confidence in entrepreneurship and innovation. It is also the premise for an enterprise to become an independent market player and a major measure for a new round of economic reforms.

This document was issued by the Supreme People's Procuratorate, which illustrates how serious the problem of dealing with entrepreneurs has been in the past.

Then, in December 2018, the Central Economic Work Conference stressed that it is necessary to support the development of private enterprises, create a legal institutional environment, and protect the personal safety and private property of entrepreneurs.

From the enterprise level, it is necessary to pay particular attention to several issues: first, they should not be so bent on becoming "high, big, and strong" and instead should work to create their own "Diamond"—core technology. Second, to make full use of government policy input is fair enough, but never forget that the most reliable road to success is to create a unique space for independent innovation, rather than wait for the government's economic stimulus. Third, it is essential to try our best to break the boundaries of innovation, strengthen basic research related to the long-term strategic objectives of relevant enterprises, and improve the nation's original innovation ability. Fourth, to guard against falling into the trap of seeking only quick success and quick profit, we must strive to promote the development of the real economy. Fifth, don't focus only on high technologies at the material level or rush to purchase foreign technologies or patents, but also be concerned about innovations in "soft" areas outside purely technical fields. Finally, shift from focusing exclusively on being a "big business" to striving to become a "good business".

**3. To strengthen basic research and futures studies**

A lack of core technology exists in many Chinese industries, and certain key technologies and components remain dependent on foreign or multinational companies. To solve this problem fundamentally, it is necessary to strengthen enterprise-led futures studies and basic research to provide a targeted knowledge source and theoretical support for the long-term development of the enterprise, and enhance its capability for innovation. It is not enough to only take shortcuts; we must recognize that some technologies cannot be brought up to date by money alone. There is no future for companies that do not care about or invest in global cutting-edge technologies. Basic research is an important way for an enterprise to acquire core technology and shape long-term competitive advantage, but it may prove difficult to generate significant benefits for the enterprise in the short term. Many of China's outstanding enterprises have gone beyond the stage of original capital accumulation, and have reached a point where they must have a special team to consider the company's long-term future, and guide its leaders to adopt a farsighted viewpoint, and plan for the future. Only then can there be a hope of establishing a company that will last for 100 years.

One of the important reasons behind Intel Corporation's enduring prosperity is that, in addition to keeping a sense of crisis, they continue to pursue technology innovation, making sure that their products remain at the world-class level. They also attach great importance to futures research. Intel set up a research institute for shaping and experiencing futures that specializes in developing improved operability and visions of future computer architecture.

Huawei Technologies Co., Ltd. headquartered in Shenzhen is one of the few enterprises in China that has set up a specialized agency for futures research. Among the top 100 most valuable brands in Forbes 2018, Huawei's brand value has entered the list for the second consecutive year, becoming the only Chinese brand on the list. Due especially to the firm's success in 5G technology, which currently leads the world, and other achievements, it should be noted that Huawei's attention to futures research and its huge investment in basic R&D, result from the firm's strategy of "always preparing for the future".

**4. Supporting and developing indigenous technologies**

In recent years, the number of patents being granted in China has grown rapidly. Especially significant are the number of applications for invention patents and effective invention patent ownership. This all indicates the potential of China's indigenous technologies.

According to the State Intellectual Property Office of China, the number of invention patents in China has grown steadily, reaching 1.382 million in 2017, a year-on-year increase of 14.2 per cent, of which the number of invention patents per 10,000 people reached 9.8. But the average conversion rate of patents in China is only 21.7 per cent (of which business enterprises account for 42 per cent and universities 10 per cent).

The only way for Chinese enterprises to escape from the status quo of lacking independent brands, original core technologies, and international competitiveness is to vigorously promote invention and creation, foster indigenous technologies, and improve the technology transfer efficiency of invention patents in China.

**5. Changing the mode of thinking, and creating new innovation platforms**

Haier's business model is one worth learning from with respect to innovation. They have developed an entrepreneurship platform serving hundreds of small and micro enterprises and created a new business model in keeping with the characteristics of the Internet era. Up to now, they have supported internal entrepreneurship to establish more than 200 small and micro companies, which enable people who are most closely following their specialized market and have the best understanding of their customers needs, to achieve their entrepreneurial dream through "problem solving". Haier is also incubating and fostering more than 2000 small and micro "Maker" companies that provide over 1 million jobs for the whole society.[20]

**6. Strengthening the soft environment construction of enterprise**

It will be necessary to create a relaxed environment inside an enterprise that will encourage innovation, tolerate failure, and allow "fanciful" imagination and design; and to encourage those employees who are determined to start their own businesses by establishing an internal entrepreneur system. Can you imagine a Chinese company that would allow one of its employees, like Intel's futurist Brian David Johnson, to make speeches everywhere, write science fiction stories and novels, and even become the director of a science fiction film? In fact, Johnson's work is called "future-casting"—through the study of ethnology, related technology, trend data, and even science fiction to create a pragmatic vision of consumers and computing.

**7. Organizational innovation of enterprises**

In this era of rapid change, the trend of organizational innovation within businesses is to adopt six specific types of change. The first is to get rid of the traditional pyramid-like management structure and realize platformization. Corporate organizations should adapt to a fully integrated platform structure, to achieve intelligent management. The second is not to seek unlimited growth in terms of scale or number of employees, but to shape a flexible organization that can quickly adapt to market changes. The third is to change from being a closed organization to becoming a borderless and open organization. The fourth is to insist on the principle of shrinking time and space (promoting cooperation, and alliances, cross-country and cross-industry boundaries as these have become a prerequisite for success in this era of globalization). The fifth is to adapt to and actively challenge the individual innovation age characterized by "platform PLUS individual". However, the resulting new individual economy urgently needs the protection of appropriate government institutions, and an effective governance system to promote the healthy development of the platform economy. And the sixth is to recognize and maintain the firm's core competence, so as to make full use of external resources as well as pay attention to the use of virtual companies and virtual research institutes, and lastly to establish an inclusive corporate culture—a culture of innovation and flexible reform.

**8. Both technology innovation and the innovation of technological institutions must be taken into account**

One of the root causes why the efficiency of technology transfer in China is low is that we do not pay enough attention to the innovation of technological institutions. Due to a lack of interdisciplinary cooperation between social science circles and natural science and technology circles, few experts on institutional research ever become involved with technological institutions. Because of this failure to systematically study technological institutions, China lacks a system of institutions, standards, and policies in key technology areas. By contrast, Japan is known worldwide as the "Kingdom of Robots" for its amazing development and popularization that involves more than twenty robot-related institutions, regulations, and plans.

While we in China may emphasize original technological innovation, innovation of relevant technological institutions must advance in step—or at least be synchronized—if we hope to take the lead in developing the game rules and eventually dominate this field.

## China's rejuvenation and future research

From the perspective of a country, futures research can be said to be a higher-level form of basic research. It provides research results that enable a country to formulate a long-term development strategy, so as to enhance its comprehensive national strength and maintain its prosperity, including pointing out the most promising direction for basic research.

German philosopher Georg Wilhelm Friedrich Hegel said that a nation is hopeless unless it has people who look up at the stars with lively interest. If a nation is only concerned with immediate things, it has no future.[21]

The era of China's rejuvenation has been marked by vast changes, and alternating periods of emphasis on old and new civilizations. China is advancing along a road to modernization very different from that followed by the developed countries, and, as a developing country, it actively seeks to promote the transformation from Industrial Civilization (which is still going on here) to Global Civilization.

This even more requires the involvement of many intellectuals, like those who have dedicated themselves to national salvation and rejuvenation over the past 100 years, heedless of personal fame or gain. They undertook to transcend themselves with the spirit of sacrifice for the new era, and made the study of, and concern for, the long-term future of the nation their personal responsibility. These people must live and work in China, study global change, the future of mankind and the future of the world wholeheartedly, and provide sober and far-sighted reference information for the whole society, especially to decision-makers at all levels.

Since the 1990s, global interest in futures research is on the rise again, and many countries have strengthened their futures research capabilities. Its characteristics are that research should not be limited to science and technology, but greatly extended to include economic, social, environmental, resource and public policy, and even to such macro-levels as global patterns, world order, global governance, and human futures generally. Today's futures research institutions show diversity, interdisciplinary, systematic thinking, globality, complexity, etc.

In short, futures research has become a global, interdisciplinary, cross-domain and cross-cultural phenomenon.

**1. The situation is pressing**

- The rapid development of China has attracted the world's attention. Every step of our reform measures has been widely discussed by foreign countries, and some agencies have been studying China's future 30/50/100 years ahead. As a new type of big country undergoing peaceful development, we urgently need to continue serious scenario analysis so as to avoid risks, setbacks and any repetition of past mistakes in the next 50 years and 100 years on the road to comprehensive rejuvenation.
- China needs not only to conduct research into international trends and perspectives but also understand how futurists and elites in other countries forecast the future, what kind of basis (theory) and methods they use and what kinds of suggestions they provide to their decision-makers for dealing with future domestic and foreign changes. More importantly, China must identify its strengths, deep-seated challenges, risks and opportunities to provide futures research results for its continued peaceful development.

**2. The gaps in China's future research requires deep reflection**

- The past 40 years of reform and opening up has been a period of constant exploration and experimentation in China, which is often described as "crossing the river by feeling the stones." Based on the challenge of China's sustainable development, it is now necessary to move toward a more rational approach and set longer-term goals and development strategies to facilitate more sensible practices under a relatively mature and more complete theoretical system of development and reform.
- Although scientific decision making has been discussed for several decades, many major decisions are not made on the basis of solid long-term futures research. As a result, major mistakes have frequently occurred, some with losses that may not be repaired for generations.
- The current tendency in China is to be keen to study antiquity, other countries, futures study methodology in the abstract (which involves no risk), but avoid research on recent events, policy failures; the lack of international integration, or of cross-sectoral, cross-disciplinary, cross-domain research.
- Lack of professional future research institutions, and even less private futures research institutions; most decision-makers pay more attention to those matters during their tenure, and rarely care about long-term futures research, let alone invest in supporting such research.

- There are more than 3,000 think tanks in China, but few of them are based on long-term, sustainable, independent and international integrated futures research for providing advice or consultation to relevant decision-making bodies.
- There are hundreds of professional futures research institutions in the world, but no department in China is dedicated to new ideas and new trends; there is no "atmosphere" or mechanism for investment in "people" and "new thinking" (especially in new thinking from Chinese people), and this is not conducive to the creation of "Chinese thought."
- China's economic strength has been enhanced and a large number of investments are being made in "all aspects". But if China does not invest in future research that enhances people's future awareness, fosters world-class future thinkers and provides wisdom to policymakers, how can it gain a voice on a global platform in the future of humanity, future civilization, future world governance, the direction of scientific and technological development among world powers?
- Few Chinese enterprises attach importance to or invest in future research. Huawei is a rare Chinese enterprise that does carry out professional futures research.

**3. For China's overall rejuvenation, future study must be strengthened**

We advocate philosophical thinking on the future vision of human beings and strengthen the futures research, which is not only related to the long-term future of a country and even mankind but also to a process of exploring the orientation of the political, economic, social, cultural, scientific, and technological development in today's society.

- China is a testing ground for the sustainable development of the world in the twenty-first century. In view of China's special national conditions in terms of social system, population, green development, and agriculture, rural areas and farmers (that feed 1.4 billion people), and the health of the whole people, every step aimed at comprehensive rejuvenation will be different from that of other countries. Therefore, it is more worthwhile to conduct independent research for China's long-term future by studying the country's history as well as the changing world and its future prospects.
- There is an urgent need to raise people's awareness of the future, so that every citizen, including decision-makers at all levels, those in science and technology circles and even teenagers, will care about the future of mankind, the future of the World and China's future, and, moreover, work jointly to create a "Chinese version" of future civilization.

- We need to rejuvenate those aspects of Oriental civilization that attach importance to spiritual and ethical values, and the traditional Chinese philosophy characterized by advocating harmony, dialectical thinking and the fundamental unity of man and nature, so as to reshape the ideological basis of human future civilization, cultivate the consciousness of a common destiny for all mankind, create and develop a new culture of sustainable human development, and guide the direction of future human evolution and civilization. For this reason, China's comprehensive rejuvenation must be integrated into the grand practice of human beings to welcome a future civilization—"Global Civilization", and even a "Great Civilization" by adopting the positive factors and discarding the negative ones in both Eastern and Western civilizations.

### 4. We need to deeply study and promote the transformation of human civilization

Nowadays, human beings are facing a variety of crises, which can be divided into two categories. The first includes various realistic crises which already threaten the sustainable development of mankind, such as geopolitical conflicts, abnormal climate change, the widening gap between rich and poor, depletion of natural resources, the eco-environmental crisis, the abuse of Technology (such as uncontrolled innovation and applications of AI, Nano- and Bio-technologies), escalating regional wars and violence, widespread pollution from micro plastics, dangers from new viruses, etc. The other category consists of long-term threats, such as disinformation and growing doubt with regard to scientific and technological progress, rapid increases in species extinction, reckless attempts to alter the direction of human evolution which could lead to the extinction of traditional human beings, and other threats to the sustainability of human civilization and Earth itself. These latter concerns may appear to be long-term future problems, which have little impact on our current situation. However, if we do not start to solve them now, humanity will surely face the danger of extinction.

To prevent both immediate and long-term crises, human beings must adopt systematic solutions in every area, from modes of development and lifestyle to straightening out our relationship with nature, from guiding the direction of technological innovation to preventing politics from being polluted by money and the threat of force. Transforming human development and shifting the paradigm on which civilization is based can never be accomplished by one country alone, but must involve all countries and ethnic groups in the world, working in cooperation with one heart and one mind. Based on its stated aims and accomplishments to date, it appears that only the United Nations organization is capable of making the long-term effort to achieve this result (The current covid-19 and global climate change once again call for human awakening).

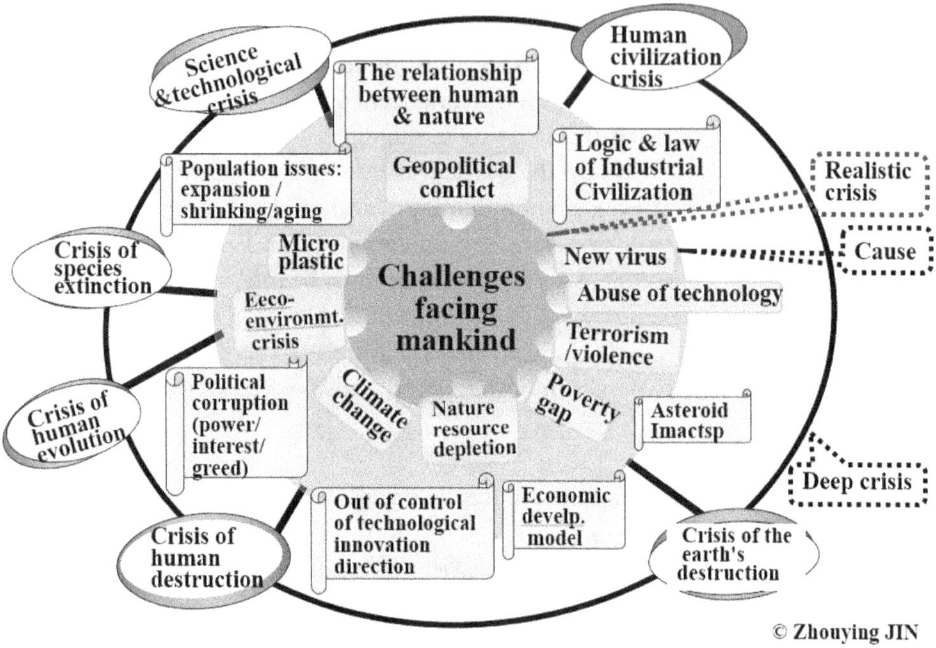


FIGURE 7.4: Challenges facing mankind.

However, given the difficulties experienced by the United Nations in its attempts to resolve armed conflicts over the past 70 years, all its efforts will be ineffective so long as no common standards are accepted by all parties. Why is there a lack of consensus? The crux is that the worldviews and values of most international elites, national leaders, and ordinary citizens in mainstream society today, are still dominated by the logic and rules of hundreds of years of Industrial Civilization (see Chapter 2 for details). Therefore, when dealing with major global issues, national interests or even group interests are often higher than global interests, it is difficult to reach a consensus. As a result, many international agreements, treaties, laws and even various technical specifications are difficult to implement. This is why we need to deeply study and actively promote the transformation from Industrial Civilization to Global Civilization (the primary stage of the advanced human civilization form), and must then strive to realize the Great Civilization (the higher stage of the advanced human civilization form).

**5. Failure is the mother of success**

Many of the lessons China has learned in formulating long-term strategies are worth summarizing.

Take our family planning policy as an example.

The establishment of a voluntary birth control mechanism and adapting the human population and growth model to the demands of sustainable development are big challenges for the entire world.

Beginning in the late 1980s, China, as the most populous country in the world, undertook an experiment in population control and began to implement a family planning policy of "one couple with one child." However, after decades of forcible control over the birth rate (at least 100 million births have been averted in the past 30 years), various drawbacks gradually began to appear:

1) Today, China's fertility rate has dropped to less than 1.5, which is well below the replacement level of 2.1.
2) The gender ratio at birth is imbalanced.[22] By the end of 2014, the male-to-female gender ratio in China was 105.06:100; among unmarried people in their 20s, 30s, and 40s, the male-to-female gender ratio at 110:100, 136:100, and 206:100, respectively.
3) Adequate supplies of labor could also be lacking. According to data from the sixth population census in China released in 2010, 16.60 per cent of the country's population as then aged 14 or younger. This figure was 33.6 per cent in the third census conducted in 1982, which shows a drop of more than 50 per cent in less than 30 years.
4) Becoming an aging society before attaining economic security for all citizens. The number of Chinese people aged 60 or older reached 241 million at the end of 2017. By 2050, it is estimated that this number will reach 487 million, accounting for 34.9 per cent of the total population.
5) The scale of empty-nesters among the elderly population continues to rise (in 2013, it exceeded 100 million people); the number of "families bereft of their only child"[23] is also gradually increasing.
6) The 145 million "only-children" have brought a series of social problems to Chinese society, such as having only one child available to support parents in their old age.
7) When the children born in the 1990s and 2000s reach working age, many of them may face the need to raise two children and also support four elderly parents. This population decline will not only cause a shortage in the labor market but also bring a sharp decline in the consumer market. If there is no reasonable solution, China will find itself facing a serious demographic crisis in another 20 years. It is thus evident that the ever-longer lifespans of the aged, combined with "fewer births" has not only produced many economic, social problems, it has even affected national security.

For this reason, in November 2013, the Third Plenary Session of the 18th CPC Central Committee proposed, that "China allow couples to have two children if either parent is an only child." This is, the so-called "Selective Two-Child Policy." However, among the more than 11 million couples who meet the "Selective Two-Child Policy", only about 1.45 million had actually applied for a second child as of May 2015.

The Fifth Plenary Session of the 18th Central Committee of CPC held in October 2015 decided to further ease the family planning policy to fully implement a two-child policy. However, two years later, in 2017, the birth rate had declined by another 0.52‰ (to 12.43‰) compared with the previous year, and was down to 10.94‰ by 2019. In 2019, only 700,000 couples filed for a second child, well below official expectations of about 2 million couples a year.

If this trend continues, births will shrink by 300,000–800,000 per year in the next decade. This may force us to adopt a policy of "fully liberalizing and even encouraging childbearing." In fact, China's current low fertility rate is not simply caused by its one-child policy, but by growing social pressures, such as the cost of housing, education, and medical services, which continue to rise. For these reasons, many couples who are able to have a second child often give up this right. Today, basic living conditions in China are widely guaranteed, so that people consider the number of offspring they could raise from the perspective of the family's quality of life including the economic burden a second child would involve.

Population resources are the basic elements of a long-term strategy of a country, and the quantity and quality of population directly affect the coordinated and sustainable development of society, economy, resources, and the environment. However, China's decision-making at that time lacked any long-term futures research of population as the basis for major national decisions. Now, population policy has needed to be changed three times within a few years.

The lessons of history remind us once again that national long-term strategies and major decisions, regarding such issues as population strategy, must be based on rigorous long-term futures research. Taking population forecast as an example, we need to integrate our policies with future development trends in economics, society, science and technology, and research into the future of human civilization. Faulty logic and inaccurate estimates of future population trends misled the country's major decision-making (e.g., if the population is not controlled, China's population could reach 4.3 billion by 2080).

In fact, the self-regulation of procreation is the fundamental basis for future human civilization. From a global perspective, family planning or self-regulation of procreation needs to avoid going to either of two extremes, namely we must not only prevent overpopulation, it is also important to note that as fertility rates continue to decline (nowadays the population growth rate of many developed countries is negative) with the enrichment of material life and the improvement of education, fertility rates that are too low can cause a country to slip into decline over time due to dwindling population.

How to gradually improve birth policy, and on the basis of guaranteeing the return of reproductive rights to family autonomy, the realization of voluntary and conscious control of fertility is an important issue for China and the world. This can only be achieved by developing the economy, improving social welfare and health care, and reforming education, so as to achieve the goal of stabilizing the population, which is not only conducive to sustainable development but also can help assure a dynamic balance with the carrying capacity of the Earth's resources.

In short, it is a great and arduous undertaking to rejuvenate an ancient civilization that has been sleeping for more than 100 years and has endured countless vicissitudes. It requires us not only to study the futures of the world and mankind with a view to realizing Global Civilization and even a Great Civilization but also to formulate China's future and determine the country's long-term strategic direction from the perspective of the country's millennium and Centennial plan, so as to provide futures research results that will promote China's great rejuvenation.

### Summary: Building an innovative country has a long way to go

In the above, we mainly focus on innovation in the field of science and technology and discussed the various challenges to be overcome in constructing an innovative country, such as ideological emancipation, strategic innovation, cracking the soft environment, freeing enterprises from the innovation dilemma, and strengthening future research.

In fact, innovation in the field of science and technology is certainly important for building a truly innovative country. However, carrying out all-round, deep-seated, systematic and up-to-date reform and reconstruction in many fields, such as culture, education, systems and institutions, as well as economic and social development modes is equally essential.

## *Realizing sustainable development by adopting a systematic solution*

As mentioned earlier, achieving sustainable survival and development will require a complex system for engineering human activities, which is a process of changing human activity patterns and their subsystems to adapt to the transformation of civilization. To illustrate what is needed, I will review China's efforts to realize green economic development by confronting various challenges and problems, and outline some of the successes that have already been achieved.

### Systems engineering for green development

After 40 years of rapid economic development following China's reform and opening up, its economy is now second in the world. However, China still faces many challenges today. Faced with these challenges, China's primary viable option is to fundamentally change its mode of development. The nation's burgeoning new technological and industrial revolution, which takes "sustainable and green" as its dominant characteristics, not only opens endless innovation space for sustainable development but also provides a new impetus for China's continued economic growth, and an effective way to improve the quality of that growth.

According to UNEP's definition, a green economy is one that results in improved human well-being and social equity, while significantly reducing environmental risks and ecological scarcity. At the same time, it is an economy of low-carbon use, resource efficiency, and social inclusivity. Recently, the concept of the green economy has further evolved into "green growth" or "green development", terms that refer to economic progress foster environmentally sustainable, low-carbon, and socially inclusive development.

China has adopted a variety of measures to achieve green development, including structural adjustment, reform of relevant institutions, improvement of the policy system, increased investment in R&D for green technology, reinforcing measures to benefit people's livelihoods, and others, which have made remarkable progress. Take industrial restructuring as an example: according to the data released by the National Bureau of statistics, the service industry accounted for 52.2 per cent of GDP in 2018, ahead of manufacturing which was 40.7 per cent of GDP. According to the UNEP's statistical standards, as early as 2010, the output value of China's green industry accounted for about 10 per cent of total national GDP.

However, it is hard to fully implement green development. Taking environmental pollution as an example, China's newly revised Environmental Protection Act, which took effect on 1 January 2015, has been called "the most stringent environmental protection law in history", but even so, solving problems such as haze could still take 30–50 years. To trace the root cause, compared with the large investments in R&D and hard infrastructure for green technology, the soft technology and soft environment aspects of green development show obvious weaknesses. For example, the lack of a comprehensive strategy, the incompatibility of legal, institutional, and policy systems, the lack of long-term management mechanisms, indifference toward capacity building, the failure to give full play to non-governmental organizations, etc.

Therefore, it is necessary to solve the imbalance between hard and soft systems in both the planning and implementation, and in the strategic management of green development. Second, green development must be integrated into the whole sustainable development system, and coordinate the operation of various systems in order to ultimately be successful.

Chinese scientist Xuesen Qian has put forward the concept of complex giant systems. If the world's geographical and ecological systems, social system, individual organisms, the human body, and brain are all regarded as examples of complex giant systems, then implementing green development will require an open complex giant system that integrates several categories of these as sub-systems, including natural resources, living things, Earth's eco-environment, and other subsystems such as the social and economic systems. Moreover, while all these systems are interdependent, each remains unique (with its own special character and function).

For example, guiding the green and low-carbon lifestyle and building a green consumption system; around the clean production mode involves the transformation of traditional industries, the construction of the green industry system, and the adjustment of industrial structure. Implementing the overall plan involves a series of soft and hard environmental protection systems, ranging from the macro to micro management, and the development and application of green technology, as well as green investment and relevant laws, regulations, policies, etc. Among them, in addition to the openness between the above-mentioned systems, the opening of the system also means that developing a green economy cannot be completed by any single nation acting alone. Instead, it will require extensive cooperation among countries, in multiple fields and at all levels, including the political level.

Thus, achieving green development will require taking nations and entire regions as a platform to design and run interconnected complex giant systems. Examples include the strategic integration of economic, social, eco-environmental, and resources systems on the macro level; and on the management level; evolving from national strategic management to the integrated management of entire industries, enterprises, and civic behaviors. Finally, on the implementation level, the implementing integrated systems composed of new strategic planning, tools and conditions, as well as establishing a complex system from concept to action must all take place.

The implementation system of green development consists of two levels (see Figure 7.5). The lower level represents the concept and background of green development. It is a complex system comprised of various soft environment elements such as concept and values (cultural dimension), development model (strategic level), system, mechanism, institution (institutional level), lifestyle, consumption patterns and urbanization model (social dimension), modes of production (industrial dimension), business models (enterprise dimension), all of which impact or cross support green development. The upper level shows the operational aspects (from idea to action) of green development—strategic management system of green development (see "Strategic management of green development and practice in China" in the next section for details), including five subsystems: (1) strategic planning, (2) tangible means, (3) intangible means and approaches, (4) support

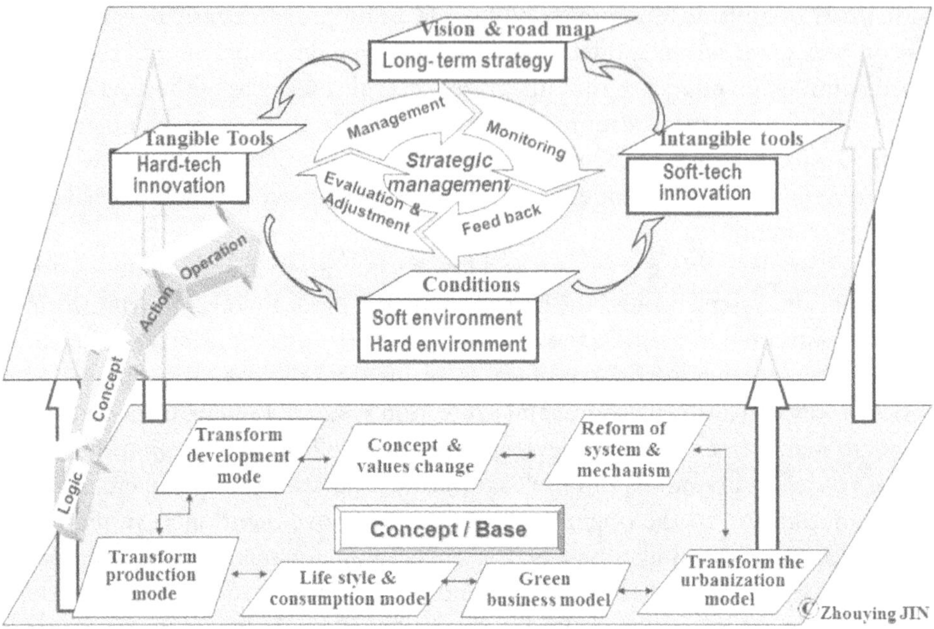


FIGURE 7.5: Complex system for implementing green development.

and guarantee—soft and hard environment and conditions, (5) tracking management and supervising implementation (operating system).

## The broad context and concept of green development

Implementing the green economy constitutes a true economic revolution, and it is an important step for human economic activity to adapt to sustainable development and even to enter a new stage of Global Civilization. To realize green development, humans will need to radically change their values, norms of behavior and lifestyles. It is not enough to rely solely on half measures such as green projects, green investment, green R&D, institutions and preferential policies promoting green development. Only by grasping the broader context as a whole can we truly realize the essence and significance of green development efforts and correctly set strategic objectives, and implementation approaches, using tools and methods appropriate to actual conditions.

### 1. Changing concepts and values

For human beings to truly change their dominant model for development from that of "high energy use, high consumption of raw materials, and high emissions" to one of "low consumption, low emissions, high efficiency, and sustainability," it is necessary to first change ways of thought and values that have prevailed for centuries. This includes altering the basic concept of business that sets maximizing profit ahead of all other economic and social goals.

The majority of people in society must come to recognize that natural resources and the eco-environment are not only the support system of human life but also the material basis for economic and social progress and that their carrying capacity has limits; they cannot endlessly take and contribute nothing in return, and that they must also consider the needs of future generations. To this, human beings must add respect for the rights of other living creatures, and a willingness to live in harmony with nature, rather than blindly pursuing the so-called "people-oriented" path. Only then can human survival and development be sustained.

For now, however, most developing countries in the world are still at the primary or intermediate stage of industrialization. From their point of view, hard power, hard infrastructure, and the accumulation of financial capital all remain top priorities for building up their national strength. Thus, when they deal with the contradiction between the growth rate (taking GDP as the indicator of progress) and genuine progress, they tend to consider only the former. Clearly, we must be prepared to put in a lot of hard work for a long time to establish a worldview and global values capable of building a sustainable future.

**2. Changing the development mode**

The various crises in today's world have largely been caused by humanity's crazy pursuit of material wealth. As mentioned in the previous section, human beings must realize the transformation of development mode in the main ways of sustainable development, such as economic development, natural resource utilization, social development, ecological environment, political system and the development of science and technology, otherwise, they will only contribute to extinction. Among them, the model changes directly related to the development of green economy include:

*Changing the mode of production*: The transformation of production mode is the most important to development and the basis for attaining a green economy. In order to change the mode of production from conquering nature, abusing natural resources and seeking immediate benefits to one that respects nature, recycles resources and harmonizes with nature, we should vigorously develop new productivity represented by various green hard technologies to help the "green" production process (reduce pollutant emissions, cause less damage to the natural environment, and improve efficiency in resource utilization). In addition, we should actively develop actively a circular economy to upgrade and update production, adjust industrial structure, redefine desired growth, and change consumption patterns. It will also be necessary to persuade the whole of society to shift from advocating hard technologies to consciously developing healthy soft technologies and soft industries, change the direction of value creation, pursue comprehensive value for the economy, society and the environmental ecology, and ultimately replace old economic ideas based on the endless expansion of material consumption and production.

***Profound changes in lifestyles and consumption patterns***: Following hundreds of years of technological progress and the success of several waves of industrial revolutions, the material life of most people in the world today has improved greatly, and some are clearly affluent. But in the process people have gradually adopted social tendencies that foster high consumption and high waste. The result is that the environment for human survival has been severely damaged and that natural disasters occur more often. More and more people are being packed into crowded cities, living in concrete skyscrapers and staying away from nature; driving instead of walking, becoming obese, and suffering from new diseases. The more affluence increases in a country, the more unhappy people there seem to be and the higher the national suicide rate becomes.[24]

For this reason, we must change lifestyles, production modes, and ways of working to establish meaningful occupations and ways of working that are no longer damaging to social systems and ecosystems, and instead reward those careers and ways of life that do not cause damage to society and ecosystems. In addition, we must also transform the current urbanization model, and rebalance urban–rural relations. These ideas must be transformed into actions and reflected in the implementation of green development at all levels and links.

In China, with the improvement of living standards, some people crazily vie with each other in material consumption. This abnormal "consumption" psychology results in excessive acquisition of luxury goods and an overall level of spending that is incompatible with China's basic conditions, causing a great waste of resources and energy. Chinese people have to ask themselves whether such a lifestyle is healthy. Is it worth continuing?

Green consumerism focuses on moderation, and the balance between meeting human needs and maintaining the environment's capacity to supply raw materials and replenish itself. Thus, it is designed to ease tensions between humans and resources, energy and environment. Accordingly it offers the choice of uncontaminated and healthy green products, while avoiding or reducing damage to the environment from overconsumption, and by paying attention to the disposal of waste, encouraging citizens to choose low-energy modes of travel, despise and resist waste, etc.

In short, to establish new social trends and promote a cultural atmosphere that considers respect for nature, environmental protection, and frugality as a kind of social morality, people must be persuaded to satisfy their needs for clothing, food, daily necessities, construction, housing, transportation, and travel, while resisting the lure of old vices and luxury consumption.

***Green business model***: Enterprises adapting green development can no longer take economic profit maximization as their sole business objective, and consequently they must change their corporate behaviors (see below for details).

**3. Reforming systems, mechanisms and institutions**

From the macro level, the development of a green economy is one of the sustainable development efforts aimed at achieving a prosperous and harmonious society for generations to come. For now, however, the existing market economy system driven by the values of Industrial Civilization has caused intensified environmental pollution and ecological damage, increased the gap between the rich and the poor, and undermined social justice. Furthermore, the costs incurred by war, violence, and social conflict not only cause great human suffering and needless loss of life but also waste huge quantities of Earth's resources and cause widespread ecological destruction. None of these problems can be wholly compensated for merely developing a green economy or changing lifestyles, consumption patterns, and production modes. Consider examples like the Gulf War, the attacks of September 11, the recent Iraq War, and the continuing unrest in Libya, Syria, and Afghanistan.

Accordingly, each country must first institute ongoing reforms and improvements within their national and regional social systems and institutions. Examples might include institutional designs to expand employment, distribute income more equitably, and improve social security, health care, and housing. The goal is to continuously upgrade the wellbeing of their people, and thus create a harmonious society that is able to properly resolve issues such as the negative impacts brought on by globalization while minimizing the threat of harm from hostile forces, domestic or foreign. In this sense, the reform of system, mechanism and institutions to promote long-term sustainability is the underlying premise of green development.

**4. Brief summary**

Having now outlined the broad context of green development, let me make clear that this does not mean that no green development can be achieved until all of its aspects have reached the level of perfection. Rather, in green development strategy and planning, and in particular in the formulation of relevant systems, policies, and long-term management mechanisms, we should take full account of the important function that is served by knowing our ultimate goal. Each aspect of the broad context has the characteristics and principles of the systems defined by Donella Meadows, and all these systems form a complex giant system that supports or helps define the broader context of green development.

## Implementation system framework of green development

As stated earlier, the implementation system for green development will depend on five interactive, interdependent, and essential systems. It is worth emphasizing here that implementing a green economy and each of its subsystems must include both soft and hard balanced systems. So far, in China as elsewhere, the general tendency in trying to develop a green economy is to let soft and hard strategic structures remain unbalanced. Developers have tended to invest financial and human resources primarily in hard technology projects and hard infrastructure construction, but have paid relatively little attention to strategic management, and have largely ignored soft industrial innovation and capacity-building. This is especially true with regard to corporate behavior and the evaluation criteria of official performance, which have not kept pace with the government's stated goal of building a green economy.

The result has been poor efficiency in technology transfer and use. Moreover, the soft environment is neither suited to encourage innovation, nor conducive to achieving the strategic objectives of green development.

### 1. Strategy/planning

For details, refer to the relevant strategic objectives and strategic planning in the section of "Strategic management of green development and practice in China" below.

### 2. Tangible tools and means: hard technology innovation

Developing green hard technology, which is an effective tool and approach to green development, involves focusing on resources, energy, ecology, and the environment. This includes technologies that help improve resource productivity (using fewer natural resources more efficiently), technologies that promote low-carbon use, recycling, and decontamination, as well as technologies that reduce or reprocess waste emissions, and renewable energy technologies. Just as important are energy saving and environmentally friendly buildings, green automobile technologies, eco-friendly agriculture technologies, etc. It is noteworthy that while vigorously promoting R&D for green technology, we need to identify technologies that use different technological systems, have different priorities and applications, and that each of these must be adapted to best suit the characteristics of the regions in which they are employed.

### 3. Intangible tools and methods: soft technology innovation

No hard technology is ever likely to wholly substitute for the services provided by natural capital, or if any does, it will be very rare.

Technophiles point to 3-D printing and fantasy machines like the "replicators" on *Star Trek* as quick ways to reproduce any substance or object with ease. However, it may require a huge amount of energy to transform matter even if the design and assembly involved are relatively simple. More importantly, most natural services, the gene pool, and other bases required for human survival are likely to be difficult or impossible to replicate efficiently using hard technologies alone. We must also change ideas, shift production modes, and change lifestyles to affect a complete transition to applying natural resources to new uses that will prevent the destruction of the Earth's ecological balance and protect non-renewable resources and services.

Soft technology plays a far more prominent role in green development than it did in the industrial economy. The mission of soft technology is to transform many of the concepts related to green development so as to produce a roadmap and operational action plan. The key components of a green economy are: (1) green industry (providing green products, equipment, technologies, and services); (2) green and clean production processes that reduce energy and material consumption as well as pollutant emissions during the production process; (3) green distribution; and (4) green consumption. Except for green industry, soft-tech innovation plays a leading role in the other components.

The significance of soft technology tools in the development of the green economy lies in:

- ***Improving the efficiency of technology transfer***: China's green technology is still in a period of transition from the introduction, exploitation, and absorption of technology to independent innovation in general; thus, effective technology transfer is essential. Even in developed countries, to successfully move from technology R&D to industrialization, effective technology transfer is critical. The ability to organize, manage, innovate, pioneer, and transfer is dependent on soft technology.
- ***Providing the core technology for soft industries***: one hallmark of soft industry is its ability to consume relatively low quantities of natural resources and energy, which is congruent with green development. Soft technologies, which take the resources of intelligence, culture, society, and the human body as their main development objectives, will become the gold mine of soft industry innovation.
- ***Enhancing implementation capacity***: implementation capacity is the ability to achieve strategic goals by relentlessly improving the ability to reform, and manage macro- to micro-level strategies. Such improvements include more effective leadership, direction setting; comprehensive and multi-level innovation ability including innovative new business models, system design capacity,

institution building, and public relations capacity (better public information and learning), etc. Therefore, we must consciously design and arrange projects to improve implementation capacity.

- ***Soft technology innovation***: soft technology innovation provides countless innovative tools and contents to drive green development. Examples include acknowledging that natural capital is no longer to be regarded as inexhaustible and essentially cost-free but instead should be reasonably assessed and incorporated as a form of multi-capital expenditure and reflected in the corporate balance sheet.
- ***Providing new content and setting new requirements for the soft environment, especially in institutions (game rules)***: in order to truly achieve green development, all the activities of mankind will have to adapt. Therefore, it is necessary to perfect existing "games" (i.e., soft technology) or design new ones in political, economic, environmental, social, and cultural contexts to solve related problems. But as mentioned earlier, the "game" itself is not necessarily sound. We need to redesign or modify the various rules of the game to accord with the principles of green development, so as to stimulate or channel innovative behaviors in sustainable directions.

**4. Creating a soft-hard balanced support system**

Implementing the green economy requires creating conditions that will attract more investment, including funds, human resources, and policy inputs for green development and that will help to increase natural capital. Such conditions must produce a balanced blend of both hard and soft environments.

Soft environment innovations in green development include building a system and mechanism to foster effective institutions for economic transition, covering numerous mandatory and optional institutional arrangements that help to bring socio-economic development in line with the requirements of the ecosystem (e.g., designing or reforming laws and regulations related to the economy, environment, and resources, and the institutions supporting public and social objectives). This can even be extended to include direct and supporting policies in the areas mentioned above, as well as in the international environment, and expanding those tendencies in society that favor green development (such as the resource conservation and environmental protection movements, and advocates for green consumption).

**5. Strategic management of green development**

The success of green development depends on linking five major systems—the determination of strategic objectives, strategic planning, effective use of tangible means and intangible ways, continuous reform and improvement of soft and hard infrastructure (conditions of support and guarantee). Follow-up monitoring, supervision/management, feedback, evaluation, adjustment, and recycling are also required for each action, so as to make the whole implementation system of green development forms a virtuous circle.

### *Strategic management of green development theory and practice in China*

If the strategy in the military sense is to defeat all deployments of the opponent, then the strategy in peacetime is to gain competitive advantage. Strategic management refers to the action of "managing" a series of key strategic "elements" or "links", in order to build and maintain competitive advantage. Therefore, we cannot talk about strategy without strategic management. Without successful strategic management, strategic objectives are empty, and strategic plans or blueprints are just beautiful visions hanging on the wall. In other words, if the process of turning the strategic blueprint into reality is called the road map, then the process of implementing or practicing the road map is strategic management.

Our past has been to "emphasize planning and neglect management". In addition, strategic management at the enterprise level has been stressed for a long time, but strategic management at the national, regional or industrial level is rarely studied in depth. Dan Schendel (Professor of Management at the Krannert Graduate School of Management, Perdue University), once said that the importance of strategy has a long history. However, it is surprising that when the word "strategy" is used today, strategic management is often not mentioned.[25]

Since green development is a revolution, it will inevitably require the carrier of its action—government, industry, business and the whole society to set off a thorough revolution from concept to behavior. This requires not only joint efforts from bottom-up and top-down but also long-term strategic management focused on ultimate strategic goals at the macro-, meso-, and micro-levels.

Over the years, based on the above concept, our team has provided effective guidance to the medium- and long-term planning for several regions in China, and has developed the Long-term Strategic Management System Integration Model (LSMSIM for short), including the so-called "seven levels plus one cycle" of LSMSIM (LSMSIM-1) and the "three stages and eight links" of LSMSIM (LSMSIM-2), in order to fully understand and implement the strategic management system.

Figure 7.6 shows a long-term strategic management system using green development at the national, regional or industry levels. It is characterized by seven levels

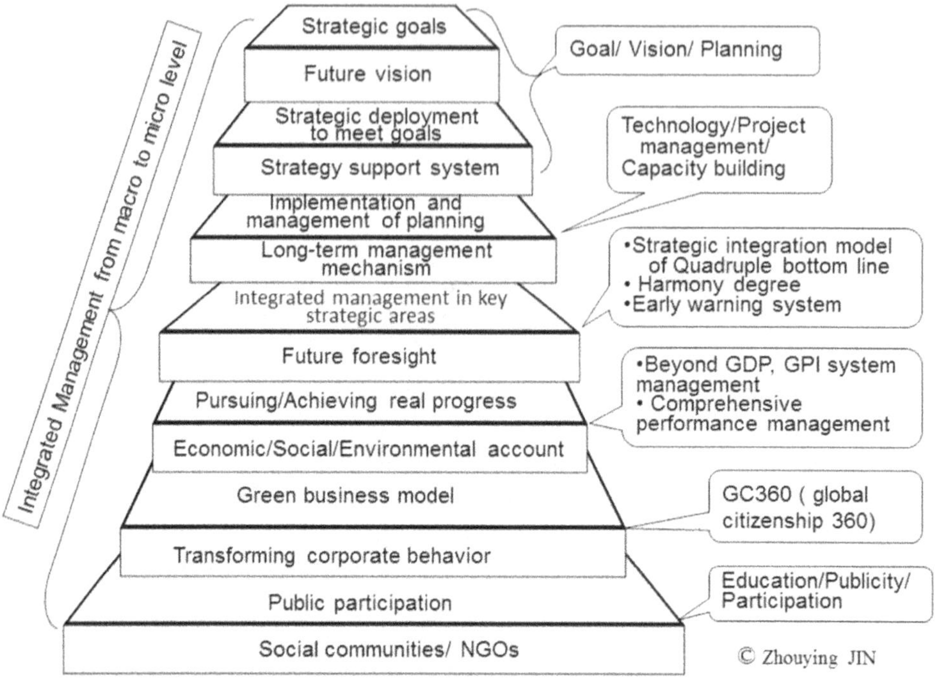


FIGURE 7.6: Long-term Strategic Management System Integration Model I (LSMSIM-1).

(dimentions) plus a cycle and provides a set of quantitative tools to periodically test the extent to which the objectives at that level have been achieved.

The so-called seven levels include:

- Defining goals and creating a future vision;
- Strategic planning: deploying key technologies, projects and strategic support system;
- Implementation and management of planning: key technology and project management, implementation capacity building, implementation of long-term management mechanism;
- The comprehensive systematic integration of key strategy and the future fore-sight (as measured by the degree of harmony achieved and early warning);
- Go beyond GDP to promote genuine progress in economic, social, and environmental areas, as well as promoting comprehensive performance management [assessing by the ratio of GPI (Genuine Progress Indicator) to GDP];

- Changing corporate behavior. A green business model of enterprises (evaluating with the grade of GC360—Global corporate Citizenship comprehensive responsibility assessment system);
- Determining the role of NGOs and public participation.

Figure 7.7 can be called "three stages and eight links of the long-term strategic management system model." Generally speaking, strategic management includes three levels or stages: the formulation of strategic goal, strategic planning, and the implementation and evaluation of strategies, which can be further divided into eight key elements (or links). LSMSIM-2 describes the internal connection between these elements of strategic management and the connotation of establishing a long-term mechanism for strategic management.

The first stage is to define strategic goals and to draw blueprints that not only refine goals but also mobilize the whole society.

The second stage is strategic planning that meets these goals, includes the deployment of key technologies, key projects and soft and hard industries, and

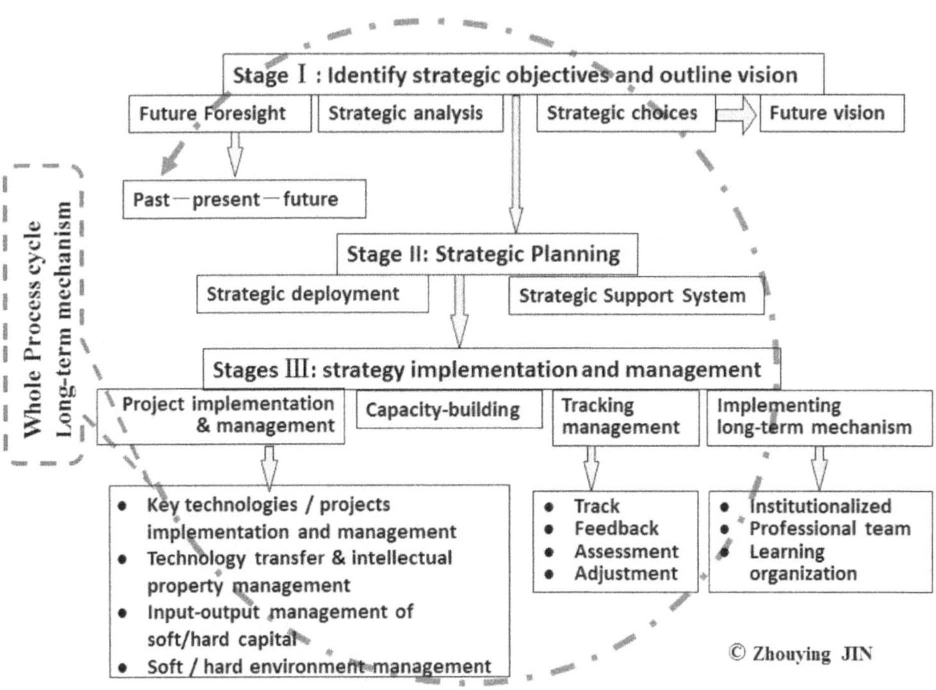


FIGURE 7.7: Long-term Strategic Management System Integration Model II (LSMSIM-2).

the deployment of strategic support system, especially the relevant institutional arrangements and policies;

The third stage is strategy implementation and management. The implementation and management of key projects and technologies (including technology transfer and intellectual property management, input–output management of soft/hard capital); implementation capacity building; tracking, evaluating, feedback and adjusting strategy throughout the whole process of strategy deployment and implementation; and the establishment of long-term mechanism to make the strategic management cycle fully institutionalized.

Thus, it can be seen that strategic management is an inseparable chain.

### Strategic goals and future vision

The formulation of strategic goals is a process of selecting the long-term future direction, scope of activities and possible goals and finally determining the objectives based on the study and analysis of the history, the current internal and external environment, and expected future objectives related to the strategic subject.

Therefore, the strategic goals must be:

1. Long-term and forward-looking. To achieve green development is an important part of the transformation from industrial civilization to ecological civilization. It should be noted said that the restoration of ecology and the environment takes a long time, but the change of ideas and values will likely require an even longer time;
2. In line with the direction of sustainable development;
3. Implementable (realistic and feasible);
4. Challenging (i.e., charismatic and likely to be achieved through hard work).

Therefore, the determination of strategic goals requires a process of future research followed by strategic analysis and strategic selection.

After the strategic goals are determined, they must be decomposed, "translated" and designed into a vision for the future, which can serve as a blueprint that can not only inspire enthusiasm and dedication from organization members but also awaken, attract and mobilize the vast number of strategic beneficiaries.

In conclusion, green development strategy must be a long-term development strategy based on the perspective of the future and be reflected in the short- and medium-term plan. Moreover, the strategic structure must conform to the characteristics of coordinated development, such as green economic development, social progress, environmental construction and protection, and effective utilization of resources.

### Strategic planning—soft/hard balanced strategic deployment that meets goals

The term "strategic planning" identifies a process through which the actual, potential or likely to be available resources within the strategic entities can be optimized, allocated, arranged, and laid out to achieve strategic goals. Therefore strategic planning includes strategic deployment and strategic support system design. This involves not only arrangements for key technologies, projects, and industrial deployments but also deployment of investment, in the forms of both hard and soft capital, as well as hard and soft infrastructure, capacity building, etc. (Figure 7.8).

*The principles of strategic planning should include:*

- ***Strategic deployment*** that considers not simply economic profit alone, but that also takes into account social progress, and ecological and environmental protection/enhancement as well as optimum use and conservation of resources.
- ***Multi-capital supports***: including both soft and hard capital.
- ***Soft and hard balanced project deployment***: in the strategy to achieve green development, project deployment is usually focused on hard technology (e.g., assuring the use of low carbon technology, ecological sustainability, recycling and reliance on renewable energy) and related projects. However, the research and development of soft technology and engineering projects for green development and the deployment of soft industries with them as the core technology must be arranged simultaneously. For example, soft technologies in green city planning should include transportation management, water circulation, energy, eco-environmental protection, medical and health, education, information management, garbage disposal and recycling, public management (including safety and emergency response), urban landscape design, urban–rural integration, etc. In this way, green development can be realized from multiple perspectives of society, culture and ecology, as well as relevant institution and policy design.
- ***Strategic support systems***: refers to a system comprising the soft-hard environment and conditions needed to enable resources to be more efficiently employed and strategic planning to be effective. In addition to the financial guarantees and the construction of hard infrastructure needed to implement soft and hard technical projects, it is also necessary to design and arrange "soft" environmental support (laws, regulations, institutions, mechanisms, policies, etc.) that directs the strategy to be implemented in the best direction for objectives to be satisfactorily achieved. This is a key area of strategic management. Of course, we must not forget to promote implementation capacity building.

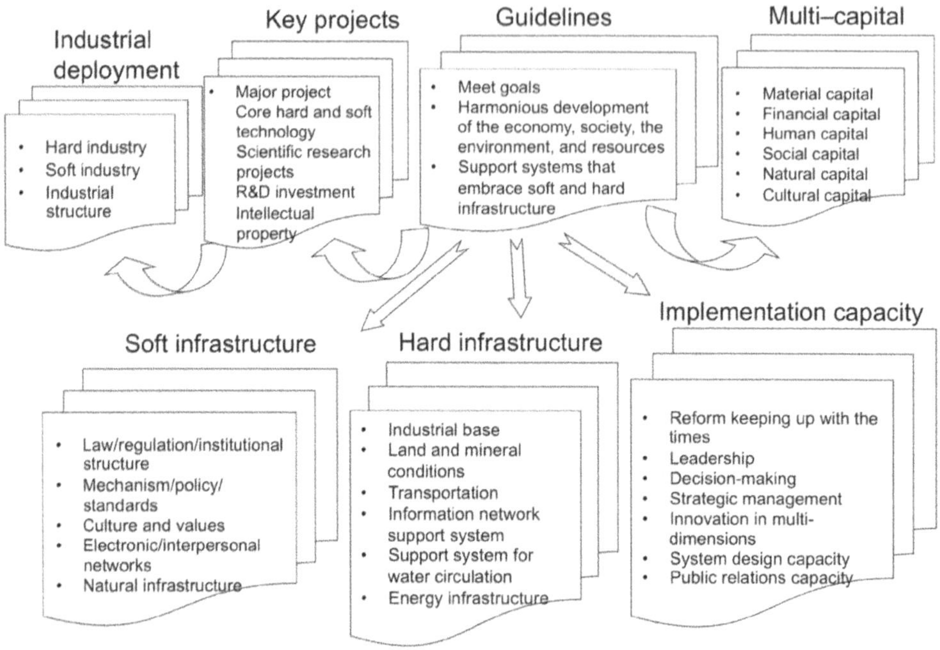


FIGURE 7.8: Soft-hard balanced strategic deployment and support system. © Zhouying Jin.

## Implementation and management of strategic planning

### 1. Project and technology management

In macro strategic management, the so-called "project" covers all the important parts of strategic deployment, and "projects" are important carriers of strategic deployment. Project management refers to the whole process of managing technology, engineering, and project construction arranged in strategic deployment (planning, organizing, coordinating, controlling, and evaluating), so as to achieve project objectives efficiently. In general, each project competes for necessary supporting funds, resources, talent, infrastructure, preference, and institutional support. Moreover, the more support a project can obtain, the more maneuvering and innovation space it will have. Strategies at the national or regional level often involve a large number of important projects. However, the resources that a country or region can mobilize are always limited. Thus, countries or regions must give up some projects in order to accomplish more important ones. At the same time, key short- and medium-term projects must be guaranteed, while the "100 Year Plan" also needs to be taken into account.

As a result, preference of policy and capital investment at different stages may be based on strengthening infrastructure as well as coordinating development of the economy, society, environment, and resources. In this context, success does not depend on project management alone, but on other relevant actions, including the optimal availability, allocation, and overall management of strategic resources, the input–output management of soft and hard capital, hard infrastructure management, and soft environment innovation, especially as related to institutions, mechanisms, and policy. The balance and coordination among these elements can also become crucial. However, all of the above factors have their own inherent systems. Therefore, project management must be integrated with all of these management systems.

**2. Capacity building for implementation**

Strategic management refers to the process of "translating" strategic goals and planning into organizational action, and transforming strategic entities into performance, by which the goals of an organization will be achieved. Therefore, strategic planning must consciously design and arrange projects or measures to improve the capacity for implementation. The core of implementation capacity building is the cultivation of soft technology talent (as explained above).

**3. Tracking management**

At each stage and at all levels of strategic management, a series of important decisions and actions are made. Therefore, some mechanism must be established and a team assembled to focus on the whole strategic plan and roadmap. This team should take on the roles of tracking, supervising, regularly evaluating, and providing early warning, feedback, and helping make timely adjustments to ensure that the strategic mission's goals are realized. Reviews and summaries of experiences and lessons cannot be made only at ten- to twenty-year intervals or after something goes wrong. This will require that the strategy must be transparent and open to the whole society. Transparency not only helps harness the enthusiasm of people, and boost their morale, it also aids in sound supervision. Periodic evaluations should include assessments by society as a whole, including supervisors, experts, and internal evaluations. These can greatly facilitate timely amendment of possible deviations and help to maintain and promote the proper measures for achieving strategic objectives.

In many cases in China, the major strategic documents at all levels are often locked in the archives of leading organizations as "confidential documents". This lack of transparency obstructs the tracking management of strategies. Generally, after a few years, it is evaluated as "achievement" and mainly praised, with little in-depth exploration and review of any problems encountered.

**4. Establishing a sustained mechanism for long-term strategic management**
As shown in Figure 7.7, strategic management is a chain that must be kept whole. Successful strategic management must establish a mechanism to make the whole process, which is composed of three stages and eight links, in line with goals. Only in this way, can we form a long-term mechanism to improve the possibility of achieving strategic objectives.

The above-mentioned logic and roadmap not only applies to the long-term strategic management at the national, regional, and corporate levels but also applies to the strategic management of building an innovative country.

Some points worth emphasizing here include:

- *Avoid a few pitfalls*: to pay attention to strategic planning but neglect the implementation management of this planning would be a serious mistake; to attach importance to the deployment of a project but neglect its strategic support system, or to focus on capital investment but ignore institutional arrangements and policy input, etc., would be equally misguided.
- *Learning process*: it is important to make the leadership and management team become a learning organization by the process of innovation strategy management.
- *Set up a special team*: it is also important to set up a special team to undertake tasks like tracking, evaluation, offering feedback and suggestions (adjusting strategy), and producing regular issue evaluation reports on the implementation of the strategy, including the evaluation of relevant regulations and policies.

## Strategic management must be combined with future foresight

For the long-term development of any country or region, integrated and coordinated development in key areas such as economy, society, environment and resources is essential for sustainable development. To ignore any of these areas is counter-productive. Therefore, we have designed an integrated model for monitoring all four of these major strategic systems—that is, a Quadruple Bottom Line Strategic Integrated Management System. It can be used not only as a tool to track and adjust the coordinated development of the long-term strategic system but also as a visual analysis tool for future foresight and early warning, providing a useful tool for decision-makers.

Key characteristics of the quadruple bottom line are: (1) to define four quadrants that represent the four key strategic fields (namely economy, society, environment, and natural resources), then to select representative indicators for each field as elements based on identifying the optimum structure and function of each subsystem, and to forecast each element for the next ten years; (2) displaying three

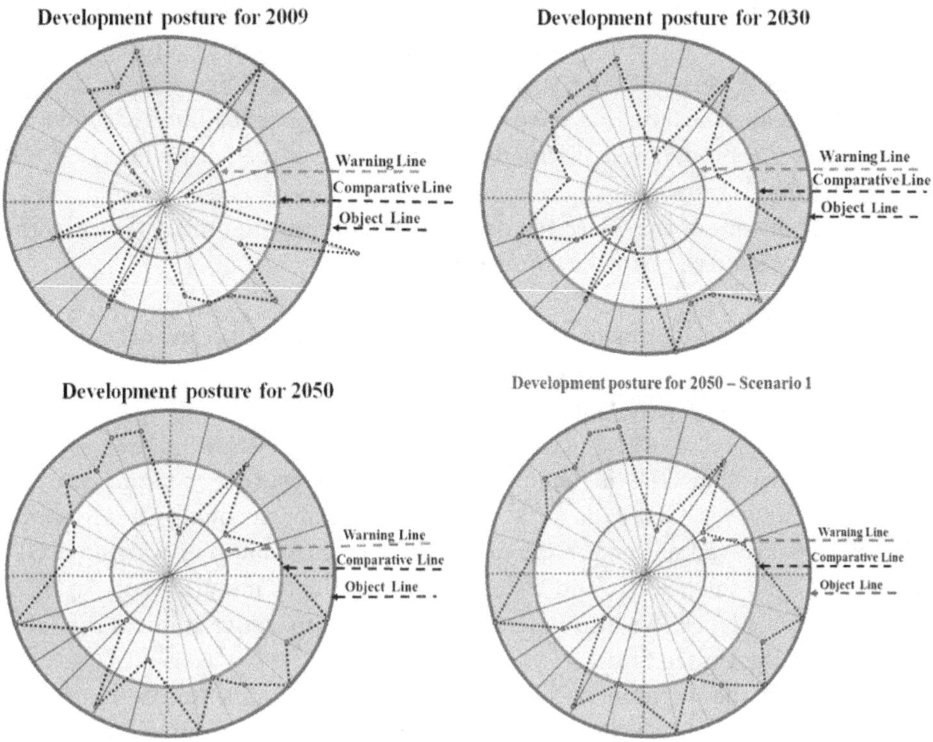


FIGURE 7.9: Regional development postures.

rings (namely a warning line, comparative line, and target line) as on a radar chart to show the development posture of a given country or region and to provide a visual support tool for decision making; (3) a behavior trajectory or strategic development posture for a country or region, which can be determined by running the software of the quadruple bottom line management system; (4) as referred to earlier "the harmonious degree", which measures the coordination among subsystems or elements with key strategic systems and within various fields under the principle of sustainable development; (5) looking to the future, adjusting the input (including financial and institutional, policy inputs) of innovation resources, so as to maintain the sustainable development posture in the future; and finally, (6) establishment of an early warning system: through tracking management will allow the strategic deployment to be adjusted to avoid risks.

We carried out tracking research on "China 2050 and Early Warning System", and by using this model, proposed some suggestions for the future development of given areas in the next 20–50 years. Using this tool, which is called "long-term strategy visual director", decision makers can correct mistakes or adjust and sublimate strategies at the same time, so as to achieve the goal of improving leadership ability and regional sustainable and coordinated development ability. Meanwhile, according to this model, we constructed China's State of the Future Index (SOFI) for international comparison.

With the advent of the era of big data, the reliability and practicability of the model are expected to be further improved.

## Green development must help the real progress of relevant countries and regions

### Beyond GDP, establishing a GPI system

It is well known that GDP is the key indicator for measuring economic growth at present. However, GDP fails to take account of either the quality of economic growth, or perceived national happiness. We have introduced and set up a GPI system in China since 2007, and have used the results to initiate demonstration projects in some cities. We also have conducted a comparative study of the GPIs in Japan and the United States.

The GPI includes separate social, economic, and environmental accounts. GPI takes full account of positive factors that contribute to real progress, including weighted personal consumption that is adjusted by income distribution, the monetary value of household work and parenting, the service value of household consumer durables and social capital stock, as well as the value of net capital investment and foreign borrowing. From these factors, it subtracts the costs of depleting natural resources and degrading the environment (e.g., water and air pollution, loss of wetlands and farmland, depletion of nonrenewable energy sources, loss of primary forests, the costs of long-term environmental damage—mainly from carbon dioxide emissions—and other costs from the services of natural capital). It also deducts the costs incurred due to crime, accidents, litigation, damage, and other negative factors, such as unequal income distribution, costs associated with work and loss of leisure time (e.g., unemployment, overwork, and under-employment), costs stemming from urbanization like the costs of commuting, automobile accidents, noise pollution, etc., as well as family breakdown and other costs related to societal dysfunction.

Our studies indicate that GPI is an effective measure to analyze the environment and social costs of GDP and that it can reflect national and regional economic health and social progress in a far more meaningful manner for both the public and policymakers. It is an ideal tool for evaluating regional sustainable development.

FIGURE 7.10: Comparison of China's GDP and GPI trends.

From 1980 to 2012, China's GDP and GDP per capita rose at an average of 9.83 per cent and 8.73 per cent, an overall increase of 22.23 times and 15.22 times, respectively (GDP per capita increased from about $500 to $4551, 2000=1.0). During the same time, China's GPI and GPI per capita increased 20.5 times and 13 times (GPI per capita increased from about $393 to $1677, 2,000=1.0), thereby indicating that while an economic miracle was being achieved during 35 years of reform and opening, "genuine" progress also took place.

However, the trajectories of GPI and GDP are different, and there is no direct linkage between them. Throughout the 1980s and 1990s, the gap between them has significantly expanded and especially during the 1990s GPI showed almost no growth.

The difference between GPI and GDP reflects the proportion of real progress in economic growth. This ratio was an average of only 26.46 per cent in the 1980s, declined to 18.65 per cent in the 1990s, then rose to 28.2 per cent in the 2000s, and reached 45.71 per cent by 2010–12, which indicates that even now, nearly 55 per cent of GDP value is counteracted by environmental and social costs as defined in the GPI calculation.

During the 35 years from 1978 to 2012, China's GDP increased more than 22 times and GDP per capita increased 15 times, yet the environmental and social costs increased 32 times and 47 times, respectively.

It is worth noting that the growth rate of GPI exceeded that of GDP, in the 2000s. This rise was mainly because investment in fixed assets surged during these ten years, and because of adjustments in the industrial structure, which led to the abnormal retirement of workers increased, while new jobs and demands for labor decreased. During this period, the average annual growth rate of labor input reached 0.56 per cent, resulting in the growth of capital stock at an average annual growth rate of 15.29 per cent, which made net capital investment grow at an average annual rate of 25.85 per cent. In addition, China's foreign debt has turned into a surplus of external assets since 2002, and in particular, net capital investment has surged since 2003, leading to the net foreign debt grew at an average rate of 64.29 per cent from 2002 to 2009. However, the above figures conceal the fact that the growth rate for personal consumption was much slower, especially as there was a relative decline in consumption by farmers. Also since 2010, the growth rates of China's net capital investments and foreign exchange reserves have both slowed significantly.

As the next step, we are ready to conduct a thorough review and adjustment of China's GPI system and to expand the scope of the model cities program. We suggest that each region can gradually build its own GPI system and use these as indicators for a comprehensive examination of local officials' performance. They may classify over 20 indicators of GPI into several clusters and use these as operational indicators for examining the performance of functional departments, and take any increase in the GPI/ GDP ratio as evidence of reduced social and environmental costs and improved levels of genuine progress.

## Changing the development mode and corporate behaviors

To implement green development, changes in the concept and transformation of government functions are certainly very important. But ultimately the behaviors and business models of enterprise must be changed as well. Ultimately changing corporate behaviors is the important basis for transforming national development. Currently, however, the business model of many companies aims merely to maximize profits. Such short-term behavior has created a series of social problems including corporate scandals related to food safety, drug safety, unsafe disposal of toxic substances, ignoring the safety of employees and customers, serious pollution of the environment, and more. These scandals have led to deep introspection and reflection throughout Chinese society. In this regard, China's Company Law,[26] for the first time, specifies that: "When undertaking business operations [...], a company shall act in good faith, [and] accept the supervision of the government and the general public...." In August 2010, the State-owned Assets Supervision and Administration Commission of the State Council (SASAC) asked that all central government-led enterprises release Corporate Social Responsibility (CSR) reports within three years. In 2018, 72 social responsibility reports were issued by central enterprises, and 38 per cent of them issued reports for 10 consecutive years.[27] Driven by government, the capital market, industry associations and other forces, the number of corporate social responsibility reports in China continues to grow, from 1,913 in 2017 to 2,097 in 2018. The number of private enterprise reports accounted for more than 50 per cent of the total number of reports for the first time.

However, releasing a CSR report is still far from fundamentally changing corporate behaviors. In order to establish a new corporate culture that values sustainable development and the implementation of a green business model, we introduced the Future 500 in early 2003.[28] The future 500 advocates that all businesses fulfill their economic, social, and environmental responsibilities, which we called the "triple bottom line, making it a corporate culture. The Future 500, encourages enterprises to change their profit model, from merely being a "big" enterprise to becoming a "good" one, and from worshiping the Fortune 500 to striving to establish the new Future 500, setting an example as "good" enterprises in the twenty-first century.

In fact, under the conditions of a market economy, the role played by government administrative orders and economic leverage is limited. Ideally, it should establish a fair and scientific evaluation system, introduce better principles and standards, and offer a model of "good" business. In short, it needs to define principles and standards that will constrain corporate behaviors, while evaluating and verifying the degree of responsibility undertaken by each enterprise as a global citizen contributing to sustainable development for the region and for the Earth as a whole, and also for future generations.

As shown in Figure 7.11, the Future 500[23] has developed a tool—GC360 (Global corporate Citizenship comprehensive responsibility assessment system), which incorporates 24 internationally recognized standards or guidelines for audits and self-evaluation to help companies and suppliers adopt a green business model. It includes 208 questions in five areas: (1) corporate governance and ethical conduct, (2) commitments to act responsibly toward employees by maintaining safe working conditions, (3) safeguarding community and societal development, (4) protecting the ecological environment, and (5) looking out for the well-being of users or consumers of products. Using such audits, seven outstanding Chinese companies have now become Future 500 members, and 13 more have used the GC360 to test their own "triple bottom lines".

To widen public awareness and increase public and social participation, Future 500 China has successfully held four international conferences with themes like "Why China Needs to Introduce the Future 500", "The Scientific Approach and the Enterprise for the Future", "Corporate Triple Responsibility and the

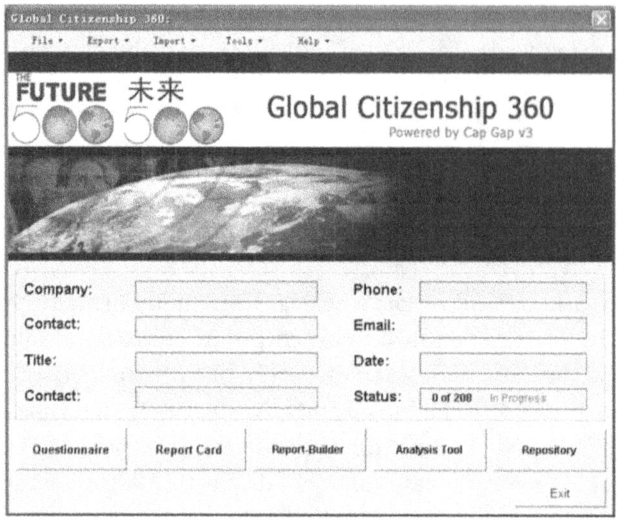

FIGURES 7.11 and 7.12: Global Citizenship 360 (top) and Future 500 members (bottom).

Harmonious Society," and "Global Corporate Citizenship and The Future 500 China." The Future 500 continues to work hard to involve more Chinese enterprises.

## The role of social organizations and public participation

Since China's reform and opening up, progress in the democratization of political life has brought an increasingly relaxed atmosphere for the development of NGOs, and China's NGOs are playing a valuable role filling a space long left vacant by past failures of the government and marketplace to achieve true green development. However, most Chinese grassroots NGOs still face a difficult choice in terms of identity and survival. Nowadays, social media provides an effective platform for citizen participation. Especially new media, such as the Internet and mobile phones, permit fast and easy dissemination of information so that exchanging public opinion on the Internet is already having a profound impact on society. By December 2020, China had 989 million Internet users, of whom mobile phone users reached 986 million, accounting for 99.7 per cent. This means that Internet exchanges have become an important part of public participation in the administration and discussion of state affairs. This innovation represents major social progress. At the same time, the impact of new media on society is enormous, and even its destructive effects are worthy of vigilance. How to responsibly use and direct expressions of public opinion via these new media, on the one hand, the masses of the people should learn and improve through participation and gradually become mature, while improving the government's ability to constructively channel public opinion for socially desirable goals presents, and correctly balance opening and control. This is both an opportunity and a challenge.

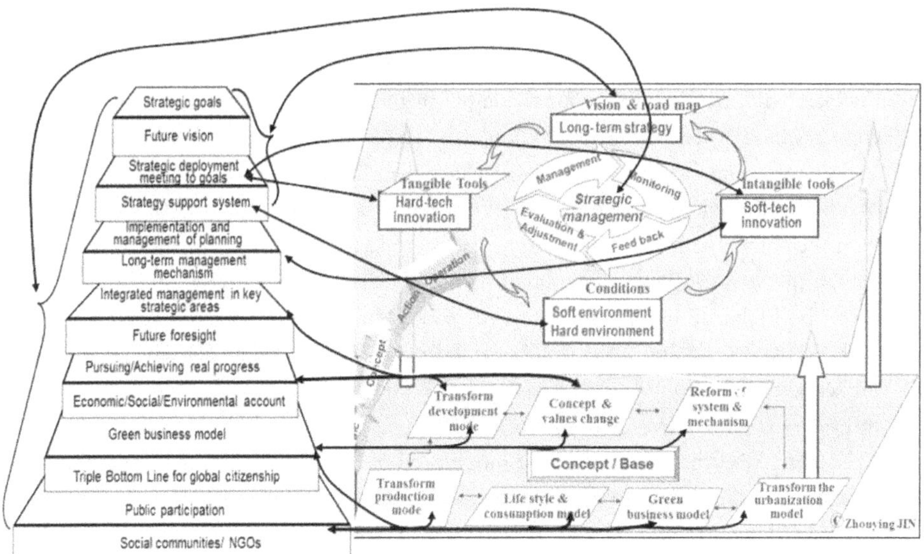


FIGURE 7.13: The relationship between the complex systems of green development and strategic management.

### Creating a tridimensional integrated system for green development

If we think of the implementation of green growth (consisting of strategic planning, tools and means, support conditions, and a tracking management), supported by philosophy, as a horizontally integrated system, then the strategic management system of green development, which consists of "six levels plus a circle" from the macro to micro is a vertically integrated system. This relationship of vertical and horizontal integration is shown in Figure 7.14. The ideal state should be to integrate and coordinate the above two systems and manage the multi-level complex giant system in order to gradually approach the green development goal and promote the green transformation of the development model.

## NOTES

1. "Five major challenges facing global sustainable development (data from UNICEF)", 24 July 2012, https://bbs.pinggu.org/thread-1530500-1-1.html.
2. "Fumbling the way to across the river" was first proposed at the 27th session of the council meeting in 1950 by Yun Chen, who was one of the leading members of the CPC at that time, in the 27th session of the council meeting in 1950. On 16 December 1980, Yun Chen proposed again at the opening session of the Central Committee of the CPC that 'although reform needed admittedly to rely on some theoretical research, economic statistics and economic forecasting, it was more important to start from the pilot, sum up experience at any time, namely, "fumbling the way to across the river."' Subsequently, Xiaoping Deng at the closing session said he fully agreed with the views of Yun Chen, and he believed that the speech of Yun Chen was "China's long-term guidelines for the future", http://blog.sina.com.cn/s/blog_494d802e010009vl.html.
3. In September and October 2013, Chinese President Jinping Xi proposed the strategic idea of building the Silk Road Economic Belt and the 21st Century Maritime Silk Road (called "One Belt One Road" for short) during his visit to Central Asia and Southeast Asian countries, http://www.360doc.com/content/15/0329/16/1014528_459065706.shtml.
4. http://baike.baidu.com/link?url=A4dC69PUNjtln6qS0oAox1uj764rgHGHiOmD4D8PQHKooXxK2jIm_CXQM5_A4vm8cd1XEFCB3BhogHCbTFjTWq.
5. https://www.in-en.com/article/html/energy-2277047.shtml.
6. https://www.sohu.com/a/201658566_362042.
7. The term "APEC blue" refers to the rare period of *blue* sky in Beijing during the APEC meeting held there in 2014 resulting from a drastic but effective government-sponsored emission reduction campaign, https://en.wikipedia.org/wiki/Special:Search/APEC_blue.
8. https://www.tuliu.com/read-48757.html.
9. http://baike.baidu.com/view/10891.htm?fromtitle=%E5%92%8C%E8%B0%90%E7%A4%BE%E4%BC%9A&fromid=279468&type=syn.

10. Whether it is from a cultural point of view or from a historical perspective, China at the current stage needs to maintain a strong central government. Lee Kuan Yew also said that the weakness of central government means chaos and turmoil.
11. The three historical stages of the development of socialism: from the publication of the Communist Manifesto in 1848, marking the birth of scientific socialism to the October Revolution in Russia in 1917; from 1917 to the drastic changes in the Soviet Union and Eastern Europe in the late 1980s; from the late 1980s to the middle of the twenty-first century. Hui Jiang, "Socialism with Chinese characteristics opens up a new realm of socialist development," *China Social Sciences Net*, 16 October 2017, http://www.cssn.cn/zzx/zwzzzdzzx/201710/t20171016_3669344.shtml.
12. "Four comprehensives" refer to "comprehensively" building a moderately prosperous society, deepening reform, advancing the rule of law and strictly governing the party, https://en.wikipedia.org/wiki/Four_Comprehensives.
13. Among the four ancient civilizations, the Mesopotamian civilization (Babylon) was Islamized in the Middle Ages, the ancient Egyptian civilization declined and disappeared in the third century CE, and the ancient Indian civilization died out due to foreign invasions around 1750 BCE.
14. www.worldbusiness.org.
15. https://baijiahao.baidu.com/s?id=1623984575865046934&wfr=spider&for=pc.
16. On 29 July 2005, Xuesen Qian put forward the famous "Xuesen Qian's question" to Premier Jiabao Wen when Premier Wen Jiabao visited him, https://baike.baidu.com/item/钱学森之问/3287915?fr=.
17. http://www.docin.com/p-772478443.html.
18. http://japan.xinhuanet.com/2014-10/14/c_133714590.htm
19. www.future500china.org.
20. http://www.haier.net/cn/abouthaier/one_person_alone/, 18 April 2016.
21. This is derived from the story of the ancient Greek philosopher Thales and G.W.F. Hegel's interpretation on it two thousand years later, http://www.360doc.com/content/14/0224/14/2198695_355282690.shtml.
22. "State Council Information Office released the operation of the national economy in 2014", *Xihua Net*, 20 January 2015, http://www.xinhuanet.com/live/20150120z/index.htm; Training Center of National Population and Family Planning Commission and Jiayuan website jointly issued "2012–2013 survey report on marriage concept in China", *Baidu*, 21 May 2013, http://wenku.baidu.com/link?url=Ebgvwax83ME8DMiuco6M6TBS3-CLD7Zd45c-0FDnNnW2a07MniJ-fqO2siU5Vk0u1uXGeuptNt8gsgU5LnbnwTGPyX-RkOXuGFLxiEpYN0G.
23. In 2013, demographers predicted that the number of families who lost their only child in China would reach 10 million in the future. Statistics from the Ministry of Health show that there are 76,000 new families losing their only child each year in China, http://news.ifeng.com/a/20151029/46045163_0.shtml.

24. "South Korea's suicide rate ranked the first in the OECD for eight consecutive years, and Japan ranked the third", 2012, http://bbs.tianya.cn/post-333-232296-1.shtml.
25. http://www.docin.com/p-478554144.html.
26. The Company Law of the People's Republic of China (adopted at the fifth meeting of the Standing Committee of the Eighth National People's Congress on 29 December 1993, and amended several times in 1999, 2004, 2005, and 2013. The current version is issued by the Standing Committee of the National People's Congress on 28 December 2013), https://baike.baidu.com/item/Company law of the people's Republic of China.
27. "Blue Book of Social Responsibility of Central Enterprises (2018)", Joint project group of the Chinese Academy of Social Sciences and Comprehensive Bureau of SASAC of the State Council.
28. www.future500.org.

# 8

# The Responsibility of Our Generation

*A better future cannot be predicted, but it can be created.*

A better future for human beings will not come automatically. If today's human beings cannot consciously promote the transformation of Industrial Civilization that has been formed over hundreds of years, and do not change their behavior patterns relative to economic, social, political, cultural, and environmental resources, the pathway leading to ultimate self-destruction appears inevitable. Therefore, we must face up to and deal with our current crises and take measures to prevent the outbreak of malignant new crises and disasters. At the same time, we must also design and create a clearer vision of a desirable long-term future for humanity in our lifetimes and for all succeeding generations. Then we must together strive to achieve it.

## *Reaching a consensus is key*

History has proven that the worldviews, philosophy of life, moral values, and ecological views of world elites, including influential national leaders, politicians, scholars (including futurists), and the heads of large multinational businesses are the driving forces that inspire social development and bring about significant social change. So, it is crucial that these leaders and mainstream society reach a consensus regarding basic issues related to the future of humankind. Among the vexing questions, we must wrestle with are these:

- What kind of future world do we need?
- What kind of future civilization should we establish?
- How can we best promote the transformation of Industrial Civilization?
- What is a human being? What is life?
- How should human beings evolve?
- Does human evolution have an end or a bottom line?

- How can we prevent the extinction of the human race (i.e., can we agree on how to achieve sustainable survival and development)?
- What is technology? What is the basic purpose of technology?
- What is the proper relationship between humans and technology?
- How can we develop and regularize the technology best suited to the kind of future civilization we desire?
- How can we avoid scientific and technological disasters (in sum: can we reach a consensus on scientific technological development and ethics)?
- How do we begin to shape a harmonious and peaceful world (can we agree on how to preserve humanity as a community)?

By achieving broad consensus on such issues, and then guiding mainstream society toward the widely shared vision of a desired human future, so as to jointly promote a series of major scientific discoveries, hard technology inventions, soft technology innovations, and their rule systems can we pave the way for realizing Global Civilization and even Great Civilization. Take the "democratic crisis" facing today's world as an example. The world's political elites should reach a consensus on the way to allocate power and select a path for national development. Without such consensus, democracy could very easily descend into chaos.

### *Changing thinking mode is the precondition for achieving consensus*

Our mode of thinking determines whether people are capable of framing effective and useful insights from the process of observing the world and analyzing complicated processes, at the same time, it is also the premise of various paradigm transformation.

To establish a world in which "groups with different cultures, different faiths, and different values can accept each other, coexist and share happiness"—that is, to realize a fair, just, and harmonious world—the human thinking mode under the logic of industrial civilization must gradually be changed starting with global elites, national leaders, corporate decision-makers, and finally the general public.

Take China–US relations as an example. The development of China is an indisputable fact. In the near future, even if China does become the world's largest economy, the United States need not be alarmed by this, because the world economy is not a zero-sum game. China's development and that of the United States can be complementary and mutually supportive. If China, with a quarter of the world's population, accelerates its development, this will create more opportunities and new markets for the United States, which is an innovative power with advanced technologies, and it will also be conducive to the prosperity of the world. But if America continues to view China's gains as losses for the United States, regard China's power as a threat to itself, strive to "contain" or limit China's influence, never give up the thinking mode of transforming the world with American values, the result will be endless contradictions and conflicts, and will not do much to slow down China's rejuvenation.

Because as explained in the section of "Socialist practice in China" in Chapter 6 and the section of "China 2050" in Chapter 7, although China's peaceful development is up against and will continue to face great challenges, the path it chooses and its ultimate successful rejuvenation are a kind of historical inevitability.

The United States and China should seize the opportunity to sincerely cooperate on various projects of mutual benefit, make an example of tolerating and respecting other countries while coexisting and sharing with them, have the courage to assume the responsibilities of both sides as world powers and jointly commit to promoting sustainable development and perpetual peace in order to create a better world.

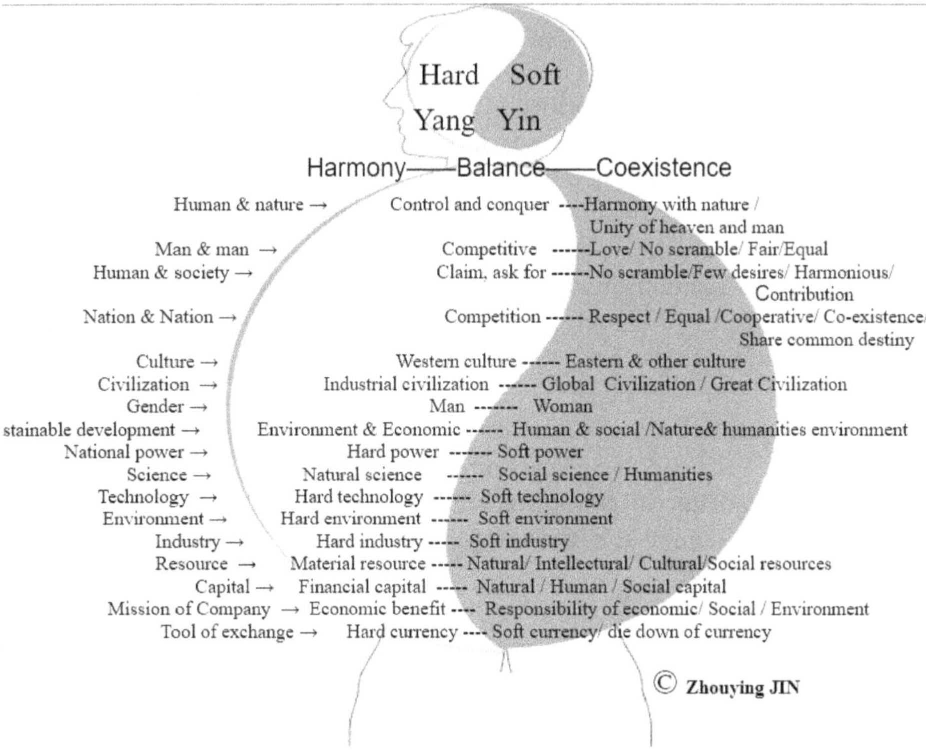


FIGURE 8.1: The principles of harmony, balance, and coexistence in the twenty-first century.

Therefore, in dealing with different development models, values, and cultures, as well as the opposing sides of various contradictions in human society and their relations, we simply need to apply the theories of "Yin-Yang" and "Soft-Hard" to achieve balance, equality, tolerance, and harmony, and make these theories the principle mode of thinking about major issues affecting human development and survival in the twenty-first century.

The principle of "Harmony, Balance and Coexistence" is in line with the ancient Chinese culture and philosophy of Yin-Yang, as it is expressed in the opening words of *Plain Questions: On the Changes of Yin and Yang of the Yellow Emperor's Inner Canon*, Yin and Yang are the laws of Heaven and Earth, the discipline of the universe, the origin of immortality and death, the parents of change, and the mansion of gods and spirits.

These words may be interpreted as follows: Yin-Yang is the basic and universal law of the movement of things in nature, the basis for understanding everything, and the cause of all occurrence, development, decline, and disappearance of things. The origin of immortality and death refers to the root cause of changes in all things, and "the mansion of gods and spirits" refers to the intrinsic motivation that causes the movement of all things in nature.

Yin-Yang theory emphasizes that both sides of Yin-Yang together form a unity of opposites. They may seem to be mutually contradictory, but actually under certain conditions each can be transformed into the other, even as they remain interdependent, reinforcing and attracting each other, and coexisting as a unified whole.

Understanding the essence and actual connotation of the philosophy of Yin-Yang and the theory of Soft-Hard will be helpful in establishing a new culture with enhanced values and a broader worldview, and will also be conducive to promoting cosmopolitanism and globalism, fostering a culture of tolerance, and creating the climate of harmony, balance, coexistence, and win-win cooperation that is essential for a sustainable future civilization.

The principles of Soft-Hard theory are readily adaptable to culture, society, the economy, technology, science, business, and other fields. Understanding the theories of Yin-Yang and Soft-Hard represents progress in thinking, deepening of insight, and the advance of the epistemology.

Figure 8.1 lists a number of the Soft-Hard thinking mode guided by the values of Global Civilization:

- *The relationship between humanity and nature*: shift from controlling and conquering nature to being in harmony with nature; comply with the principle of the unity of Heaven and Man.
- *The relationship between man and man*: shift from competition to a relation that is loving, caring, non-competitive, just, and fair.

- *The relationship between man and society*: shift from demanding (welfare, public services, and jobs) to non-contention, having few desires, living in harmony, and willingly contributing to others.
- *State-to-state relations*: shift from competition to respect, equality, cooperation, coexistence, and faith in a common destiny.
- *Culture*: practice mutual respect, coexistence, and harmony among Western, Oriental, and other cultures. For example, Western culture propels Industrial Civilization, promotes the increase of social wealth, and advances science and technology, while Oriental culture stresses the unity between humans and nature, and provides the philosophical basis for a sustainable future civilization. Different cultures should respect each other, learn from each other, and freely share their special gifts with one another.
- *Civilization*: transition from the Industrial Civilization epoch to the epoch of Global Civilization or even the Great Civilization.
- *Gender relations*: achieve mutual respect and equality of rights between men and women.
- *Sustainable development*: shift from focusing only on the environment to seeking sustainability in human relations with other creatures in nature, the economy and society, and work to assure sustainable human survival and development.
- *Science*: seek to balance hard and soft elements in the natural and social sciences as well as expanding non-traditional methods of studying natural phenomena and human behavior.
- *Technology*: transition from hard technology to soft technology, and then to a technology that integrates and merges soft and hard elements.
- *National strength*: seek balance between the use of soft and hard power.
- *Economic development*: transition from today's brown economy to a new green economy (including modifying methods for economic accounting to reflect true benefits to humanity and not simply monetary profit).
- *Industrial structure*: seek to balance hard and soft industries.
- *Environment for development*: balance hard and soft environment.
- *Resource use*: shift from the exploitation of material resources to the sustainable use of natural, intellectual, cultural, and social resources.
- *Capital*: seek to balance hard and soft capital. In other words, move from investing mainly in tangible man-made capital to acknowledging the value of natural capital, human capital, social capital, etc. as worthwhile investments.
- *Tools of exchange*: move from "Yang" currency to "Yin" currency, electronic or digital currency, until the need for currency itself gradually disappears.
- *Corporate identity and goals*: shift companies self-image from that of economic entities whose highest duty is maximizing profit, to global citizens who strive to meet economic, social, ethical, and environmental responsibilities.

## *Education is fundamental*

The foreseeable future will be shaped by ourselves and our children. But we also need to expect that our descendants, too, will take on the responsibility of creating the future and be personally involved in creating an ideal future of their own choosing. We must therefore take the responsibility to cultivate the next generation so that they will continue to work for a better future of sustainable human development. Moreover, we must educate people everywhere so as to improve public awareness and convince decision-makers to make fair and responsible choices related to the future civilization from one generation to the next.

This requires that the content and direction of education must also change to reflect the changes of the times and the continuous emergence of disruptive technologies. For example, there must be new connotations on how to cultivate both the morality and wisdom of the next generation. In terms of moral education, in an environment with highly developed technology and extremely rich material, it is a great challenge to endow the next generation with the spirit of hard work, integrity, love, and social responsibility (as opposed to being "self-centered"). In terms of intellectual education, it needs to replace traditional educational methods such as the memorization of rote knowledge, or the emphasis on outdated business values (such as always placing economic interests first, and the desire for quick success and instant benefits, that lead to excessive competition, etc.).

To create a future civilization that enables the sustainable development of mankind, what we really need are a new mindset and way of thinking that encourages young people not to shy away from complicated problems, to be capable of independent thinking and persistent in pursuit of truth, to dare to question accepted wisdom, to desire to explore the unknown, and to persevere in searching for its essence and laws. There are too many natural and social science problems for human beings to ever become complacent. Let us rather cultivate our insights and patience by seeking to understand things and apply facts to solve problems and actively promote the positive sublimation of human nature by observing and analyzing the origin of various conflicts and contradictions in society. We must also learn to identify the characteristics of different cultures, promote their essence, and remove their dross through studying history, so as to create an advanced culture that adapts to or supports future civilization. This kind of education is much more difficult than simply passing on existing knowledge. The difficulty lies in how to guide and cultivate values or thinking modes that are conducive to the construction of Global Civilization and even Great Civilizations, in particular, to cultivate a sense of responsibility for creating a better future for humanity.

To shape young minds, we must implement a new educational model, infiltrate the above-mentioned educational concepts and values not only in the teaching process from elementary school to university but also in all sectors of society, including politics, academia, business, literature, and art, and even in the daily life of the general public, so as to create a healthy and supportive environment.

### *A better future cannot be predicted, but it can be created*

It is difficult to accurately predict a society that adapts to the future of humanity. Of course, if we simply allow the future of humanity to proceed at random, every aspect of that future will remain uncertain. But I believe one thing is certain, that is, in the future, not only due to the rapid development of science and technology but to the progress of human thought, human wisdom and ability will vastly improve compared with today. It is possible that people's ideas and ways of thinking, their way of life and work ethic, the concept of family, and even the way economics and social governance operate will be "completely different" from what they are now. Coupled with the new global culture formed by the progress of globalization, human consciousness and identity may undergo major changes.

However, exactly "where and how" and "in which direction these changes are made" depend on us. That is to say, no matter what kind of future it is, it will be created by human beings. The behavior patterns guided by our values determine the direction and speed of the transformation to future civilization.

Therefore, it is not a question of how to accurately predict the future, but a question of what kind of vision humans take as the ideal goal for the future (e.g., what I suggest is that we transform first into a Global Civilization, and then realize a Great Civilization). This is the value of long-term future study—namely, to clarify the development goals of human beings and human society through future foresight, and strive to realize them.

We need to take a different attitude towards the future of humanity.

The road to a better future lies before us, for the future is what we create. Our mission is not to accurately predict the future, nor to be led by our romantic imagination, let alone just to worry, evaluate or comment on unknown consequences. The purpose of this book is to guide people to apply the right thinking, move towards a future that can be achieved as long as efforts are made, to set goals, and jointly design and plan a better future for sustainable human development, and work to achieve it.

As the Venus Project[1] has advocated, we should not be content merely to debate what the future *might* be, but should explore what the future *can* be if we apply what we already know to achieve a sustainable new world civilization. This calls for a straightforward redesign of our existing culture to create one in which the age-old scourges of war, poverty, hunger, debt, and unnecessary human suffering are at last seen to be not only avoidable but totally unacceptable. Anything less will only perpetuate the same catalog of problems inherent in today's world.

Edward Cornish (1927–2019), the founder of the World Future Society, said 50 years ago: "We can do nothing to change the past, but we have enormous power to shape the future. Once we grasp that essential insight, we recognize our responsibility and capability for building our dreams of tomorrow and avoiding our nightmares."

Of course, this does not negate the role of futures forecasting, which offers effective means for carrying out scenario analysis, early warning, and risk prevention—all tasks that help us determine the right future direction. In particular, we need studies of medium- and short-term future trends or future forecasts in specific industries and domains to help identify opportunities and manage or prevent risks.

But for the long-term future of mankind, what we need above all else is to design and continuously improve uplifting and inspiring goals obtained through sustained long-term futures research. In addition, we should strive to create a development mode (and roadmap for implementation) appropriate to these goals–including cultural standards, institutional reform, new ways of governance, capacity building, etc., and encourage people to strive from generation to generation to promote the sustainable human society and to evolve towards Global Civilization and even the Great Civilization.

I mentioned here the different research ideas for the short- and medium-term future, and the long-term future. The short- and medium-term future discussed in this book refers to the next 20–50 years, while the long-term future refers to the future over centuries or even thousands of years, as discussed in Chapter 5 (see Figure 5.1).

As for the time scale of the future, David Christian, in his *Maps of Time—An Introduction to Big History*, decomposes the future into the near future (next 100 years), the medium future (next centuries and next Millennium) and the long-term future (the future of the solar system, the galaxy and the universe). In view of the long-term future of billions of years as he defined in his book, the necessity for future forecasting has increased. For example, it needs to consider the risk of life extinction on the earth and the way out to avoid disaster in the life cycle of the sun.

## *Tolerance and visionary thinking*

I believe that one day humans will be able to achieve the Global Civilization, and then enter an era of Great Civilization. In the process of realizing Global Civilization, the systems of various countries may gradually converge, but cultures do not need to converge totally, and in fact we should welcome the uniqueness of every culture, past and present, respect their varied contributions to the advancement of human civilization, and maintain those sound traditional values that can still be used in modern societies of every kind. The routes that individual countries use to reach a desirable future may be different due to the discrepancies in their historical backgrounds or the state of their cultural, economic, and social development. Therefore, we should respect each country's choice of development path, and moreover, pay attention to, and become tolerant of, the various experiments and practices that countries and regions carry out in order to build a better future, even if these do not always succeed.

### *Be bold to take responsibility*

Regarding the human civilization of the future, I believe that future generations will be better able to answer this question than we can, but if we do not begin to consider such questions, define the right direction and goals for the future, and lay a solid foundation for it, who will?

If the seventeenth century was the incubation period for Industrial Civilization, then today—the twenty-first century–is the incubation period of the Great Civilization. In the seventeenth century, there was no ability to design mechanisms that would make the industrial age more humane and livable.

Today we can see that we are in the midst of a metamorphosis and have the ability to shape our future at least to some degree. Although this evolution will be slow and long, and may sometimes relapse, at least we now have clear goals and have already begun to consciously promote the transformation of civilization. Moreover, we have grasped increasingly powerful tools—soft and hard technologies as well as their impact on the progress of human civilization and will continue to promote their development.

Our generation is the first in history to recognize the true importance of human sustainability and to consciously promote the replacement of an existing civilization. Therefore, our generation has the responsibility to actively seek answers to serious issues like which path human civilization should follow to improve itself, and how to stay on the right road to achieve the Great Civilization.

### *Transmitting the goal of realizing the Great Civilization to the next generation*

The celebrated dictum—"The future will depend upon young people"—is not only suitable for a family or a country but is also even more applicable to creating a better future world for humanity as a whole. The younger generation is always the most creative, full of passion and vitality, full of yearning for a better future, and willing to work and sacrifice to realize their dreams. In this era of a new round of globalization and the Internet, the young are also the generation with the most common languages, and the fewest cultural barriers and ethnic prejudices. They find it easier to communicate with one another; they have less desire for power, they are less arrogant, and they are willing to boldly take on reform and innovation. Of course, they are also more susceptible to distraction and more likely to go to extremes. With this in mind, it is important to guide young people towards a correct understanding of themselves, to enhance their independent thinking ability and their ability to distinguish between right and wrong, while attracting more young people to participate in, and take seriously future education and research. Above all, we must enhance their sense of responsibility for a global society, humanity, and their future. Chairman Mao once talked about the opportunities that lie with the young people as follows: "The world is yours, as well as ours, but in the last analysis, it is yours."[2]

In conclusion, I believe that after long and arduous efforts, humans will finally be able to create Global Civilization and even the Great Civilization, ensuring all peoples a bright future together.

## NOTES

1. www.thevenusproject.com.
2. The speech of Zedong Mao to the Chinese students studying abroad at Moscow State University on 17 November 1957.

# References

## INTRO

UNEP (2011), "Towards a Green Economy", https://sustainabledevelopment.un.org/index.php?page=view&type=400&nr=126&menu=35. Accessed 15 August 2019.

## CHAPTER 1

Alfred, Nordmann (2004), "Converging Technologies – Shaping the Future of European Societies", Brussels: European Commission.

Anhuinews.com (2020), "Intelligent robots stand on the front line of the anti-epidemic: AI technology helps companies to show their abilities", 13 February, http://news.anhuinews.com/system/2020/02/13/008341157.shtml. Accessed 15 August 2019.

Anon, (n.d), "Chinese scientists have developed artificial liver cells", *Life Times*, 14 March 2014.

Anon (2010), "Human organs can be 'printed on demand' with the world's first 3D bio-printer", *Science and Technology Daily*, 16 March.

Anon (2010), "The United States invents new technology to transform body kinetic energy into electrical energy", *China Energy News*, 8 March.

Anon (2017), "The consequences of the arms race of killer robots are worrying", *Reference News*, 21 November.

Baidu.com (2016), "Stuart Russell, Professor of Berkeley University: Basic concepts of artificial intelligence and 34 misunderstandings", 21 November, https://baijiahao.baidu.com/s?id=1551588314566245&wfr=spider&for=pc. Accessed 25 October 2017.

Baidu.com (2018), "Congratulations to China, another major scientific and technological breakthrough has been made", *Baidu*, 14 November, https://baijiahao.baidu.com/s?id=1617113342396561934&wfr=spider&for=pc. Accessed 6 May 2019.

Baidu.com (2018), "HE is the world's first AI robot boyfriend", Baidu, 8 April, https://baijiahao.baidu.com/s?id=1597180165495983170&wfr=spider&for=pc. Accessed 18 May 2019.

Baidu.com (2018), "Visiting the humanoid robot laboratory in Japan: making your own replica", *Baidu*, 14 September, http://baijiahao.baidu.com/s?id=1611575739672132677. Accessed 5 July 2019.

Baidu.com (2019), "National Health Commission of China: Projects such as gene editing technology are to be approved by the competent health department of the State Council, *Baidu*, 27 February, https://baijiahao.baidu.com/s?id=1626596590833936664&wfr=spider&for=pc. Accessed 2 September 2019.

Baidu.com (2021a), "EU plans to legislate to limit the abuse of AI", *Baidu*, 15 April, https://baijiahao.baidu.com/s?id=1697096795261713079&wfr=spider&for=pc. Accessed 11 May 2021.

Baidu.com (2021b), "How to achieve AI co-governance? The top 10 Global AI Governance Events in 2020 are thought-provoking", *Baidu*, 19 January, https://baijiahao.baidu.com/s?id=1689295359590818463&wfr=spider&for=pc. Accessed 25 March 2021.

Bill, Joy (2000), "Why the future doesn't need us", *Wired*, April.

Bioon.com (2007), "Bioluminescence at the service of a novel cerebral imaging technique", *Bioon News*, 25 April, http://www.bioon.com/biology/bioenginering/291152.shtml. Accessed 22 January 2019.

Cankaoxiaoxi.com (2012), "Seven ways to change the world by nanotechnology", *Reference News Online*, 18 November, http://world.cankaoxiaoxi.com/2012/1118/121677.shtml. Extract of a news report on the website of *Popular Science*, 14 November 2012. Accessed 6 February 2016.

Cankaoxiaoxi.com (2013a), "'Mind-reading' might become a reality", *Reference News Online*, 17 October, http://science.cankaoxiaoxi.com/2013/1017/287535.shtml. Extract of a news report from the website of *Time*, 15 October 2013. Accessed 8 October 2016.

Cankaoxiaoxi.com (2013b), "Print liver slices with 3D printer for organ transplantation", *Reference News Online*, 8 November, http://science.cankaoxiaoxi.com/2013/1108/298634.shtml. Extract of a news report from the website of *LiveScience*, 6 November 2013. Accessed 3 February 2016.

Cankaoxiaoxi.com (2013c), "Space exploration 'creates' 30,000 products", *Reference News Online*, 7 November, http://science.cankaoxiaoxi.com/2013/1107/298004.shtml. Accessed 8 October 2016.

Cankaoxiaoxi.com (2014), "Ready to meet the 4D printing revolution", *Reference News Online*, 12 October, http://k.cankaoxiaoxi.com/weizhan/article/102683959/31142090205/236492?from=groupmessage&isappinstalled=0. Extracted the article from the website of *Foreign Affairs* magazine, 8 October 2014. Accessed 8 October 2016.

Cankaoxiaoxi.com (2015a), "3-D printing will change future war", *Reference News Online*, 7 January, http://www.cankaoxiaoxi.com/mil/20150107/620606.shtml. Extract of a news report from *Agence France Presse*, 5 January 2015. Accessed 6 October 2016.

Cankaoxiaoxi.com (2015b), "Biohackers may change life", *Reference News Online*, 11 August, http://www.cankaoxiaoxi.com/science/20150811/898900.shtml. Accessed 8 October 2016; Tuxi.com (2015), "Biohacking technology: Let the human body have infinite possibilities", *Tuxi News*, 6 May, http://news.tuxi.com.cn/news/43/430021.html. Accessed 5 November 2016.

Cankaoxiaoxi.com (2018a), "According to British media, space junk endangers space exploration: Maybe 'shoot down' the spacecraft", *Reference News Online*, 4 September, http://www.cankaoxiaoxi.com/science/20180904/2320621.shtml. Accessed 8 January 2019.

Cankaoxiaoxi.com (2018b), "In the future, hackers can manipulate human memory", *Reference News Online*, 4 November, http://www.cankaoxiaoxi.com/science/20181104/2348342.shtml. Accessed 8 December 2018.

Cankaoxiaoxi.com (2020), "Adolescent depression is associated with social media", *Reference News Online*, 27 January, http://www.cankaoxiaoxi.com/science/20200127/2400932.shtml. Accessed 8November 2020.

Changyan, Ding (2014), "Problem in the modernization of political party governance: Analysis of transition in the soft power of the CCP", *Theory Journal*, 9, p. 20.

Chao, Sun (2002), "Philosophical thinking brought by nanotechnology", *Journal of Anhui Agricultural University*, 2, pp. 66-68.

China.com (2013), "The European Space Agency's 'Amaze Project' will bring 3D printing into the age of metal", *China.com*, 16 October, http://tech.china.com/news/company/international/11066130/20131016/18092751.html. Accessed 11 September 2018.

China Electronics Standardization Institute (2018), "White Paper on Artificial Intelligence Standardization (2018)".

Chinanews.com (2013), "Who will destroy mankind? Scholars claim that technology is a 'double-edged sword,'" *China News*, 25 April, http://www.chinanews.com/gj/2013/04-25/4762996.shtml. Accessed 20 July 2013.

Chinareview.com (2019), "Facing the arrival of intelligent robots, experts and scholars have given us some countermeasures", *Chinareview*, 9 September, http://www.chinareview.com.cn/html/muyingpindao/buruweiyang/20191009/46529.html. Accessed 10 December 2019.

Chinese Academy of Sciences (2003), "National Nanotechnology Initiative (NNI) of the United States and ten recommendations of NNI from American Academy of Sciences", *Website of Chinese Academy of Sciences*, 29 July, http://www.cas.cn/xw/kjsm/gjdt/200906/t20090608_623423.shtml. Accessed 29 July 2012.

Chuanqi, He (2011), *Strategic Opportunities on the Sixth Revolution of Science and Technology*, Beijing: Science Press.

Cn-healthcare.com (2018), "The world's first genetically modified fetus immunized against AIDS is born. Is the vaccine really about to be out?" *Cn-healthcare*, 27 November, https://www.cn-healthcare.com/articlewm/20181127/content-1041311.html. Accessed 29 March 2019.

Cnhubei.com (2005), "How will humans evolve? Future evolution depicts five paths (a group of pictures)", *Cnhubei*, 26 August, http://www.cnhubei.com/200508/ca852694.htm. Accessed 20 November 2012.

Cntv.cn (2011), "Ten ideas that will change the world", *Xinhua Net*, 25 November 2011, http://jingji.cntv.cn/20111125/104921.shtml. Extracted the article from *Scientific American* 12 (2011). Accessed 5 January 2016.

Definition of AI, https://baike.baidu.com/item/%E4%BA%BA%E5%B7%A5%E6%99%BA%E8%83%BD/9180?fr=aladdin. Accessed 20 May 2017.

Duoyi, Fei (2004), "Gray sorrow: Social risks of the technology of nanometer", *Philosophical Trends*, 1, pp. 23-36.

Duozhishidai.com (2018), "Google announced seven principles for their use of AI", *Duozhishidai*, 10 November, http://www.duozhishidai.com/article-17354-1.html. Accessed 18 April 2019.

Ed., Regis (1994), *Great Mambo Chicken and the Transhuman Condition: Science Slightly over the Edge* (trans. Mingde Zhang and Qingqing Liu), Beijing: China Translation & Publishing Corporation.

Elecfans.com (2018), "The achievement, current progress and future development trend of BCI in application system implementation", *Elecfans*, 8 February, http://www.elecfans.com/d/632703.html. Accessed 12 May 2019.

Gang, Pei, Yan, Xiong and Liubin, Gao (2007), "Converging technology: Is it a new opportunity for China?", *Chinese Medicinal Biotechnology*, 2:1, pp. 46-50.

Gerald M., Edelman and Giulio, Tononi (2004), *A Universe of Consciousness: How Matter Becomes Imagination* (trans.Fanji Gu), Shanghai: Shanghai Science and Technology Press.

Gov.cn (2019), "Responsible artificial intelligence: The governance principles of China's new generation of artificial intelligence are released", *Chinese Government Website*, 17 June, http://www.gov.cn/xinwen/2019-06/17/content_5401006.htm. Accessed 12 May 2020.

Haosou.com, "New media art design", n.d., http://baike.haosou.com/doc/2381157-2517710.html. Accessed 28 November 2020.

Hazel, Henderson (2014), *Mapping the Global Transition to the Solar Age*, London: ICAEW and The Centre for Tomorrow's Company.

Hazel, Henderson (2021), "Can AI algorithms ever be ethical?", Ethical Markets, 4 February, http://www.ethicalmarkets.com. Accessed 10 February 2021.

Huanqiu.com (2014), "The IEA claimed that solar energy will probably become a major source of electricity before 2050", *Global Times Online*, 30 September, http://finance.huanqiu.com/view/2014-09/5156457.html. Extract of a news report from *Reuters*, 29 September 2014. Accessed 5 January 2018.

Ifeng.com (2013), "Scientists used stem cells to produce an artificial kidney", *ifeng*, 16 December, http://tech.ifeng.com/discovery/special/artificial-organs. Accessed 10 April 2016.

Intelligence Research Group (2016), "Report on in depth research and investment prospect analysis of China's metamaterial market from 2016 to 2022", *Chyxx.com*, 25 August, https://wenku.baidu.com/view/05f635090242a8956aece4c9.html. Accessed 6 April 2018.

Jerome, Glenn and Theodore, Gordon (2005), *2005 State of The Future*, The Millennium Project, CD Chapter 3.

Jie, Yan and Xianlun, Pang (2004), "Ethical thinking on pre-implantation genetic diagnosis (PGD)", *Medicine and Philosophy*, 4, pp. 19–20.

John, Smart (2013), "Leadership of technological change: Ten areas of strategic disruption, opportunity and threat", *World Future 2013 Conference*, Chicago, Illinois.

Jules, Verne (2012), "For twenty years, the people who move forward have been doing a Jules Verne": Hubert Lyautey, quoted in Jean-Michel Margot, "Editorial," *Verniana* 4, https://en.wikiquote.org/wiki/Jules_Verne#Quotes_about_Jules_Verne. Accessed 2 March 2013.

Kankanews.com (2018), "More like human beings! Atlas, a humanoid robot, has learned to run and jump in the wild", *Kankanews*, 14 May, http://www.kankanews.com/a/2018-05-14/0038440723.shtml. Accessed 2 March 2019.

Kevin, Kelly (2011a), *What Technology Wants* (trans. Xiang Xiong), Beijing: China Citic Press.

Kevin, Kelly (2011b), *What Technology Wants* (trans. Xiang Xiong), China: China Citic Press, p. 11.

Kevin, Kelly (2014), *Out of Control: The New Biology of Machines, Social Systems, and the Economic World* (trans. Xinwu Chen), Beijing: New Star Press.

Li, Chen (2014), "Target selection and social ethics of gene technology", *Science and Technology Daily*, 28 September.

Liming,Wang (ed.) (1994), *New Theory of Personality Right Law*, China: Jilin People's Publishing House.

Linda, Groff (2014), "Views of the possible future human", *World Future 2014 Conference*, Orlando, 22 July.

Luc, Ferry (2017), *La Revolution Transhumaniste* (trans. Xing Zhou), Hunan: Hunan Science and Technology Press.

Martin, Rees (2003), *Our Final Century*, New York: Random House.

Mihail C., Roco and William Sims, Bainbridge (eds) (2003), *Converging Technologies for Improving Human Performance*, New York: Springer.

National Intelligence Council (NIC) (2017), "Global Trends: Paradox of Progress", Washington: NIC.

Ofweek.com (2019), "The Japanese sex robot was sold out one hour after it went online. In the age of AI, is there a future for human beings?", *Ofweek*, 13 May, http://mp.ofweek.com/robot/a745683023006. Accessed 17 December 2019.

People.cn (2000), "20 natural and man-made disasters threatening mankind", *Beijing Youth Daily*, 30 November, http://www.people.com.cn/GB/channel2/570/20001130/332300.html. Accessed 8 January 2013.

People.com (2018), "AI is a 'double-edged sword': Machines liberate humans or replace humans", *People.cn*, 23 August, http://scitech.people.com.cn/n1/2018/0823/c1007-30245635.html. Accessed 15 August 2019.

Peter Douglas, Ward (2001), *Future Evolution*, New York: W.H. Freeman & Company.

Pinlue.com (2018), "The incident of genetic baby is not over yet! Google issued a shocking prophecy", *Pinlue*, 3 December 2018, https://www.pinlue.com/article/2018/12/0312/507757184251.html. Accessed 20 January 2019.

Qiang, Zhang (2002), "Negative effects of Biotechnology", *Studies in International Technology & Economy*, 3, pp. 25–31.

Qingli, Zhang (2016), "Gene editing technology has unknown risks, which may impact human dignity. We should keep the ethical bottom line of the gene era", *Chinese Social Sciences Today*, 16 January.

Qq.com (2012), "Watson, the IBM supercomputer systems: The new interaction behind big data", *Tencent*, 9 March, http://tech.qq.com/a/20120309/000266.htm. Accessed 23 November 2015.

Qq.com (2019), "The 30th anniversary of the birth of the World Wide Web: Is it becoming a 'runaway monster'?" *Tencent*, 6 March 2019, https://tech.qq.com/a/20190306/003943.htm. Accessed 5 December 2019.

Ray, Kurzweil (2006), *The Age of Spiritual Machines: When Computers Exceed Human Intelligence* (trans. Zhiyan Shen et al.), Shanghai: Shanghai Translation Publishing House, p. 27.

Ray, Kurzweil (2011a), *The Singularity Is Near* (trans. Qingcheng Li et al.), China: China Machine Press, pp. 9 and 15.

Ray, Kurzweil (2011b), *The Singularity Is Near* (trans. Qingcheng Li et al.) China: China Machine Press, p. 15.

Ray, Kurzweil (2011c), *The Singularity Is Near* (trans. Qingcheng Li et al.), China: China Machine Press.

Richard, Dobbs, James, Manyika and Jonathan, Woetzel (2015) "The four global forces breaking all the trends", *McKinsey & Company*, 6 April, http://www.mckinsey.com/insights/strategy/the_four_global_forces_breaking_all_the_trends. Accessed 5 May 2015.

Sina.com (2015), "Hawking and others issued an open letter: Beware of the potential risks of AI", *Sina Tech*, 14 January, http://tech.sina.com.cn/d/i/2015-01-14/doc-icesifvy3684641.shtml. Accessed 20 January 2016.

Sina.com (2017a), "Experts warn: Brain computer interface technology will cause many problems, which should be treated with caution", *Sina Tech*, 8 May, http://tech.sina.com.cn/d/i/2017-05-08/doc-ifyeycfp9335388.shtml. Accessed 22 January 2018.

Sina.com (2017b), "Scientists solve the mystery of consciousness: human brain may operate in 11 dimensions", *Sina Tech*, 18 June, http://tech.sina.com.cn/d/i/2017-06-18/doc-ifyhfhrt4657081.shtml. Accessed 25 September 2019.

Sina.com (2018a), "More than 20 countries have legislated against gene editing, but there is no special legislation in China", *Sina Finance*, 27 November, http://finance.sina.com.cn/chanjing/cyxw/2018-11-27/doc-ihmutuec4064755.shtml. Accessed 3 June 2019.

Sina.com (2018b), "The report on the social role and ethics of artificial intelligence, the cornerstone of the future, has been released", *Sina*, 9 July, http://news.sina.com.cn/o/2018-07-09/doc-ihezpzwu0952522.shtml. Accessed 10 October 2019.

Sina.com (2019), "Russia has created a force of 'killer robots'", *Sina*, 24 March, http://news.sina.com.cn/o/2019-03-24/doc-ihtxyzsm0039236.shtml. Accessed 10 January 2020.

Sohu.com (2012), "Ten major assumptions of human evolution", *Sohu*, 9 July, https://it.sohu.com/20120709/n347682780.shtml. Accessed 20 January 2015.

Sohu.com (2018a), "Scientists believe that humans have at least 11 senses", *Sohu*, 14 December, https://www.sohu.com/a/281818358_114911. Accessed 12 July 2019.

Sohu.com (2018b), "The three most noteworthy brain technologies of the year", 4 January, http://www.sohu.com/a/214581535_473283. Accessed 18 February 2019.

Sohu.com (2019), "The only robot in the world with a citizen's ID card said in an interview that I would destroy human beings", *Sohu*, 25 January, https://www.sohu.com/a/291482346_120046613. Accessed 25 January 2020.

Sohu.com (2020), "South Korea is developing artificial skin that can 'make soldiers invisible'. Will the rules of special night combat be changed?", 17 December, https://www.sohu.com/a/4388644294_98343. Accessed 8 April 2021.

Szhk.com (2019), "3-D print out breathing lungs", *Szhk.com*, 4 May, http://news.szhk.com/2019/05/04/283029943930604.html. Accessed 18 August 2019.

Thomas, Frey (2014), "162 Future jobs: Preparing for jobs that don't yet exist", *Futurist Speaker*, 21 March, https://futuristspeaker.com/category/business-trends/162-future-jobs-preparing-for-jobs-that-dont-yet-exist/. Accessed 25 January 2016.

Tiina, Kymäläinen (2015), "Innovative leap to future technology experiences—Science fiction prototypes advancing emerging technology research and foresight", *International Conference on Foresight*, Athens, Greece, 22–25 June.

Tom, Lombardo (2015), "Science fiction: The evolutionary mythology of the future", *World Future 2015 Conference*, July; *Center for Future Consciousness*, n.d., http://www.centerforfutureconsciousness.com/. Accessed 5 July 2017.

Weiguang, Wang (2015), "Information world and informatization of the world", *China Social Sciences Today*, 3 July.

Wenxin, Wu (2000), "Should science and technology be God?" *Studies in Dialectics of Nature*, 11:10.

Xinhuanet.com (2010), "The birth of artificial life cells: Is a blessing or a curse?" *Xinhua Net*, 24 May, http://news.xinhuanet.com/2010-05/24/c_121345652.htm. Extract of a news report on the website of *The New York Times*, 21 May 2010. Accessed 25 September 2015.

Xinhuanet.com (2011), "Ten things that may change future life", *Xinhua Net*, 29 August, http://news.xinhuanet.com/world/2011-08/29/c_121924961.htm. Accessed 20 January 2019.

Xinhuanet.com (2012), "Due to concerns that technological progress might destroy mankind one day, Cambridge set up a research center for human-machine confrontation", *Xinhua Net*, 27 November, http://news.xinhuanet.com/world/2012-11/27/c124008628.htm. Extract of a news report from the website of *The Sunday Times*, 25 November. Accessed 20 November 2013.

Xinhuanet.com (2012), "Future computer can simulate human senses", *Xinhua Net*, 20 December, http://news.xinhuanet.com/world/2012-12/20/c_124122874.htm. Extract of a news report from *Agence France Presse*, 17 December 2012. Accessed 28 December 2016.

Xuan, Jiang (2014), "The development and ethical challenge of human enhancement technology", *Studies in Dialectics of Nature*, 5, pp. 7–11.

Xuyan, Tu, Zhonggui, Ma and Yanhui, Guo (2012), *Artificial General Intelligence*, Beijing: National Defense Industry Press.

Yinhe, Li (2017), "Google issued a shocking prediction: mankind will begin to achieve immortality in this year", 23 July, https://mp.weixin.qq.com/s?_biz=MzU2OTEwNjU3Ng==&mid=2247492154&idx=2&sn=8f2371c9b408d6ffbdc0c1a0f1504770&source=41#wechat_redirect. Accessed 20 January 2019.

Yong, Fang (2018), "Important progress and trend of world space development in 2017", *Satellite Application*, 2, pp. 8-14.

Zhouying, Jin ([2005] 2011), *Global Technological Change—From Hard Technology to Soft Technology*, Bristol: Intellect.

Zhouying, Jin (2016), *What Kind of Future Does Humanity Need? Global Civilization and China's Comprehensive Rejuvenation*, Hunan: Hunan Science and Technology Press.

## CHAPTER 2

Anon (2017), "The earth is still shrouded in the cloud of war", *Reference News*, 25 December.

Baidu.com (2020), "Russia is surrounded by 200 American biochemical laboratories", *Sputnik News Agency*, 15 January, https://baijiahao.baidu.com/s?id=1622962335770072300&wfr=spider&for=pc. Accessed 3 October 2020.

Cankaoxiaoxi.com (2013), "'Animals' brains are more advanced than those of humans", *Reference News Online*, 17 December, http://science.cankaoxiaoxi.com/2013/1217/318519.shtml. Extract of a news report from *The Daily Mail*, 12 December 2013. Accessed 5 November 2016.

Chunyou, Yan (2015), *Wisdom of Nature*, Beijing: China Social Sciences Press.

David, Orrell, David (2010), *Apollo's Arrow: The Science of Prediction and the Future of Everything* (trans. Yangxun Huang), Beijing: Hainan Publishing House, p. 263.

Douban.com (2020), "What did the pandemic that infected 500 million people teach humans?", *Douban*, 3 March, https://www.douban.com/note/752890817/. Accessed 20 November 2020.

Francis, Fukuyama (2001), "For the first time, human beings have the opportunity to change human nature", *World Affairs*, 3.

Fred, Spier (2019), *Big History and The Future of Humanity* (trans. Yue Sun), Beijing: China Citic Press.

Jerry, Kaplan (2016), *Humans Need Not Apply: A Guide to Wealth and Work in the Age of Artificial Intelligence* (trans. Pan Li), Hangzhou: Zhejiang People's Publishing House.

John, Keegan (2010), *A History of Warfare* (trans. Yinhong Shi), Beijing: Commercial Press.

Kevin, Kelly (2011), *What Technology Wants* (trans. Xiang Xiong), Beijing: China Citic Press, p. 11.

Lao Tzu (2011a), *Tao Te Ching*, Beijing: New World Press (Chapter 25).

Lao Tzu (2011b), *Tao Te Ching*, Beijing: New World Press (Chapter 42).

Lewis, Mumford (2009), *Technics and Civilization* (trans. Yunming Chen et al.), Beijing: China Architecture & Building Press.

Luc, Ferry (2017), *La Revolution Transhumaniste* (trans. Xing Zhou), Shanghai: Hunan Science and Technology Press.

Martine, Rothblatt (2016), *Virtually Human: The Promise – And The Peril – Of Digital Immortality* (trans. Xue Guo), Hangzhou: Zhejiang People's Publishing House.

Mike, Floorwalker (2013), "10 Incredible ways technology may make us superhuman", *Listverse*, 12 May, http://listverse.com/2013/05/12/10-incredible-ways-technology-may-make-us-superhuman/. Accessed 5 May 2016.

Nick, Bostrom (2015), *Superintelligence: Paths, Dangers, Strategies* (trans. Tiwei Zhang and Yuqing Zhang), Beijing: China Citic Press.

Nsfc.gov.cn (2018), "Science magazine released 125 cutting-edge scientific questions in the world", *Nsfc*, 29 January, http://www.nsfc.gov.cn/csc/20340/20289/22023/index.html. Accessed 9 February 2018.

Pinlue.com (2014), "Yuval Harari: Making inquiries about the meaning of life in human history", *Pinlue*, 28 September, https://www.pinlue.com/article/2018/12/1723/007860866317.html. Accessed 5 January 2016.

Qq.com (2013), "The 'Iron Man' armor developed by the US military can make soldiers become 'Superman'", *Tencent*, 12 October,https://news.qq.com/a/20131012/002640.htm. Accessed 5 October 2015.

Ray, Kurzweil (2011), *The Singularity Is Near* (trans. Qingcheng Li et al.), Bejing: China Machine Press, pp. 9 and 15.

Shengbai, Guo (2009), "Life instinct system theory", *Baidu Library*, 23 December, http://wenku.baidu.com/link?url=4OYU9RhwagGBBmS2C18IPQK1NpMG2TnPtHTazIKgE0-bz9Y-wykfR1_SV3Ot_iwYfKe9PCrqtSJQS91G31NuKibELYgRxUhV5YaJ8m834BGW. Accessed 25 October 2017.

Skinner, B.F. (2018), *Beyond Freedom and Dignity* (trans. Hong Fang), Beijing: China Renmin University Press.

Sohu.com (2017), "The man who built the rocket wants to connect our brains to the computer this time!", 7 April, http://www.sohu.com/a/132625138_204826. Accessed 30 October 2017.

Xunqing, Chen (1997), "What exactly is life?", *Science and Technology Daily*, 19 February.

Yuval, Harari (2014a), *Sapiens: A Brief History of Humankind* (trans. Junhong Lin), Beijing: China Citic Press, p. 95.

Yuval, Harari (2014b), *Sapiens: A Brief History of Humankind* (trans. Junhong Lin), Bejing: China Citic Press, pp. 261 and 376.

## CHAPTER 3

Anon (2008), "What is the future civilization?", *Reference News*, 31 August. Extract of an article in *Fun Magazine*, August 2008.

Anon (2014), *Mencius*, Beijing: Chinese Overseas Chinese Publishing House; last chapter.

Anon (2016), *The Analects of Confucius*, Beijing: Zhonghua Book Company.

Adam, Rosenberg (2015), "'Star Wars: The Force Awakens' makes $1 billion in record time", *Mashable*, 27 December, https://mashable.com/2015/12/27/star-wars-1-billion-record/. Accessed 20 February 2016.

Al, Gore (2013), *The Future: Six Drivers of Global Change* (trans. Jieyin Feng et al.), Shanghai: Shanghai Translation Publishing House, p. 273.

Arnold Joseph, Toynbee (2010), *A Study of History* (trans. Xiaolin Guo et al.), Shanghai: Shanghai People's Publishing House, 2010.

Baidu.com (2007), "Human sociality", *Baidu Library*, 23 April, http://wenku.baidu.com/view/812f988d680203d8ce2f24c9.html?from=search. Accessed 4 November 2011.

Baidu.com (2020), Community of Human Destiny, *Baidu Library*, 10 June, https://baike.baidu.com/item/%E4%BA%BA%E7%B1%BB%E5%91%BD%E8%BF%90%E5%85%B1%E5%90%8C%E4%BD%93/1096715?fr=aladdin. Accessed 10 October 2020.

Cankaoxiaoxi.com (2014), "American scientists performed the most dangerous experiment: To develop new variants of deadly virus", *Reference News Online*, 3 July, http://science.cankaoxiaoxi.com/2014/0703/411514.shtml. Extract of an article from the website of *The Independent*, 1 July 2014. Accessed 8 May 2017.

Carl, Zimmer (2011), "Steven Pinker: If you wish for peace, you must first understand psychology", *Science Human*, 20 December, http://www.guokr.com/article/80943/. Extract of "Human nature's pathologist" from *The New York Times*, 28 November 2011. Accessed 6 June 2015.

Chaoxia, Yang (2011), "An era of environmental rights concerning ecological civilization", *Environmental Economy*, 11.

## CHAPTER 4

Anon (2015), "Human history of using tools may be 800000 years in advance", *Chinese Social Sciences Today*, 20 April.

China.com (2017), "The Soviet military officer died silently, who had prevented the outbreak of the US-Soviet nuclear war", *Haiwai Net*, 21 September, https://3g.china.com/act/military/62/20170921/31495052.html. Accessed 10 October 2019.

Dashen, Li (2005), "The progress and breakthroughs of 'Convergence Technology' in recent years", *China SciTechnology Business*, 6, p. 59.

David S., Landes (2001), *The Wealth and Poverty of Nations* (trans. Honghua Men et al.), Beijing: Xinhua Press, 2001.

E-Square Inc. (2007), *Sustainable Agriculture Survey, Japan: E-Square Inc., December; Development Path of Sustainable Agriculture* (trans. the Future Center of Beijing Academy of Soft Technology), Beijing: Xinhua Press, p. 61.

Francis, Fukuyama (2015), "Democracy is still the end of history", *Reference News Online*, 6 January, http://column.cankaoxiaoxi.com/2015/0106/619750.shtml. Extract of a news report from *Nihon Keizai Shimbun*, 4 January 2015. Accessed 8 October 2016.

Guancha.cn (2014), "The 80th anniversary of the birth of Donald Duck", *Guancha Syndicate*, 10 June, http://m.guancha.cn/Celebrity/2014_06_10_236387. Accessed 20 June 2015.

Guanghua, Fang (2015), "Destiny community highlights the essence of Chinese culture", *Chinese Social Sciences Today*, 19 November.

Institute of Electrical and Electronics Engineers (2017), "Ethically Aligned Design", *Advancing Technology for Humanity*, 18 December.

Jiping, Guo (2015), "Promising a better future for the world – On the human destinies community", *People's Daily*, 18 May.

John, Naisbitt (2005), "What kind of era will we enter", *Witsee*, 4 December, http://www.witsee.com/article/qyzl/41968.html. Accessed 6 October 2015.

Joseph, Schumpeter (1990), *The Theory of Economic Development* (trans. Wei He and Jiaxiang He), Beijing: Commercial Press.

Jyuji, Misumi (1955), *Introduction of Social Technology*, Chalk Shobo.

Keli, Fang (2003), "The unity of heaven & man and ecological wisdom of ancient China", *Social Science Front*, 4.

Keli, Fang and Cunguang, Lin (2012), "The rational view of the Chinese nation on civilization", *Chinese Social Sciences Today*, 15 February.

Kevin, Kelly (2011), *What Technology Wants* (trans. Xiang Xiong), Beijing: China Citic Press.

Lao Tzu (2011), *Tao Te Ching*, Beijing: New World Press, Chapter 8, 13, 25 and 46, 51, 67.

Lieyunwang.com (2015), "Biohacking technology: Let the human body have infinite possibilities", *Lieyunwang*, 6 May, https://www.lieyunwang.com/archives/84478. Accessed 5 November 2016.

Min, Yang (2014), "Cross and integration is in line with the development trend of social science", *Chinese Social Sciences Today*, 15 October.

Olaf, Helmer, Bernice, Brown and Theodore, Gordon (1966), *Social Technology*, New York: Basic Books.

Oswald, Spengler (1963), *The Decline of the West* (trans. Shirong Qi et al.), Beijing: Commercial Press, p. 125.

Pengpeng, Zhou (2015), *The Book of Changes*, Beijing: Beijing Joint Publishing Company.

Qian, Gu (2016), *The Book of History*, Beijing: Zhonghua Book Company.

S. L., Anderson (2008), "Asimov's 'three laws of robotics' and machine metaethics", *AI & Society*, 22:4, pp. 477-493.

Shanghai Library et al. (2004), "What will the world be like when the four technologies converge? – NBIC converging technology will enable new revival of science and technology in the 21st century", *World Science*, 5, pp. 8-12.

Sheng, Dai (2016), *The Book of Rites*, Beijing: Zhonghua Book Company, the chapter on the "Conveyance of Rituals".

Shide, Cheng, Hongtu, Wang and Zhaolin, Lu (eds) (1982), *Collection of Explanatory for "Plain Questions" of the Yellow Emperor's Inner Canon*, Beijing: People's Hygiene Press.

Shiro, Kurihara (1987), *Technology Philosophy in the Future*, Japan: Ohm Publishing House.

Shuro, Honda (1975), *Anthropology of Technology*, Japan: Asakura Publishing House.

Sina.com (2008), "The bomb scare: Four little-known wrong nuclear alerts during the Cold War", *Sina*, 18 July, http://blog.sina.com.cn/s/blog_4bf657990100a167.html. Accessed 30 June 2017.

Sina.com (2014), "Commentary of the TV documentary, – The Internet Age", *Sina*, 21 September, http://blog.sina.com.cn/s/blog_4dd66e9a0102v54t.html. Accessed 12 February 2017.

Sohu.com (2017), Five Principles of Peaceful Coexistence, *Sohu*, 9 November, https://www.sohu.com/a/203309106_792383. Accessed 5 August 2019.

Sohu.com (2018), "Hawking's Super Human Prophecy: The law can prohibit humans from editing genes, but human nature cannot resist the temptation", 27 November, https://www.sohu.com/a/2780361022_23764. Accessed 4 June 2019.

Sohu.com (2018), "Top ten hotspots of global AI policy in 2017", *Sohu*, 3 January, http://www.sohu.com/a/214438566_323203. Accessed 4 October 2019.

Songqin, Shen (2014), *The New Translation of Fan Zhongyan Anthology*, Taipei: Sanmin Book Company (quote originally from *Memorandum of Yueyang Tower* by Zhongyan Fan [Song Dynasty]).

Stuart, Russell (2016), "Twenty-three questions and answers give you a deep understanding of artificial intelligence", *CIO Times*, 29 November, http://www.ciotimes.com/recommend/121302.html. Accessed 4 February 2018.

Thepaper.cn (2015), "Were biochemical crises self-created by the U.S. military? U.S. troops mistakenly sent live anthrax bacteria to nine states and U.S. military bases in South Korea", *The Paper*, 28 May, http://www.thepaper.cn/newsDetail_forward_1336012. Accessed 4 October 2018.

Trevor, Williams (1989) (ed.), *A History of Technology*, 6: 1, Changhsa: Central South Industrial University Press, p. 37.

Tzu, Chuang (2015), *Chuang Tzu: The Chapter of Heaven and Earth* (trans. and annot. Yong Fang), Beijing: Zhonghua Book Company.

Weidong, Chen (2014), "Big data brings animation industry revolution.", *People.cn*, 29 October, http://culture.people.com.cn/n/2014/1029/c172318-25932800.html. Accessed 25 November 2015.

Wikipedia.org, "Nikolay Danilevsky", *Wikipedia*, http://en.wikipedia.org/wiki/Nikolai_Danilevsky. Accessed 15 October 2019.

Xianglong, Zhang (2016), *The Book of History*, Beijing: SDX Joint Publishing Company, the chapter on "Canon of Yao".

Xiaofen, Chen (2016), *The Analects of Confucius*, Beijing: Zhonghua Book Company, the chapter of Zilu – A student of Confucius.

Xiaozhou, Mai (2012), *A Reborn of Lao Tzu*, Beijing: Academy Press.

Xinhuanet.com (2014), "Kevin Kelly introduced 12 rules for the new economy in Beijing", *Xinhua Net*, 15 June, http://news.xinhuanet.com/world/2014-06/15/c_1111150520.htm. Accessed 25 January 2016.

Xinhuanet.com (2015), "China explicitly put forward the idea of global governance for the first time", *Xinhua Net*, 14 October, http://www.xinhuanet.com/world/2015-10/14/c_1116824064.htm. Accessed 10 November 2019.

Xinmin.cn (2014), "Scientists create a deadly flu virus which causes controversy", *Xinmin Net*, 13 June, http://tech.xinmin.cn/2014/06/13/24529806.html. Accessed 30 November 2015.

Yanwu, Gu (2013), *Annotation of the Explanation of Daily Understanding* (annot. Yuan Chen), Anhui: Anhui University Press.

Yi, Wang (2016), "Work together to create a human destiny community", *People's Daily*, 31 May 2016.

Yuval, Harari (2014), *Sapiens: A Brief History of Humankind* (trans. Junhong Lin), Beijing: China Citic Press, pp. 261 and 376.

Zhe, Zhong (2019), "Speeding up the construction of 'three systems' of philosophy and social sciences with Chinese characteristics", *Chinese Social Sciences Weekly*, 20 February.

Zhouying, Jin ([2005] 2011), *Global Technological Change – From Hard Technology to Soft Technology*, Bristol: Intellect.

Zhouying, Jin (2002), *Soft Technology*, Beijing: Xinhua Press.

Zhouying, Jin (2010a), *Global Technological Change – From Hard Technology to Soft Technology*, China: Peking University Press, Preface 1.

Zhouying, Jin (2010b), *Global Technological Change – From Hard Technology to Soft Technology*, China: Peking University Press, Preface 3.

Zhouying, Jin (2010c), *Global Technological Change – From Hard Technology to Soft Technology*, China: Peking University Press, Preface 2.

Zhouying, Jin (2010d), *Global Technological Change – From Hard Technology to Soft Technology*, China: Peking University Press, Preface 4.

Zhouying, Jin (2010e), *Global Technological Change – From Hard Technology to Soft Technology*, Beijing: Peking University Press.

Zhongshu, Dong (2011), *Luxuriant Dew of the Spring and Autumn Annals*, Beijing: Zhonghua Book Company.

Zhouying, Jin (2013), "What kind of future do we need? – Reflections from China", *World Future 2013 Conference*, Chicago, IL, 21 July.

Zhouying, Jin (2016), *What Kind of Future Does Humanity Need? Global Civilization and China's Comprehensive Rejuvenation*, Hunan:Hunan Science and Technology Press.

Zhouying, Jin et al. (2006), *Long-term Strategy – System Integration and Sustainable Development*, China: Social Sciences Academic Press, Chapter 5.

## CHAPTER 5

Anon (2013), "Dialogue with Klaus Roland: Development is a full range of system engineering", *Chinese Social Sciences Today*, 16 January.

Anon (2015), "Africa which is in the '30 years of glory'", *Reference News*, 25 August. Extracted the article from *Le Monde*, 6 August.

Anon (2018), "World War will break out no later than 2150", *Reference News* 4 March.

Cankaoxiaoxi.com (2014a), "A regime cycle of bipartisan confrontation makes America paralyzed", *Reference News Online*, 26 November, http://www.cankaoxiaoxi.com/waimeishuo/fgssj/. Extracted the article from the website of *Frankfurter Allgemeine Zeitung*, 26 November 2014. Accessed 12 October 2018.

Cankaoxiaoxi.com (2014b), "The one hundred anniversary of World War I: War, endless war", *Reference News Online*, 1 August, http://column.cankaoxiaoxi.com/2014/0801/445515.shtml. Accessed 10 August 2017.

Cankaoxiaoxi.com (2015a), "Former U.S. President Jimmy Carter: The United States is no longer a democratic country", *Reference News Online*, 12 August, http://column.cankaoxiaoxi.com/2015/0812/901804.shtml. Article extracted from the website of *Huffington Post*, 3 August 2015. Accessed 8 November 2017.

Cankaoxiaoxi.com (2015b), "Today American dream really becomes a dream", *Reference News Online*, 25 August, http://column.cankaoxiaoxi.com/2015/0825/918112.shtml. Extracted the article from the website of *The New York Times*, 9 August 2015. Accessed 8 January 2018.

China.com (2008), "Statistics of casualties during the 5 years of the Iraq war", *China.org.cn*, 20 March, http://www.china.com.cn/international/txt/2008-03/20/content_13106729.htm. Accessed 20 October 2019.

China.com (2009), "China's ethnic policy and common prosperity and development of all ethnic groups", *Xinhua Network*, 27 September, http://news.china.com/zh_cn/domestic/945/20090927/15654318.html. Accessed 1 May 2016.

Chinanews.com (2013), "A total of 4500 American soldiers died in the Iraq war during 10 years, and reconstruction still has a long way to go", *China News*, 19 March, http://www.chinanews.com/mil/2013/03-19/4654468.shtml. Accessed 20 October 2019.

Chunyan, Wang (2014), "The review of World War I & II: China is a staunch force for world peace", *Chinese Social Sciences Today,* 28 July.

Dante, Alighieri (1985), *De Monarchia* (trans. Hong Zhu), Beijing: Commercial Press.

Delegation of Party School of the Central Committee of CPC to Norway and Sweden (2007), "Characteristics and Enlightenment of the 'Nordic Model'", *Scientific Socialism*, 6.

Francis, Bacon (2012), *The New Atlantis* (trans. Xin He), Beijing: Commercial Press.

George, Friedman (2009), *The Next 100 Years: A Forecast for the 21st Century* (trans. Zonglei Wei and Ningna Jie) Shenzhen: Haitian Publishing House.

Guanhong, Sun et al. (2008), *Introduction to Political Science*, Fudan: Fudan University Press, 2ed.

Herman, Kahn et al. (1984a), *The Next 200 Years: A Scenario for America and the World* (trans. Shenzhang Cai), Taipei: Taiwan Zhiwen Publishing House.

Herman, Kahn et al. (1984b), *The Next Two Hundred Years* (trans. ShenzhangCai), Taipei: Taiwan Zhiwen Publishing House.

Herman, Kahn, William, Brown and Leon Martel (1976), *The Next Two Hundred Years*, New York: William Morrow & Co.

Honore, de Balzac (1989), *Pere Goriot* (trans. Lei Fu), China: The People's Literature Publishing House.

Ian, Morris (2014), *War: What Is It Good for?*, New York: Farrar, Straus & Giroux (FSG).

Immanuel, Kant (2005), *Perpetual Peace* (trans. Zhaowu He), Shanghai: Shanghai People's Publishing House.

Jerome, Glenn and Theodore, Gordon (2005), *2005 State of the Future*, The Millennium Project, CD Chapter 3.

John, Rawls (2001), *The Law of Peoples* (trans. Xiaohui Zhang et al.), Jilin: Jilin People's Publishing House.

Jurgen, Habermas (2002), *The Inclusion of the Other* (trans. Weidong Cao), Shanghai: Shanghai People's Publishing House, p. 209.

Karl, Marx and Frederick, Engels (1960), *Karl Marx and Frederick Engels*, Vol. 3, China: People's Press.

Karl, Marx and Frederick, Engels (1965), *Karl Marx and Frederick Engels*, Vol. 4, China: People's Press, pp. 357–374.

Keping, Yu (2002), "Introduction to Global Governance", *Marxism & Reality*,1, pp. 20–32.

Lawrence, Freedman (2018), *The Future of War: A History*, NewYork: Penguin.

Marq, De Villiers (2012), *Our Way Out: First Principles for a Post-Apocalyptic World* (trans. Qi Tang), Beijing: Renmin University Press.

Michael, Zgurovsky (2012), "Sustainable development global modeling: Quality of life and security of the world population", *International Academic Forum on Promoting the Green Economy and Sustainable Development by Science and Technology in the 21 Century*, Beijing, 7 April.

Misao, Murayama and Takashi Asai (2000), *Meditation on East and West Civilizations* (trans. Wenzhi Ping and Wenda Xia), China: China International Broadcasting Publishing House.

Nicholas, Spencer (2014), "Human beings have the wisdom to stop the next war", *Chinese Social Sciences Today*, 28 July.

Plato (1986), *The Republic /Πολιτεία* (trans. Binhe Guo, Zhuming Guo), Beijing: Commercial Press.

Qichao, Liang (2011), *Introduction to the Learning of the Qing Dynasty*, Shanghai: Shanghai Classics Publishing House.

Rulun, Zhang (2013), "China Dream cannot lack the guidance of philosophy", *Chinese Social Sciences Today*, 24 April.

Ruolin, Zheng (2013), "Exposing 'five principles of deceptive propaganda on war' in western countries", *Xinhua Net*, 14 October, http://news.xinhuanet.com/world/2013-10/14/c_125529923.htm. Accessed 5 October 2016.

Sheng, Dai (2016), *The Book of Rites*, Beijing: Zhonghua Book Company, Li Yun Essay.

Theodore, Gordon (1965), *The Future*, New York: St. Martin's Press.

Theodore, Gordon (2005), "Moral business in the future", *2005 the Future 500 China Forum*, Beijing, 18-19 October.

WWF (2014), Living Planet Report 2014.

Xinhuanet.com (2005), "China unveiled a position paper on the reform of the United Nations", *Xinhua Net*, 7 June, http://news.xinhuanet.com/world/2005-06/07/content_3056686.htm. Accessed 2 October 2016.

Xinhuanet.com (2013), "*War! What Is It Good For?* Can a war lead to a more peaceful world?" *Xinhua Net*, 18 November, http://news.xinhuanet.com/cankao/2013-11/18/c_132897828.htm. Accessed 10 November 2019.

Xintian, Yu (2004), "The new features of war and peace – China's foreign strategy for peaceful rise from the angle of the trend of the future war", *World Outlook*, 10.

Zhengjun, Jiang (2011), "Hope or myth: Interpretation of Marx's national demise", *Studies on Marxism*, 11, pp. 124-132.

Zhouying, Jin (2010), *Global Technological Change – From Hard Technology to Soft Technology*, Peking: Peking University Press, pp. 212–213.

Baidu.com (2013), "Can the world be peaceful?" *Baidu*, 25 August, http://zhidao.baidu.com/question/585473458.html. Accessed 10 December 2017.

## CHAPTER 6

163.com (2010), "The founding father of science fiction – Jules Verne's impression of China", *NetEase*, 6 April, http://news.163.com/10/0406/15/63JJ643F000146BD_2.html. Accessed 10 February 2017.

Al, Gore (2013), *The Future: Six Drivers of Global Change* (trans. Jieyin Feng et al.), Shanghai: Shanghai Translation Publishing House, pp. 406-408.

Angus, Maddison (2004), *The World Economy: A Millennial Perspective* (trans. Xiaoying Wu et al.), Peking: Peking University Press, p. 259.

Baidu.com (2013), "2013 World Happiness Report", *Baidu,* 9 September 2013, http://baike.baidu.com/link?url=LvsN33PqLBz44gm_I4qQt9dAyXN1jnhIsrxSx-2oSE_JWjuizPPfqR-JTuMqW55WYgDqO9LWQvIbXHo65-KD0hK. Accessed 6 January 2019.

Baidu.com (2016), "On the exploration of the early stage of socialism in the Soviet Union", *Baidu*, 4 January, http://zhidao.baidu.com/link?url=XIQBtBEZDW4HRn4wiAeFLrjP-jiB1u3OkjzRFf1uC6XNl1OXyyP8gmkI1VwKhPMnm6CWaFcfFKIMZHH5rVm697K. Accessed 1 January 2018.

Civilcn.com (2010), "Interviews about productive landscapes", *Civilcn*, 2 July, http://www.civilcn.com/news/jzxw/1278036656122778.html. Accessed 10 January 2018.

Economic Institute of the Soviet Academy of Sciences (ed.) (1982), *Soviet Socialist Economic History*, Vol. 3, Shanghai: SDX Joint Publishing Company.

Enyuan, Wu (2016), "Did Lenin's thought lead to the disintegration of the former Soviet Union?" *Chinese Social Sciences Today,* 1 February.

Immanuel, Kant (2005), *Perpetual Peace* (trans. Zhaowu He) Shanghai: Shanghai People's Publishing House.

Jintai, Zhang (2011), *Lao Tzu Who Benefits the World*, China: House of the China Literary Federation.

Jizhi, Li and Qian, Xu (2014), "The notion of abiding by the law has penetrated into the Finns' blood", *Reference News Online*, 3 November, http://world.cankaoxiaoxi.com/2014/1103/551751.shtml. Accessed 8 October 2016.

Lane, Jennings (2015), "The growing acceptance of women as economic and political equals to men", E-mail communication from Lane Jennings, former editor-in-chief of World Future Review, World Future Society, 30 November.

Lao Tzu (2011), *Tao Te Ching*, Beijing: New World Press.

Theodore, Gordon (2005), "Moral business in the future," *2005 The Future 500 China Forum*, Beijing, 18-19 October.

Thomas, More (1959), *Utopia* (trans. Liuling Dai), Beijing: Commercial Press.

Tian, Xia (2010), "A comparison of the socialist thoughts of Saint-Simon Fourier & Owen", *China Market*, 48, p. 183.

Tommaso, Campanella (2010), *The City of the Sun* (trans. Dawei Chen, Sifu Li, and Tingbi Li), Beijing: Commercial Press.

Weiwei, Liu (2015), "On the active exploration of global non ruling Communist Party on socialist movement", *Chinese Social Sciences Today*, 25 March.

Xiaozhou, Mai (2012), *Lao Tzu's Rebirth*, London: Academy Press.

Zhimin, Yan (2013), "The emergence and development of utopian socialism", *Scientific Socialism*, 5, pp. 30-32.

Zhouying, Jin (2013), "What kind of future do we need? – Reflections from China", *World Future 2013 Conference*, Chicago, IL, 21 July.

## CHAPTER 7

Anon (2015), "China's clean energy investment expands its advantage compared with the United States", *Reference News*, 11 January. Article extracted from the website of *Financial Times*, 10 January 2015. Accessed 20 January 2015.

(2001), "The proportion of China's GDP invested in environmental protection is rising", *People's Daily Overseas Edition*, 3 December.

(2006), "In the next 15 years, 21 major minerals in China will be difficult to meet the demand", *Guangdong Audit*, 1, p. 27.

(2011), "Three challenges facing global sustainable development", *China Securities Journal*, 18 April.

163.com (2014), "MEPC: China's environmental protection investment has risen by $32.26 billion USD per year", *NetEase*, 8 March, http://money.163.com/14/0308/15/9MQUU2AO00254TI5.html. Accessed 12 January 2019.

66law.cn (2020), "Approximately 700,000 couples in China filed separate second-child applications, which is less than official expectations", *Hualv.com*, 5 March, https://www.66law.cn/laws/852903.aspx. Accessed 10 August 2020.

Baidu.com (2018), "IEEFA: China is a leader in global clean energy investment", 10 January, https://baijiahao.baidu.com/s?id=1589196074014402025&wfr=spider&for=pc. Accessed 11 April 2018.

Baidu.com (2020), "China's energy market analysis in 2019: total energy consumption increased by 3.3%, and the proportion of clean energy increased", *China Business Intelligence Net*, 2 February, https://baijiahao.baidu.com/s?id=1657353300433972508&wfr=spider&for=pc. Accessed 10 April 2020.

Baisong, Jin (2014), "'New capitalism' and 'new socialism'", *ccb.com*, 23 June 2014, http://www.ccb.com/Info/71896908?marker=3. Accessed 18 March 2018.

Bjx.com (2018), "It took only 7 years for China's cumulative installed photovoltaic capacity to grow from 1GW to 130GW", *Bjx.com.cn*, 30 January, http://guangfu.bjx.com.cn/news/20180130/877659.shtml. Accessed 3 March 2019.

Bjx.com (2018), "The '2017 Bulletin of the State of China's Ecological Environment' was released on May 31", *Daqi.bjx.com.cn*, 1 June, http://huanbao.bjx.com.cn/news/20180601/902631.shtml. Accessed 20 April 2019.

Cankaoxiaoxi.com (2015), "The heritage left to the world by Lee Kuan Yew: Myth of 'Asian capitalism'", *Reference News Online*, 1 April, http://column.cankaoxiaoxi.com/2015/0401/727388.shtml. Accessed 8 October 2018.

Changyan, Ding (2015), "National governance moves towards daily politics", *China Social Sciences Today,* 25 November.

Chengyou, Tian (2014), "Where is the difficulty of judicial independence?" *Caixin.com*, 28 October, http://opinion.caixin.com/2014-10-28/100743846.html. Accessed 2 September 2018.

China.com (2015), "As of May 2015, 1.45 million Chinese couples applied for a second child", *China.org.cn*, 10 July, http://news.china.com.cn/2015-07/10/content_36028510.htm. Accessed 18 October 2018.

Chinanews.com (2013), "Temporarily exempt some small and micro enterprises' from VAT and sales tax", *China News*, 24 July, http://www.chinanews.com/cj/2013/07-24/5080886.shtml. Accessed 6 September 2018.

Chinanews.com (2015), "Qingyanliu village of Yiwu, the first village of online Taobao store: The street of online retailers encounters a spending spree", *China News*, 10 April, http://www.chinanews.com/df/2015/04-10/7199675.shtml. Accessed 20 September 2018.

Chundong, Deng (2014), "Solid footprint for exploring the basic problems of socialism with Chinese characteristics", *Chinese Social Sciences Weekly*, 26 May.

Chyxx.com (2015), "The analysis of the status quo of China's environmental protection industry investment in 2015 and suggestions for its optimization", *chyxx*, 29 June, http://www.chyxx.com/industry/201506/325594.html. Accessed 25 May 2019.

Chyxx.com (2018), "Analysis of the development status of China's photovoltaic industry in 2018 and forecast of future development prospects", *Chyxx*, 29 March, http://www.chyxx.com/industry/201803/624728.html. Accessed 26 January 2019.

Cnhubei.com (2018), "China's elderly population will reach its peak in 2050, and the total number will reach 487 million, accounting for 34.9% of the total population", Cnhubei.com, 21 September, http://news.cnhubei.com/guonei/p/4139345.html. Accessed 12 October 2018.

Cssn.cn (2014), "It needs to adjust the economic structure in order to keep 'APEC blue' as long as possible", *Chinese Social Sciences Network*, 29 November, http://www.cssn.cn/dybg/201411/t20141129_1421715.shtml. Accessed 5 June 2019.

Cyol.com (2017), "'Being a scientist' loses its appeal. Who stole the scientific dreams of Chinese children?", Cyol.com, 13 January, http://news.cyol.com/content/2017-01/13/content_15280046.htm. Accessed 25 September 2018.

Doc88.com (2014), "The problems facing China's talent are too serious", 30 November, http://www.doc88.com/p-9009316342559.htm. Accessed 2 November 2019.

Docin.com (2015), "Special topics on the theory and practice of socialism with Chinese characteristics", *Docin*, 7 September, http://www.docin.com/p-1282050812.html?t_t_t=0.7314207321032882. Accessed 1 August 2019.

Donella H., Meadows (2008), *Thinking in Systems*, Chelsea: Chelsea Green Publishing House.

Gov.cn (2015), "Guideline of the State Council on accelerating the construction of support platform for popular entrepreneurship and mass innovation", *GOV.cn*, 26 September, http://www.gov.cn/zhengce/content/2015-09/26/content_10183.htm. Accessed 21 April 2018.

Herman Daly (2001), *Beyond Growth: The Economics of Sustainable Development* (trans. Dajian Zhu et al.), Shanghai: Shanghai Translation Publishing House.

In-en.com (2018), "China Electricity Council: As of 2017, China's installed wind power capacity totaled 163.67 million kilowatts", *IN-EN.com*, 9 February, http://www.in-en.com/article/html/energy-2265521.shtml. Accessed 11 January 2019.

Ji, Liu (2009), "Three prospects: China's next 30 years", *Green Leaf*,6.

Jjckb.cn (2018), "'China Corporate Social Responsibility Report 2018' was released in Beijing", *Economic Information Daily*, 28 December, http://www.jjckb.cn/2018-12/28/c_137704919.htm. Accessed 2 November 2019.

John Stuart, Mill (2013), *Principles of Political Economy* (trans. Di Jin and Yi Jin), China: Huaxia Publishing House, p. 701.

John, Talberth, Clifford, Cobb, and Noah, Slattery (2007), "The Genuine Progress Indicator 2006", *Redefining Progress*, February.

Jorgen, Landers (2013), *2052: A Global Forecast for the Next Forty Years* (trans. Xuezheng-Qin et al.), Yilin Press.

Laurence C., Smith (2010), *The World in 2050*, Boston: Dutton.

Li, Li (2012), "During the 20 year period, China's young population was reduced by 30%, and the experts suggest that family planning should be released", *China News*, 25 April, http://www.chinanews.com/jk/2012/04-25/3845830.shtml. Accessed 5 October 2018.

Li, Mao (2015), "China's rise can make more contributions to the world", *Chinese Social Sciences Today*, 17 April.

Linsu, Kim (1998), *Imitation to Innovation: The Dynamics of Korea's Technology Leaning* (trans. Xiaomei Liu and Hongji Liu), Beijing: Xinhua Publishing House.

MEPC (2002), National Surface Water Quality Standards.

Paul, Hawken, Amory, Lovins, and L. Hunter, Lovins (2002), *Natural Capitalism* (trans. Naili Wang et al.), Shanghai: Shanghai Science and Technology Press, pp. 182–187.

Paul, Krugman (2009), *The Accidental Theorist and Other Dispatches from the Dismal Science* (trans. Yufeng Chen), Peking:Peking University Press.

Peilin, Li (2013), "Social system reform in the context of transformation", *Qiushi,*15.

People.com (2013), "Communique of the Third Plenary Session of the CPC Central Committee: Speed up the institutionalization, standardization and proceduralization of socialist democratic politics", *People's Daily Online*, 12 November, http://politics.people.com.cn/n/2013/1112/c1001-23519064.html. Accessed 19 May 2019.

People.com (2013), "The current anti-corruption campaign focuses on palliative approaches and gains time for treating the root cause", *People's Daily Online*, 20 February, http://yuqing.people.com.cn/n/2013/0220/c210123-20538871.html. Accessed 26 July 2018.

People.com (2015), "The situation of 'abandoned wind power' is grim, which wind power companies cannot afford", *People's Daily Online*, 15 December 2015, http://energy.people.com.cn/n1/2015/1215/c71661-27929744.html. Accessed 18 October 2018.

People.com (2017), "Jinping Xi: Winning the goal of building a moderately prosperous society in an all round way and winning the great victory of socialism with Chinese characteristics in the new era – report at the 19th National Congress of the Communist Party of China", *People.cn*, 28 October, http://cpc.people.com.cn/GB/n1/2017/1028/c64094-29613660.html. Accessed 20 November 2018.

Pinlue.com (2019), "Number of college graduates in China over the years (1949–2017)", *Pinlue*, 26 March, https://www.pinlue.com/article/2019/03/2600/518411894412.html. Accessed 7 October 2020.

Qi, Wu (2017), "The development trend of China's energy conservation and environmental protection industry", *China National Conditions and Strength*, 2017, 3:12, pp. 18-21.

Qing, Mei (2012), "China urgently needs to speed up wetland protection", *China Green Times,* 13 December.

Sen, Wei (2012), *The Great Transformation: The Current Situation, Problems and Feasible Choices of China*, China: China Citic Press.

Sheng, Jin (2018), "Essays on life aesthetics", 30 October.

Shuai, Yuan, Jie, He and Fei, He (2019), "The total global R&D investment continues to grow, of which China has the fastest growth rate, but the proportion of basic research funding is still the lowest", *Science & Technology Review*, 19.

Shunhong, Zhang (2009), "How can we adhere to the socialist road? Reflections on the occasion of the 90 anniversary of the October Revolution", *Sina*, 10 February, http://blog.sina.com.cn/s/blog_59d6bbd60100cb5n.html. Accessed 17 April 2018.

Sina.com (2006), "Xiaoping Deng: The reform of the political system determines the success or failure of all reforms", 26 January, http://news.sina.com.cn/c/2006-01-26/08598973281.shtml. Accessed 16 January 2019.

Sina.com (2019), "Liepin.com released '2018 Trend Report on Overseas Students Returning'", *Sina*, 15 January, http://edu.sina.com.cn/a/2019-01-15/doc-ihqfskcn7232347.shtml. Accessed 8 October 2019.

Sohu.com (2015), "In fact, China is still short of talents, and you will understand after reading these two groups of comparative data", *Sohu*, 28 August, https://www.sohu.com/a/29709404_114901. Accessed 10 October 2019.

Sohu.com (2016), "What is the level of technological innovation after all in Japan?", *Sohu*, 30 November, https://www.sohu.com/a/120234070_465915. Accessed 1 November 2019.

Sohu.com (2017), "Summary of the main data of China's wind power development in 2016", *Sohu*, 29 June, https://www.sohu.com/a/153004787_146947. Accessed 10 November 2018.

UNEP (2008), *Green Jobs: Towards Decent Work in a Sustainable*, Low-Carbon World.

UNEP (2011), "Towards the Green Economy: Pathways to Sustainable Development and Poverty Eradication".

Water8848.com (2014), "Bulletin of national soil pollution survey", *Water8484.com*, 18 April, http://www.water8848.com/news/201404/18/16655.html. Accessed 26 May 2019.

World Commission on Environment and Development (1997), *Our Common Future* (trans. Zhijia Wang et al.), China: Jilin People's Publishing House.

Xianjichina.com (2019), "In 2018, China's wind power development was generally stable, and the abandonment rate of wind power continued to decline", *XianJiChina.COM*, 9 May, https://www.xianjichina.com/news/details_118852.html. Accessed 21 April 2020.

Xinhuanet.com (2012), "German parliament has adopted its 2013 financial budget", *Xihua Net*, 24 November, http://news.xinhuanet.com/fortune/2012-11/24/c_113786258.htm. Accessed 16 January 2019.

Xinhuanet.com (2014), "Key topics of the United Nations Conference on the environment: Sustainable development goals", *Xinhua Net*, 24 June, http://news.xinhuanet.com/energy/2014-06/24/c_126663969.htm. Accessed 1 November 2017.

Xinhuanet.com (2016), "Wind power and photovoltaic power are hard-earned, why they are frequently abandoned?", *Xinhua Net*, 29 March, http://news.xinhuanet.com/2016-03/23/c_1118420544.htm. Accessed 1 September 2018.

Xinhuanet.com (2017), "The daily order volume of the takeaway platform is 20 million. How to deal with the takeaway garbage?", *Xinhua Net*, 28 August, http://www.xinhuanet.com//info/2017-08/28/c_136560769.htm. Accessed 30 June 2019.

Xinhuanet.com (2021), "General Secretary Xi Jinping's concern: the battle against poverty has been won in an all-round way", *Xinhua Net*, 25 February, http://www.xinhuanet.com/2021-02/25/c1127140205.htm. Accessed 10 April 2021.

Xuesen, Qian, Jingyuan, Yu, and Ruwei, Dai (1990), "A new field of science-open complex giant system and its methodology", *Nature Magazine*,1, pp. 3-10.

Ying, Bai (2015), "Report of China's Genuine Progress Indicator", Beijing.

Yingyi, Qian (2017), "'Why Chinese schools always fail to produce outstanding talents?' Look at how Professor Yingyi Qian of Tsinghua University answered 'Xuesen Qian's Question?'" 17 December, http://www.sohu.com/a/211054328_682840. Accessed 5 September 2018.

Yongnian, Zheng (2012), "Look forward to the acceleration of social reform after the 18th CPC National Congress", *Global Times*, 11 January.

Youran, Wang (2014), "Building a 'degrowth' steady-state economy", *Chinese Social Sciences Weekly*, 11 October.

Yu, Chu (2010), *Critique of Chinese Thinking Mode – The Root Cause of China's Backwardness Is the Traditional Mode of Thinking*, China: People Press.

Zhangping, Xing and Jian, Zhang (2011), "To promote green economy in China with incentive policies – Interview with Fei Feng, director-general of Department of Industrial Economy, DRC", *Economy*, Z1, pp. 40-41.

Zhenning, Yang (2016), "The influence of the book of changes on Chinese culture", *Caixin*, 11 May, http://china.caixin.com/2016-05-11/100942176.html. Accessed 7 October 2019.

Zhixiong, Gao, Lianzhen, Zhang and Jiye, Quan (2014), "Transfer of patented technology in China: Conditions, problems and solutions", *Science & Technology and Economy*, 4.

Zhouying, Jin ([2005] 2011), *Global Technological Change – From Hard Technology to Soft Technology*, Bristol: Intellect, p. 171.

Zhouying, Jin (2005), "The source of creativity", the speech at the *First Festival of World Thinkers*, March.

Zhouying, Jin (2008), "Beijing node report", *MP Project Planning Committee Meeting*, NW, Washington, DC, 23-26 July.

Zhouying, Jin (2010), "China's Genuine Progress Indicator (GPI) system – A tool for promoting sustainable development", *Bulletin of the Chinese Academy of Sciences*, 25.

Zhouying, Jin (2011), "Changing development mode and long-term strategy management", *Bulletin of the Chinese Academy of Sciences,* May.

Zhouying, Jin (2012), "Technological innovation needs 5 driving forces", *China News Weekly,* September.

Zhouying, Jin and Kenneth W., Hunter (2013), "Systemic solution to achieving green economic growth and sustainable development", *World Future Review, 5,* p. 2.

Zhouying, Jin and Ying, Bai (2009), *Policy Research Report of the Robot in China*, Brazil: Weapons Industry Press, p. 12.

Zhouying, Jin and Ying, Bai (2011a), "Sustainable development and long-term strategic management", *The World Future Review,* 3:2, by World Future Society.

Zhouying, Jin and Ying, Bai (2011b), "'Twelfth Five-year' Plan of ×× City – Long-term Development Strategy Management System", Beijing.

Zhouying, Jin et al. (2006), *Long-Term Strategy System Integration and Sustainable Development*, Beijing: Social Sciences Academic Press, pp. 157-180.

## CHAPTER 8

David, Christian (2007), *Maps of Time – An Introduction to Big History* (trans. KejiaYan et al.), Shanghai: Shanghai Academy of Social Sciences Publishing House.

Hongtu, Wang (ed.) (2002), *Lecture Notes in the Yellow Emperor's Inner Canon*, Beijing: People's Medical Publishing House.

Shide, Cheng, Hongtu,Wang and Zhaolin,Lu (eds) (1982), *Selected Notes on Plain Questions of the Yellow Emperor's Inner Canon*, Vol. 1, Beijing: People's Medical Publishing House, p. 68.

Timothy, Mack (2011), "20 Forecasts 2011–2025", *The Futurist*, 1.

Yongnian, Zheng (2014), "The crisis of democracy and its future", *Reference News*, 26 May.

Zhouying, Jin ([2005] 2011), *Global Technological Change – From Hard Technology to Soft Technology*, Bristol: Intellect, pp. 183-189.

Zhouying, Jin (2010), *Global Technological Change – From Hard Technology to Soft Technology*, Beijing: Peking University Press.

Zhouying, Jin (2015), "Achieving a sustainable Global Civilization: The case for enhancing long-term futures study", *World Future Review* 6, (4).

# Notes on the Author

Zhouying Jin is a senior researcher and professor at the Chinese Academy of Social Sciences (CASS); Founder and former Director of the Center for Technology Innovation and Strategy Studies of CASS; President and Founder of the Beijing Academy of Soft Technology.

She graduated from University of Science and Technology of China (USTC); a researcher, Institute of Mechanics, Chinese Academy of Sciences (CAS); a researcher, Research Institute of a National Defense Science and Technology; Deputy Chief Engineer of Changchun Electric Industrial Administration; Vice secretary-general, China enterprise Directors (Managers) Association of State Economic Committee of China. From 1988, she has served at CASS. At the same time, since the beginning of the 1990s, she served for the China S863 Plan, has been appointed as the Strategy Experts Team Leader for the S863 Plan (China High-Tech Research & Development Plan for 2001–10) by the Ministry of Science & Technology. At present, she is Chair of China Node of millennium project (MP), Chair of China Chapter of World Future Society (WFS), Senior Advisor of the United Nations International Collaboration and Coordination Agency (UNICCA), Fellow of the World Business Academy (Ojai, CA, U.S.), Global Advisory Board member of Ethical Markets Media (U.S.), Member of the editorial board or Advisory Committee of several magazines, such as "AI & Society" (UK) etc.

She was a Member of Professional Committee of Chinese Academy of Social Sciences; Visiting professor of Case Western Reserve University (Cleveland, U.S.A), University of Nebraska-Lincoln (Lincoln, U.S.A), University of Aix-Marseille III (France); Senior Research Fellow, Institute for The Future (U.S. CA, Menlo Park);

IC2 Institute (The University of Texas at Austin); Special researcher, Institute of Science and Technology policy of Japan; Guest Professor of University of Science and Technology of China (Hefei), Tsinghua University (Beijing), Hohai University (Nanjing); Academic member of Shanghai Academy of Systematic Science; Adviser for Soft Power Research Center of Jinan University; Chair of the "Future 500 China"; Global knowledge leader (E-100) etc.

The major field of her recent research are soft technology and soft environment, future research, long-term strategy management, Innovation, etc. She was invited by more than twenty countries and over 40 universities, research institutes and international conferences to present about her theory of soft technology, soft environment and the future of humanity. For instance she was invited as one of the ten "world thinkers" and as a speaker for the first 'Festival of Thinkers' with ten Nobel Laureates in 2005.

She is listed as the Global Foresight Professionals as an only Chinese mainland futurist (http://www.globalforesight.org) and listed as the world's top female futurists (http://rossdawson.com).

Among her publications, there are 21 monographs, 6 translated books, more than 20 joint publications; more than 30 important research reports; more than 30 enterprise diagnosis and consultation reports, and hundreds of papers. Major monographs including: *Management Consultation* (Guiyang, 1982); *Management and Enterprises Diagnosis* (Beijing, 1987); *Soft Technology* (Tokyo, 2000); *Soft Technology—The Essence and Space of Innovation* (Beijing and USA, 2002); *Service Innovation and Social Resource* (Beijing, 2004); long-term strategy integration and sustainable development (China, 2006); *Global Technological Change—From Hard Technology to Soft Technology* (UK and USA, 2005 and 2011; China, 2010; Korea, 2018); *What Kind of Future Does Humanity Need— Global Civilization and China's Comprehensive Rejuvenation* (China, 2016); *The Future of Humanity—Global Civilization and China's Rejuvenation (*UK and USA, 2018; Hungary, 2019); The *Future of Humanity—From Global Civilization to Great Civilization* (China, 2019 and 2021; Korea, 2021).

Over the past several decades, she led more than 30 important projects and consulted for over 40 medium and large-scale companies, which were asked by the central government, CASS, international organizations and companies. Through these studies and practice, she developed a model of "China 2050 and early warning system"; designed "Long-term Strategy Management System Integration Model-I and Model-II" adapted to the green development; introduced and established "Beyond GDP, China's Genuine Progress Indicator (GPI) system" in line with international standards in order to improve the quality of GDP and the official performance evaluation standard. During 1989–1999, as a volunteer for poverty alleviation, she worked with Care Japan to help China's Poor area such as Tong County of Hubei Province, Nanchong County of Sichuan Province, etc.

www.ingramcontent.com/pod-product-compliance
Lightning Source LLC
LaVergne TN
LVHW060727310826
846742LV00016B/46
* 9 7 8 1 7 8 9 3 8 6 1 6 5 *